MY NAME IS "LEGION"

Palestinian Judaic Traditions in Mark 5:1-20 and Other Gospel Texts

Roger David Aus

Studies in Judaism

University Press of America,® Inc.
Dallas · Lanham · Boulder · New York · Oxford

BS
2585.2
.A869
2003

Copyright © 2003 by
University Press of America,® Inc.
4501 Forbes Boulevard
Suite 200
Lanham, Maryland 20706

12 Hid's Copse Rd.
Cumnor Hill, Oxford OX2 9JJ

All rights reserved
Printed in the United States of America
British Library Cataloging in Publication Information Available

Library of Congress Control Number: 2003111862
ISBN 0-7618-2667-X (paperback : alk. ppr.)

∞™ The paper used in this publication meets the minimum
requirements of American National Standard for Information
Sciences—Permanence of Paper for Printed Library Materials,
ANSI Z39.48—1984

Studies in Judaism

EDITOR

Jacob Neusner
Bard College

EDITORIAL BOARD

Alan J. Avery-Peck
College of the Holy Cross

Herbert Basser
Queens University

Bruce D. Chilton
Bard College

José Faur
Bar Ilan University

William Scott Green
University of Rochester

Mayer Gruber
Ben-Gurion University of the Negev

Günter Stemberger
University of Vienna

James F. Strange
University of South Florida

Dedicated

to

Jacob (Jack) Neusner, now having turned seventy, in gratitude for his many methodological studies and English translations of Judaic sources, thereby making them more easily accessible, also to students of the "New" Testament, and whose editorial generosity throughout the years has been more than laudable – *'ad me'ah we'esrim*

and

Elsge, dear wife, true helpmate, and best friend

Table of Contents

Chapter One

My Name is "Legion": Palestinian Judaic Samson Traditions in Mark 5:1-20

Introduction 1
I. The Gerasene Demoniac Characterized as a Madman,
   and Psalm 91 3
   1. A Madman...3
   2. Psalm 91 6
      2.1 The Most High God 9
      2.2 The Name...10
      2.3 Legion...11
II. The Gerasene Demoniac Described in Terms of Judaic
    Traditions Centering on Samson..19
    1. Living in a Rock Cave 21
    2. Uncleanness..24
    3. Phenomenal Strength, Binding, Hand-chains and
       Foot-shackles..25
    4. Shouting Loudly, Running and Meeting......................30
    5. Swearing Not to Torment or Injure Someone..............33
    6. What is Your Name? 36
    7. Legion..39
       7.1 Support and Food 42
       7.2 Fighting Alone 43
    8. Swine and Swineherd 45

- 9. Panicking by Rushing Down a Steep Slope, and Drowning 48
  - 9.1 Panicking 49
  - 9.2 A Steep Slope 51
  - 9.3 Drowning 52
- 10. Survival of Only One, Who Proclaims the Miracle Elsewhere 54
- 11. Begging Someone to Leave the Land out of Fear 59
- 12. About Two Thousand 63

III. The Site of the Miracle / Exorcism: Kursi 69
  1. The Location 72
  2. The Name Kursi 73
  3. The Size 80
  4. A Mixed Population 80

IV. The Extent of the Original Narrative, and Markan Editing 83

V. Provenance, Language and Date of the Original Narrative 85
  1. Provenance 85
  2. Language 86
  3. Date 89

VI. Form and Historicity 89
  1. Form 89
  2. Historicity 90

VII. The Purposes of the Narrative 92
  1. Jesus Is Lord of the Unclean Spirits / Demons 92
  2. Jesus as the Son of the Most High God Is Stronger Than the Strongest Human 93
  3. Ridicule of the Unclean and Idolaters 94
  4. The Beginning of a Christian Mission in the Decapolis 96

Chapter Two

Catchword Connections and Day of Atonement Imagery in Luke 4:16-30

Introduction 101
I.   Catchword Connections...103
     1. Synagogue 103
     2. All 103
     3. Acceptable 104
         3.1 The Proverb in Luke 4:24......................................104
         3.2 Isa 61:1-2 in Luke 4:18-19.....................................107
         3.3 Isa 58:6 in Luke 4:18..108
         3.4 The Benediction Spoken Before the Reading
              from the Prophets 111
         3.5 Words of "Grace" 112
II. Day of Atonement Imagery..113
     1. The High Priest as Reading Aloud................................114
     2. Isa 58:6 as Part of the Prophetic Reading on the
         Day of Atonement 118
     3. The Jubilee Year, the Day of Atonement, the
         Messiah, and Isa 61:1-2 120
     4. Jesus as the Scapegoat in Luke 4:29..............................123
         4.1 The Negative Connotations in Luke 4:22a 124
         4.2 The Proverb "Physician, Heal Yourself!" 125
         4.3 The Widow of Zaraphath and Elijah....................126
         4.4 The Healing of the Leper Naaman the Syrian
              and Elisha...129
         4.5 Jesus as the Scapegoat 132
III. The Original Language, Provenance and Date 142
     1. The Original Language 142
     2. The Provenance..146
     3. The Date..147
IV. The Question of Historicity...148
V.   The Purposes of the Narrative 149

Chapter Three

The Name Judas "Iscariot" and Ahithophel in Judaic Tradition

Introduction		155
I.	Ahithophel as a Disciple of David, and Judas as a Disciple of Jesus, the Son of David	158
II.	Ahithophel Eats of David's Bread and Betrays Him, and Judas Eats of Jesus' Bread and Betrays Him	160
III.	The General Setting of Ahithophel's Betrayal of David, and the General Setting of Judas' Betrayal of Jesus	164
IV.	David Betrayed by Ahithophel When Weary and Discouraged, and Jesus Betrayed by Judas When Weary and Discouraged	165
V.	Ahithophel's Plan When He Captures / Betrays David That All Those with Him Will Flee, and the Flight of Jesus' Disciples When Judas Betrays Him	165
VI.	Ahithophel's Plan When He Captures / Betrays David That Only David Will Be Killed, and Judas' Betrayal Only of Jesus, Who Is Killed	165
VII.	Get Up!	166
VIII.	Elders, Chief Priests and the Sanhedrin	167
IX.	Judas as a Guide, and Ahithophel as a Guide	169
X.	Judas and a Crowd with Swords and Clubs, and Ahithophel's Band, Swords and Clubs	171
XI.	Rabbi and Friend	176
XII.	Judas and Ahithophel as Informers / Betrayers	179
XIII.	Ahithophel's Motivation for Betraying David, and Judas' Motivation for Betraying Jesus	183
XIV.	Falsehood / Betrayal	186
XV.	Ahithophel's Suicide, and Judas' Suicide	188
XVI.	Ahithophel's Remorse / Repentance, and Judas' Remorse / Repentance	190
XVII.	Ahithophel and the Name Judas "Iscariot"	191
Summary		207

Chapter Four

Jesus' Weeping over the Destruction of Jerusalem in Luke 19:41-44, and David's Weeping over the Destruction of Jerusalem in Judaic Tradition

Introduction	209
I. The Geographical and Eschatological Setting (Zechariah 14)	210
II. David's Weeping at the Mount of Olives	216
III. David as a Prophet, and the Messiah as the Son of David	218
1) David as a Prophet	218
2) The Messiah as the Son of David	219
IV. David's Weeping over the Future Destruction of Jerusalem in Judaic Tradition	220
1) Josephus	220
2) Psalm 3	220
3) The Ninth of Ab	221
4) Psalm 137	221
V. 2 Sam 17:13	230
VI. Isaiah 29	232
VII. The Genre, Original Language and Provenance	242
1) The Genre	242
2) The Original Language	242
3) The Provenance	243
VIII. The Question of Historicity and the Date of the Narrative	243
1) The Question of Historicity	243
2) The Date of the Narrative	245
IX. Lukan Editing	246
X. The Emphases in the Narrative	248
1) Jesus as a Prophet	248
2) Jesus as the Son of David	249
3) True Lamentation over the Fate of Jerusalem	249
4) Jerusalem's Last Opportunity to Repent and to Acknowledge Jesus as the Son of David, the Messianic King	251

Chapter Five

Abraham's Prophetic Vision of the Messiah: The Judaic Background of John 8:56-58

Introduction	253
I. Genesis 15	255
1) Jubilees	257
2) Pseudo-Philo	258
3) Philo	259
4) The Genesis Apocryphon of Qumran (1QapGen ar)	261
5) Josephus	261
6) The Apocalypse of Abraham	262
7) Fourth Ezra	263
8) 2 (Syriac) Baruch	264
II. Tannaitic Interpretation of Genesis 15	265
III. The Messianic Interpretation of Gen 15:11	267
1) Abram's Prophetic Vision	268
2) The Fifteenth of Nisan	269
3) The Messiah as the Bird of Prey of Gen 15:11	271
IV. Jesus' Day	278
V. Jesus' True Age	280
VI. Abraham's Rejoicing	282
VII. Our Father Abraham	286

Chapter Six

The Messiah as a Vulture in Matt 24:28 // Luke 17:37b

Introduction	289
I. Job 39:30b	293
II. The Carrion Vulture in Judaic Tradition	296
III. Gathering	297
IV. The Meaning of the Saying	298

Chapter Seven

The Rejection of the Mother Bird Messiah in Luke 13:34b // Matt 23:37b

Introduction	303
I. Isa 31:5	305
II. Deut 22:6–7	306
1. Brood and Young Ones / Children	308
2. Often	309
3. Protective and Merciful Care	310
III. Deut 32:11	313
1. Desiring / Yearning / Longing	314
2. Young	316
3. To Be Anxious About, Care For	316
4. Wings as Protection	317
5. The Messiah and Gathering	319
IV. Protection from Judgment	322
Sources and Reference Works	329
About the Author	339
Index of Modern Authors	341

Preface

I would like to thank the members of the Society of New Testament Studies seminar "The Gospels and Rabbinic Judaism" for their helpful comments on chapters two and four at the 2001 and 2002 meetings of the Society in Montreal, Canada, and Durham, England. Professor Maurice Casey of the University of Nottingham encouraged me to deal with the contents of chapter one, and he also read it. Professor Peter von der Osten-Sacken of Berlin's Humboldt University kindly read chapters one and two, and Dr. Niko Oswald of the "Institut für Judaistik" at Berlin's Free University not only did the same for all the essays, but also generously helped me with some Aramaic phrases. The now retired fisherman and hobby archaeologist Mendel Nun, as well as Yoel Ben-Yosef of Kibbutz Ein-Gev on the Sea of Galilee, graciously shared with me their knowledge of the site "Kursi" and its environment.

Taking time off from working on his own dissertation, my son Jonathan Aus typed and formatted the manuscript on his computer, and the Rev. Dr. Thomas Day of Berlin kindly proofread it. Professor Jacob Neusner, now of Bard College in Annandale-on-Hudson, New York, graciously accepted the volume in his series "Studies in Judaism." To them all I express my heartfelt thanks.

Since I write as my "hobby" in addition to my full-time position as a parish pastor, I hope that the reader will understand my efforts to dialogue primarily with the most important secondary literature as it has been available to me in Berlin, thus not overburdening the footnotes. The many Judaic and other sources employed throughout are described in "Sources and Reference Works" at the end. In the text only the standard abbreviations are employed. An index of modern authors is also included, especially in order to indicate where I differ from many modern interpreters.

Those today who attempt to point out the relevance of rabbinic sources to New Testament scholarship, especially on the Gospels, are forced to swim against a strong current. This is due primarily to the fact that, despite their expertise in Greek, most New Testament scholars have only a working knowledge of biblical, not rabbinic Hebrew. Thus they usually have no direct access to rabbinic sources in the original, and many end up citing only (H. Strack and) P. Billerbeck in their footnotes (Str-B) – a work over eighty years old and theologically problematical.

In spite of vexing problems such as the dating of individual Judaic traditions, swimming against the current can not only be good exercise, but also deeply rewarding: the proposals made in the following seven chapters are to my knowledge all new. I thus hope that I can persuade the reader to join me and others in some fine swimming.

Roger David Aus
Easter, 2003
Berlin, Germany

Chapter One

My Name is "Legion" : Palestinian Judaic Samson Traditions in Mark 5:1-20

Introduction

Jesus' healing the Gerasene demoniac in Mark 5:1-20 has been labeled "a strange story,"[1] "difficult, obstinate,"[2] and an ancient *crux interpretum*.[3] R. Pesch maintains that a *"cantus firmus* of perplexity permeates the history of research" on the text.[4] Yet E. Lohmeyer could also state that there is hardly another narrative in the Gospel of Mark which is so vivid and descriptive.[5] Like R. Pesch, F. Annen wrote a monograph on this pericope. Among other things he concluded that the form and wording of the original report are no longer retrievable.[6]

---

[1] J. Schniewind, *Das Evangelium nach Markus* (NTD 1; Göttingen: Vandenhoeck & Ruprecht, 1960⁹) 53.
[2] R. Pesch, *Der Besessene von Gerasa*. Entstehung und Überlieferung einer Wundergeschichte (SBS 56; Stuttgart: Katholisches Bibelwerk, 1972) 9 – "spröde, widerspenstig."
[3] E. Haenchen, *Der Weg Jesu* (Berlin: de Gruyter, 1968²) 190. Cf. J. Donahue and D. Harrington, *The Gospel of Mark* (Sacra Pagina 2; Collegeville, Minnesota: The Liturgical Press, 2002) 169: "The narrative is by far the most elaborate and enigmatic gospel miracle story."
[4] *Der Besessene* 11. Cf. the statement by H. van der Loos, *The Miracles of Jesus* (NovTSup 9; Leiden: Brill, 1965) 394 that "this account ... lies heavily on the exegete's stomach."
[5] *Das Evangelium des Markus* (Meyer I 2; Göttingen: Vandenhoeck & Ruprecht, 1963¹⁶) 99.
[6] Cf. his *Heil für die Heiden*. Zur Bedeutung und Geschichte der Tradition vom besessenen Gerasener (Mk 5, 1-20 par.) (Frankfurter

Other views of the narrative are even more negative. J. Weiß maintained that "we would lose nothing if we took a complete farewell from it."[7] M. Dibelius even spoke of its "striking opposition to every kind of evangelical ethos...."[8]

Jesus' exorcizing a "legion" of unclean spirits from a man described as mad, however, is a truly fascinating tale, with its twenty verses the longest in the Gospel of Mark. Today's reader asks for example where "the country of the Gerasenes" was located (v 1); why Jesus must ask the unclean spirit what its name is (v 9) when it knows his name (v 7);[9] what the unclean spirit's name "Legion" actually means (v 9); why a herd of swine numbering about 2000 would suddenly rush down a steep slope into the Sea of Galilee and drown (v 13); why the healed demoniac did not follow Jesus' advice in v 19, but instead went off to the Decapolis to proclaim what Jesus had done for him (v 20); and whether an originally independent anecdote about a herd of swine was later added to the narrative of Jesus' exorcizing unclean spirits from a madman.

In addition, the high number of *hapax legomena* in the narrative, found only here and in the parallel accounts of Matthew (8:28-34) and Luke (8:26-39) in the Gospels (Γερασηνοί, κατοίκησις, ἅλυσις, πέδη, διασπάω, δαμάζω, κατακόπτω, ὁρκίζω, λεγιών [elsewhere only Matt 26:53] ; ἀγέλη, ὁρμάω, κρημνός, ἱματίζω, σωφρονέω and Δεκάπολις [elsewhere only 7:31]), points to special traditions behind the

---

Theologische Studien 20; Frankfurt: Josef Knecht, 1976) 199. See also the secondary literature cited by him on pp. 222-238, as well as in R. Guelich, *Mark 1 - 8:26* (WBC 34 A; Dallas: Word Books, 1989) 271, and in J. Marcus, *Mark 1 - 8* (AB 27; New York: Doubleday, 2000) 341-354.

[7] Cf. his *Die drei älteren Evangelien* (Göttingen: Vandenhoeck & Ruprecht, 1907²) 120, cited by W. Schmithals, *Das Evangelium nach Markus, Kapitel 1 - 9,1* (ÖTKNT 2/1; Gütersloh: Gerd Mohn; Würzburg: Echter, 1979) 266.

[8] *From Tradition to Gospel* (New York: Scribner's, n.d.) 89; cf. also 101.

[9] Well stated by E. Gould in *The Gospel According to St. Mark* (ICC; Edinburgh: Clark, 1896/1955) 90: "It is a curious question, why Jesus asked this question of the demoniac, and it has been curiously answered...."

narrative. Where did they come from? In what language was the original account narrated, and is it historical?

I attempt to answer the above and other relevant questions concerning Mark 5:1-20 in the following study. Part I deals with the Gerasene demoniac characterized as a madman, and Psalm 91. Part II is on the Gerasene demoniac described in terms of Judaic traditions centering on Samson. After an introduction on Samson in Judaic traditions, I point out the relevance of the latter to the motifs and expressions of 1. living in a rock cave; 2. uncleanness; 3. phenomenal strength, binding, hand-chains and foot-shackles; 4. shouting loudly, running and meeting; 5. swearing not to torment or injure someone; 6. the question "What is your name?" 7. legion; 8. swine and swineherd; 9. panicking by rushing down a steep slope, and drowning; 10. survival of only one, who proclaims the miracle elsewhere; 11. begging someone to leave the land out of fear; and 12. about two thousand.

Part III deals with the site of the miracle / exorcism, Kursi; Part IV with the extent of the original narrative, and Markan editing; Part V with the provenance, language and date of the original account; Part VI with its form and historicity; and Part VII with the purposes of the narrative.

I. The Gerasene Demoniac Characterized as a Madman, and Psalm 91

1. A Madman

The Mishna at *Terumoth* 1:1 states that a שׁוֹטֶה, usually translated as "imbecile," is one of five persons ineligible to give a heave offering.[10] Yet the term primarily means a "madman" or insane person.[11] The Tosefta at *Ter.* 1:3 supplements the above Mishnah passage by defining who a madman is:

> He who goes out alone at night, and
> who lodges / stays over night in a cemetery,

---

[10] Albeck 1.179; Danby 52; Neusner / Avery-Peck 93.
[11] Cf. the many examples cited by Jastrow, *A Dictionary* 1531.

tearing his clothing, and
who destroys what people give him.

The opposite of his being mad is then stated as חָלוּם, "sane," "well,"[12] one who is mentally alert (פִּקֵּחַ)[13] in every respect.[14] This tradition is commented upon in several other sources.[15]

The Gerasene demoniac of Mark 5:1-20 displays the above characteristics and was thus perceived as a "madman" by the first Palestinian Jewish and Jewish-Christian hearers and readers of this episode:

1) The Gerasene demoniac is described throughout as being alone; nowhere is another demoniac mentioned. He ventures out alone not only by day, but also by night (v 5).[16]

2) He lodges / stays over night among the tombs. Mark 5:3 has ὃς τὴν κατοίκησιν εἶχεν ἐν τοῖς μνήμασιν : "who had his dwelling among the tombs." The latter are variously called μνήματα in vv 3 and 5, and μνημεῖα in v 2. This is similar to the two plural forms of קֶבֶר , grave, tomb, in Hebrew: קְבָרוֹת and קְבָרִים.[17]

Contact with a corpse rendered one "unclean," טָמֵא , as in Num 5:2 and 9:7, 10. There were even persons who deliberately "lodged" (לוּן)[18] in cemeteries in the hope that an "unclean spirit" (רוּחַ טוּמְאָה) would rest upon them

---

[12] Jastrow 465 and 471.
[13] Jastrow 1208, 3): bright, smart, prudent.
[14] Lieberman 107. Cf. also the English translation of Avery-Peck in Neusner 1.130.
[15] Cf. y. Ter. 1:1, 40b (Neusner / Avery-Peck 6.55); b. Hag. 3b (Soncino 12); and y. Git. 7:1, 48c (Neusner 25.178-179).
[16] In the Markan setting, the whole episode occurs in the evening, when it had become dark (4:35; 5:1). This is due either to the editorial work of the Evangelist, or more probably to the collector of the pre-Markan material, who already had 5:1-20 follow the stilling of the storm on the same Sea of Galilee in 4:35-41.
[17] Jastrow 1312-1313. Cf. the (בית ה)קברות) in the above Tosefta passage, and (בית ה)קברים) in b. Ber. 18b (Soncino 111) for "cemetery." On the two Greek terms, see BAGD 524 and LSJ 1139.
[18] Jastrow 699, BDB 533. The term is used in the above Tosefta passage.

and they could then foretell the future.¹⁹ While the latter does not apply to the Gerasene demoniac, it does account for the association of "tombs" and an "unclean spirit" (πνεῦμα ἀκάθαρτον) in Mark 5:2. The latter is repeated in v 8, and as the plural in v 13. A madman who lived among tombs automatically had contact with "unclean spirits."

3) After his cure by Jesus, the Gerasene demoniac is described as sitting "clothed" (5:15 – ἱματισμένον). This contrasts with his previous state, when he is assumed to have ripped or torn off at least parts of his original clothing while bruising himself with stones (v 5).²⁰

4) The demoniac is thought of as "destroying"²¹ his clothes, the shackles and chains placed upon him (5:3-4), and even destroying / injuring his own body by bruising it with stones (v 5).

5) After Jesus heals him, the former demoniac is described as sitting with him, clothed and "being in his right mind" (5:15 – σωφρονοῦντα).²² It corresponds to the opposite mental state of a madman, שׁוֹטֶה , in the above Tosefta passage: חָלוּם.²³

---

¹⁹ Cf. b. Ḥag. 3b (Soncino 12); Sanh. 65 b (Soncino 446); and Nidd. 17a (Soncino 113). They are simply called "spirits" in b. Ber. 18b (Soncino 110-111). For the phenomenon, see already Isa 65:4, including the LXX, and Deut 18:11. On "spirit of impurity," "unclean spirit," see the sources cited in Str-B 4.503-504.

²⁰ The above Tosefta passage has the verb קָרַע for tear, rip (Jastrow 1424, BDB 902) and the noun כְּסוּת for clothing (Jastrow 652). Luke 8:27 expands the motif by stating that "for a long time he had worn no clothes."

²¹ The Tosefta passage employs הַמְאַבֵּד, which does not mean "he who loses," as translated by Avery-Peck, but "he who destroys." Cf. Jastrow 3, citing b. Ḥag. 4a, and the English translation in Soncino 12.

²² Cf. BAGD 802.1. on σωφρονέω : of mental health (in contrast to μαίνεσθαι); LSJ 1751.

²³ Cf. again Jastrow 471, where it is the passive participle of חלם. I consider נִפְקָד much less probable in the context, for it usually is in contrast to שָׁטַף (Jastrow 1208, 3).

The above four characteristics of a "madman," together with the opposite state of being of sound mind, found in the Tannaitic document *t. Ter.* 1:3, thus describe the "before" and "after" condition of the Gerasene demoniac very closely. This is important to note not only in regard to the question of the provenance of the account, but also in regard to the relevance of the particular psalm employed in early Judaism for people who were considered mad or insane. To this I now turn.

2. *Psalm 91*

This psalm is known to Christians primarily through Jesus' quoting vv 11-12 to the devil (the head of all demons) when he is tempted by him in Matt 4:6-7 // Luke 4:10-11. In regard to Num 6:24, "The Lord bless you and keep you," the Tannaitic midrash *Sifre* Naso 40 for example interprets the latter as "He will keep you from 'demons' (המזיקים)."[24] This is then buttressed by Ps 91:11.[25]

---

[24] Cf. Jastrow 755 on מַזִּיק. The root is נזק, to hurt, injure, damage (Jastrow 892), signifying a demon's main activity. For an overview of Judaic demonology, see the art. "Demonology" by K. Kohler in *JE* (1903) 4.514-520; Str-B 4.501-535; the art. δαίμων etc. by W. Foerster in *TDNT* 2.1-20; the art. "Demons, Demonology" by T. Gaster in *IDB* (1962) 1.817-824; and the art. "Demons, Demonology" by D. Hillers and L. Rabinowitz in *EJ* (1971) 5.1521-1528. Several of these authors refer to Psalm 91.

[25] Horowitz 44; Neusner 1.191-192. Cf. the similar tradition in *Num. Rab.* Naso 11/5 on Num 6:24, which cites Ps 91:7 and 11 (Mirqin 9.298; Soncino 5.433-434). See also *Tanh.* Wayyeṣe 3 on Gen 28:10 (Eshkol 1.120-121) with R. Meir, a third generation Tanna (Strack and Stemberger, *Introduction* 84), as well as Mishpaṭim 19 (Eshkol 1.255). The 1993 Cambridge Ph.D. dissertation of R. Burrelli, *A Study of Psalm 91 with Special Reference to the Theory That It Was Intended as a Protection Against Demons and Magic*, has not been available to me. J. Marcus in *Mark 1 - 8*, 344, says he also calls attention to the use of "Most High" in Psalm 91. R. Glöckner in *Neutestamentliche Wundergeschichten und das Lob der Wundertaten Gottes in den Psalmen* (Mainz: Matthias-Grünewald-Verlag, 1983) does not note Psalm 91 in his treatment of Mark 5:1-20 (pp. 80-104).

The pre-Christian Septuagint already attributes this psalm to David.[26] In *b. Sanh.* 103 a-b, vv 1-10 are interpreted as David's addressing his son Solomon, vv 11-13 as Bathsheba's doing so, and vv 14-16 as God's doing so.[27]

The Targum, certainly reflecting popular tradition, has David say v 2 to the Lord, then v 3 to "Solomon, my son." David continues addressing Solomon, stating in v 5 that he should definitely not fear "demons" (מזיקי) who go about at night, nor the arrow of the angel of death, (the angel) of the demons (שׁד) of the daytime. In v 6 he tells his son not to fear a troop (or company, סִיעָא)[28] of demons (שׁדין) who inflict wounds at noon. Verse 7 opens by recalling a frequent means of incantation or exorcism: "Remember the Holy Name!"[29] Solomon is then represented as answering in v 9, and the Lord of the Universe as replying in turn to him in v 10, with a demon (מזיקא), and in the following verses.[30]

One reason for Psalm 91's being interpreted as providing aid from demons lies in Judaic interpretation of the verb יְשׁוּד in v 6, thought of as a particular demon.[31] The Septuagint already renders the Hebrew as δαιμόνιον. The term שֵׁד / שִׁיד was

---

[26] Another, later tradition attributes it to Moses, probably deduced from the beginning of the preceding psalm, 90: "A prayer of Moses, the man of God." Yet this variant tradition also maintains that Moses composed it while ascending Mount Sinai because "he was afraid of the harmful demons." See for example *Num. Rab.* 12/3 on Num 7:1 (Mirqin 10.12; Soncino 5.453) and *Midr. Pss.* 91/1 on Ps 91:1 (Buber 396, Braude 2.101).
[27] Soncino 701. Note 7 should read: "*Ibid.* 11-13." *Midr. Pss.* 91/1 on Ps 91:1 also states: it is thought that Solomon composed Psalm 91 (Buber 395, Braude 2.100).
[28] Jastrow 984.
[29] Verse 14 also states: "I will lift him up on account of his knowing My name."
[30] Cf. the Aramaic in Merino 149-150, with a Latin translation at 277-278. At times, for example שׁדי for Merino's שׂרי in v 5, I prefer readings found in de Lagarde, 55. The letters ר and ד were frequently confused by scribes.
[31] Cf. *b. Pesaḥ.* 111b (Soncino 573) and *Num. Rab.* Naso 12/3 on Num 7:1 (Mirqin 10.13; Soncino 5.454).

seen in it: "demon."[32] I suspect that this was also true for v 1, interpreted as: "He who lives in the shelter of the Most High, who (nevertheless) abides in the shadow of demons (שדי)."[33]

Psalm 91, as employed in the exorcism of demons, is already found in the pre-Christian Qumram writings. In the 11Q Apocryphal Psalms (11Q11), exorcism terminology is employed in connection with Solomon[34] and David. Columns one and two mention: an oath (שבועה), exor(cizing) / causing to swear (משבנ]יע]), the demon (השד), Solomon, [the spiri]ts ([הרונ]חות]), the demons (השדים), cure (רפואה), and your name (שמך - Solomon's, or more probably God's).

Column five deals with "those who are afflicted / possessed" ([הפגועןים]), "of (by) David," and an incantation "in the name of the Lor[d]." To a demon who comes upon one during the night, one should say: "Who are you (מי אתה) ... ? ... You are the chief of the army (שר הצבה) [of evil spirits]." Another de[mon] (ש[ד]) is then mentioned. Column six continues with the "sons of Bel[ial]." Then Psalm 91 is quoted through v 13.[35]

The above question "Who are you?" recalls Jesus' asking the unclean spirit in Mark 5:9, "What is your name?" And when the demon which is being exorcized is labeled "the chief of the

---

[32] BDB 993, Jastrow 1523.
[33] Cf. K. Kohler's statement in his art. "Demonology" in *JE* 4.515 that "For a long time the name שד was erroneously connected with 'the Almighty' (שדי)." See also the general statement by M. Tate in *Psalms 51-100* (WBC 20; Dallas: Word Books, 1990) 455: "the content of the psalm reflects a thought world in which the presence of demons, demonical possession, and malignant spirits and powers was considered commonplace."
[34] On Solomon's great repulation as an exorcist, cf. Wisd Sol 7:20; Josephus, *Ant.* 8.45-49; Pseudo-Philo 60 in *OTP* 2.373, with n. "e," and Harrington 1.368; and the Second Targum on Esth 1:2 (Grossfeld, English 106 and n. 2 on p. 108). The Testament of Solomon (*OTP* 1.960-987) also confirms this reputation. In 11:1-7 (*OTP* 1.972-973) there is even a retelling of Mark 5:1-20 because it is an exorcism.
[35] Martínez and Tigchelaar, *The Dead Sea Scrolls, Study Edition* 2.1200-1205.

army," this is reminiscent of the military term "Legion" in the same Markan verse.

According to Tannaitic rabbinic tradition, Ps 91:1-9 was called "The Song Against Plagues" (שִׁיר שֶׁל נְגָעִים), based on v 10. Yet it was also labeled "The Song of Afflictions / the Afflicted" (שִׁיר שֶׁל פְּגָעִים / פְּגוּעִין), the latter a term found above in the Qumran exorcism material and here referring to v 7. The noun פֶּגַע means evil occurrence; *affliction,* plague.[36] The "Song of the Afflicted" was customarily recited in Jerusalem in the Temple for those afflicted with madness / insanity.[37]

The "Song of the Afflicted," Ps 91:1-9, was thus well-known in Palestine while the Temple still stood, i.e. up to 70 CE. It was then almost automatically associated with a person considered to be a madman, like the Gerasene demoniac. The psalm is relevant to the Markan pericope in three ways.

2.1 The Most High God

In Mark 5:7 the demoniac shouts at the top of his voice: "What have you to do with me, Jesus, Son of 'the Most High God'?" The Greek of the latter is τοῦ θεοῦ τοῦ ὑψίστου. Except for the parallel passage in Luke 8:28, the expression is found in the NT only in Acts 16:17 and Heb 7:1.[38]

The "Song of the Afflicted" begins in 91:1 with "He who lives in the shelter of 'the Most High'" (עֶלְיוֹן, LXX τοῦ ὑψίστου). It ends in v 9 with "you have made 'the Most High' your dwelling

---

[36] Jastrow 1135.
[37] Cf. *b. Šebu.* 15b (Soncino 75); *y. Šabb.* 6:2, 8b as שיר פגועין (Neusner 11.198); and *y. 'Erub.* 10:11, 26c (Neusner 12.290), very similar to the latter. One reason for the Psalm's being recited in the Temple lay in its opening two verses, which deal with someone entering there. For the "Song of the Afflicted," see also *Num. Rab.* Naso 12/3 on Num 7:1 (Mirqin 10.12; Soncino 5.453) and *Midr. Pss.* 91/1 (Buber 198b, Braude 2.101). For Isaac's blessing his son Jacob with this Song of the Afflicted, see *Bereshit Rabbathi* Toledoth on Gen 28:1 (Albeck 113). This is an example of the preventive use of the Song.
[38] See also "the Son of the Most High" in Luke 1:32, "the power of the Most High" in v 35, "the prophet of the Most High" in v 76, "children of the Most High" in 6:35, and "the Most High" in Acts 7:48.

place": עֶלְיוֹן, LXX τὸν ὕψιστον. That is, the entire "Song" is framed by עֶלְיוֹן, "the Most High." Of only twenty-nine Hebrew occurrences as a name of God in the OT, two are found in Ps 91:1 and 9.[39] This makes it very probable that the madman's designation of Jesus as son of "the Most High God" in Mark 5:7 derives from the Psalm connected very closely in early Judaism with madness, 91. The term "Most High God" here thus does not necessarily point to the demoniac as a pagan, as maintained by numerous commentators.[40]

2.2 *The Name*

In Mark 5:9 Jesus asks the Gerasene demoniac, "What is your name?" The latter then replies, "My name is Legion, for we are many."

As I will point out below in section II.6, the "name" imagery here primarily derives from Judaic tradition on the Samson

---

[39] The Aramaic form is found in Dan 7:18, 22, 25 and 27. See also עַלְיָא as the Most High God (BDB 1106).

[40] Cf. for example W. Grundmann, *Das Evangelium nach Markus* (THKNT 2; Berlin: Evangelische Verlagsanstalt, 1977⁷) 143; J. Gnilka, *Das Evangelium nach Markus (Mk 1 – 8,26)* (EKK II/1; Zurich: Benziger; Neukirchen-Vluyn: Neukirchener, 1989³) 204; and M. Hooker, *The Gospel According to St Mark* (Black's; London: Black, 1991) 143. Only Babylon in Isa 14:14 and Balaam in Num 24:16 are definitely pagan speakers employing "the Most High." Melchizedek in Gen 14:18-20 is hardly conceived as such. It should also be noted that the *Shemoneh 'Esreh* or Eighteen Prayer, which was to be recited three times daily, begins in 1. in both the Babylonian and Palestinian recensions with "Blessed art Thou... great, mighty and fearful God, 'God Most High' (אֵל עֶלְיוֹן)...." See Schürer, *The history* 2.256 and 260; I. Elbogen, *Der jüdische Gottesdienst in seiner geschichtlichen Entwicklung* (Frankfurt am Main, 1931³; reprint Hildesheim: Georg Olms, 1962) 43; and Str-B 4.211. When the Gerasene demoniac addresses Jesus as "Son of the Most High God" in Mark 5:7, this is thus typically Palestinian Jewish terminology. Also against J. Derrett in "Spirit-Possession and the Gerasene Demoniac" in *Man* 14 (1979) 289, who maintains that "Most High" is "not a contemporary Jewish expression for the deity," but a "pagan morality deity of Asia Minor."

narrative in Judg 13:17-18. Yet Psalm 91 encouraged the author of Mark 5:1-20 to employ such imagery.

The second half of Ps 91:14 has God say: "I will protect him, for he knows 'My name.'" Verse 7 reads: "A thousand may fall at your side, ten thousand at your right hand, but it [assumed to be one of the demons] will not approach you." The Targum at this point intentionally changes "it" to "they," referring back to the 1000 and 10,000 (demons). It also begins the verse with the admonition, "Remember the holy Name" (תדכר שמא קדישא).[41] That is, the divine Name (יהוה) should be employed in an incantation to exorcize a demon, to make it depart. This is shown in 11Q Aprocryphal Psalms, where column two begins with the fragment שם, which could be "name." After mention of Solomon, spirits and demons, the text continues: "his people ... cure, ... have relied [upon] your name (שמך)."[42] The context makes it probable that this is the name of God, "Your name." This is buttressed by column five, where before the citation of Psalm 91 the phrase occurs: "[An incanta]tion in the name of YHW[H]."[43]

The above remarks indicate that elements of Psalm 91, employed in pre-70 CE Judaism to treat those afflicted with madness / insanity, probably encouraged the author of Mark 5:1-20 to have Jesus ask the "name" of the Gerasene madman.

2.3 Legion

When Jesus asks the unclean spirit within the Gerasene madman "What is your name?" he replies: "My name is 'Legion' (λεγιών), for we are many" (Mark 5:9). While the term "legion" primarily derives from Palestinian Judaic tradition on the Samson narrative (see section II. 7. below), it is also closely connected to Psalm 91. Before analyzing the latter, however, it will be helpful to note a number of other unclean spirits /

---

[41] Merino 149 and 278. Cf. also *Num. Rab.* Naso 12/3 on Num 7:1, where Ps 91:2 is interpreted to mean that Moses said: "Through His [the Lord's] name I drive out the harmful demons and the destroying angels" (Mirqin 10.11; Soncino 5.453).
[42] Martínez and Tigchelaar 2.1200-1201.
[43] *Ibid.*, 2.1202-1203.

demons with specific names, as well as the popular conception that there were "myriads" of demons.

a) Names of Specific Demons

The Gospels mention only the name "Beelzebul," the ruler of the demons (Mark 3:22 par.).[44] Yet Judaic sources reveal numerous others such as the following:

1. Ashmedai (אַשְׁמְדָאִי),[45] the chief of the demons,[46] perhaps the same as Shimadon (שִׁמָדוֹן), a destroyer.[47]
2. Joseph.[48]
3. Ben Temalion (בֶּן תְּמַלְיוֹן).[49]
4. The Princess (בַּת מֶלֶךְ).[50]
5. Shibeta (שִׁיבְתָא), an evil spirit attacking those who eat without washing their hands.[51]
6. Lilith (לִילִית), the night demon.[52]
7. Igrath (אִגְרַת),[53] daughter of Mahalath and queen of the demons.[54]

---

[44] Cf. also Matt 10:25, and 12:27 // Luke 11:18-19.
[45] Jastrow 129.
[46] Cf. b. Pesaḥ. 110a (Soncino 566); Giṭ. 68a (Soncino 323); and Num. Rab. Naso 11/3 on Num 6:23 (Mirqin 9.288; Soncino 5.421). See also "the wicked demon Asmodeus" in Tob 3:8.
[47] Jastrow 1592, from the root שָׁמַד , in the hiphil to destroy. See Gen. Rab. Noah 36/1 on Gen 9:18 (Theodor and Albeck 335, Soncino 1.288) and 36/3 on Gen 9:20 (Theodor and Albeck 338; Soncino 1.290). In both incidents the demon talks to human beings, as "Legion" does with Jesus.
[48] Cf. b. Pesaḥ. 110a (Soncino 566 and 567) and ʿErub. 43a (Soncino 299).
[49] Cf. Jastrow 1677 and b. Meʿil. 17b (Soncino 64).
[50] Cf. Jastrow 791, and b. Šabb. 109a (Soncino 529; Goldschmidt 1.577, n. 3) in the name of R. Yose, a third generation Tanna (Strack and Stemberger, Introduction 84).
[51] Cf. Jastrow 1557, b. Yoma 77b (Soncino 377), Taʿan. 20b (Soncino 102), and Ḥull. 107b (Soncino 595 as "evil spirits").
[52] Cf. Jastrow 707 and b. Šabb. 151b (Soncino 773).
[53] Jastrow 15.
[54] Cf. b. Pesaḥ. 112b (Soncino 579-580), where she converses with R. Ḥanina b. Dosa. In Num. Rab. Naso 12/3 on Num 7:1 (Mirqin 10.13; Soncino 5.454), R. Simeon b. Yoḥai, a third generation Tanna (Strack

8. Tezazith (תְּזָזִית), a demon causing shaking, epilepsy, madness.[55]
9. Qeteb (קֶטֶב), a demon of pestilence and destruction.[56]
10. Qeteb Meriri (קֶטֶב מְרִירִי), a demon of "'bitter' pestilence / destruction."[57]

Passages such as *b. Pesaḥ.* 110a-112b[58] mention numerous others, especially those found in Babylonia, where belief in the demonic was very widespread. Yet the above ten suffice to show that just as "Legion" was the name of a particular demon in Mark 5:9, so too others had their specific designations. In the notes I have also called attention to the fact that various demons known in Palestine were connected to Psalm 91, the "Song of Those Afflicted (with Madness)."

b) *Myriads of Demons and "Legion"*

Mark 5:9 has the demon inside the Gerasene madman tell Jesus his name is Legion, "for we are 'many' (πολλοί)." That is, there was not only one, but numerous demons who tortured him. In the exorcism narrative in Mark 1:21-28, the (one) unclean spirit cries out, "What have you to do with *us*, Jesus of Nazareth? Have you come to destroy *us*?" (v 24). Here too more than one unclean spirit is within the victim, yet only one of them

---

and Stemberger, *Introduction* 84), interprets her to be the "terror of the night" in Ps 91:5.
[55] Jastrow 1660. In *Num. Rab.* Ḥukkath 19/8 on Num 19:2 (Mirqin 10.227-228; Soncino 6.757), R. Yoḥanan b. Zakkai, a first generation Tanna (Strack and Stemberger, *Introduction* 74-75), asks a heathen whether he has never seen someone possessed by this demon (lit. spirit) of madness.
[56] BDB 881, Jastrow 1346. Derived from Ps 91:6, it is described in *Num. Rab.* Naso 12/3 on Num 7:1 (Mirqin 10.13, Soncino 5.454-455). See also *Midr. Pss.* 91/1 on Ps 91:1, referring to v 6 (Buber 397, Braude 2.102), in the name of R. Yose, a third generation Tanna (see n. 50).
[57] The term "Bitter pestilence / destruction" in Deut 32:24 is labeled a demon in *Sifre* Ha'azinu 321 on that verse (Finkelstein 368, Hammer 331), and is described by R. Yose in the same *Midr. Pss.* 91/1 passage cited in n. 56 above.
[58] Soncino 566-580.

addresses Jesus.[59] Luke 8:2 also notes that Jesus had cured Mary Magdalene, resulting in seven demons leaving her. In 11:24-26 (// Matt 12:43-45) an unclean spirit brings seven others more evil than himself to join him within the body of a person he had once left.

Judaic sources, however, speak of many more than seven demons / unclean spirits together. R. Yoḥanan, a second generation Palestinian Amora active first at Sepphoris and later at Tiberias,[60] maintains in *b. Giṭ.* 68a: "There were three hundred kinds of demons (שדים) in Shiḥin...," a place near Sepphoris.[61] Abaye, a fourth generation Babylonian Amora,[62] says in *b. Ber.* 6a that demons (מזיקין) "are more numerous than we (humans) are and surround us like the ridge round a field."[63] R. Levi, a third generation Palestinian Amora and pupil of R. Yoḥanan,[64] states that "In the wide space of the universe there is no place – even one so small that it holds no more than a fourth of a *ḳab* of seed – that is without nine *ḳab* of demons, so that wherever a man reaches, his hand is in the midst of demons...."[65] R. Joshua b. Levi, a first generation Palestinian Amora,[66] also notes regarding Titus' siege of the Jewish capital: "When the enemies came to destroy Jerusalem there were sixty myriads of evil spirits (מזיקין) standing at the gate of the Temple ready to

---

[59] In the other two Markan exorcisms (7:24-30 and 9:14-29), only one unclean spirit is mentioned.
[60] Strack and Stemberger, *Introduction* 94-95.
[61] Soncino 322, and Jastrow 1559 on שיחין. See also *Midr. Pss.* 78/12 (Buber 351, Braude 2.31).
[62] Strack and Stemberger, *Introduction* 104.
[63] Soncino 23.
[64] Strack and Stemberger, *Introduction* 98.
[65] Cf. *Midr. Pss.* 17/8 on Ps 17:8 (Buber 130-131, Braude 1.212). In 2.438, n. 36, Braude remarks that "A fourth of a *ḳab* is the equivalent of a pint." Parallels are found in *Midr. Pss.* 55/3 on Ps 55:19 (Buber 292, Braude 1.493); *Pesiq. R.* 5/10 on Num 7:1 (Friedmann 21b, Braude 1.112); and *Deut. Rab.* Re'eh 4/4 on Deut 11:22 (Mirqin 11.75, Soncino 7.92) in the name of Abba b. Ze'ira, a Palestinian rabbi active ca. 330 CE (Str-B 5/6.108).
[66] Strack and Stemberger, *Introduction* 92-93.

engage them in battle...."[67] The term "myriad" here is רִבּוֹא, ten thousand,[68] thus meaning 600,000 demons.

The expression "myriad" also occurs in v 7 of the "Song of Those Afflicted (with Madness)," Psalm 91. It reads:

> A thousand my fall at your side,
> ten thousand at your right hand,
> but it will not come near you.

"Ten thousand" here is the Hebrew רְבָבָה, meaning "multitude, myriad, ten thousand," of which רִבּוֹא / רְבּוֹ is a later synonym.[69] "It" in the third clause refers to one of the demons, called δαιμόνιον already in the LXX of v 6. The Targum of v 7 maintains regarding all these demons: "they will not approach you to injure you."[70] Ps 91:7 is the prooftext for the harmful demons (מַזִּיקִין) who surround a person in *Num. Rab.* Naso 11/5 on Num 6:24, "The Lord ... keep you" (from these demons),[71] as well as elsewhere.[72]

Other Judaic sources, however, interpret the "thousand" and "ten thousand" of Ps 91:7 as the number of angels God assigns to protect a person from the myriads of demons seeking to do him harm.[73] The passage most relevant in this respect to the term "Legion" in Mark 5:9 is *Midr. Pss.* 17/8 on Ps 17:8, here interpreting the phrase "will not come near you" in 91:7. It asks:

---

[67] Cf. *Deut. Rab.* Debarim 17 on Deut 2:3 (Mirqin 11.21, Soncino 7.20).
[68] Jastrow 1440.
[69] BDB 914, Jastrow 1439.
[70] Merino 149 and 278.
[71] Mirqin 9.298; Soncino 5.433.
[72] Cf. *b. Ber.* 6a (Soncino 23, with n. 8), as well as the exposition of R. Ḥanina b. R. Abbahu in *Num. Rab.* Naso 12/3 on Num 7:1 (Mirqin 10.14-15; Soncino 5.456), with parallels in *Midr. Pss.* 17/8 on Ps 17:8 (Buber 213, Braude 1.213) and 91/4 on Ps 91:7 (Buber 398, Braude 2.103).
[73] Cf. *Exod. Rab.* Mishpaṭim 32/6 on Exod 23:20, in connection with Ps 68:18 (Mirqin 6.84, Soncino 3.410-411); the incident which "the Rabbis taught" in *Midr. Pss.* 17/8 on Ps 17:8 (Buber 131, Braude 2.212-213); and 91/4 on Ps 91:7 (Buber 398, Braude 2.103). See also 55/3 on Ps 55:2, with 55:19 and 91:11 (Buber 292, Braude 1.493). Matt 26:53 also has Jesus in Gethsemane mention twelve legions of angels God would send him (to protect him) if he requested it.

What is meant by the words "will not come near you"? They mean that the Holy One, blessed be He, said: "It is the way of the world that when a (mortal) king goes forth on a journey, and all His 'legions' (לגיונות) go forth with him to protect him, he is obliged to give them provision and food. But I, I assigned a thousand (angels) at your left hand, and ten thousand at your right hand to protect you, and not one (of these angels) 'will come near you' and say, 'Feed me and provide for me.'"[74]

This narrative is found in two other sources as well,[75] and ultimately derives from haggadic interpretation of Ps 136:13 and 25 in connection with Exod 15:3.[76] I shall analyze the great significance of the latter verse for the term "legion" in section II. 7. below. Here, however, it is important to note the connection between "legion" and early Judaic interpretation of "thousand" and "myriad" in v 7 of Psalm 91, the "Song of Those Afflicted (with Madness)." The Palestinian Jewish Christian author of Mark 5:1-20 may also have known of this association, aiding him in choosing the term "Legion" in v 9.

A complete Roman *legio* at the time of Jesus consisted of ca. 6,000 foot soldiers, in addition to some cavalry and auxiliary troops with special tasks.[77] The Latin term was a loanword both in Greek (λεγιών), Hebrew and Aramaic.[78] In the latter two

---

[74] Buber 131; I modify Braude's translation in 1.213.
[75] Cf. *Midr. Pss.* 91/4 on Ps 91:7 (Buber 398; Braude 2.103), and *Num. Rab.* Naso 12/3 on Num 7:1 (Mirqin 10.15, Soncino 5.456).
[76] Cf. *Midr. Pss.* 136/8 on Ps 136:13 in Buber 521, Braude 2.327-328.
[77] Cf. the art. "Legio" in PW 23 (1924) 1194-1199 for the older, republican period; λεγιών by H. Preisker in *TDNT* 4.68-69; "Legion" by F. Gealy in IDB 3.110; and BAGD 468. As of ca. 120 CE there was even a civilian village near Megiddo named "Legio" next to the headquarters of the Legio VI Ferrata. It was later renamed Maximianopolis. See Z. Safrai, "The Roman Army in the Galilee" in *The Galilee in Late Antiquity*, ed. L. Levine (New York: Jewish Theological Seminary, 1992) 105, 111-112.
[78] For the latter two, cf. S. Krauss, *Griechische und lateinische Lehnwörter* 2.304-305, and Jastrow 692. Only a very small number of the occurrences are in Aramaic. This makes the commentators' assertion that the "Legion" of Mark 5:9 is found in Greek and Aramaic (and not Hebrew) very strange. It is uncritically repeated again and again. See

languages it could simply mean a vast number, as in *Gen. Rab.* Bereshith 20/6 on Gen 3:16. R. Eleazar b. R. Shimeon, a fourth generation Tanna,[79] for example says there: "It is easier for a man to grow 'a legion' (ליגיון) of olives in Galilee than to rear one child in the Land of Israel."[80]

Yet the expression "legion" very soon developed negative connotations in Palestine. At the latest in 6 CE, the Legio X Fretensis was stationed in nearby Syria. Along with several other legions it had a wild boar as part of its military standards.[81] The wild boar as a pig was an unclean animal for the Jews (Lev 11:7 and Deut 14:8 - טָמֵא)[82] and stood metaphorically for a ravaging, destructive power (Ps 80:14, Eng. 13).[83] Many segments of the population, even those who were not Zealots, would have attributed these two connotations to a Roman legion stationed as an occupational power in Palestine.

---

for example E. Klostermann, *Das Markusevangelium* (HNT 3; Tübingen: Mohr / Siebeck, 1950[4]) 49; E. Lohmeyer, *Das Evangelium des Markus* (Meyer; Göttingen: Vandenhoeck & Ruprecht, 1967[17]) 96, n.2; W. Lane, *The Gospel According to Mark* (NICNT 2; Grand Rapids, Michigan: Eerdmans, 1974) 184; and R. Guelich, *Mark 1 - 8:26*, 281.

[79] Cf. Strack and Stemberger, *Introduction* 87.

[80] Cf. Theodor and Albeck 190. Soncino 1.165 has "myriads of olives." After finishing my own research on this expression, I discovered that J. Lightfoot had already called attention to this passage in *A Commentary on the New Testament from the Talmud and Hebraica* (Peabody, MA: Hendrickson, 1989; original 1859) 2.411. He died in 1675 (1.iii).

[81] Cf. the art. "Legio X Fretensis" by Ritterling in PW 24 (1925) 1671-1678, especially 1671-1672. Schürer, *The history* 1.362 maintains three legions were already stationed in Syria in 4 BCE, and four as of Tiberius, including X Fretensis. See also PW 24 (1925) 1363 for four in Syria ca. 20 CE, and 1362 for three in Syria as of 6 CE.

[82] Cf. the art "Swine" by G. Davies in *IDB* 4.469.

[83] Cf. the imagery of a "severe" (קשה) legion in *Gen. Rab.* Bereshith 4/6 on Gen 1:7 (Theodor and Albeck 30, Soncino 1.32); *y. Ta'an.* 2:1, 65b (Neusner 18.182); and *Exod. Rab.* Va'era 12/4 on Exod 9:24 (Mirqin 5.146, Soncino 3.146-147). For the wild boar of Ps 80:14 as the Roman emperor, see *'Avot R. Nat.* A 34 (Schechter 100, Goldin 138). See also *Gen. Rab.* Toledoth 65/1 on Gen 26:34, with Ps 80:14 (Theodor and Albeck 713, Soncino 2.581), where the Roman state is compared to a swine which maintains it is clean.

Another early reference associates a Roman legion with uncleanness. According to *m. Ḥull.* 9:2, the skin of a human being, the domestic pig and a wild boar are unclean.[84] The Tosefta at this point (8:16) states: "A legion (לגיון) which is passing from place to place – he who overshadows it is unclean (טמא). You have no legion (לגיון) in which there are no (human) scalps."[85] Commenting on the latter phenomenon, *b. Ḥull.* 123a maintains that "Our Rabbis taught: If a [Roman] legion (ליגיון) which passes from place to place enters a house, the house is unclean (טמא), for there is not a legion (ליגיון וליגיון) that does not carry with it several scalps."[86] Both Rashi and Jastrow believe the latter were used as charms in battle.[87]

A Roman legion in Palestine was thus definitely considered by the Jewish population to be "unclean" (טמא) because a) Gentiles or idolatrous heathen by definition were unclean;[88] b) the Tenth Legion, Fretensis, had a wild boar, an unclean animal, as part of its insignia; and c) it carried with it human scalps, unclean, probably as charms in battle. This helps to explain why the destructive "unclean spirit" of the Gerasene demoniac in Mark 5:1-20, whose name is "Legion," asks permission to enter a great heard of "swine," which are also unclean.

---

[84] Albeck 5.140-141, Danby 525, Neusner 782.
[85] Zuckermandel and Liebermann 510; Neusner 5.92.
[86] Soncino 685. A legion, and not an individual legionary, is meant here. J. Jeremias in *Jesus' Promise to the Nations* (London: SCM Press, 1958) 30-31, n.5, thinks one "legionary" was originally meant in Mark 5:9. When the translator rendered the Aramaic into λεγιών, "the mistaken idea arose that the demoniac was possessed by a whole regiment of demons." There is no basis for this view, especially in light of the phrase "for we are many," and the "myriads" of demons in Judaic interpretation of Ps 91:7.
[87] Soncino 685, n.1, and Jastrow 1426 on קרקפל.
[88] Cf. the sources cited in Str-B 4.374-375, especially "b," and 2.759-760.

II. The Gerasene Demoniac Described in Terms of Judaic Traditions Centering on Samson

Introduction

Five motifs and expressions from the terrible incident of the Levite's concubine in Judges 19 appear to have influenced the Emmaus narrative in Luke 24:13-35.[1] The Palestinian Jewish Christian author of the account now found in Mark 5:1-20 has borrowed heavily from chapters just before that, the story of Samson in Judges 13-16.[2] He applies motifs and expressions from the positive presentation of Samson in Judaic tradition to the negative figure of a madman, a demoniac.

Josephus, a native of Jerusalem whose mother tongue was Aramaic, completed his *Jewish Antiquities* ca. 93-94 CE.[3] In 5.275-317 (viii. 1-12) he retells the Samson narrative, including Palestinian haggadic traditions known to him.[4] In spite of his womanizing, says the Jewish historian, one should bear testimony to Samson for "his surpassing excellence in all the rest."[5] According to Judg 15:20 (and 16:31) Samson "judged Israel in the days of the Philistines twenty years." *Eccl. Rab.* 1:4

---

[1] Cf. my *The Stilling of the Storm*. Studies in Early Palestinian Judaic Traditions (Binghamton, New York: Global Publications, 2000) 193-202.
[2] On Samson in Judaic sources, cf. Ginzberg, *The Legends* 4.47-49 and the relevant notes in 6.204-209; the art. "Samson" by J. Lauterbach in *JE* 11 (1905) 1-2; and the art. "Samson" by M. Siff, A. Rothkoff, the editors and B. Bayer in *EJ* (1971) 14.771-777.
[3] Cf. *Ant.* 20.267 for the date, and the LCL edition (I. vii-xi and IV. xii-xiii) for the rest.
[4] Pseudo-Philo 42-43 (*OTP* 2.355-357; Latin in SC 229, pp. 288-298) also deal with Samson, including many haggadic elements. One such is phraseology from Judg 6:21 employed of the angel in 42:9, found also in Josephus' *Ant.* 5.284. D. Harrington in *OTP* 2.298-300 maintains that Pseudo-Philo is Palestinian and was written originally in Hebrew about the time of Jesus.
[5] Cf. Thackeray's translation in 5.317. Before this Josephus emphasizes that it is appropriate to admire Samson for his brave deeds, strength, generosity (in sacrificing himself) at the end of his life, and his anger toward his enemies (the Philistines) up to his death.

§ 4 states that his Beth Din (court) was then as great and important as that of Aaron.⁶ Samson could even be labeled a "righteous man" (צדיק) because he was unwilling to speak the Divine Name in vain in Judg 16:17.⁷ The latter verse has Samson tell Delilah, "I have been a Nazirite to God from my mother's womb." Since a Nazirite is "holy" (קָדֹשׁ) to the Lord according to Num 6:5 and 8, this explains why the angel tells Manoah's wife in Pseudo-Philo 42:3, "And behold, you will conceive and bear a son, and you will call his name Samson. For this one will be *sanctificatus* (holy, consecrated, dedicated) to your Lord."⁸

The latter statement is based on Judg 13:5, where the angel also states that Samson is "he who shall begin 'to deliver' (לְהוֹשִׁיעַ) Israel from the hand of the Philistines."⁹ The Tannaitic midrash *Sifre* Wezot Habberakah 357 on Deut 34:1, "As far as Dan," notes in this respect that shortly before his death God showed Moses the tribe of Dan worshiping idols, and then He "showed him 'the redeemer of Israel' (גואל ישראל) who was to arise from that tribe in the future. And who was this man? Samson the son of Manoah."¹⁰ This helps to explain the statement in *Gen. Rab.* Vayechi 98/14 on Gen 49:17, "Dan shall be a snake by the roadside" : "Our ancestor Jacob saw [Samson]

---

⁶ Soncino 8.12-13, where the Danite Samson is identified with Bedan ("of Dan") in 1 Sam 12:6. On the latter, cf. also *b. Roš Haš.* 25 a-b (Soncino 111).

⁷ Cf. *b. Soṭ.* 9b (Soncino 43) and *Num. Rab.* Naso 9/24 on Num 5:27 (Mirqin 9.196, Soncino 5.286). See also the Hellenistic Jewish sermon "De Sampsone" 44-46 (F. Siegert, *Drei hellenistisch-jüdische Predigten* 81-83).

⁸ Harrington in SC 230.290, and *OTP* 2.356. This refutes L. Ginzberg's statement in *Legends* 6.205 that "there is no Hebrew word meaning 'holy' which can in any possible way be connected with the word Samson." "Holy" here is not connected to Samson's name, but to his being a Nazirite.

⁹ Cf. BDB 446 on ישע, hiphil "deliver." Targum Jonathan here (Sperber 2.75) has פרק with the same meaning (Jastrow 1239,3), and both the A and B texts of the LXX employ the verb σώζω. See also Josephus, *Ant.* 5.275.

¹⁰ Finkelstein 425, Hammer 378.

and thought that he was the Messianic King. But when he saw him dead, he exclaimed: He too is dead! Then 'I wait for Your salvation, O Lord' (v 18)."[11]

The above Palestinian haggadic traditions, some of them very early, demonstrate how Samson played an important role in the imagination of the people. L. Ginzberg maintains, for example, that Samson "was the greatest hero of the period and, except [for] Goliath, the greatest hero of all times."[12] Samson's great popularity thus helps to explain why the Palestinian Jewish Christian author of the incident found in Mark 5:1-20 employed major verbal expressions and motifs from the Samson account within his narrative.[13] The following twelve sections describe these.

1. Living in a Rock Cave

A. Mark 5:2-3 state that when Jesus disembarked from the boat in the country of the Gerasenes, "immediately a man 'out of the tombs' (ἐκ τῶν μνημείων) with an unclean spirit met him, 3) 'who had his dwelling among the tombs' (ὃς τὴν κατοίκησιν εἶχεν ἐν τοῖς μνήμασιν)." Verse 5 notes that "All night and day[14] among the tombs (ἐν τοῖς μνήμασιν) and the hills[15] he was shouting and bruising himself with stones." After Jesus cured him of the unclean spirit(s) within him, the man begged for permission to follow Jesus. However, the Galilean

---

[11] Theodor and Albeck 1265, Soncino 2.964.
[12] *The Legends* 4.47.
[13] While several commentators have very briefly alluded to Samson in regard to the Gerasene demoniac, no one up to now has made a full-scale analysis of these factors. See E. Lohmeyer, *Das Evangelium des Markus* 94; C. Cave, "The Obedience of Unclean Spirits" in *NTS* 11 (1964/65) 96, from Swete; and R. Gundry, *Mark* (Grand Rapids, Michigan: Eerdmans, 1993) 259.
[14] The day's beginning at sunset is Jewish (Gen 1:5); therefore "night" is mentioned here before "day."
[15] The term ὄρος means both "mountain" and "hill" (BAGD 582), true also for the Hebrew הַר (BDB 249), "mountain, hill, hillside." Interestingly, the NRSV has "hillside" for ὄρος in v 11. As will be shown in section III. below, the hills surrounding Kursi on the east side of the Sea of Galilee are meant.

miracleworker and exorcist refused, saying to him: "Depart to your home (οἶκος : house, dwelling, home),[16] to your relatives and friends (πρὸς τοὺς σούς) ..." (v 19). That is, in the narrative his permanent "home" is contrasted with his temporary "dwelling" (κατοικία)[17] as a madman. It is among the tombs (of a cemetery).

In the first half of the first century CE burials in Palestine still took place primarily in caves, usually natural as caused by the rocky soil, or hewn out of the rock. An example of the first was the "cave" (σπήλαιον)[18] in which Lazarus was buried in John 11:38, and of the second "the tomb that had been hewn out of the rock" in which Jesus was buried in Mark 15:46. Since such caves were used for multiple (family) burials, they were large enough for the Gerasene madman to live in.[19]

The description of the Gerasene demoniac as having his "dwelling" among the tombs (rock caves) is based on Samson's dwelling in such a place.

B. Judg 15:8b states that Samson went down "and stayed in the cleft / cave of the rock of Etam" (וַיֵּשֶׁב בִּסְעִיף סֶלַע עֵיטָם). The "cleft / cave of the rock of Etam" is repeated in v 11, and v 13 notes that the men of Judah "pulled up" Samson from the rock, showing it to be a cave-like structure. While J. Myers considers Etam to be "somewhere in the vicinity of [Samson's] home but not certainly identified,"[20] and R. Boling thinks it was

---

[16] BAGD 560.
[17] BAGD 424: dwelling – (place), habitation.
[18] BAGD 762; LSJ 1627: grotto, cavern.
[19] Cf. Str-B 1.1049-1051, especially 1049: "Besonders beliebt zur Herrichtung von Familienbegräbnisstätten waren *Felsenhöhlen* oder *Felsenspalten*, die durch Aushauen künstlich vertieft und erweitert wurden, bis sie die gewünschte Größe erlangt hatten" (my italics). See also the art. "Cemetery" by K. Kohler in *JE* (1902) 3.637-642, who calls attention (638) to the term מְעָרְתָא as "burial cave" (Jastrow 819), often equivalent to a cemetery. M. Ydit in the art. "Cemetery" in *EJ* (1971) 5.272 also notes that until Talmudic times Palestinian custom led to the employment of caves.
[20] Cf. his "The Book of Judges" in *IB* (1953) 2.788.

"somewhere in the southern hills,"[21] J. Gray says it was "probably some unidentified locality in the western escarpment of the mountains of Judah, which abound in large caves."[22]

The verb יָשַׁב in v 8b means "to dwell, have one's abode 'in' (בְּ)."[23] The LXX translates it with κατῴκει, also found at Josephus at this point (*Ant.* 5.297.) The expression is the basis for τὴν κατοίκησιν εἶχεν in Mark 5:3.

The noun סָעִיף is the "cleft" of a crag, found only here and in Isa 57:5 and 2:21.[24] In the latter passage it is set in parallelism to "'the caverns' of the rocks."[25] LXX A Judg 15:8b employs the noun σπήλαιον, the same term employed for the "cave" in which Lazarus was buried in John 11:38.[26] R. Boling also translates סָעִיף as "cave."[27]

A סֶלַע is a crag or cliff,[28] and in later Hebrew and Aramaic simply "rock."[29] Isa 22:16 states that "you have cut out a tomb (קֶבֶר) here for yourself, cutting a tomb on the height, and carving a habitation for yourself 'in the rock' (בַּסֶּלַע)."

In light of the above it seems probable that imagery from Samson's "living / dwelling in the cleft / cave of the rock of Etam" in Judg 15:8b was the basis for the Palestinian Jewish Christian author of Mark 5:1-20 when he described the Gerasene demoniac as "taking his dwelling among the tombs" (of rock) in v 3. As pointed out in section A. above, such tombs in the first century CE were usually to be found in rock caves or those hewn out of the rock.

---

[21] Cf. his *Judges* (AB 6A; Garden City, New York: Doubleday, 1975) 236.
[22] Cf. his *Joshua, Judges and Ruth* (NCB; London: Oliphants, 1977) 265.
[23] BDB 443,3.
[24] BDB 703.
[25] Cf. BDB 669 on נִקְרָה : only here and Exod 33:22.
[26] The first term in the A text, χείμαρρος , is a stream which can be swollen by winter rain, a wadi (LSJ 1982), translating a variant in the Hebrew text: אָפִיק (BDB 67).
[27] Cf. his *Judges* 234.
[28] BDB 700.
[29] Jastrow 996.

2. Uncleanness

A. The Gerasene demoniac in Mark 5:2 is a man with an "unclean spirit" (πνεύματι ἀκαθάρτῳ). This is repeated in v 8 (τὸ πνεῦμα τὸ ἀκάθαρτον), and v 13 has the plural, "unclean spirits" (τὰ πνεύματα τὰ ἀκάθαρτα). The madman's impurity is not only due to his living in tombs (vv 2-3, 5), causing him to have uncleanness due to contact with the dead (see section 1. above). The spirit(s) within him are also those of "uncleanness" (טוּמְאָה). The Palestinian Jewish Christian author of Mark 5:1-20 employed this motif in his narrative in part because Samson was closely associated with "uncleanness."

B. In Judg 13:3 the angel of the Lord tells Manoah's wife she shall conceive and bear a son. Verse 4 continues: "Now be careful not to drink wine or strong drink, or to eat 'anything unclean' (כָּל־טָמֵא)." This is repeated in vv 7 and 14 with כָּל־טֻמְאָה, "any uncleanness." Targum Jonathan in these three verses employs כל מסאב, anything "repulsive, unclean,"[30] and the LXX πᾶν ἀκάθαρτον.[31] Pseudo-Philo 42:3 transfers this motif from Manoah's wife during her pregnancy to Samson himself. The angel tells Eluma, as she is called here: "But see that he does not taste from any fruit of the vine and eat 'any unclean thing' (*omne immundum*), because (as He has himself said) he will free Israel from the hand of the Philistines."[32]

The Mishnah at *Naz.* 1:2 differentiates between a lifelong Nazirite and one in the status of Samson. When a Nazirite like Samson "becomes unclean" (נִטְמָא), for example, he does not bring the offering for "uncleanness" (טֻמְאָה).[33] This offering for

---

[30] Sperber 2.75. See Jastrow 803 on מְסָאָב .
[31] Only at A 13:7 does πᾶσαν ἀκαθαρσίαν occur.
[32] Harrington in SC 229. 290, and *OTP* 2.356. The name Eluma is given in 42:1, 4 and 43:1. Josephus apparently interprets the uncleanness as Samson's refraining from any drink stronger than water, and as a frugal diet; see *Ant.* 5.278 and 285.
[33] Albeck 3.195-196; Danby 281, Neusner 431. Cf. also *y. Naz.* 1:2, 51b (Neusner 24.23). It should be noted that in the Palestinian triennial lectionary system Num 6:1 ff. and Judg 13:2 ff. were the Pentateuchal

a Nazirite's defiling himself by corpse uncleanness is described in Num 6:10-12. The Tosefta comments on the above Mishnah passage in *Naz.* 1:5 by quoting R. Judah (the Prince, the compiler of the Mishnah and a fourth generation Tanna)³⁴ : "A Nazir in the status of Samson is permitted 'to become unclean with corpse – uncleanness' (ליטמא למתים). For Samson himself 'became unclean with corpse-uncleanness' (היה מיטמא למתים)."³⁵ In *b. Naz.* 4b the latter is repeated, and two Scriptural passages are adduced to prove it. Judg 15:16 states that Samson slew 1,000 men, and 14:19 that he killed thirty men of Ashkelon, (thus incurring corpse uncleanness). This was known by tradition.³⁶

The threefold repetition of "uncleanness" in the Samson narrative in Judg 13:4, 7 and 14, and Tannaitic emphasis on the Nazirite Samson's deliberately becoming unclean through contact with the dead, provided the Palestinian Jewish Christian author of Mark 5:1-20 with at least part of the background for his description of the Gerasene demoniac. The latter was plagued by an unclean spirit(s) and lived among the dead in tombs.

3. *Phenomenal Strength, Binding, Hand-chains and Foot-shackles*

A. Mark 5:3 states regarding the Gerasene demoniac that no one could "bind" (δέω)³⁷ him any more, even with a "chain" (ἅλυσις).³⁸ This may imply that other means such as ropes had been unsuccessfully tried out before. Verse 4 continues by noting that the madman had frequently been bound with

---

and haftarah readings for the fourth Sabbath in the second year of the month Adar. This most probably facilitated the association of motifs from these two chapters. See the table in the art. "Triennial Cycle" in *EJ* (1971) 15.1387-1388, as well as the table in the similar article by J. Jacobs in *JE* 12 (1906), between pp. 256-257.

³⁴ Strack and Stemberger, *Introduction* 89-90; he died in 217 CE.
³⁵ Zuckermandel and Liebermann 284, Neusner 3.124.
³⁶ Soncino 11. For other comment on Samson's longing for something unclean (a heathen wife – Judg 14:1), cf. *b. Soṭ.* 9b (Soncino 44) and *Num. Rab.* Naso 9/24 on Num 5:27 (Mirqin 9.197, Soncino 5.286).
³⁷ BAGD 177; the NRSV has "restrain."
³⁸ BAGD 41,1.

"fetters / shackles" (on his feet: πέδη)³⁹ and chains (on his hands), but⁴⁰ the chains were "torn apart" (διασπάω)⁴¹ and the fetters were "broken / shattered" (συντρίβω)⁴² by him. And no one was able to "subdue" (δαμάζω)⁴³ him. Matthew in 8:28 omits the above description from Mark and summarizes by stating that (the two) demoniacs "were extremely fierce (χαλεπός)⁴⁴ so that no one could pass that way." In 8:29 the Evangelist Luke notes that the unclean spirit had seized the demoniac many times. The latter was kept under guard and bound with chains and fetters / shackles, yet he would "break" (διαρρήγνυμι)⁴⁵ the fetters (δεσμός)⁴⁶ and be driven by the demon into the wilderness.

The Markan narrative, which is of primary concern in this study, thus describes the Gerasene madman as having superhuman strength, tearing apart and breaking all the hand-chains and foot-shackles frequently employed by others in order to subdue him. This description is also based on the superhuman strength of Samson.

B. Rabbinic sources emphasize the tremendous strength of Samson. In *b. Soṭ.* 10a a baraitha has R. Simeon the Pious⁴⁷ say:

---

³⁹ BAGD 638: only here and in the parallel passage Luke 8:29 in the NT.
⁴⁰ The adversative meaning of καί here is Semitic, corresponding to the waw (ו). Cf. BDF 458 (p. 239) for καί as waw, and BDB 252, 1. e., for the meaning "but."
⁴¹ BAGD 188.
⁴² BAGD 793.
⁴³ BAGD 170. The verb is also used of "taming" a wild animal. Except for James 3:7-8, the verb only occurs here in the NT.
⁴⁴ BAGD 874: hard, difficult; here hard to deal with, violent, dangerous.
⁴⁵ BAGD 188: tear, break, shatter, destroy.
⁴⁶ BAGD 176.
⁴⁷ Cf. Str.-B 5/6 240 for him as Babylonian, ca. 210 CE, yet he appears to be the same as Bar Nezira, a Palestinian of the third century CE (5/6.126). Billerbeck himself thought he was the same as Shim'on the Pious (n. 3); see W. Bacher, *Die Agada der Tannaiten* (Strassburg: Trübner, 1890) 2.178, n. 2. Yet if he is cited in a baraitha, he was probably Tannaitic.

"The width between Samson's shoulders was sixty cubits," as Judg 16:3 is interpreted, "and there is a tradition that the gates of Gaza were not less than sixty cubits [in width]."[48] Here the Israelite hero is pictured as carrying the two doors and posts of the city gate on his very broad shoulders all the way from Gaza to Hebron.[49]

In *Num. Rab.* Mattoth 22/7 on Num 32:1, "Our Rabbis taught" that "two strong men arose in the world, one in Israel and one among the nations of the world – Samson in Israel and one among the nations of the world...."[50] Here one would expect the Greek hero Hercules, who is similar to Samson in a number of ways,[51] yet Palestinian Jews remained faithful to the character in their own Bible and named the giant Goliath as Samson's Gentile counterpart.

Tanḥ. B Waethannan 1 on Deut 3:23 states that Samson is one of the seven people who were similar to the first man (Adam, in his original strength at creation), yet he died after having his eyes gouged out (Judg 16:21).[52] *Pirq. R. El.* 53 relates this of six people, Samson resembling Adam in his strength (כֹּחַ).[53] In *b. Soṭ.* 10a "Our Rabbis have taught: Five were created after the likeness of Him Who is above, and all of them incurred punishment on account of [the feature which distinguished] them: Samson in his strength...," and Samson was punished "in his strength," for which Judg 16:19 is cited.[54] This divine strength is also alluded to in *Gen. Rab.* Vayyechi 98/13 and 99/11 on Gen 49:16, where Samson in needing no assistance in battle is like the Unique One of the world. Samson needed no sword or aid from others, but killed 1000 men with the fresh

---

[48] Soncino 45.
[49] Cf. *Eliyyahu Zuṭa* 24 on Jer 9:22 (Eng. 23), "do not let the mighty boast in their might." It maintains that "from his crotch to his shoulders there was a span of sixty cubits" (Braude and Kapstein 519).
[50] Mirqin 10.302, Soncino 6.859. Cf. *Eccl. Rab.* 1:18 § 1 (Soncino 8.50).
[51] Six similarities are listed in J. Gray, *Joshua, Judges and Ruth* 183.
[52] His death then occurs in v 30. See Buber on Deuteronomy, 8, and Bietenhard 2.448.
[53] Cf. Eshkol 214, Friedlander 432.
[54] Soncino 46.

jawbone of an ass (Judg 15:15-16).⁵⁵ Finally, Judg 13:25 notes regarding Samson that "The spirit of the Lord began to stir him in Mahaneh-dan, between Zorah and Eshtaol." R. Assi, a first generation Babylonian Amora,⁵⁶ said in *b. Soṭ.* 9b that the latter are "two great mountains, and Samson uprooted them and ground one against the other."⁵⁷ R. Judah, perhaps b. Ilai, a fourth generation Tanna,⁵⁸ noted in this regard that "when the holy spirit rested on Samson, it enabled him to traverse a distance as long as from Zorah to Eshtaol in one step."⁵⁹

The above haggadic material, emphasizing Samson's superhuman strength, corroborates the first century Jewish writer Josephus' summary statement that it is right to admire Samson's brave deeds and "strength" (ἰσχύς : *Ant.* 5.317; cf. 277). The biblical account itself emphasized this motif, including "binding" and "chains," employed also of the Gerasene demoniac.

Within the four chapters of Judges 13-16 Samson performs seven feats of strength beyond those connected with binding him. They are: 1) his tearing apart a lion barehanded in 14:6;⁶⁰ 2) his killing thirty men from Ashkelon in 14:19; 3) his catching 300 foxes and putting torches on their tails in 15:4-5; 4) his striking down the Philistines alone, "hip and thigh" with great slaughter in 15:8; 5) his killing 1000 men with the jawbone of an ass in 15:15-16; 6) his pulling down the doors and two posts of

---

⁵⁵ Theodor and Albeck 1264 and 1282, Soncino 2.962-963 and 985. On divine strength given to Samson at the end of his life (Judg 16:28), see *Gen. Rab.* Toledoth 66/3 on Gen 27:28 (Theodor and Albeck 747, Soncino 2.602).

⁵⁶ Strack and Stemberger, *Introduction* 94; he was also called Issi and Assa.

⁵⁷ Soncino 44. Cf. also the saying of R. Samuel b. Naḥmani, a third generation Palestinian Amora (Strack and Stemberger, *Introduction* 97) in *Lev. Rab.* Tzav 8/2 on Lev 6:13 (Soncino 4.102).

⁵⁸ Strack and Stemberger, *Introduction* 84. He could also be Judah the Prince, a fourth generation Tanna (pp. 89-90), who comments several times elsewhere on the Samson narrative.

⁵⁹ Cf. *Lev. Rab.* as in n. 57.

⁶⁰ The lion is called "strong" (עז : BDB 735 - strong, fierce) in vv 14 and 18.

the city gate of Gaza and carrying them to Hebron in 16:3; and 7) his causing the pillars of a large house in Gaza to collapse, killing at least 3000 men and women, in 16:30, 27.

The term "strength" (כֹּחַ)[61] is used here seven times of Samson (16:5, 6, 9, 15, 17, 19 and 30), who is stronger than (עָז מִ') a lion in 14:6, 14 and 18, and who prays at the end of his life that God will "strengthen" (חזק)[62] him one final time in 16:28.

Of most relevance to the description of the Gerasene demoniac, however, is the depiction of Samson's tearing apart the ropes and chains by which he was frequently bound. The term "to bind" (אסר)[63] is emphasized by twelvefold repetition in 15:10, 12, 13 (twice), and 16:5, 6, 7, 8, 10, 11, 12 and 21; the "prison" in 16:21 and 25 is בֵּית הָאֲסִירִים ; and Samson's "bonds" (אֱסוּר)[64] occur in 15:14. The LXX always employs δέω for the Hebrew verb, and δεσμοί for "bonds" in 15:14.

The Gerasene demoniac's having been "frequently" (πολλάκις) bound, unsuccessfully (Mark 5:4), is based on Samson's having been bound unsuccessfully (except at the very end of his life). The Philistines want to do so in Judg 15:10, 3,000 men of Judah in vv 12-13, the Philistines again in 16:5, and Delilah in vv 6, 7, 8, 10, 11 and 12. Yet two new ropes with which the men of Judah bound Samson on his arms in 15:13 "became like flax that has caught fire, and his bonds melted off his hands" (v 14). When Delilah then used seven fresh bowstrings to bind Samson (16:7-8), he "snapped" (נתק)[65] them "as a strand of fiber 'snaps' when it touches the fire" (v 9). LXX A employs διαρρήγνυμι in the first instance, as in Luke 8:29 of the Gerasene demoniac, and διασπάω for the second instance, as in Mark 5:4. When Delilah then employed new ropes to bind Samson (16:11), he "snapped" these off his arms too like a thread (v 12). Here both LXX A and B employ the verb διασπάω. When Delilah wove the seven locks of Samson's hair with a web

---

[61] BDB 470.
[62] BDB 304-305.
[63] BDB 63, 3: "bind" with cords, fetters, etc., as a prisoner.
[64] BDB 64.
[65] BDB 683, piel.

and tightened the latter with a pin (16:13), he awoke and "pulled away" the pin, the loom and the web (v 14). When Samson finally revealed the secret of his strength to Delilah, and she had his hair shaved off, he awoke and wanted to "shake himself free" – as before (16:20).[66] Yet his superhuman strength had left him, and the Philistines could now bind him with "bronze shackles" (נְחֻשְׁתַּ֫יִם - v 21)[67] on his feet. Both LXX A and B have the plural of πέδη here, as of the Gerasene demoniac in Mark 5:4.

The above narrative of Samson's being frequently bound, unsuccessfully (except for the time he revealed the secret of his strength), including both bonds on his hands and shackles on his feet, and his tearing them apart, meaning that no one could subdue him, provided the concrete imagery employed to describe the Gerasene demoniac in a similar way in Mark 5:3-4.

4. Shouting Loudly, Running and Meeting

A. Mark 5:6-7 says that when the Gerasene demoniac saw Jesus from a distance, "he ran and bowed down before him, 7) and having shouted with a loud voice, he said: 'What have you to do with me, Jesus, Son of the Most High God?'"

In section I. 2.1 above I pointed out that the expression "Most High God" derives from Ps 91:1 and 9, the opening and concluding verses of the psalm spoken in the Jerusalem Temple to treat a madman.

The Palestinian Jewish Christian author of Mark 5:1-20 was also aware of the exorcism narratives in Hebrew or Aramaic which later entered the Gospel of Mark in Greek form. From another anecdote of a man with an "unclean spirit" (1:21-28) he borrowed the terminology of a) "crying out," b) "What have

---

[66] Cf. נָעַר II in BDB 654, and the Lord's shaking off the Egyptians into the Reed Sea in Exod 14:27.

[67] BDB 638-639, 2: fetters of copper or bronze, usually dual. The only instance with a demon being chained in rabbinic sources, to my knowledge, is found in *Midr. Pss.* 78/12 on Eccl 2:8 (Buber 352-353, Braude 2.33-35), where Solomon has someone throw a "chain" (שׁוּשִׁילְתָּא, Jastrow 1590) on which the Ineffable Name was engraved over Ashmedai, the king of the demons. A parallel is found in *b. Giṭ.* 68a (Soncino 322).

you to do with us?" and c) a further designation of Jesus. In 1:23 the man with an unclean spirit (ἐν πνεύματι ἀκαθάρτῳ) a) "cried out (ἀνακράζω),[68] 24) saying: b) 'What have you to do with us (τί ἡμῖν καὶ σοί), Jesus of Nazareth? Have you come to destroy us? I know who you are, c) the Holy One of God.'" Then in v 26 the unclean spirit convulses the man, a) "crying out in a loud voice" (φωνῆσαν φωνῇ μεγάλῃ).

In the fourth Markan exorcism, that of a Syrophoenician woman's little daughter who also has an "unclean spirit" (7:24-31), the woman first heard of Jesus, then came and "bowed down at his feet" (προσέπεσεν πρὸς τοὺς πόδας αὐτοῦ - v 25), requesting Jesus to cast out the demon. Yet this was the mother of the sick child.

Mark 3:11 describes the behavior of the "unclean spirits" themselves. Whenever they saw Jesus, "they fell down before him and shouted, 'You are the Son of God!' (προσέπιπτον αὐτῷ καὶ ἔκραζον λέγοντες ὅτι σὺ εἶ ὁ υἱὸς τοῦ θεοῦ)."[69]

While the unclean spirit's "bowing down" and "shouting" thus appear to be standard early Jewish Christian exorcism terminology, they may have been "triggered" in Mark 5:6-7 by a statement in the Samson narrative.

B. Judg 15:14 states that when Samson came to Lehi, the Philistines "came shouting to meet him" (הֵרִיעוּ לִקְרָאתוֹ). Lehi, meaning "jawbone," was "probably in the region of Bethshemesh, between Zorah and Timnah."[70] It was a town of Judah, where the Philistines had camped in order to raid the site (v 9).

Originally meaning "to shout a war-cry" or "alarm of battle," the Hebrew verb רוּעַ in the hiphil could also simply mean "to

---

[68] BAGD 56.
[69] On Satan's "falling on his face" when he sees the Messiah, cf. *Pesiq. R.* 36/1 (Buber 161b, Braude 677-678). In the future the Messiah will cause him and all the (angelic) princes of the nations of the earth to "fall" (= die a violent death; BDB 657, 2.a. on נפל) in Gehenna, as Isa 25:8 is interpreted.
[70] Cf. V. Gold, art. "Lehi" in *IDB* 3.111. Josephus in *Ant.* 5.300 says it was still called "Jawbone" in his day.

shout" or "to cry out in distress."[71] It was at any rate a very loud shouting. The Targum's יְבַב is similar.[72]

Both LXX A and B add at this point: "and ran" (ἔδραμον) to meet (Samson). I suggest that the Judaic tradition behind this addition was known to the Palestinian Jewish Christian author of Mark 5:1-20. It caused him to state that the Gerasene demoniac "ran" (ἔδραμεν - v 6) and bowed down before (Jesus) and cried out in a loud voice....

Mark 5:3-5 serve to characterize the Gerasene demoniac. Verse 6 in its content actually follows v 2, which states that when Jesus had disembarked from the boat, "immediately a man out of the tombs with an unclean spirit 'met him' (ὑπήντησεν αὐτῷ)." The Greek verb ὑπαντάω, to meet (someone),[73] is employed here, corresponding to the Hebrew קְרָא [74] of Judg 15:14.

It is thus quite possible that in addition to other (Jewish Christian) exorcism narratives, Judaic tradition on Judg 15:14 influenced the terminology in Mark 5:6-7 in regard to the Gerasene demoniac's "running" and "shouting loudly." His "meeting" Jesus in v 3 may also ultimately derive from the same verse in Judges.

The above proposal becomes more probable if one considers that the Gerasene demoniac's staying in (rock) tombs is derived from Samson's staying in the cleft / cave of the rock of Etam in the nearby verses of Judg 15:8 and 11 (see above, section 1.), and that Samson's request in 15:12, "Swear to me that you will not attack / kill me," lies behind the terminology of Mark 5:10 and the "adjuring / causing someone to swear" in v 7 (see the next section, 5.) The argument here is thus cumulative.

---

[71] BDB 929.
[72] Cf. Sperber 2.79, and Jastrow 560: to sound an alarm, in the ithpael to shout. Both LXX A and B have here ἠλάλαξαν, which appears to derive from λαλάζω = λαλαγέω, to babble (LSJ 1025), certainly not what the Philistines were up to.
[73] BAGD 837. Matthew employs the cognate noun ὑπάντησις in the same narrative at 8:34.
[74] BDB 896, 1. meet, encounter. The verb קָרָה means the same (899).

5. Swearing Not to Torment or Injure Someone

A. Mark 5:8, "For [Jesus] had said to [the Gerasene demoniac], 'Come out of the man, you unclean spirit!'" is a parenthesis explaining the content of v 7. Such a parenthesis is typical of originally oral folk tales and can be found in the Samson narrative, for example, in Judg 13:16 b; 14:4; and 16:12 b. It therefore should not be considered a later editorial insertion by Mark, as maintained by numerous commentators.[75]

The unclean spirit says to Jesus in v 7 b, "I adjure you by God, do not torment me" (ὀρκίζω σε τὸν θεόν, μή με βασανίσῃς). Just before he had acknowledged Jesus as "Son of *God* the Most High / the Most High *God*." Demons, invisible to humans, were thought to be able to view mortals and to have supernatural knowledge, for "they hear from behind the Veil [before God's throne in heaven] like the ministering angels."[76] Imbued with this special knowledge, the unclean spirit knows that Jesus is the Son of "God."

By adjuring Jesus by "God," the demon also acknowledges that he himself is ultimately subject to the divine "authority." This is shown for example in a baraitha found in *b. Pesaḥ.* 112 b. "One should not go out alone at night, i.e. on the nights of neither Wednesday nor Sabbaths, because Agrath the daughter of Mahalath, she and 180,000 destroying angels go forth, and each has 'permission' to wreak destruction independently."[77] The latter term is רְשׁוּת, which means both "permission" and "authority."[78] Demons and unclean spirits can do nothing

---

[75] Cf. F.C. Grant, "The Gospel According to St. Mark" in *IDB* (1951) 7.714; E. Klostermann, *Das Markusevangelium* 49; and W. Schmithals, *Das Evangelium nach Markus. Kapitel 1 – 9,1* 265 as a "Verschlimmbesserung," a supplement of the original text by the Evangelist.
[76] Cf. *b. Ḥag.* 16a (Soncino 101) as one of six things concerning demons which "Our Rabbis taught." They also die, as humans do. See also *'Avot R. Nat.* A 37 on this (Schechter 109, Goldin 153).
[77] Soncino 579-580. Cf. the motif of "permission" also in *b. Ḥull.* 105b (Soncino 586), and in *Num. Rab.* Naso 14/9 on Num 7:89 (Mirqin 10.129, Soncino 6.632).
[78] Jastrow 1499.

without divine permission / authority. The unclean spirit's adjuring Jesus by "God" is thus not merely due to the narrator's desire to create a touch of irony at this point, for usually the exorcist adjured the demon to leave the victim, not the reverse.[79] It also adumbrates Jesus' "giving" the unclean spirits "permission" (ἐπιστρέφω) to leave the Gerasene demoniac and to enter a great herd of swine nearby in v 13.[80]

The term "adjure" in Mark 5:7 is ὁρκίζω, in the sense of "causing someone to swear." It translates the hiphil of the Hebrew שׁבע in the LXX. The Greek can also mean "to implore."[81] Thus in the present Greek form of the Markan narrative it is very similar to the unclean spirit's "earnestly begging" Jesus not to send him and the other unclean spirits out of the country in 5:10. The Greek of "to beg earnestly" here is παρακαλέω πολλά, whereby the verb alone can also mean "to request, implore, appeal to, entreat."[82] This "imploring / begging" is repeated in v 12 on the part of the unclean spirits, and in v 18 on the part of the healed demoniac. The threefold repetition helps to unite the narrative.

Mark 5:7 has the unclean spirit adjure Jesus not to "torment" him. This is the Greek βασανίζω, meaning to torture or torment someone.[83] For the unclean spirit(s) this torment would mean Jesus' sending them out of the country (v 10). The Palestinian Jewish Christian author of 5:1-20 also employed irony at this point. The tormentor earnestly begs not to be tormented. A standard designation of a "demon" in Hebrew was מַזִּיק, from the root נזק, to hurt, injure, damage.[84] A demon was thus by nature one who injured, damaged or

---

[79] Against for example R. Guelich in *Mark 1 – 8:26*, 279, who even speaks of a "double irony" here; R. Gundry in *Mark* 250; and J. Gnilka, *Das Evangelium nach Markus (Mk 1 - 8, 26)* 204, who calls it a "parody."
[80] BAGD 303: allow, permit.
[81] BAGD 581.
[82] BAGD 617, 3.
[83] BAGD 134. In another exorcism story, the unclean spirits ask whether Jesus has come to "destroy" them (Mark 1:24).
[84] Cf. Jastrow 755 and 892.

"tormented" others. Precisely this being asks not to be tormented itself, but to remain alive.

The above imagery of swearing and not being tormented or even killed, found in the narrative of the Gerasene demoniac, is based on similar imagery employed of Samson.

B. When the men of Judah go down to the cleft / cave of the rock of Etam where Samson is staying, they inform him that they have come to bind him and give him into the hands of the Philistines. He then answers them, "Swear to me that you yourself will not attack me" (הִשָּׁבְעוּ לִי פֶּן־תִּפְגְּעוּן בִּי אַתֶּם - Judg 15:12). The men of Judah respond in v 13 by saying, "No, we will only bind you and give you into their hands; we will not kill you."

The verb פָּגַע means to meet, encounter, yet here with the element of hostility, thus "to fall upon" someone.[85] It is the same verb as employed in one designation of Ps 91:1-9, the "Song of Those 'Fallen Upon / Stricken / Afflicted' (by Madness - פְּגוּעִין)," intoned in the Jerusalem Temple for those like the Gerasene demoniac. While LXX B at this point translates with συναντάω, to meet, encounter,[86] the A version is more explicit with ἀποκτείνω, to kill. Targum Jonathan renders the Hebrew verb with "to have power over."[87]

The latter is reflected in Josephus' retelling of this incident. Certainly influenced by Palestinian haggadic traditions, the Jewish historian notes in *Ant.* 5. 299 that only when Samson received an "oath" (ὅρκους) from the men of Judah that they would merely commit him into the enemy's hands, did he put himself under the "authority" (ἐν τῇ ... ἐξουσίᾳ) of these tribal

---

[85] BDB 803, 3; Jastrow 1135: attack, strike.
[86] LSJ 1696.
[87] Sperber 2.79, Harrington and Saldarini 88, with שְׁלַט בּ' , Jastrow 1581: to rule, have power over, control. An example is given of an evil spirit's "seizing" someone.

representatives.⁸⁸ The passage became a prooftext for Samson's "fearing" an oath in the sense of "respecting" it.⁸⁹

The Palestinian Jewish Christian author of the narrative now found in Mark 5:1-20 appropriated the motifs of "swearing" and not "tormenting / injuring" from Judaic tradition on Judg 15:12 in regard to Samson. The unclean spirit in the Gerasene madman, modeled to a great extent on Samson, "adjures" or swears an oath in regard to Jesus in v 7.⁹⁰ The latter should not torment or injure him, for example by sending him out of the country. Samson too requests the men of Judah to swear by oath to him that they themselves will not fall upon / attack / injure (פָּגַע in later Hebrew) him. Only then will Samson submit to their "authority," only then will the unclean spirit(s) willingly leave their victim, the Gerasene demoniac, and take their abode elsewhere (vv 10-13).

6. What is Your Name?

A. After the unclean spirit in the Gerasene demoniac adjures Jesus by God not to torment him, Jesus asks him in Mark 5:9: "What is your name?" (τί ὄνομά σοι). As pointed out in section I. 2. 3) a) above, many demons were called by distinct names. The name usually was connected with the particular injury or sickness inflicted by the demon. For example, the demon Ḥamath (חַמָּת) caused an eruption or blister on a person's face through "heat,"⁹¹ and the (evil) spirit Ben ha-Nephilim (בֶּן הַנְּפִילִים) caused nervous prostration through "falling

---

⁸⁸ Cf. other haggadic tradition in 298, where the Judeans are represented as 3,000 men-at-arms.

⁸⁹ Cf. for example *Eccl. Rab.* 9:2 § 1 (Soncino 8.227) and *Lev. Rab.* Aḥare Moth 20/1 on Lev 16:1, with Eccl 9:2 (Soncino 4.251).

⁹⁰ Cf. the Hebrew אֲנִי מַשְׁבִּיעֲךָ בּ׳ in Delitzsch's Hebrew New Testament (p. 69), and אֲנִי מַשְׁבִּיעַ אוֹתְךָ בּ׳ in the United Bible Societies' Hebrew New Testament (p. 100). This is the same hiphil form as in Judg 15:12.

⁹¹ Cf. *b. Sanh.* 101a (Soncino 685) and Jastrow 480. The root חמם means to be hot (Jastrow 478).

(down)".⁹² When the unclean spirit answers Jesus in Mark 5:9 by stating: "My name is 'Legion,' for we are many" (λεγιὼν ὄνομά μοι , ὅτι πολλοί ἐσμεν), this explanation of his name was thus not unusual. "Legion" was not only the designation of a Roman military unit, but also a term meaning extremely many, uncountable (see section I. 3) b) above).

The specific question "What is your name?" also derives from the Samson narrative, as does the term "Legion" from Judaic tradition on it (see section 7. below).

B. After an angel informed the barren wife of Manoah that she would become pregnant and bear Samson, she went to her husband and said: "I did not ask him where he came from, and he did not tell me 'his name' (שְׁמוֹ - Judg 13:6). When Manoah later gets to meet the angel himself, he asks him: "'What is your name' (מִי שְׁמֶךָ),⁹³ so that we may honor you when your words come true?" (v 17). The angel replies with a counterquestion: "Why do you ask 'my name' (שְׁמִי)? It is פֶּלִאי ," translated by the NRSV as "too wonderful" (v 18). Manoah then takes a kid and offers it to the Lord, to "Him who works wonders (מַפְלִא לַעֲשׂוֹת)."

Speculation about this special "name," emphasized by threefold repetition, occurred at a very early date as shown in the Qere, פֶּלִי or פֶּלִיא, and the Ketab פֶּלִאי .⁹⁴ The LXX in both A and B has θαυμαστόν , "wonderful, marvelous," and Targum Jonathan מפרש ,⁹⁵ probably "distinguished, made wonderful."⁹⁶ The Hebrew root פָּלָא in the niphal means to be

---

⁹² Cf. *b. Bekh.* 44b (Soncino 301) as a Tannaitic tradition. See Jastrow 923 under נָפִיל , and the root נפל as to fall (down) in Jastrow 924.

⁹³ R. Boling in *Judges* 222 points out that in his excitement Manoah uses the wrong pronoun here. As in Gen 32:28 and Exod 3:13, the מִי should be מָה .

⁹⁴ Cf. the apparatus of *Biblia Hebraica* ad loc.

⁹⁵ Sperber 2.76.

⁹⁶ Jastrow 1243 on פָּרַשׁ , pael 5). Harrington and Saldarini 86 translate "interpreter," from 6) to explain, interpret. This is improbable in the context.

surpassing, extraordinary. The hiphil participle in v 19 means "working wonders in doing."[97] The noun פֶּלֶא is a "wonder," as in the "marvel of a counselor" / "wonderful counselor" of Isa 9:5. After having caused Pharaoh and his hosts to drown in the Reed Sea, the Lord is also praised in the Song of Moses at Exod 15:11 as doing a "wonder" (פֶּלֶא),[98] of relevance to the drowning of a herd of swine in the Sea of Galilee (see section 9. B. 3. below). The adjective פִּלְאִי means "wonderful, incomprehensible," and in Judg 13:18 it is used as a proper name.[99]

The first century CE Palestinian work Pseudo-Philo 42:10 has Manoah say in this context: "'It is not enough that I have seen [the angel] but I even asked his name (*nomen eius*), not knowing that he was the minister of God.' Now the angel who came was named Fadahel (*dicebatur Fadahel*)."[100] The original Hebrew here was probably פלאיאל , deformed when Λ was mistaken for Δ in the Greek, from which the Latin translation was made.[101]

As pointed out above, Judges 13 was the prophetic reading for that Sabbath in the triennial lectionary system when Numbers 6 was read from the Torah, the connection being the theme of being a Nazirite. Num 6:2 reads: "When either a man or a woman 'makes a special vow' (יַפְלִא לִנְדֹּר), the vow of a Nazirite...." This occurrence of the root פלא caused rabbinic comment on the name פִּלְאִי in Judg 13:18 to be gathered at this point of Numbers.

In *Num. Rab.* 10/5 on Num 6:2 Manoah addresses the angel by saying: "Tell me your name..." (אֱמֹר לִי שְׁמֶךָ). The angel maintains it is "hidden," for he himself "would be hidden (מְכֻסֶּה)[102] from him and never see him again."[103] Another

---

[97] BDB 810, 3.
[98] BDB 810.
[99] BDB 811: only here and in Ps 139:6 in the feminine.
[100] Harrington in SC 229, 292, and *OTP* 2.356.
[101] Cf. *OTP* 2.356, n. "o," and C. Perrot and P.-M. Bogaert together with D. Harrington in SC 230, p. 196.
[102] Jastrow 653 on כסי , בָּסָה , piel passive participle.

comment asserts that the angel cannot tell Manoah his name because for each wonder (פֶּלִאיָה) God performs through His angels, He gives them a (different) name.[104] A third comment notes that the angel called his own name (שֵׁם שְׁמוֹ) "Peli" according to his task, that of making Samson a Nazirite in Judg 13:5. Here "Peli" is derived from the יַפְלִא of Num 6:2.[105]

The above Judaic traditions, some of them pre-Christian like the LXX, and others definitely Tannaitic, show how much attention early Palestinian Judaism attached to the question Samson's father Manoah asked of the angel in Judg 13:17 – "What is your name?" The Palestinian Jewish Christian author of the Gerasene demoniac narrative in Mark 5:1-20, borrowing heavily throughout from Judaic Samson traditions, appropriated this question and had Jesus ask it of the unclean spirit in v 9. The demon answers "My name is Legion," which also derives from very early Judaic comment on Samson.

7. Legion

A. In Mark 5:9 the unclean spirit answers Jesus' request for his name by stating: "My name is 'Legion,' for we are many." The noun is repeated in v 15. The Latin term *legio*, λεγιών / λεγεών in Greek, soon became a loanword in Hebrew and Aramaic, at the latest after Pompey's conquering Jerusalem in 63 BCE.[106] It was connected not only with Judaic comment on Ps 91:7, part of the "Song of Those Afflicted (with Madness)" intoned in the Jerusalem Temple for people like the Gerasene demoniac (see

---

[103] Mirqin 9.254, Soncino 5.368. Here "wonderful" is considered to have this meaning.
[104] On this, cf. also *Sifre* Naso § 42 on Num 6:26 (Horowitz 48, Kuhn 138, with n. 77), and *Gen. Rab.* Vayyishlach 78/4 on Gen 32:30 (Theodor and Albeck 921-922, Soncino 2.718) with Rabbi in the name of Abba Yose b. Dosai, probably a third generation Tanna (Strack and Stemberger, *Introduction* 86). On the latter, see also *Num. Rab.* Naso 11/7 on Num 6:26 (Mirqin 9.305, Soncino 5.444).
[105] For the above comments, cf. Mirqin 9.254-255 and Soncino 5.368-369. For the latter combination, see also 10/6.
[106] Cf. Josephus, *Ant.* 14.66 for the date. See p. 17, n. 81 above for a Roman legion in Syria as of 6 BCE.

section I. 2. 3) b) above). It was also intimately associated with early Judaic traditions on Samson.

B. Samson is mentioned three times in the Mishnah, the first two occurrences being in *Nazir* 1:2 and 9:5. The third is in *Soṭah* 1, which deals with a wife suspected of adultery (Num 5:11-31). In 1:7 the principle is stated: "With what measure a man metes, it shall be measured to him again." Examples are then given of parts of the woman's body which sinned as suffering divine retribution precisely there.[107] The first example of the principle of one-to-one retribution on the part of a person from the Bible is then given in 1:8. It states, "Samson went after [the desire of] his eyes – therefore the Philistines put out his eyes, as it is written, 'the Philistines seized him and gouged out his eyes' (Judg 16:21)."[108]

The Tannaitic supplement to the Mishnah, the Tosefta, comments on *m. Soṭ.* 1:7-8 by listing nine examples of those who acted arrogantly before God or rebelled against Him. Therefore He punished them accordingly. They are listed in 3:6-19 as 1) The generation of the Flood; 2) The men of the Tower of Babel; 3) The men of Sodom; 4) The Egyptians; 5) Sisera; 6) Samson; 7) Absalom; 8) Sennacherib; and 9) Nebuchadnezzar.[109]

The examples of the Egyptians, Sisera and Samson are most important in regard to the term "Legion" and the drowning of the large herd of swine in the Sea of Galilee (for the latter see section 9. below), therefore they are cited here *in toto*.

> 3:13 A. The Egyptians took pride before the Omnipresent, blessed be He, only on account of water, as it is said, "Then Pharaoh commanded all his people, 'Every son that is born to the Hebrews you shall cast into the Nile'" (Exod 1:22).
> B. So the Omnipresent, blessed be He, exacted punishment from them only by water, as it is said, "Pharaoh's chariots and his host He cast into the sea" (15:4).

---

[107] Albeck 3.235; Danby 294 (the translation here); Neusner 449.
[108] Albeck 3.236; Danby and Neusner *ibid*.
[109] Lieberman, *Soṭah* 160-166; Neusner 3.156-159.

3:14 A. Sisera took pride before the Omnipresent, blessed be He, only on account of his [volunteer] legions which do not receive a reward [for their service to him], since it is said, "The kings came, they fought; then fought the kings of Canaan" (Judg 5:19).

B. So the Omnipresent, blessed be He, exacted punishment from them only by [volunteer] legions which do not receive a reward, as it is said, "From heaven fought the stars, from their courses they fought against Sisera" (5:20).

C. And in the end they did not pay him honor or take heed of him because [he ran away by foot] like an ordinary foot-soldier.

3.15 A. Samson rebelled by using his eyes, as it is said, "Then Samson said to his father, 'I saw one of the daughters of the Philistines at Timnah; now get her for me as my wife'" (14:3).

B. So he was smitten through his eyes, as it is said, "And the Philistines seized him and put out his eyes" (16:21).

C. Rabbi says, "The beginning of his corruption took place in Gaza, so his punishment took place only in Gaza."[110]

The term "legions" in 3:14 is לִגְיוֹנוֹת in MS Vienna, לִגְיוֹנוֹת in MS Erfurt.[111] It cannot be emphasized too much that it occurs in direct connection with early Judaic tradition on Samson. The Palestinian Jewish Christian author of the narrative in Mark 5:1-20 knew of this close connection and appropriated the singular of the term "legions" here as the name of the unclean spirit which dwelt inside the Gerasene demoniac. He in turn was modeled after Samson.

The above tradition in *t. Soṭ.* 3:13-15 is also found in *Num. Rab.* Naso 9/24 on Num 5:27, where an unfaithful wife is punished "measure for measure." Here too the term "legions"

---

[110] Translation Neusner 3.157-158, which I only slightly alter. The Hebrew is in Lieberman, *Soṭah* 163-164, with MS Vienna in the right column and MS Erfurt in the left.

[111] Cf. Lieberman, *Soṭah* 164 and 163 respectively.

(לְגְיוֹנוֹת) occurs twice.¹¹² *Mek. R. Ish.* Shirata 2 on Exod 15:1, "for He is highly exalted," notes that God is "exalted above all those who exalt themselves. For with the very thing with which the nations of the world pride themselves before Him, He punishes them." The nine examples given in *t. Soṭ.* 3:6-19 are then supplemented by Tyre and the prince of Tyre.¹¹³ In Shirata 6 on Exod 15:7, "In the greatness of Your majesty You overthrew Your adversaries," Pharaoh and all "his host" (חֵילוֹ) are cited with Exod 14:7 and 15:4, and then Sisera with Judg 4:13 and 5:20.¹¹⁴

The Lord's victory alone at the Reed Sea over the Egyptians, Pharaoh and his "host" or "army" (חַיִל),¹¹⁵ causing them to drown in that Sea, provides the major background to the term "legion" in Mark 5:9 and 15, and to the drowning of the large herd of swine in the Sea of Galilee (see the next section). Two strands of Judaic tradition developed in regard to the term "legion," the first about the difference between a mortal king and the Lord as providing support and food for their armies at the Reed Sea, and the second about the Lord's fighting alone there.

7.1 Support and Food

Midr. Pss. 136/8 deals with 136:13, "To Him Who divided the Reed Sea in two," and v 25, "Who gives food to all flesh." These two verses are illustrated by the following. "A mortal king when engaged in battle cannot feed¹¹⁶ his troops (חיילוותיו)¹¹⁷ or supply other provisions for them. Yet He who spoke and the world came into being is not so. Rather, 'the Lord is a warrior

---

¹¹² Mirqin 9.194, Soncino 5.284.
¹¹³ Lauterbach 2.13-19. For the Egyptians Exod 14:7 and 15:4 are cited, and for Sisera Judg 4:13 and 5:20 (Lauterbach 2.16).
¹¹⁴ Lauterbach 2.46.
¹¹⁵ BDB 299, 4. It is found extensively for example in Exod 14:4, 9, 17 and 28, as well as in 15:4.
¹¹⁶ Cf. Jastrow 387 on זוּן : to provide, outfit; to sustain, esp. to feed.
¹¹⁷ The plural of the above חיל ; cf. Jastrow 454. Braude in 2.521, n. 15, explains the statement: "The soldiers are obliged to live off the country."

(lit., man of battle),' (Exod 15:3) who made war against the Egyptians. 'The Lord is His name' (*ibid.*), for He fed and provided for all His creatures. Thus it is stated, 'To Him who divided the Reed Sea into two,' and it is written, 'Who gives food to all flesh.'"[118]

This is the foundation for the explanation of "but he will not come near you" (Ps 91:7), part of the "Song of Those Afflicted (by Madness)," as found in *Midr. Pss.* 17/8. "The Holy One, blessed be He, said: It is the way of the world that when a king departs on a journey, all his legions (הלגיונות) depart with him to protect him, and he is obligated to give them their support and food. Yet I assigned you 1000 [angels] at your right hand and 10,000 at your left who protect you. Not even one will 'come near you' and say, 'Feed me and provide support for me.'"[119]

Here the angels of the Lord, the "King of Kings," are His "legions" who protect a person from demons. In contrast to a mortal king's legions, they need neither provisions nor food. This tradition is found elsewhere in *Midr. Pss.* 91/4 on Ps 91:7 [120] and in *Num. Rab.* Naso 12/3, also commenting on Ps 91:7.[121]

7.2 Fighting Alone

Num. Rab. Naso 11/7 on Num 6:26, "and give you peace," has R. Simeon (b. Yoḥai), a third generation Tanna,[122] state: "Come and see that the way of the Holy One, blessed be He, is not like the way of a mortal. When a mortal king goes forth to battle he goes with troops (אוֹבְלוֹסִין)[123] and legions (לְגְיוֹנוֹת), but when he goes on a peaceful mission he goes alone. Yet the way of the Holy One, blessed be He, is not so. When He goes on a peaceful mission He goes forth with troops and legions (לְגְיוֹנוֹת), as it is said: 'He makes peace in His high heaven' (Job 25:2), and after this it is written: 'Is there any number to His

---

[118] Buber 521; Braude 2.327-328, whom I modify.
[119] Buber 131; Braude 1.213, whom I modify.
[120] Buber 398, Braude 2.103. It has "1,000 men" instead of "legions."
[121] Mirqin 10.15, Soncino 5.465. It also has "1,000 men."
[122] Strack and Stemberger, *Introduction* 84.
[123] Jastrow 25: a levy of troops.

armies?' (v 3).[124] It also says: 'With mighty chariotry, twice ten thousand, thousands upon thousands, the Lord came from Sinai into the holy place' (Ps 68:18, Eng. 17). It also says: 'A thousand thousands served Him, and ten thousand times ten thousand stood attending Him' (Dan 7:10). Yet when He goes to battle He only goes alone, as it is said: 'The Lord is a man of battle, the Lord is His name' (Exod 15:3). Through His name He fights, and He needs no assistance. It also says: 'I have trodden the wine press alone' (Isa 63:3)."[125]

Emphasis is put here upon the Lord's being a man of war who fights alone when He rescues the Israelites and causes the Egyptians to drown in the Reed Sea. He employs His "legions" on other occasions.[126] This tradition is found in numerous other sources, showing its popularity.[127]

Finally, R. Jonathan, a third generation Tanna,[128] asks in b. Sanh. 39b: "What is meant by 'one did not come near the other all night' (Exod 14:20, at the Reed Sea). In that hour the ministering angels wished to utter the Song (of praise – Isa 6:3) before the Holy One, blessed be He. Yet He rebuked them, saying: 'My handiwork [the Egyptians] is drowning in the Sea.

---

[124] The expression לִגְדוּדָיו may have triggered "*leg*ion" here.

[125] Mirqin 9.304; Soncino 5.443.

[126] Cf. also the fourth plague in Egypt designated the Lord's "legions" in *Pesiq. Rav Kah.* 7/11 on Exod 12:29 (Mandelbaum 132, Braude and Kapstein 151); *Pesiq. R.* 17/7 on the same verse (Friedmann 89b, Braude 1.374); and 49/8 (Friedmann 197a, Braude 2.838-839), also on the same verse.

[127] Cf. *Midr. Pss.* 18/17 on Ps 18:13 (Buber 146-147, Braude 1.246-247) in the name of the third generation Tanna R. Judah the Prince, with legions; *Pesiq. R.* 21/9 (Friedmann 104a, Braude 1.430) in the name of R. Judah II. the Patriarch, Rabbi's grandson and a first generation Palestinian Amora (Strack and Stemberger, *Introduction* 92) with legions; *Exod. Rab.* Yithro 29/8 on Exod 20:1 (Mirqin 6.26-27, Soncino 3.337-338; אֲמִירָה means "das Zusammengehen, daher auch das Geben und Annehmen (Austausch) der Geissel, als Unterpfand des Friedens, zur Sicherheit" – Levy 1.101); and *Sifre* Beha'alothecha § 102 on Num 12:5 (Horowitz 100, Neusner 2.121-122).

[128] Cf. Strack and Stemberger, *Introduction* 83.

Would you utter Song before Me?"[129] This is repeated in the name of R. Yoḥanan in *b. Meg.* 10b.[130] The latter rabbi states the tradition slightly differently in *Exod. Rab.* Beshallaḥ 23/7 on Exod 15:1: "My legions (לְגִיוֹנוֹתַי) are in distress, and you wish to utter Song before Me?"[131]

Here the Egyptians are labeled God's "legions." Yet even the persecutors of His children the Israelites remain His creatures. This designation of Pharaoh and his hosts, drowning in the Reed Sea, as "legions" is of direct relevance to the drowning of the large herd of swine in the Sea of Galilee, into whom the unclean spirit(s) "Legion" entered. To this I now turn.

8. *Swine and Swineherd*

A. After the unclean spirit in the Gerasene demoniac informs Jesus that his name is "Legion, for we are many," he begs the prophet from Nazareth earnestly not to send "them" out of the country (Mark 5:9-10). The narrative continues by stating that "on the hillside 'a great herd of swine' (ἀγέλη χοίρων μεγάλη) was feeding" (v 11). The unclean spirits then begged Jesus: "Send us into 'the swine' (τοὺς χοίρους - v 12)." After Jesus permitted this, they came out (of the Gerasene demoniac) and then entered the swine (τοὺς χοίρους), which rushed down the steep bank into the Sea (of Galilee) and drowned there (v 13). At this point the "swineherds" (οἱ βόσκοντες αὐτούς) ran off and told it in the city and in the country (v 14). The swine are again referred to in v 16 (τῶν χοίρων).

The fourfold mention of "swine" here emphasizes their importance in the narrative. Except for the parallels in Matthew and Luke, the term χοῖρος occurs in the NT only in Matt 7:6 and Luke 15:15-16.[132] The expression "swineherds" in Mark 5:14 is literally "those feeding / tending them," with the Greek verb

---

[129] Soncino 251, which I modify.
[130] Soncino 59.
[131] Mirqin 5.263, Soncino 3.285. See also *Midr. Pss.* 106/2 on Ps 106:2 (Buber 454, Braude 2.189), and *Lam. Rab.*, proem 24 (Soncino 7.37-38).
[132] Cf. also the noun ὗς for "sow" in 2 Pet 2:22.

βόσκω. The active participle ὁ βόσκων is then a herdsman, here a "swineherd."[133]

Before pointing out the connection between swine and swineherd and the Egyptians and Pharaoh at the Reed Sea, it will be helpful to show how other demons could also change their appearance. In *b. Qidd.* 29b a demon appears in the guise of a seven-headed dragon.[134] In *Sanh.* 101a a demon (turns itself into a cedar tree and) swallows up a rabbi.[135] *Midr. Pss.* 78/12 relates that Ashmedai sat down on Solomon's throne in the guise of the king and acted like a madman.[136] Demons also take the appearance of humans in *b. Yebam.* 122a [137] and *Giṭ.* 66a.[138] The general statement is made in *'Avot R. Nat.* A 37 regarding demons: "They also change their appearance to any likeness they please."[139]

The above examples show that the unclean spirits' taking on the appearance of swine in the narrative of Mark 5:1-20 was behavior typical of demons.

B. Because the swine/pig was an unclean animal for the Jews, there are understandably few references to them in Judaic writings. This is especially true for the rare term "swineherd." The noun חֲזִירָא [140] is found only in *y. Ter.* 8:10, 46d. The students of R. Judah the Patriarch made fun of Diocletian as a "swineherd," but not later when he was the Roman emperor (284-305 CE).[141] A longer form of this narrative is found in *Gen.*

---

[133] BAGD 145. The Jewish "Prodigal Son" had to become one simply in order to stay alive when abroad in Luke 15:15.
[134] Soncino 141.
[135] Soncino 685, with n. 5.
[136] Buber 353, Braude 2.35.
[137] Soncino 865.
[138] Soncino 312.
[139] Schechter 109, Goldin 153. The verb הפך is employed: to turn, to change; hithpael, to be changed, to disguise oneself (Jastrow 361). P. Billerbeck also translates *b. Yoma* 75a as: "wie ein Sched sich in wer weiß wie viele Arten (von Gestalten) verwandelt...." Soncino 364 has: "even as the demon changes into many colours...."
[140] Jastrow 444.
[141] Neusner / Avery-Peck 6.421.

Rab. Toledoth 63/8 on Gen 25:25, where, however, it is stated that Diocletian was first a רעי חזירין, a "herder of swine" near Tiberias.[142] Here the Aramaic verb רעי, to feed, pasture,[143] corresponds exactly to the Greek βόσκω employed in Mark 5:14 of those who "herded / pastured / fed" the swine.

Another rare occurrence of the term "swineherd" is employed of Pharaoh, and "swine" of the Egyptians, in regard to the Passover event in *Exod. Rab.* Beshallaḥ 20/1 on Exod 13:17, "And it came to pass, when Pharaoh had let the [Israelite] people go."[144] The passage "and a rod for the back of fools" (Prov 26:3) is interpreted here of Pharaoh, who first refused to let the Israelites leave Egypt. Only after bearing all the plagues (the "rod") placed upon him by God and having his people and own son killed, did he send them out, crying "Woe! Woe!"

The narrative begins: "A parable of Pharaoh. To what can the matter be compared? To a herdsman 'who was herding swine' (שֶׁהָיָה רוֹעֶה חֲזִירִים). He discovered a lamb and drove / herded it among them." Each time its owner demanded it back, the swineherd refused, suffering a greater punishment. The parable is resolved by the statement: "The king (owner) is the King of Kings, blessed be He; the lamb is Israel; the swineherd is Pharaoh."[145] Then the various plagues are enumerated which lead to Israel's departure from Egypt and Pharaoh's crying out: "Woe! Woe!"

The above very rare imagery of Pharaoh as a "swineherd" and the Egyptians as "swine" provides the background of the imagery of "a large herd of swine" and "swineherds" in Mark 5:1-20. This is made certain by the following sections.[146]

---

[142] Theodor and Albeck 688-689; the expression occurs twice. Soncino 2.563-564.
[143] Jastrow 1486. The Hebrew is the same. BDB 945, 1. d. has רֹעֶה as herdsman.
[144] Mirqin 5.232-234, Soncino 3.241-244. Ezek 29:3 calls Pharaoh by a similarly opprobrious term, "the great serpent / dragon." On this, see its quotation in 20/6 on Exod 13:17 (Mirqin 5.236, Soncino 3.248).
[145] Mirqin 5.232-233; Soncino 5.241-242.
[146] To my knowledge only very few scholars have noted the relevance of the scene of Exodus 14-15 to Mark 5:1-20. Cf. C. Cave, "The Obedience

9. Panicking by Rushing Down a Steep Slope, and Drowning

A. After Jesus gave them permission to do so, the unclean spirits in the Gerasene demoniac came out of him and entered the large herd of swine feeding on the nearby hillside. Numbering about 2,000, the herd then "rushed down the steep bank into the Sea (of Galilee), and were drowned in the Sea" (Mark 5:13).

Several commentators note that this reaction, caused by the legion of unclean spirits' suddenly entering a herd of animals, is typical of a "panic."[147] When large dogs for example attacked and killed several sheep in a herd grazing near Guben in Brandenburg, Germany, in 1999, the rest of them panicked, ran into the Neiße River and drowned.[148]

The Palestinian Jewish Christian author of the narrative now found in Mark 5:1-20 was not, however, describing animal psychology. In v 13 he continued to employ specific motifs and expressions from Exodus 14-15, where Pharaoh and his army also end up drowning in the Reed Sea.

---

of Unclean Spirits" in *NTS* 11 (1964/65) 93-97, who asks: "Does the editor see the destruction of Pharaoh and his hosts here?" (p. 97). Cave, however, cites no concrete sources. O. Betz in "The Concept of the So-called 'Divine Man' in Mark's Christology" in *Studies in the New Testament and Early Christian Literature*, Festschrift A. Wikgren, ed. D. Aune (Suppl. NovT 33; Leiden: Brill, 1972) 238 also states: "As the army of the Egyptians was drowned in the Red Sea, so the legions of demons perished in the Galilean Sea...." J. Derrett in "Contributions to the Study of the Gerasene Demoniac" in *JSNT* 3 (1979) 2-17 deals more extensively with the Egyptian army at the Reed Sea in pp. 6-8, which he basically repeats in "Legend and Event: The Gerasene Demoniac: An Inquest into History and Liturgical Projection" in *JSNT* Suppl. Series 2 (1980) 63-73, especially pp. 64-69. See also his "Spirit-Possession and the Gerasene Demoniac" in *Man* 14 (1979) 286-293 on the pericope. J. Marcus in *Mark 1 – 8*, pp. 345-348, makes use of Derrett's studies.

[147] Cf. the definition of panic as "a sudden overpowering fright," which is "often accompanied by mass flight," in *Webster's Ninth Collegiate Dictionary* (Springfield, MA: Merriam-Webster, 1987) 850. See in this regard the commentators V. Taylor, *The Gospel According to St Mark* 278, and W. Grundmann, *Das Evangelium nach Markus* 145.

[148] Cf. the Berlin "Tagesspiegel" of March 19, 2001, in connection with another episode of mass panic.

B.
9.1 Panicking

Mark 5:13 employs the verb ὁρμάω [149] of the herd of swine's suddenly "rushing headlong" down the steep bank into the Sea (of Galilee) and drowning there. In the Gospels it is only employed in this narrative.[150] The term and the motif are borrowed from Judaic tradition on the Egyptians at the Reed Sea, compared in section 8. above to swine.

In his retelling of the Exodus event, Josephus notes in *Ant.* 2.340 regarding Exod 14:23-24 that when the Egyptians saw the Israelites enter the Reed Sea, they first thought they were mad (μαίνεσθαι). Yet when these proceeded unharmed, the Egyptians "'rushed' to pursue them" (διώκειν ὡρμήκεσαν αὐτούς), descending after them. In 344 they all perish, as in Exod 14:28. Here the perfect of the verb ὁρμάω is employed, just as in Mark 5:13.

In *Mos.* 2.254 Philo of Alexandria also states that the Egyptians at this point "rushed on" in unresting pursuit, speeding to their own destruction.[151] He continues in 255 by noting that "the enemy met their doom, sent to their last sleep by the fall of the frozen walls, and overwhelmed by the tides, as they 'rush down' upon their path as into a ravine!" The verb ἐπιφέρω in the passive is employed in the latter, meaning to rush upon or after.[152]

Exod 14:23-24, paraphrased above by Josephus in *Ant.* 2.340, reads: "The Egyptians pursued, and went into the sea after them, all of Pharaoh's horses, chariots, and chariot drivers. 24) At the morning watch the Lord in the pillar of fire and cloud looked

---

[149] BAGD 581; LSJ 1252, II. 2. rush headlong. The middle and passive also mean to rush. Cf. LXX A and S of Isa 5:29 with "rushing like lions."
[150] Cf. also Acts 7:57, where all "rush" together against Stephen, and 19:29, where a crowd of people "rushed" into the theater.
[151] The noun ἐφόρμησις is employed here: onset, attack, approach (LSJ 747). Yet the verb ἐφορμαίνω means to rush on, and ἐφορμάω to rush upon (746), justifying the translation here.
[152] LSJ 670, III. Translation F. H. Colson in the LCL edition.

down upon the Egyptian army, and 'threw' the Egyptian army 'into panic.'" The NRSV's "and threw into panic" translates the Hebrew verb וַיָּהָם , from הָמַם, confuse, discomfit.¹⁵³ The related verb הִים, הוּם means the same, and the cognate noun מְהוּמָה tumult, confusion, discomfiture.¹⁵⁴ The LXX and the targums translate similarly in v 24.

Philo of Alexandria in *Mos.* 1.178 notes at this point regarding the Egyptians: "'tumult and confusion' prevailed everywhere among them,"¹⁵⁵ and they all perished in the Sea (179).

The Tannaitic midrash on Exodus, *Mek. R. Ish.* Beshallaḥ 6 on Exod 14:24, "and threw the Egyptian army into panic," interprets this phrase by saying the Lord "confounded them and 'brought confusion among them'" (ערבבן).¹⁵⁶

Exod 14:27 states regarding the Reed Sea's returning to its normal depth: "As the Egyptians fled before it, the Lord tossed the Egyptians into the Sea," causing them all to drown (v 28). *Exod Rab.* Bo 15/15 *ad loc.* interprets נָסִים לִקְרָאתוֹ , lit. "they fled to meet it," by saying this actually should have read: "the Egyptians fled back." Yet God deceived them so that the Egyptians could find no way to escape, "and they ran towards the Sea until they sank in the depths." Here the piel of the verb נער is also interpreted as the Lord's "throwing" the Egyptians "into confusion" or "panic."¹⁵⁷ Finally, Isi the son of Shammai comments on Exod 15:1, "the horse and his rider," by citing in *Mek. R. Ish.* Shirata 2 the passage: "I will strike every horse with panic, and its rider with madness" (Zech 12:4).¹⁵⁸

---

¹⁵³ BDB 243, 2., with additional passages. Cf. also Jastrow 355, 1) to confound, with reference to *Mekilta* on Exod 14:24.
¹⁵⁴ BDB 223. The noun is found in rabbinic Hebrew (Jastrow 737), but not the verb.
¹⁵⁵ Cf. LSJ 803-804, II. for θόρυβος as tumult, confusion, and 1758, 3. on ταραχή as confusion.
¹⁵⁶ Lauterbach 1.241. See Jastrow 1111-1112 on עִרְבֵּב . The verb is also employed by *Targum Neofiti* at this point (Díez Macho 2.93 and 2.448).
¹⁵⁷ Mirqin 5.179; Soncino 3.179, with n. 4. On נער piel, see BDB 654 and Jastrow 921: to shake, stir up.
¹⁵⁸ Lauterbach 2.21-22. On the identity of this Tanna, see W. Bacher, *Die Agada der Tannaiten* 2.373, n. 2, and the longer note on p. 372.

The above passages suffice to show that the Palestinian Jewish Christian author of the narrative of the Gerasene demoniac borrowed the motif of "panicking" for the large herd of swine's "rushing down" to the Sea of Galilee and drowning in Mark 5:13 from the Lord's causing the Egyptians, elsewhere called swine, to panic, rush down and drown in the Reed Sea.

9.2 A Steep Slope

Mark 15:13 relates that after the unclean spirits left the Gerasene demoniac and entered the large herd of swine feeding on the nearby hillside, "the herd rushed 'down the slope' into the Sea ... and drowned in the Sea."

The Greek of "down the slope" is κατὰ τοῦ κρημνοῦ . The noun κρημνός is found in the NT only here and in the parallel accounts in Matt 8:32 and Luke 8:33. It means a steep slope or bank, cliff.[159] This refers back to the hillside (or mountainside) of Mark 5:11, πρὸς τῷ ὄρει. Philo employs the term κρημνός in *Agr.* 76 of a steep "slope" down which the maddened horses (of a chariot) are swept and perish, imagery similar to that employed of the herd of swine.[160]

The expression "steep slope," however, also derives from the scene of the Exodus event in Judaic tradition. The Israelites camped at the Reed Sea by Pi-hahiroth, in front of Baal-zephon (Exod 14:9; cf. v 2). "As Pharaoh drew near, the Israelites looked back, and there were the Egyptians advancing on them" (v 10). Philo notes in *Mos.* 1. 169 that the Israelites saw "the enemy's forces, armed and drawn up for battle," "on a high ridge" (ἐπὶ λόφου μετέωρος).[161] In *Mos.* 2.255 the Alexandrian states that the Egyptians then "rushed down their path as into a ravine" and drowned in the Reed Sea.[162]

Josephus, also reflecting early Judaic interpretation of the Exodus event, notes that the Israelites when encamped at the Sea

---

[159] BAGD 450, LSJ 994. In the LXX it is only found in 2 Chr 25:12.
[160] Cf. also *Leg. All.* 1.73 on this, as well as the noun in *Som.* 2.161 and 276, also situations leading to complete destruction.
[161] Cf. LSJ 1062 on λόφος : crest of a hill, ridge.
[162] Cf. LSJ 1916 on φάραγξ : cleft, chasm, esp. in a mountain side, ravine, gully.

were hemmed in by "mountains/hills" (ὄρεσι - *Ant.* 2.328).[163] Elsewhere in the same narrative he has the singular, "mountain/hill."[164] In 2.340 the Egyptians "rushed [down] to pursue" the Israelites, "and with their cavalry leading they proceeded to 'descend' (κατέβαινον)." Here the same verb for "to rush" is employed as in Mark 5:13, ὁρμάω.

In *Ant.* 2.324 the Jewish historian notes in regard to the above scene that the Egyptians confined the Israelites between inaccessible κρημνῶν and the Sea. That is, the Egyptians rushed down after the Israelites from κρημνοί, cliffs, steep slopes, on the nearby mountain / hill and then drowned in the Reed Sea. Exactly the same phenomenon and even the same term are employed in Mark 5:13 of the large herd of swine's feeding on a hillside / mountainside, rushing down a "steep slope" on the hillside / mountainside to drown in the Sea of Galilee.[165]

The traditional site of the swines' stampede is located at Kursi ca. 2.5 km south of where Naḥal Samakh enters the Sea of Tiberias on the east shore. A ridge forty-four meters high descends to the Lake at this point.[166] I will discuss the site Kursi below in section III.

9.3 *Drowning*

Mark 5:13 notes that the herd of swine, ca. 2,000, rushed down the steep slope and "drowned" in the Sea. The term "to drown" here is the imperfect passive of πνίγω, to be choked or drown.[167] It occurs only here in the NT in this sense. This expression also derives from the event described in Exodus 14-15.

---

[163] For the plural, see also 333.
[164] Cf. 325 and 337.
[165] For the phrase κατὰ τοῦ κρημνοῦ in Josephus, cf. also *Bell.* 1.313 (//*Ant.* 14.429) and *Ant.* 14.426, and for κατὰ κρημνῶν 14. 70.
[166] Cf. the map "Christian Sites Around the Sea of Galilee," ed. S. Reuveni and Y. Roman (Tel-Aviv: The Survey of Israel, 2000), New Israel Grid 260.746: the Cliff of Nuqeib. See also M. Nun, *Gergesa (Kursi). Site of a Miracle. Church & Fishing Village* (Kibbutz Ein Gev: Tourist Department and Kinnereth Sailing Co., 1989) 28. The precipice is pictured on p. 30.
[167] BAGD 679.

After the Lord threw Pharaoh and his chariots into panic while they were pursuing the Israelites at the Reed Sea, they rushed into it. The waters then returned, so that not one of them remained (Exod 14:29).

The Song of Moses also reads in 15:4-5 : "Pharaoh's chariots and his army He cast into the Sea; his picked officers were sunk in the Reed Sea. 5) The floods covered them; they went down into the depths like a stone." The Hebrew verb for "were sunk" here is the pual of טָבַע , to sink, sink down.[168] In rabbinic Hebrew it means to sink, be drowned.[169]

All the military of the Egyptians, elsewhere called swine, drown here. This is the basis of the unclean spirits of the demon Legion, now in a large herd of swine, all drowning in Mark 5:13. It cannot be overemphasized that in Judaic tradition the figure of Samson, on whom the Gerasene demoniac is modeled, is intimately associated with "legions" and precisely the verse cited above, Exod 15:4 (see section 7. B. above).

Two other expressions in the narrative of the Gerasene demoniac may also derive from Exod 15:4-5. Verse four mentions the Sea (יָם) twice, in Hebrew parallelism. Mark 5:13 rather clumsily repeats the noun θάλασσα twice. The word "there" (ἐκεῖ) could easily have been employed instead of "and they drowned 'in the Sea.'" The author may have unconsciously been influenced by the two "seas" in Exod 15:4.

Secondly, Luke 8:31 does not follow Mark 5:10, where the unclean spirits (Legion) beg Jesus eagerly not to send them out of the country. Rather, it has them beg Jesus not to command them to depart into the "abyss."[170] Here the latter refers to the adjacent Sea of Galilee. The Greek ἄβυσσος means abyss, depth, underworld.[171] It appears to derive here from the Hebrew "depths" (NRSV "floods") in Exod 15:5, תְּהֹמֹת . The

---

[168] BDB 371.
[169] Jastrow 518. He calls attention to *b. Sanh.* 39b (Soncino 251) cited above, where God rebukes the angels for wanting to utter the Song of Isa 6:3 to Him while the work of His hands is "drowning" in the Sea.
[170] There is no justification for the NRSV to translate ἀπελθεῖν as "to go back."
[171] BAGD 2.

term תְּהוֹם means deep, sea, abyss.[172] The unclean spirits beg not to be ordered to depart into the abyss, Sea (of Galilee) - and drown. It is ironic that after Jesus grants this wish by allowing them to enter a large herd of swine (8:32), these then rush down the steep bank in panic and nevertheless drown in the Lake (v 33).[173]

10. Survival of Only One, Who Proclaims the Miracle Elsewhere

A. Mark 5:13 states that the entire herd of swine, about 2,000, into which the unclean spirits within the Gerasene demoniac entered, drowned in the Sea (of Galilee). It is assumed that the unclean spirits perished simultaneously, for demons were also considered capable of dying.[174]

Only the former demoniac, now healed and in his right mind (v 15), survived. When Jesus begins to leave the scene by entering his boat, the man who had been possessed by demons begs Jesus that he might be with him, i.e. follow him and become his disciple (v 18). Yet the prophet from Nazareth, who had just graciously granted the request of unclean spirits, strangely denies this request. Instead, he tells him: "Depart to your home, to your relatives and friends, and proclaim (ἀπάγγειλον)[175] to them the things the Lord [God] has done to you, and how He

---

[172] BDB 1062-1063. Cf. early comment on the "deeps/abysses" of Exod 15:5 in *Mek. R. Ish.* Shirata 5 *ad loc.* (Lauterbach 2.37-38). G. Schwarz in "'Aus der Gegend' (Markus V. 10b)" in *NTS* 22 (1975-1976) 214-215 unconvincingly maintains that the Aramaic $t^e homa$, abyss, stood originally in Mark 5:10b. It was somehow heard or read as $t^e huma$ and rendered χώρα , region. Yet the unclean spirits want to remain somewhere in the "region."

[173] Imagery from Judaic tradition on Exodus 14-15 thus provides the major background to the drowning of the herd of swine, and not "direct parallels" from Pausanius and elsewhere, as maintained by B. Kollmann in *Jesus und die Christen als Wundertäter. Studien zu Magie, Medizin und Schamanismus in Antike und Christentum* (FRLANT 170; Göttingen: Vandenhoeck & Ruprecht, 1996) 208. He also incorrectly maintains there are no indications of an Aramaic or Hebrew "Vorlage."

[174] Cf. for example *'Avot R. Nat.* A 37 (Schechter 109, Goldin 153).

[175] BAGD 79: 1. report, announce, tell. 2. proclaim.

has had mercy on you" (v 19). Then the man departs and begins to make known / proclaim (κηρύσσειν)[176] in the Decapolis the things Jesus did to him, causing everyone to marvel (v 20).

This is the only narrative in Mark in which Jesus even encourages someone he has healed or exorcized to make the event known elsewhere. All other related instances demand the opposite: they should keep the matter to themselves (1:43-44; 3:12; 5:43; 7:36; 8:26 v. l.). In addition, when blind Bartimaeus for example regains his sight, he "follows" Jesus "on the way" (10:52), i.e. becomes his disciple. Yet in 5:19 Jesus refuses such a request. The Evangelist Mark, however, has *not* put here a muzzle on the man formerly possessed by demons, the Evangelist's "messianic secret" which must be kept until later. This alone points to Mark's probably leaving the basic contents of 5:1-20 intact.

The Gerasene demoniac's survival and his later fulfilling in the Decapolis (v 20) Jesus' command to proclaim to his relatives and friends what the Lord has done to him, how He has had mercy on him (v 19), is also due to Judaic tradition on Pharaoh at the Reed Sea.

B. Pharaoh took six hundred picked chariots and all the other chariots of Egypt with officers over all of them (Exod 14:7) into the Reed Sea in pursuit of the Israelites. Then, when the waters returned and covered the Egyptians, "not one of them remained" (v 28).

Ps 106:11 states literally in this regard: "one of them was not left over" (אֶחָד מֵהֶם לֹא נוֹתָר), i.e. all definitely drowned. The formulation in Exod 14:28, however, is somewhat ambiguous: לֹא־נִשְׁאַר בָּהֶם עַד־אֶחָד . While this statement is normally understood as in the NRSV, "not one of them remained," the phrase עַד־אֶחָד can also mean "up to / except for one."

In *Mek. R. Ish.* Beshallaḥ 7 on the above verse, R. Judah (bar Ilai), a third generation Tanna,[177] says the verse means not even

---

[176] BAGD 431: announce, make known; preach, proclaim something.
[177] Strack and Stemberger, *Introduction* 84-85.

Pharaoh himself remained. He buttresses his assertion with the important verse Exod 15:4, "Pharaoh's chariots and his army He cast into the Sea; his picked officers were sunk / drowned in the Reed Sea." Often debating with Judah bar Ilai, R. Nehemiah, another third generation Tanna,[178] counters by stating no one remained "except for Pharaoh himself" (חוץ מפרעה). Regarding him Exod 9:16 has the Lord say: "But this is why I have let you live: to show you My power, and to proclaim My name in all the earth."[179]

The above phrase "to proclaim" is the Hebrew piel infinitive construct form, סַפֵּר(לְ), to recount / relate / rehearse (the glorious deeds of the Lord's name).[180] The *Palestinian Targum* also interprets the latter part of the verse in regard to Pharaoh: "and that you might tell of My holy name in all the earth."[181] In the Bible, Exod 9:16 precedes the seventh of the ten plagues leading up to the Israelites' exodus from Egypt. Yet early rabbis could cite it already at this point to mean the future task of Pharaoh, for "no strict order as to 'earlier' and 'later' is observed in the Torah."[182]

It is quite probable that R. Nehemiah borrowed his interpretation of Exod 14:28's "except for one" from earlier Judaic tradition on this complex. In *Pirq. R. El.* 43, a chapter dealing with repentance, R. Neḥunya ben ha-Qanah, a first generation Tanna,[183] for example cites Pharaoh as the main positive example of repentance. Earlier he had made such

---

[178] *Ibid.*, 85.
[179] Lauterbach 1.246. A parallel is found in *Midr. Pss.* 106/5 on Ps 106:11 (Buber 455, Braude 2.191). As so often, only the beginning of the biblical verses is given, the rabbis knowing them by heart. For a better understanding, I quote them *in toto*. Paul cites Exod 9:16 in Rom 9:17.
[180] BDB 708.
[181] Rieder 2.93 with דתתני , the verb תני meaning to tell, and often associated with wonders (Jastrow 1681); Maher 183. Targum Neofiti 1 is similar, but emphasizes the Lord's keeping Pharaoh alive until now (Díez Macho 2.53 and 429).
[182] Cf. *Mek. R. Ish.* Shirata 7 on Exod 15:9 (Lauterbach 2.54-55).
[183] Strack and Stemberger, *Introduction* 74.

prideful statements as Exod 5:2.[184] Yet he repented and then spoke 15:11a, "Who is like You, O Lord, among the gods?" God delivered Pharaoh from the dead [Egyptians in the Reed Sea] for him to declare (לְסַפֵּר) the might of His power, as in 9:16. Then Pharaoh went to the city Nineveh[185] and ruled there. When the prophet Jonah was later asked by God to prophesy its destruction, Pharaoh did public penance in order to encourage the wicked citizens of the city to repent.[186]

A later midrash, Wa-Yosha,[187] comments on Exod 15:11 by elaborating on the above narrative, for example by stating that the angel Gabriel placed an iron chain on Pharaoh's neck and made him descend to the depths of the Sea, where he tortured him in order to have him acknowledge God's strength.[188]

---

[184] Cf. this verse contrasted to what Pharaoh will say in the future, "I have sinned against the Lord" (10:16), and similar statements in *Exod. Rab.* Shemoth 5/14 on Exod 5:1-2 (Mirqin 5.98-99, Soncino 3.96).
[185] For Nineveh as a "great city," cf. Jonah 1:1; 3:2-3; and 4:11.
[186] Cf. Friedlander 341-342, based on the A. Epstein MS of Vienna, with extensive notes on the texts of the various editions; Eshkol 167; and Higger, *Horeb* 10 (1948) 225. Interestingly, the stilling of the storm in Mark 4:35-41 is based on Judaic traditions regarding the storm in Jonah One (see my *The Stilling of the Storm* 3-55), and the activity of the healed demoniac from Kursi in the adjacent narrative, Mark 5:1-20, is portrayed in terms of Judaic traditions on Pharaoh (later the king of Nineveh) in Jonah Three. The two Gospel units may thus have been composed by the same Palestinian Jewish Christian(s) from the area around Capernaum on the Sea of Galilee, and could even have been brought together *before* a pre-Markan redactor collected the miracle stories.
[187] Cf. וַיּוֹשַׁע in Exod 14:30 for the source of the term.
[188] Cf. Jellinek, *Bet ha-Midrasch* 1.52-53, and a German translation in Wünsche, *Aus Israels Lehrhallen* 1.112-113. For Pharaoh as the only one to not drown in the Reed Sea, and then reigning in Nineveh, see also "Dibrē ha-Yamin shel Moshe Rabbenu" in Jellinek, *Bet ha-Midrasch* 2.11, with an English translation in M. Gaster, *The Chronicles of Jerahmeel* (London, 1899; reprint New York: KTAV Publishing House, 1971) 128 as 48:12. This is also found in *Sepher ha-Yashar* 81:40-41 (L. Goldschmidt, *Sepher hajaschar* [Berlin: Harz, 1923] 273, English in M. Noach, *The Book of Jashar* [New York, 1840; reprint Salt Lake City: Parry, 1887] 231).

Many elements in the present version of the latter midrash are patently late. Yet the basic content of the Pharaoh narrative found in *Pirq. R. El.* 43 appears to be very early. There is no reason not to attribute it to the first generation Tanna R. Neḥunya ben ha-Qanah, for R. Nehemiah, a third generation Tanna, seems to be citing only a small section of the tradition.

I suggest that the Palestinian Jewish Christian author of Mark 5:1-20 also knew of an early form of this complex of haggadic tradition and borrowed motifs and expressions from it for his narrative. After all the evil spirits left the Gerasene demoniac, entered a herd of swine and drowned in the Sea of Galilee, the former demoniac, the sole surviver of the incident so to speak, was told to "proclaim" to his relatives and friends the things the Lord (God) had done to him, the mercy He had shown him (v 19). This is probably based on Exod 9:16, where Pharaoh in Judaic tradition after the miracle at the Reed Sea also is to "proclaim" the Lord's name in all the land / earth.[189] Jesus' exorcism of the legion of unclean spirits from the Gerasene demoniac and their drowning inside swine in the Sea of Galilee were a wonder or miracle reminiscent of the miraculous drowning of the Egyptian army, elsewhere called "legions" and "swine," in the Reed Sea. This explains why the cured Gerasene demoniac is not allowed to follow Jesus as his disciple and is not told to remain silent concerning the exorcism. Instead, like Pharaoh who does not return to his native city in Egypt but rather goes off to the great city of Nineveh, he makes known in the Decapolis the things Jesus did for him (Mark 5:20).

Since the narrative of the Gerasene demoniac is pictured as taking place just south of Kursi on the east shore of the Sea of Galilee (see section III. below), the reference to the Decapolis in v 20 can only refer to its nearest city, Hippos, called in Aramaic Susitha. It lay less than 4 km or 2.4 miles southeast of the

---

See also the Koran, surah 10.91-93 in M. Pickthall, *The Glorious Koran* (New York, 1960) 163-164.

[189] The MS variant διάγγειλον at Mark 5:19 recalls the διαγγελῆ in LXX Exod 9:16. The Semitic would have been the same: סַפֵּר. J. Marcus in *Mark 1 - 8*, p. 354, also calls attention to Exod 9:16 at this point.

traditional site of the drowning of the swine, and directly east of the present-day kibbutz Ein-Gev.[190] It had a large harbor on the Lake, and possibly also a smaller one.[191]

Mark 5:14 states that after the large herd of swine drowned in the Sea of Galilee, those who had been herding it fled and told it in the "city" and in the (nearby) hamlets. The term "city" here is πόλις and does not refer to Hippos / Susitha, but to Kursi, a site just south of where the Naḥal Samakh enters the Sea of Galilee. The Semitic behind πόλις is עִיר , which can mean both a city and a "town," the latter intended here.[192] It is from this site that people came to see what had happened to the swine and to the demoniac (vv 14-16). When Luke in 8:39 has the Gerasene demoniac proclaim "throughout the entire city" how much Jesus had done for him, he seems to have the same city as in v 34 in mind.[193] He intentionally omits the reference to the "Decapolis" in Mark 5:20.

11. *Begging Someone to Leave the Land out of Fear*

A. The unclean spirit(s) Legion "begged" (παρεκάλει) Jesus earnestly not to send them out of the country in Mark 5:10. Then they "begged" (παρεκάλεσαν) him to send them into the

---

[190] Cf. the map "Christian Sites Around the Sea of Galilee," New Israel Grid 262.742-743. On this city, see the article by Beer-Hepding in PW (1913) 8.1913-1914; Schürer, *The history* 2.130-132; and *Jesus & His World* (Minneapolis: Fortress, 1995) 127-128. On the Decapolis and its cities in general, see H. Bietenhard, "Die syrische Dekapolis von Pompeius bis Trajan" in *ANRW* II. 8., ed. W. Haase and H. Temporini (Berlin: de Gruyter, 1977) 220-261. Hippos has an elevation of 127 m (Pilgrims' Map, "Christian Sites Around the Sea of Galilee," New Israel Grid 262. 742.5). That is, it is 337 m above the Sea of Galilee, at - 210 m. For this reason J. Rousseau and R. Arav in *Jesus & His World* 127 think Hippos may have been the "city built on a hill" of Matt 5:14, (whose light) cannot be hid.
[191] For a description of it, cf. M. Nun, *Sea of Galilee. Newly Discovered Harbours From New Testament Days* (Kibbutz Ein Gev: Tourist Department and Kinnereth Sailing Co., 1992³) 16-18.
[192] Jastrow 1075.
[193] Hardly Gerasa, some 60 km or 36 miles southeast of the Sea of Galilee; it was far inland and thus distant from a major body of water.

swine grazing nearby (v 12). And after the man who had been exorcized of demons by the prophet from Nazareth saw Jesus entering the boat in order to depart, he "begged" (παρεκάλει) him that he might go along with him and be his disciple (v 18).

A fourth example of begging in this narrative is found in v 17. The swineherds, upon viewing the stampeding and drowning of their large herd of swine in the Sea of Galilee, ran off and told it in the town (of Kursi) and the nearby hamlets. Then people from there came to see what had happened (v 14). First they saw the ca. 2,000 dead swine floating in the water, and then Jesus and the healed demoniac. This caused them to be afraid (v 15). Verse sixteen adds parenthetically: (Those who had seen what had happened to the demoniac and in regard to the swine had related this to them.) Then verse seventeen states about the people just mentioned: "And they began 'to beg' him (Jesus) to depart from their region."[194]

The latter term, "to beg," is the fourth occurrence of the Greek παρακαλέω : to request, implore, appeal to, entreat, "beg."[195] The people's "fearing" in v 15 is ἐφοβήθησαν, from φοβέομαι, to be afraid, to fear.[196] The two motifs of begging someone to depart from the land, out of fear, also derive from the Exodus event.[197]

B. In spite of nine terrible plagues, Egypt's Pharaoh did not allow the Israelites to leave the land. Before the tenth and final one, the death of all the firstborns, Moses told Pharaoh: "all these officials of yours will come down to me, and bow down to me, saying, 'Leave us, you and all the people who follow you.' After that I will leave" (Exod 11:8).

Exod. Rab. Bo 18/1 on Exod 12:29 has Moses say to Pharaoh in regard to the above verse: "You will come to me, and not only

---

[194] On the term τὰ ὅρια for region, district, see Mark 7:31, "through 'the region' of the Decapolis," and BAGD 581.
[195] BAGD 617.
[196] BAGD 862-863.
[197] To my knowledge no one has called attention to this before except C. Cave, "The Unclean Spirits" in *NTS* 11 (1964-1965). There he refers in one sentence to Mark 5:17 (p. 97), and then to Exod 12:31 in n. 6.

you, but also this chief of your armies at your side, and your governor and all your courtiers shall come running with you to me, 'imploring and prostrating themselves to me for us to depart from here.'"[198] Here "imploring" is מְבַקְשִׁים, from בָּקַשׁ, piel, to seek, desire, "beg," ask.[199] "To depart from here" is literally "that we depart from here," שֶׁנֵּצֵא מִכָּאן.

Yet only after the tenth and final plague did Pharaoh finally summon Moses and Aaron and tell them in Exod 12:31-32: "Rise up, go away from my people, both you and the Israelites! Go, worship the Lord, as you said. 32) Take your flocks and your herds, as you said, and be gone. And bring a blessing on me too!" Verse 33 comments on this: "The Egyptians 'urged'[200] the people to hasten their departure from the land, for they said, 'We shall all be dead.'"

Judaic comment on these verses provides the primary background for the people's begging Jesus to leave their district, especially after the death of ca. 2,000 swine, causing them to be afraid.

Josephus in *Ant.* 2.310 first comments on Exod 10:28-29 by having Moses tell Pharaoh that "it was the king himself, along with the chief of the Egyptians, who would 'implore' (παρακαλέσειν) the Hebrews to depart." Then, after the tenth plague killed all the firstborn in the entire land, "multitudes of those whose dwellings surrounded the palace trooped to Pharaoh 'to urge' (συμβουλεύειν)[201] him to let the Hebrews go. And he, summoning Moses, 'ordered' (προσέταξεν)[202] him to depart..." (313-314).   This is an haggadic retelling of Exod 12:31-33.[203]

Here exactly the same verb, παρακαλέω, is employed as in Mark 5:17, where the people also beg Jesus to leave the district / land.

---

[198] Mirqin 5.210, Soncino 3.217.
[199] Jastrow 188.
[200] Cf. חזק in BDB 304, I. 3. : to press, be urgent, with עַל .
[201] LSJ 1677: advise, counsel.
[202] LSJ 1526 on προστάσσω : command, prescribe, enjoin, order.
[203] Cf. the biblical verses in the margin of the LCL edition of Josephus.

In *Mos.* 1. 138-139 Philo describes the same scene, noting in 138 that the people "were filled with fear of the destruction of those who still lived." The Alexandrian is also dependent on earlier tradition at this point.[204]

The best rabbinic example of comment on Exod 12:31-33 is the following.

Tanḥ. B Bo 19 on Exod 12:30-33 has Pharaoh inquire in the night in every lane where Moses is and where he lives. When he finally finds him, he says to him: "Rise up, go away from my people." Moses replies by asking whether the Israelites are thieves, for God had told them not to leave their houses before morning (v 22). Pharaoh then says to Moses: "*I beg you,* 'rise up, go away' (v 31)." Moses then asks him: "Why do you *persistently beg* so much?" Pharaoh answers: "Because I am a firstborn and fear that I could also die." Moses then tells him: "Do not fear that; you are destined for something greater than that." Do not say that Pharaoh alone *did the urging*. Rather, all the Egyptians *did the urging,* as in v 33. God then spoke to them: "By your life! You will not all die here, but in the Sea!"[205]

The Hebrew for "I beg you" above is בבקשה ממך,[206] the same verbal root as found in the *Exodus Rabbah* passage cited above. It should be noted that Pharaoh addresses here one person, Moses, thus in the singular, just as the people beg the one person Jesus to leave their district in Mark 5:17.

The Hebrew for "you persistently beg so much" above is אתה מטריח הרבה. The verb טרח can mean to trouble, "beg persistently."[207]

The "urging" above, not only of Pharaoh, but of all the Egyptians, is the verb דחק, to press, force, "urge," impel.[208]

---

[204] Cf. the "as we are told," φασι, in 135 and elsewhere.

[205] Buber 2.52-53; Bietenhard 1.345. A further elaboration of this is found in *Midr. Wa-yosha* (Jellinek 1.48; Wünsche 5.105-106).

[206] Jastrow 188 on בַּקָּשָׁה.

[207] Jastrow 551, 3.

[208] Jastrow 293. On this motif, cf. also Wisd Sol 19:3, where the Egyptians "pursued as fugitives those whom they had begged and compelled to leave." This writing is from Egypt, perhaps from the first half of the first century CE (Nickelsburg, *Jewish Literature* 184).

Pharaoh's "fearing" here is from the root יָרֵא , to fear, be afraid.²⁰⁹ It is thus very probable that early Judaic tradition on Pharaoh and the Egyptian people's "urging / begging" Moses (and the Israelites) to leave the land, out of "fear" that they too could die, provides the major background to the people's "being afraid" in Mark 5:15 and their "begging" Jesus to leave their land in v 17. They are afraid that they too could die, just as they consider the drowning of ca. 2,000 swine to be due to Jesus.

12. About Two Thousand

A. Mark 5:11 says there was a large herd of swine feeding on the hillside near the Gerasene demoniac. When Jesus gave the unclean spirits ("Legion, for we are many" – v 9) permission to enter these swine, they rushed down the steep slope into the Sea of Galilee, drowning there. They were "about two thousand" (ὡς δισχίλιοι - v 13). Verse 14 mentions "those herding them," i.e. the swineherds. The number of the latter, however, is not given.

The number 2,000 was extremely large for a herd of swine. Marcus Terentius Varro, born some 83 km or 50 miles from Rome in 116 BCE and who is thought to have died in 27 BCE, worked in early years on his father's estates, in part with the herdsmen. At an advanced age he wrote his *Res Rusticae* on farming.²¹⁰ He also may have been a Roman governor of Syria whom Josephus mentions in *Bell*. 1.398 and *Ant*. 15.345.²¹¹ In IV. 1-22 Varro deals with the raising of swine and notes the Latin term for "swineherd," *subulcus*.²¹² In 22 he mentions that ten boars suffice for 100 sows, yet some farmers employ even fewer.

---

²⁰⁹ Jastrow 593. Cf. also Ps 105:38, "Egypt was glad when they departed, for 'dread' of them had fallen upon them." See also the Israelites' "fearing" the Lord in Exod 14:31 after the Egyptians drowned in the Reed Sea, as well as 15:14-16, dealing with the peoples' trembling, terror and dread when they hear of the Egyptians drowning.
²¹⁰ For these dates, cf. B. Tilly, *Varro, The Farmer*. A Selection from the Res Rusticae, 1-2, 4 and 13. She only summarizes the section on swine (92-93).
²¹¹ This was in ca. 23 BCE, which makes the dating of Varro's death difficult. Cf. Schürer, *The history* 1.256.
²¹² Cf. Chambers Murray, *latin-english Dictionary* 721.

Varro himself considers a herd of 100 swine as appropriate; some, however, have 150. The number of young pigs is doubled by some, and others even go beyond this.[213]

Conditions in central Italy, in the middle of the Mediterranean, will hardly have differed from those in Palestine on the eastern side of that Sea. A normal herd of swine will have numbered between 100 and 150 there too, for the special case of piglets is not envisioned in Mark 5:1-20. This means that the number ca. 2,000 has nothing to do with reality.

Other figures in the Gospels are also greatly exaggerated. Mark 6:44 has Jesus feed 5,000 people with five loaves and two fish, and the similar story in 8:9 has "about" (ὡς) 4,000.[214] Matt 18:24 notes that one of his servants owes a king 10,000 talents. In Luke 14:31 Jesus asks whether a king with 10,000 troops will wage war with a king with 20,000. And in Matt 26:53, the only other "legion" passage in the NT, Jesus states that his heavenly Father would be willing at once to send him more than twelve legions of angels. These examples justify the question: Is the number "about 2,000" thus simply oriental hyperbole? I suggest it was not.

The phrase "Legion, for we are many" in Mark 5:9 seems to have triggered the number "about 2,000" because it was generally known that a Roman legion was comprised of several thousand.[215] Therefore the Palestinian Jewish Christian author of the narrative in Mark 5:1-20 considered it appropriate for the "legion" of unclean spirits within the Gerasene demoniac to enter a "large" herd of swine, indeed, one comprising some 2,000 animals. The graphic image of ca. 2,000 drowned swine, bloated and floating on the surface near the eastern shore of the Sea of Galilee, will have impressed itself deeply into the minds of the

---

[213] Cf. Marcus Terentius Varro, *Gespräche über die Landwirtschaft, Buch 2*, 92-100 (Latin) and 147-153 (German). Section 22 is on pp. 99-100 and 153.

[214] On "about," cf. also Matt 14:21 and John 6:10. See also "about (כְּ) 600,000 men on foot, besides children," in Exod 12:38.

[215] Cf. p. 16 above for some 6,000 as a complete legion. Most Jews in Palestine will not have known this figure. For them a legion was simply several thousand.

first hearers and later readers of the anecdote. This is another sign of the narrator's skill.

The phrase "about 2,000," however, also seems to derive from the Exodus event commemorated by Jews annually at Passover.

B. The triennial cycle of readings from the Torah and the Prophets (the "haftarah") prevailed in the synagogues of Palestine, in contrast to the annual system in Babylonia, which later became generally dominant. While its dating in specific cases is difficult, the readings for the festival days and the special Sabbaths seem to have been fixed at an early time.[216] Passover, the most important religious set festival (מוֹעֵד) in the entire year next to the Day of Atonement, acquired readings appropriate to its character.

In the second year of the triennial cycle, for the first day of Passover Exod 12:29 ff. were read, dealing with the tenth plague, the death of all firstborn. In the previous section (11.) I pointed out the importance of the verses 31-33 for the motif of "urging someone to leave the land." Joshua 5, dealing in vv 10-12 with the Passover in Gilgal, was the corresponding reading from the Prophets. Exactly one year later, i.e. in the third year of the cycle, Numbers 9 was read from the Torah on the first day of Passover, for vv 1-14 deal explicitly with the Passover in the wilderness of Sinai. The haftarah for this was Joshua 3, where Israel's crossing the Jordan River is portrayed in terms strongly reminiscent of the Israelites' crossing the Reed Sea in Exodus 14.[217]

---

[216] A. Büchler, J. Jacobs and I. Dobsevage in their art. "Haftarah" in *JE* (1904) 6.135-137 think the system of prophetic readings was probably even pre-Christian, beginning with the festivals and special Sabbaths (p. 136). Cf. also the articles "Triennial Cycle" by J. Jacobs in *JE* (1906) 12.254-257, and by the editors in *EJ* (1971) 15.1386-1389. See also J. Mann, *The Bible as Read and Preached in the Old Synagogue* (Cincinatti, Ohio, 1940), vol. I (he died before finishing the intended section on the Passover in vol. II), and C. Perrot, *La Lecture de la Bible dans la Synagogue. Les anciennes lectures palestiniennes du Shabbat et des fêtes* (Hildesheim: Gerstenberg, 1973).

[217] For these readings, cf. J. Jacobs in *JE* 12.257. In their art. "Haftarah" in *JE* 6.135-137, A. Büchler, J. Jacobs and I. Dobsevage have Exod 12:21-

The expression "about 2,000" (כְּאַלְפַּיִם) occurs only twice in the entire Hebrew Bible, once in Josh 7:3 in the phrase "about two or three thousand men should go up and attack Ai." The second occurrence is in Joshua 3. The officers tell the Israelites encamped at the Jordan River to follow the ark of the covenant carried by the levitical priests. Verse 4 then states: "Yet there shall be a space between you and it, a distance of 'about two thousand' cubits; do not come any nearer to it."

I suggest that this occurrence of "about two thousand," part of the reading from the Prophets on the first day of Passover in the third year of the triennial cycle, provided the inspiration for the phrase "about 2,000" in Mark 5:13,[218] just as other imagery from the Exodus event also influenced the narrative of the Gerasene demoniac, as pointed out in sections 8.-10. above.

Josh 3:4, with "about 2,000," may even have been associated in early Judaic tradition with the term "legion." *Exod. Rab.* Ki Thissa 45/3 cites Exod 33:7, "Now Moses used to take the tent and pitch it outside the camp, far off from the camp." This midrash asks: "How far away was it?" R. Isaac, probably II, a third generation Palestinian Amora,[219] answers: "A mile." It is equal to 2,000 cubits.[220] This is known because the term "far off" (הַרְחֵק) occurs here, and the related term "a space" (רָחוֹק) occurs in Josh 3:4, which is then cited. Moses' anger with the Israelites for squandering the precious gift God had given them, (weapons on which the Ineffable Name was inscribed, said R. Simeon b. Yoḥai, a third generation Tanna),[221] is then explained by R. Simeon b. Laqish, a second generation Palestinian Amora,[222] as follows. "It can be compared to a king whose

---

51 and Josh 3:5 - 4:1 for the first day of Passover, but this seems to be based on the later annual cycle (p. 137), for only fifty-four Sabbaths are noted.

[218] Against P. Lapide, *Ist die Bibel richtig übersetzt?* (Augsburg: Weltbild Verlag, 1999) 119, who posits an original "in herds" (ba'alafim), misread as ka'alafim, which became k'alpaim.

[219] Strack and Stemberger, *Introduction* 98.

[220] Cf. Jastrow 773 on מִיל .

[221] Strack and Stemberger, *Introduction* 84.

[222] *Ibid.,* 95.

'legion' (לְגְיוֹן) rebelled against him. What did its commander do? He took the ensign of the king and fled. Moses did likewise when Israel performed that deed [the sin of the golden calf in Exodus 32]. He took the tent and departed. Thus it is said: 'Now Moses used to take the tent,' etc."[223] *Tanḥ.* B Ki Thissa 15 repeats this tradition with very few exceptions.[224]

If Josh 3:4, including "about 2,000," was associated with the term "legion" in early Judaic tradition because a legion was thought to have "thousands" of soldiers, this too may have influenced the Palestinian Jewish Christian author of Mark 5:1-20 in noting the number "about 2,000" in v 13 after mentioning the name "legion" in v 9.

* * *

The six motifs and expressions described above in sections 7. - 12. derive from early Palestinian Judaic comment on the Exodus event, including the plagues leading up to it and the biblical readings assigned to the annual festival of Passover, commemorating this event.

In *t. Meg.* 3:5 it is said that "In the council they ask questions concerning the laws of Passover thirty days before Passover."[225] This relatively long period included synagogue lectures on the relevant biblical passages,[226] certainly also embracing haggadic materials such as those adduced above. For these reasons it is understandable that when the author of Mark 5:1-20 described the Gerasene demoniac in terms of Palestinian Judaic traditions on Samson, he also included motifs and expressions from Judaic comment on Exodus 14-15 and the Passover event, for Exod 15:4

---

[223] Mirqin 6.170; Soncino 3.520, with notes. I have slightly altered the latter's translation.
[224] Buber 2.115; Bietenhard 1.411-412. Here R. Simeon is mentioned without b. Yoḥai, and R. Isaac's name is missing. Part of this tradition is found in *Midr. Pss.* 25/6 on Ps 25:4 (Buber 211-212, Braude 1.350-351), and in *Ruth Rab.* 2:5 § 3 (Soncino 9.106). It is enigmatic how J. Derrett in "Spirit-Possession" 291 maintains the number 2,000 "comes from Ps. 8."
[225] Zuckermandel / Liebermann 225; Neusner 2.289. See also *b. Meg.* 29b (Soncino 178-179).
[226] Cf. *b. Pesaḥ.* 6a (Soncino 23-24).

was intimately associated with Samson (see *t. Soṭa* 3:13-15 in section 7. above). There the Lord's casting Pharaoh's chariots and his army into the (Reed) Sea, causing them to drown, inspired him to describe the unclean spirits in the Gerasene demoniac, legion in number, as panicking and drowning in the Sea of Galilee. Before, they had entered ca. 2,000 swine, which the Egyptians were also labeled in Judaic tradition, as Pharaoh was described as their swineherd. The author's borrowing specific elements from these haggadic materials was not only part of his artistic freedom, but also due to their great popularity, for they described Israel's central redemptive act.

It should also not be forgotten that the third section of the basic confession of Judaism, the *Shema'*, recited daily by Palestinian Jews both in the morning and the evening, ended with Num 15:41, "I am the Lord your God, 'who brought you out of the land of Egypt,' to be your God; I am the Lord your God." In *m. Ber.* 1:5 it is maintained that "The going forth from Egypt is rehearsed [also] at night."[227] In 1:4 it is noted that two benedictions are said before the *Shema'* and one afterwards in the morning; in the evening there are two each.[228] The Tosefta at 2:1 states regarding this: "One who recites the *Shema'* must mention the exodus from Egypt in [the benediction following the *Shema'* which begins] 'True and firm.' ... Others say, 'In it one must mention the smiting of the firstborn [in Egypt] and [the miracle of] the splitting of the Reed Sea.'"[229]

The benediction spoken after the *Shema'*, אֱמֶת וְיַצִּיב , "True and firm," also includes the following:

> From Egypt You redeemed us, O Lord our God,
> and from the house of servitude You liberated us.
> All their firstborn You killed, but You redeemed Your firstborn (sing. – Israel).
> You split the Reed Sea, and You drowned the wicked (pl.).
> Your beloved (pl.) You led across (to the other side),

---

[227] Albeck 1.15, Danby 3.
[228] Albeck 1.15, Danby 2.
[229] Zuckermandel / Liebermann 3; I modify Neusner 1.6 somewhat. On the *Shema'* and its benedictions, cf. Schürer, *The history* 2.454-455, and Elbogen, *Der jüdische Gottesdienst* 16-26.

but the waters covered their oppressors.
Not one of them was left over.[230]

The latter two lines are a quotation of Ps 106:11. The benediction goes on to mention praises to "God Most High" (אֵל עֶלְיוֹן), a term found in Mark 5:7, and God is also addressed as "He who does miracles" (עֹשֵׂה פֶלֶא), alluding to Exod 15:11.

The drowning of the Egyptians in the Reed Sea was thus an event which devout Palestinian Jews were reminded of every day. This too probably aided the Palestinian Jewish Christian author of Mark 5:1-20 in basing his narrative in part on haggadic Samson materials, including Exod 15:4 with the drowning of Pharaoh's army in the Reed Sea. This he transformed into a large herd of swine which drowned in the Sea of Galilee.

III. The Site of the Miracle / Exorcism: Kursi

The narrative of the Gerasene demoniac opens in Mark 5:1 by stating that "they (Jesus and his disciples) came to the other side of the Sea (of Galilee), to the country of the Gerasenes." Here Jesus disembarks (v 2), exorcizes the demoniac, and then boards the same boat again (v 18). It is assumed he returns with the disciples, mentioned nowhere else in the entire narrative, to that site on the Sea from which they embarked.

The present Markan context indicates that the incident takes place on the eastern shore of the Sea of Galilee, for 4:35 has Jesus tell his disciples: "Let us go across to the other side." This is assumed to be spoken in Capernaum, his new "home" (2:1; 3:19b, 31-35) after having left Nazareth (1:21; cf. 6:1). Thus after the stilling of the storm in 4:35-41, Jesus and his disciples are presented as landing on the (east) shore of the Sea, from which they again cross back to the other side in 5:21. There Jesus then

---

[230] Cf. the Hebrew in W. Stark, *Altjüdische liturgische Gebete* (Bonn: Marcus und Weber, 1910) 7. I owe this reference to O. Betz, "The Concept of the So-called 'Divine Man' in Mark's Christology" 239. On a variant text, see Str-B 4.194, where it is the first benediction following the evening *Shema'*.

heals the little daughter of the synagogue leader Jairus (in Capernaum).

This whole framework is patently artificial, for according to 4:35 it had already turned evening before the ferocious storm took place. This would logically mean Jesus' healing of the Gerasene demoniac took place in the dark. That is impossible, however, for the demoniac can "see" Jesus, even from a distance, in 5:6; people come to "see" what had happened in v 14; and in v 15 they "see" the demoniac sitting there, clothed and in his right mind. This means the collector before the Evangelist Mark, without reflecting too long, simply appended 5:1-20 to 4:35-41. Perhaps he knew that the most severe storms on the Lake took place on the east and northeast side.[231]

In addition, "crossing to the other side" (from Capernaum) never means towards Tiberias in the west,[232] for Jesus purposefully avoided the new capital of Herod Antipas, who could easily arrest him there (cf. Luke 13:31-32). Instead, "the other side" meant eastward, in the direction of Bethsaida, which was on the north/northeastern side of the Sea (Mark 6:45).[233]

Mark 5:1 states that Jesus (and the disciples) came to the other side of the Sea, "to the country of the Gerasenes" (εἰς τὴν χώραν τῶν Γερασηνῶν). The latter is the best attested reading of the MSS. It is also the most difficult, which on text-critical

---

[231] Cf. M. Nun, *The Sea of Galilee and its Fishermen in the New Testament* (Kibbutz Ein Gev: Tourist Department and Kinnereth Sailing Co., 1989) 54, who speaks of the "well-known eastern storm, called 'Sharkia' in Arabic ('shark' ... means east in Arabic). Even today this storm, which usually starts in the early evening, is good cause for apprehension among fishermen." M. Nun himself was for decades a fisherman on the Sea of Galilee. Such a storm from the east is pictured in his *Gergesa (Kursi)* 13.

[232] The one exception seems to be Mark 6:53, where after a storm forced the boat with Jesus and the disciples to the east, they cross over and land at Gennesaret. This settlement, however, was not located at the modern site of Ginnosar, but only slightly west of Tabgha, i.e., some 3.5 km west of Capernaum. Cf. the map "Christian Sites Around the Sea of Galilee," New Israel Grid 251.753.

[233] Cf. the map "Christian Sites Around the Sea of Galilee," with New Israel Grid 259.757, for Bethsaida.

principles alone makes it preferable. The only other clue as to the identity of the "Gerasenes" is that the healed demoniac at the end of the narrative goes off to proclaim in the (nearby) "Decapolis" what Jesus had done for him (v 20).

While Luke omits the reference to the Decapolis at 8:20, he retains "the country of the Gerasenes" in 8:26. Since it is probable that the Evangelist Matthew composed his Gospel in a bilingual community in nearby Syria, perhaps in Antioch,[234] he knew that Mark's "Gerasenes" could not apply to the Decapolis city Gerasa (modern Jerash in Jordan). It was some 60 km or 36 miles south-southeast of the Sea of Galilee and not near a body of water.[235] Also omitting Mark's reference to the Decapolis, Matthew considered "Gerasenes" an error in his copy of Mark for "Gadarenes" (8:28). This was logical on his part, for Gadara was also a city of the Decapolis, lying only 9 km or 5 miles southeast of the Lake. It is the modern Um Qeis in Jordan, with its famous hot springs located on the Yarmuk River some 3 km below and north of it.[236] Most importantly, it had a very large harbor with a breakwater some 250 m long, located at Tel Samra, probably a daughter settlement of Gadara on the east side of the very bottom of the Sea of Galilee.[237] Thus Matthew probably himself intentionally changed "Gerasenes" into "Gadarenes."

---

[234] Cf. U. Luz, *Das Evangelium nach Matthäus (Mt 1-7)* (EKK 1/1; Zurich, Benziger; Neukirchen / Vluyn: Neukirchener, 1992³) 75: "certainly a larger Syrian city," and R. Gundry, *Matthew. A Commentary on His Handbook for a Mixed Church under Persecution* (Grand Rapids, Michigan: Eerdmans, 1994²) 608 for Syria.
[235] Cf. the art. "Gerasa" by K. Clark in *IDB* 2.382-384, and Schürer, *The history* 2.149-155. J. Ådna in "The Encounter of Jesus with the Gerasene Demoniac" in *Authenticating the Activities of Jesus*, ed. B. Chilton and C. A. Evans (Brill: Leiden, 1999) 279-301, argues for Gerasa as the site of the exorcism, to which the incident of the pigs was later added.
[236] Cf. Schürer, *The history* 2.132-136, and M. Nun, *The Land of the Gadarenes. New Light on an Old Sea of Galilee Puzzle* (Kibbutz Ein Gev: Sea of Galilee Fishing Museum, 1996).
[237] For a description of this harbor and Gadara's commercial use of it, cf. M. Nun, *Sea of Galilee. Newly Discovered Harbours From New Testament Days* 20-23. Its location on the Lake is shown in his *Gergesa (Kursi)* 4, and in J. Rousseau and R. Arav, *Jesus & His World* 23.

Yet it is very improbable that Jesus is pictured in Mark 5:1 as crossing over the Sea of Galilee to its other extremity at the southern end, a distance of at least 18 km or 12 miles. Nowhere else in the Gospels is Jesus portrayed as making such a long boat trip, especially to the south. His realm of activity was rather the northern half of the Lake, centering on Capernaum. As almost all the commentators agree, the area of Kursi on the eastern side of the Lake is thus more probable as the area of the "Gerasenes."

1. The Location

The site Kursi lies somewhat below the point where Naḥal (Wadi) Samakh, coming down from the Golan Heights, flows into the Sea of Galilee.[238] It is 9 km or 5 miles across the Lake from Capernaum, and ca. 5 km or 3 miles north of the modern Kibbutz Ein Gev. As remarked above, the Decapolis city

---

[238] Cf. the map "Christian Sites Around the Sea of Galilee," New Israel Grid   260-261. 748-749.   See also the *Tübinger Bible Atlas*, ed. S. Mittmann and G. Schmitt (Stuttgart: Deutsche Bibelgesellschaft, 2001) B VI 10, northern part: 2111.2480. Y. Ben-Yosef in a letter of February 6, 2001 informs me that some 650 m lie between the Kursi harbor and the outlet of Naḥal Samakh into the Sea of Galilee to the north. On Kursi, see also G. Dalman, *Palästinajahrbuch* 7 (1911) 20-23; *ibid.*, *Orte und Wege Jesu* (Gütersloh: Bertelsmann, 1924³) 190-191; F.-M. Abel, "Koursi" in *JPOS* 7 (1927) 112-121; C. Kopp, *Die heiligen Stätten der Evangelien* (Regensburg: Pustet, 1959) 282-287; D. Urman, "The Site of the Miracle of the Man with the Unclean Spirit," in *Christian News from Israel* 22 (1971) 72-76, with a sketch of the area on p. 73; M. Avi-Yonah, *Encyclopedia of Archaeological Excavations in the Holy Land* (London: Oxford University Press, 1976) 2.459-460; G. Reeg, *Die Ortsnamen Israels nach der rabbinischen Literatur* (Beihefte zum Tübinger Atlas des Vorderen Orients, Reihe B 51; Wiesbaden: Reichert, 1989) 329-330; M. Nun, *Gergesa (Kursi)*; V. Tzafaris, art. "Kursi" in *The New Encyclopedia of Archaeological Excavations in the Holy Land*, ed. E. Stern etc. (Jerusalem: The Israel Exploration Society and Carta; New York: Simon & Shuster, 1993) 3.893-896, with illustrations; *ibid.*, art. "Kursi" in *The Oxford Encyclopedia of Archaeology in the Near East*, ed. E. Meyers (New York and Oxford: Oxford University Press, 1997) 3.314-315; and B. Pixner, *Wege des Messias und Stätten der Urkirche* (Giessen / Basel: Brunnen, 1996³) 142-148.

Hippos / Susitha was located only a good 2 km directly east of Ein Gev.

From the very outset Kursi was a fishing settlement since nutrients from Naḥal Samakh produce the best sardine fishing in the Lake at this point. The sardines deposit their eggs in the Lake before this confluence.[239] Remnants of the ancient settlement of Kursi can be found on the shore of the Lake for about half a kilometer. In 1975 M. Nun discovered segments of the Roman road which led to Kursi from the main road further east.[240] The settlement had a harbor, with its opening at the northern end. Its ruins north of Tel Kursi, including the breakwater ca. 150 m long, can still be observed when the water level is low.[241] A Byzantine church from the middle of the sixth century CE, as well as a small chapel with a cave, probably venerated as the dwelling of the Gerasene demoniac, are found in the immediate area.[242]

2. *The Name Kursi*

When one looks east into the Samakh Valley, i.e. toward the Golan Heights, the mouth of the canyon, says M. Nun, is "wide, rectangular, steep, and closed at the back, to the east. It looks like a giant armchair [viewed from the front], which is probably

---

[239] Cf. M. Nun, *Gerasa (Kursi)* 3 and 6, and the picture of a sardine catch on p. 8. "Samakh" in Arabic means "fish."
[240] *Ibid.*, 11.
[241] Cf. M. Nun, *Sea of Galilee. Newly Discovered Harbours From New Testament Days*, 8-11. It is depicted in pictures on p. 9 and in a drawing by Y. Ben-Yosef on p. 10, the latter also reproduced in *Gergesa (Kursi)* 9. M. Nun discovered it in 1970 (*Sea of Galilee* 8), as the first of sixteen ancient harbors now known on the Lake.
[242] Tel Kursi itself has not yet been excavated. On the Byzantine church first discovered by M. Nun in 1969, see his *Gergesa (Kursi)* 16-29, and on the cave in the chapel, p. 27. Eusebius of Caesarea, who died ca. 340 CE (LCL I xiii), noted in his *Onomasticon* in regard to Mark 5:1, "And now a village on the mountain / hill is shown next to Lake Tiberias, into which the swine rushed down." See *Das Onomastikon der biblischen Namen*, ed. E. Klostermann 74-75. In a letter of January 7, 2002, Y. Ben-Yosef informs me that C. Page and V. Tzafiris discovered a small but well preserved Roman bath at Kursi in September 2001.

the origin of its name – Kursi (Kursa), meaning 'armchair' in Semitic languages."[243]

The Aramaic כָּרְסָא means "chair."[244] The masc. pl. form used as the singular is כּוּרְסְיָא , כּוּרְסְיָה , כּוּרְסְיָא . The construct form is כּוּרְסֵי , כָּרְסָא , and כורסי is also found alone, i.e. in the non-construct state. The latter most closely resembles the modern name, כּוּרְסִי . The basic meaning of the noun is "divan, upholstered chair, throne,"[245] or as above, "armchair." The Arab writer Yaqout noted in 1229 CE regarding the name of the site Kursi that "it means the seat on which kings sit." It is a village "where the Messiah, they say, reunited the apostles and from where he sent them out to the countries. There is a place there made for sitting on which they say the Messiah sat down."[246]

The latter reflects local Christian tradition ("they say"), which developed regarding Mark 5:15. There it is related that the people from the town (Kursi) and the surrounding hamlets came to Jesus and saw the demoniac "sitting" there, clothed and in his right mind. It was assumed that if the former demoniac was "sitting," Jesus himself would certainly have done the same – on a "chair," the same word behind the name of the site, "Kursi." The Messiah's sending the apostles out to "countries / districts" from here could in part be based on 5:19-20, where Jesus tells the exorcized demoniac to go home to his relatives and friends and to tell them how much the Lord (God) had done for him, the mercy He had shown him. Therefore the man went off to proclaim this in the Decapolis.

The above Arab report, certainly based on local Christian tradition, shows that the name of the site Kursi was still associated with the term "chair, seat" in the thirteenth century CE.

---

[243] Cf. his *Gergesa (Kursi)* 4. Y. Ben-Yosef further elucidated this to me in his letter of February 6, 2001.
[244] Cf. Jastrow 672 and BDB 1097, with Dan 5:20 and 7:9.
[245] Jastrow 626, with the latter reference from *Yalquṭ* Esther 1055.
[246] From his Mou'djam al Buldân, quoted by F.-M. Abel in his art. "Koursi" in *JPOS* 7 (1927) 115.

My Name is "Legion" 75

Cyril of Scythopolis (Beth Shean), who probably died in 558 CE, became a follower of Sabas when the latter visited there in 531-532. In his "Life of Sabas" 24 Cyril relates that this Palestinian monk and his disciple Agapêtus were "journeying a good distance between the Sea of Tiberias and the Jordan and praying at Chorsia [εἰς τὸν Χορσίαν], Heptapêgus [Tabgha] and other revered places...."[247] This sixth-century CE travel narrative mentions Kursi as Χορσι or more probably Χορσια, whereby the *chi* was pronounced hard like a "k" (as כְּנַעַן became Χαναάν in the LXX). It also reflects an alternate spelling with a qameṣ, כָּרְסֵי or כָּרְסְיָא , instead of the form with a waw, כּוּרְסֵי or כּוּרְסְיָא . This is important for the discussion below of the term Γερασηνοί in Mark 5:1.

It has been maintained that the site Kursi is mentioned in *b. 'Avoda Zarah* 11 b, which enumerates as one of five appointed temples of idol worship: "the temple of Nebo 'in Kursi'" (בכורסי).[248] Yet Kursi on the east shore of the Sea of Galilee was a village or small town and had no temple. The MS variant "Borsippa" in Babylonia makes much more sense here, for Nebo was closely associated with it.[249] Nor does the Tanna R. Jacob b. "Korshai" have anything to do with Kursi. The latter noun rather appears to be his father's name, קוֹרְשִׁי .[250]

The only mention of Kursi in rabbinic writings is found in *y. Mo'ed Qaṭan* 3:5, 82 c. It states regarding Gamaliel of

---

[247] Cf. R. Price, together with J. Binns, *Cyril of Scythopolis: Lives of the Monks of Palestine*, xxxviii and xl on the dates, and 117 on the text. The Greek is found in E. Schwartz, *Kyrillos von Skythopolis* 108.
[248] Soncino 59.
[249] Cf. the art. "Nebo," 1., by J. Gray in *IDB* 3.528.
[250] Cf. *b. Hor.* 13b (Soncino 103), where he is active at the time of the academy president R. Simeon b. Gamaliel, and *y. Šabb.* 12:5, 12 c (Neusner 11.329) and *Pesaḥ.* 10:1, 37 b (Neusner / Bokser 13.475), where he is named as (a) teacher of R. Judah the Prince. The MSS in part have ד for ר, a frequent scribal mistake, and a second yod. This is against M. Avi-Yonah, *Encyclopedia of Archaeological Excavations in the Holy Land* 2.459.

Quntiah[251] that גבון כורסאיי קברוניה, "The Kursites / people of Kursi buried him in their area / country."[252] After three days they thought about the matter again, (wanting to bury him in his hometown), yet the original grave in Kursi had already been sealed. R. Joshua b. Levi, a first generation Palestinian Amora,[253] then gave a ruling on the question of from when the rites of mourning are to be counted.

It is interesting that the only occurrence of כּוּרְסָאיֵי, "the Kursites" or "people of Kursi," is found precisely in connection with burying someone in their own vicinity. The cemetery area will have been the same as that envisioned for the Gerasene demoniac, one of the rock caves or graves hewn out of the abundant rock in the area.

I suggest that varying pronunciations of two specific consonants in Hebrew and Aramaic explain how the original Semitic "area of the כורסאיי" became the "area of the גרסאיי," i.e. "the people of Gerasa," behind the Greek τῶν Γερασηνῶν in Mark 5:1.

The Judeans in the south of Palestine made fun of the Galileans in the north because of their inexact pronunciation, exchanging certain consonants for others.[254] One aspect of pronunciation common to most Jews of the time, however, furthers the discussion here. Already in 1911 G. Dalman had noted that the local Bedouin pronounced in Arabic the name of

---

[251] He may have been Gamaliel III, the son of Rabbi, and a fifth generation Tanna (Strack and Stemberger, *Introduction* 90). His brother was Simeon, which might explain why the people of Kursi went to R. Simeon to ask about the legal propriety of reburying him elsewhere. The reading "Quntiah," however, is difficult (Jastrow 1336 on קוּנְתְיָה; קְנָת ? See p. 1395). See also *y. Ned.* 10:8, 42b (Neusner 23.192).
[252] Cf. Neusner's translation in 20.196: "Gamaliel of Quntiah was buried by the people of Kursai in their place." See Jastrow 203, 2) for גב as a preposition with this meaning (cf. the German "bei sich"). Jastrow (626) is wrong in associating the כורסאיי with the people of Karsa or Karsana.
[253] Strack and Stemberger, *Introduction* 92-93.
[254] Cf. the examples cited in *b. 'Erub.* 53 a-b (Soncino 370-372).

the tower at "Kursi" as "Gourzeh,"[255] turning the כ into a ג, and the ס into a ז. The latter was true in rabbinic Hebrew and Aramaic also,[256] but the former is most important at this point.

The letter כ frequently interchanges with the letter ג.[257] Several examples from M. Jastrow's *Dictionary* are the following. כּוֹחִילְנָא, the name of a bird, is גְּחִילְנָא in the Aruch.[258] כַּרְזִימִין, "nibblings, dessert," is also spelled גַּרְזִימִין.[259] The Hellenized form of Lake Chinnereth, the Sea of Galilee (כִּנֶּרֶת), is גִּינֵּיסָר.[260] "Cleopatra" becomes גַּלְפַטְרָה,[261] as *castra* becomes גַסְטְרָא.[262]

The example most relevant to "Kursi," however, is that of another settlement in the MT and in rabbinic writings. Josh 19:29 mentions the town אַכְזִיבָה, which Judg 1:31 labels אַכְזִיב: "Achzib." It is the modern ez-Zib, some 15 km or 9 miles north or Acco / Acre.[263] In rabbinic writings it is the most northern town inside the borders of Palestine, which was very important in regard to matters of impurity and tithing. It is mentioned four times in the Mishnah: *Dem.* 1:3; *Šebi.* 6:1 (twice); and *Ḥall.* 4:8. In all occurrences the standard spelling is כְּזִיב, with a kaph.[264] Yet in the Jerusalem Talmud, i.e. of the Land of

---

[255] Cf. the *Palästinajahrbuch* 7 (1911) 22. He repeats this in his *Orte und Wege Jesu* 190-191 as "gurze." F.-M. Abel refers to the first in his art. "Koursi," 119.

[256] Cf. Jastrow 947 for ס interchanging not only with שׁ, but also ז.

[257] Cf. Jastrow 605, who also notes ק. He states the reverse regarding ג on p. 201. See also G. Dalman, *Grammatik des jüdisch-palästinischen Aramäisch* (Leipzig: Hinrichs, 1905²) 99. N. Oswald of Berlin kindly called my attention to the latter.

[258] Jastrow 618 and 233.

[259] Jastrow 666 and 267, with the passage from *Esther Rabbah*.

[260] Jastrow 240.

[261] Jastrow 250.

[262] Jastrow 260. Cf. *b. Ber.* 32 b, where for each "legion" thirty "camps" are created. The reverse is found in the Hebrew גָפְרִית, "sulphur." In Aramaic it is כִּבְרִיתָא (Jastrow 609).

[263] Cf. the art. "Achzib" by I. Ben-Dor in *IDB* 1.27-28.

[264] Cf. Albeck 1.74, 154 and 286, respectively. See also the English in Danby 21, 46 and 87.

Israel, once two spellings are given directly after another, as in *y. Dem.* 1:3, 22a (three times כֹזיב , two times גֹזיב).²⁶⁵ Otherwise גֹזיב is employed, as in *y. Dem.* 1:1, 21c;²⁶⁶ *Šebi.* 6:1, 36b and d;²⁶⁷ and *Ḥall.* 4:8(4), 60a.²⁶⁸

The place-name כְּזִיב , northwest of the Sea of Galilee on the Mediterranean coast, was thus usually pronounced and even written גְּזִיב in Palestine, the kaph becoming a gimmel. I therefore suggest that this also took place with the place-name "Kursi." Not only local Arabic-speaking Bedouin at the turn of the twentieth century were accustomed to pronouncing Kursi as Gourzeh, with a hard "g." Local Palestinian Jews and Jewish Christians in a much earlier time did the same, pronouncing כּוּרְסִי as גּוּרְסִי . The waw could also have dropped out when written under the kaph, as כְּ . Or the place-name was vocalized with a qameṣ in the form known for "chair," כָּרְסָא .

The Semitic *oral* original of Mark 5:1, τὴν χώραν τῶν Γερασηνῶν , thus may have been in Aramaic: בְּעַרְעָא דְּגָרְסָאֵי , "in the land / area of the people of Gorsi (the Gorsians)." Since Kursi / Korsi was pronounced locally with a ג instead of a כ , the original listeners knew exactly which site was meant, that fishing settlement just south of Nahal Samakh on the east shore of the Sea of Galilee.

The major problem arose when a Greek-speaking Jewish Christian who knew Aramaic translated this account into his mother tongue. He was not aware of the local usage with ג instead of כ and logically changed גרסאיי (גְּרְ or גֵּרְ) into "the people of Gerasa," οἱ Γερασηνοί , the inhabitants of Γέρασα.²⁶⁹ The fact that the city belonged to the Decapolis,

---

²⁶⁵ Cf. Neusner / Sarason 3.49.
²⁶⁶ Neusner / Sarason 3.25.
²⁶⁷ Neusner / Avery-Peck 5.195 and 214. A citation of *t. Ohol.* 18:4 has אכזיב twice in 6:1, 36b (Neusner / Avery-Peck 5.201-202), yet Zuckermandel / Liebermann cite the Tosefta as כֹזיב (p. 617).
²⁶⁸ Neusner 9.129.
²⁶⁹ Cf. *Bell.* 2.480, where Josephus relates that the Γερασηνοί did not harm the Jews who remained with them in 66 CE at the time of the Jewish uprising against Rome.

mentioned in the narrative in 5:20, aided him in doing so, even though he probably knew that Gerasa was far away and an inland city not bordering on water. He remained slavishly true to what he had heard, even though he probably sensed that it now sounded strange.

If the above proposal is basically correct, it means Origen's suggestion that οἱ Γεργεσαῖοι should be read in Mark 5:1 is wrong. This great biblical scholar, who died in 251 or 254 CE in Palestine,[270] wrote in his commentary on John 1:28 that Gerasa and Gadara were improper solutions to the problem. Rather, one should think of Γέργεσα and οἱ Γεργεσαῖοι because of the ancient city once near Lake Tiberias with the name "Gergesa." He maintains this means παροικία ἐκβεβληκότων, i.e. it prophetically alluded to the "dwelling place of those [spirits in the swine] driven out" by Jesus, whom the citizens then asked to leave.[271] Origen probably was thinking here of the Hebrew root גָּרַשׁ, meaning to send off or banish.[272]

By the "Gergesines" Origen meant הַגִּרְגָּשִׁי, the Girgashites, as in Josh 3:10, one of the local peoples God will drive out before the Israelites enter Canaan.[273] The LXX translates here and elsewhere with Γεργεσαῖος, enabling Origen to propose Γεργεσαῖοι for Mark 5:1 par. Yet in Judaic tradition the Girgashites took up Joshua's offer of a peaceful exit, and God gave them another land as beautiful as their own: Africa.[274]

---

[270] W. Walker, *A History of the Christian Church* (New York: Charles Scribner's Sons, 1959) 74.
[271] Cf. the text in E. Preuschen, *Origines Werke* 4.150, lines 3-20. It is Book VI.41. See also Book X.12(10) on John 2:12 (p. 182).
[272] Jastrow 273.
[273] Cf. BDB 173 for the other occurrences.
[274] Cf. *Deut. Rab.* Shofeṭim 5/14 on Deut 20:10 (Mirqin 11.94, Soncino 7.116). Parallels are found in *Lev. Rab.* Metzora 17/6 on Lev 14:34 (Mirqin 7.197, Soncino 4.221), and *y. Šebi.* 6:1, 36c (Neusner / Avery-Peck 5.208). The reference before the latter passage to Susitha (Hippos) is in a different context and should not be related to the Girgeshites. Against Dalman, *Orte und Wege Jesu* 190. See also Josephus, *Ant.* 1.139 on the "Girgashites" of Gen 10:16. He states regarding them and others: "we have no record in the sacred Scriptures beyond their names; for the Hebrews destroyed their cities...." If Josephus, who knew the area of

Origen's great influence in biblical scholarship[275] also affected the MS traditions in Mark 5:1 par. Due to his fanciful interpretation, for which there is absolutely no other basis, the alternative reading Γεργεσηνῶν unfortunately crept into many texts.

3. The Size

Kursi cannot have been very large in the first century CE. If it had been a purely Jewish settlement, larger and worth fortifying, Josephus would certainly have mentioned it when he discussed the major Jewish sites in the area he helped to fortify for the upcoming Jewish-Roman war.[276] The Jewish historian even calls nearby Capernaum in the north, to which he was carried after falling from his horse and breaking his wrist, a "village" (κώμη - *Vita* 403), and no mention is made of its special fortifications. J. Reed estimates that at the time of Jesus Capernaum had only some 600 – 1,500 inhabitants.[277] If it was called a כְּפָר / כַּפְרָנָא, a village or country town,[278] Kursi would have been only a small village with considerably fewer inhabitants. One probable indication of this is the fact that it is only mentioned once in all of rabbinic literature, in the passage quoted above.

4. A Mixed Population

It is very probable that Kursi had a mixed population of both Gentiles and Jews in the first half of the first century CE. This is

---

the Sea of Galilee very well, had known of a "Gergesa," he would not have written as he did here.

[275] Cf. T. Baarda, "Gadarenes, Gerasenes, Gergesenes and the 'Diatessaron' Tradition" in *Neotestamentica et Semitica*, Festschrift for Matthew Black, ed. E. Ellis and M. Wilcox (Edinburgh: Clark, 1969) 181-197, esp. 185-188.

[276] Cf. *Vita* 187-188, including Tarichaeae (Magdala) and Tiberias, as well as *Bell.* 2.573, and 568 for Gamala in the Golan. Since Kursi probably had a mixed Jewish-Gentile population (see below), Josephus would have met resistance there anyway.

[277] Cf. his *Archaeology and the Galilean Jesus* (Harrisburg, PA: Trinity Press International, 2000) 152. He considers Nazareth to have had fewer than 400 inhabitants (p. 131).

[278] Jastrow 662.

because it lay in the domain of the Decapolis city Hippos / Susitha, the Naḥal Samakh just above Kursi probably forming the natural northern border of the district.[279] In *Bell.* 3.37 Josephus speaks of the "territory of Hippos" (Ἱππηνῇ) as an eastern border of Galilee, and in *Vita* 42 of its villages (to the SW). In *Vita* 153 he also describes how he once embarked in a boat with others (from Tarichaeae / Magdala on the western side of the Sea of Galilee) and "crossed over 'to the frontiers of the district of Hippos' (ἐπὶ τὴν μεθόριον τῶν Ἱππηνῶν)" – a journey similar to that of Jesus in Mark 5:1.

Alexander Jannaeus conquered Hippos in the Maccabean period, but the Roman general Pompey later returned it to Gentile rule. Caesar Augustus bequeathed it to Herod the Great, placing it again under Jewish dominance. Yet at Herod's death in 4 BCE the city was joined to Syria.[280] Hippos also had a mixed yet primarily Greek population, for when more than 20,000 Jews were slaughtered by Syrians in Caesarea in 66 CE, parties of Jews in retaliation destroyed or burned everything before them when they attacked Hippos (Josephus, *Bell.* 2.459 – 460). After the slaughter of 13,000 Jews in the Decapolis city Scythopolis / Beth Shean, some 27 km or 16 m south of the Sea of Galilee, the people of Hippos killed the rebellious Jews in

---

[279] Hippos / Susitha got its fresh water via an aquaduct from the upper part of this stream, some 24 km away. The whole southern side of the Valley, extending west to Kursi, was thus probably a part of its domain (letter from Y. Ben-Yosef and M. Nun of Feb. 6, 2001). See also M. Avi-Yonah, art. "Historical Geography of Palestine" in *The Jewish People in the First Century*, ed. S. Safrai and M. Stern (Amsterdam: Van Gorcum, 1974) 1.103: "Its [Hippos'] territory included Gergesa (Kursi) on the lake, which is regarded by many authorities as the site of the miracle of the 'Gadarene' swine."

[280] Cf. the sources given in Schürer, *The history* 2.130-132. It should be noted that in *Bell.* 2.97 Josephus describes Gaza, Gadara and Hippos as "Greek" cities which were detached by Caesar Augustus from Archelaus' principality and annexed to Syria after Herod the Great died in 4 BCE. Schürer in *The history* 1.337 is certainly wrong in maintaining that the tetrarch Philip's territory, including Gaulanitis, extended on the eastern shore of the Sea of Galilee down to its southern tip. That section belonged to the "Hippenene" and to Gadara.

their midst, while imprisoning those who were less daring (2.477-478). Hippos / Susitha thus itself had a mixed population up until the outbreak of the Jewish-Roman War.

Susitha (Hippos) and the villages surrounding it are listed in *t. Ohol.* 18:4 as an example of "cities surrounded by the Land of Israel."[281] Kursi is lacking in the list of towns near Susitha mentioned in *t. Šebi.* 4:10 which are subject to Jewish tithing. Yet "Aynosh," a very small Jewish settlement on the south side of Naḥal Samakh 2 km east of Kursi, is found in this list.[282] This shows Kursi cannot have been a completely Jewish site. Like the nearby Decapolis city of Hippos / Susitha itself, it most probably had a mixed population.

The "Geresene" demoniac there could have been a Jew or a Gentile. Since he goes off to proclaim in (nearby Hippos of) the Decapolis how much Jesus had done for him (Mark 5:20), however, it is *probable* that he is depicted as being a non-Jew. In the Gospel of Mark, this would mean that even before Jesus exorcized the unclean spirit / demon from the little daughter of a Gentile, Syrophoenician woman in 7:24-30, he had exorcized unclean spirits / demons from another Gentile.[283] The event took place in the region of Kursi, not a major distance from Jesus' new hometown, Capernaum.

---

[281] Zuckermandel / Liebermann 616, Neusner 6.130.

[282] Cf. Lieberman, *The Tosefta* 1.181 with וְעֵינִישָׁה; Neusner 1.221. See also *y. Dem.* 2:1, 22d (Neusner / Sarason 3.72-73, and 333, n. 128 on "Ayanosh" – the spelling varies). For the distance I am indebted to Y. Ben-Yosef and M. Nun in a letter of Feb. 6, 2001, who call the settlement "Avanish." On the above, see also M. Nun, *Gergesa (Kursi)* 4.

[283] The healing of a deaf and dumb man "in the region of the Decapolis" in 7:31 may also refer to the area around Hippos. The route described in the verse, however, is difficult.

IV. The Extent of the Original Narrative, and Markan Editing

Verse one of the narrative in Mark 5:1-20 may originally have been something like the following: "Once Jesus and his disciples crossed the Sea (of Galilee) to the district of the Kursites / people of Kursi." There is no reason to presume he walked there alone all the way from Capernaum. It is assumed Jesus let himself be rowed there by his disciples, in part experienced fishermen on the Lake, or they all sailed there, as in other similar instances (3:9; 4:35; 5:21; 6:32; 6:53; 8:14). When the narrative of the Gerasene demoniac was combined in a pre-Markan stage with the other miracle accounts in 4:35 - 5:43,[1] the opening verse was shortened to "And they came to the other side of the Sea, to the district of the Gerasenes." While the boat is mentioned in vv 2 and 18, the disciples are only passively present. The entire focus of the narrative is on Jesus and his power / authority.

If this is true, it means there was not an original story which took place at far-off Gerasa and was later transferred to the Sea of Galilee.[2] Nor was the account of a Jewish exorcist later transferred to Jesus.[3] R. Bultmann even called the anecdote "a popular jest applied to Jesus."[4] Jesus, however, was involved centrally in the narrative from the outset.

Others have viewed the incident of the swine as a secondary addition.[5] Yet I have shown above that in Judaic thought the Egyptians were characterized as swine, and it was they who all drowned after rushing down from cliffs into the Reed Sea (Exod 15:4). This was the model for the original Palestinian Jewish Christian narrator. In addition, the drowning of ca. 2,000 swine in the Sea of Galilee accents not only the terrible number of unclean spirits in the Gerasene demoniac. It also explains why

---

[1] Cf. R. Bultmann, *The History of the Synoptic Tradition* 210, and Pesch, *Der Besessene* 15.
[2] Against Pesch, *Der Besessene* 44. Cf. Gnilka, *Das Evangelium nach Markus (Mk 1 - 8,26)* 201.
[3] Cf. M. Dibelius, *From Tradition to Gospel* 101.
[4] Cf. his *The History* 210.
[5] Cf. for example E. Haenchen, *Der Weg Jesu* 197.

the local people ask Jesus to leave their district: they are afraid (Mark 5:15) he might remain and continue to do similar deeds in their midst.

The healed Gerasene demoniac went off to proclaim in the Decapolis the things Jesus had done for him (5:20). As shown above, this motif also derives from Judaic tradition on Pharaoh as the only Egyptian who survived the drowning of the Egyptians in the Reed Sea. He was thought to have then gone off to the great city of Nineveh, becoming an example of repentance to the inhabitants, thus proclaiming God's name through all the earth / land (Exod 9:16). The final verse in the Gospel narrative (5:20) is thus not due to Mark, as so often proposed.[6] This also argues against the view that 5:18-20 are a later, secondary conclusion.[7]

Finally, a number of scholars consider v 8 to be Markan.[8] Yet it is a parenthesis typical of Jewish oral narratives, especially the "tales" (see below on the genre of this narrative), and of biblical accounts such as those of Samson (cf. Judg 13:16; 14:4; and 16:13), upon which the entire narrative is ultimately based.

I thus observe almost no editorial activity on the part of the Evangelist Mark in 5:1-20. He left it remarkably unchanged when he appropriated it in Greek from the unit 4:35 – 5:43 already available to him. This agrees with my similar conclusion in regard to the stilling of the storm in 4:35-41, just before the narrative of the Gerasene demoniac, and in regard to 6:45-52 with Jesus' walking on the Sea of Galilee.[9]

---

[6] Cf. for example Gnilka, *Das Evangelium nach Markus (Mk 1 - 8,26)* 202, and R. Guelich, *Mark 1 - 8:26*, 274.

[7] Cf. Pesch, *Der Besessene* 41 and M. Dibelius, *From Tradition to Gospel* 87; J. Marcus in *Mark 1-8*, 347, also considers some of vv 17-20, or all of it, to be from Mark. O. Bauernfeind in *Die Worte der Dämonen im Markusevangelium* (Stuttgart: Kohlhammer, 1927) 35 would even extend this to vv 16-20.

[8] Cf. R. Bultmann, *The History* 210; Gnilka, *Das Evangelium nach Markus (Mk 1 - 8,26)* 202; V. Taylor, *The Gospel According to St Mark* 281; and J. Marcus, *Mark 1 - 8*, 347.

[9] Cf. my *The Stilling of the Storm* 71. For a similar conclusion in regard to Mark 6:45-52, see my *"Caught in the Act," Walking on the Sea, and the*

V. Provenance, Language and Date of the Original Narrative

1. Provenance

As I have shown above, the account of the Gerasene demoniac is heavily dependent on Palestinian Judaic haggadic development of the Samson story, which includes the term "legion" and the drowning of the large Egyptian host when they rush down from cliffs into the Reed Sea. All of these haggadic materials are in Hebrew, with the exception of several Talmudic passages and references from the Targums, which are in Aramaic. Only Philo of Alexandria describes the Exodus event in Greek,[10] but he too was dependent here in part on earlier Judaic traditions, as indicated by the phrase "as they say" (φασι). There was a synagogue of the Alexandrians in Jerusalem, where Palestinian and Alexandrian haggadic traditions were certainly also exchanged.[11] The linguistic background of the sources thus also speaks strongly for Palestine as the home of the narrator.

The area around Capernaum on the north shore of the Sea of Galilee may even have been the author's home. It was the center of Jesus' active ministry, and after the Resurrection appearances it was also the center of those disciples who had returned from Jerusalem to their homes on or near the Lake (cf. Mark 14:28 and 16:7; John 21). One modern author even thinks this area was also the home of "Q" and the Q community.[12]

Release of Barabbas Revisited (Atlanta, Georgia: Scholars Press, 1998) 116-117.
[10] Josephus' writings are now in Greek, yet his mother tongue was Aramaic (cf. *Bell.* 1.3 and LCL II. ix-xi and IV. xii, xvii).
[11] Cf. Str-B 2.663-664 on this synagogue.
[12] Cf. J. Reed, *Archaeology and the Galilean Jesus* 170-196. If this is correct, which seems plausible, the mention of Jonah's being a sign to the people of Nineveh in Q 11:30 may be a cross-connection to the early haggadic account of Pharaoh's not drowning in the Reed Sea, but surviving and going off to become the king of Nineveh, where he became an example of repentance in connection with Jonah. Cf. also n. 186.

The narrator of Mark 5:1-20 knew the local terrain well, presupposing his being at home nearby.[13] The name of the "town" noted in v 14 also did not have to be mentioned. It was clear to the original hearers of the narrative, for "to the district of the Kursites / people of Kursi" in Mark 5:1 made it explicit from the very outset.

For the above reasons Palestine, more specifically Galilee,[14] and probably the area around Capernaum, can be considered the provenance of the narrative of the Gerasene demoniac.

2. Language

Mark 5:1-20 betrays the following signs of its Semitic background.

1) "The country of the Gerasenes" in v 1 is a misunderstanding by the Greek-speaking translator of the Semitic "the country of the Kursites / people of Kursi," as explained above in section III. 2.
2) The expression ἄνθρωπος ἐν πνεύματι ἀκαθάρτῳ in v 2 is not Greek. The preposition ἐν, "in," betrays the Semitic בְּ, "with."[15]
3) The Greek in v 4, " καί the chains he wrenched apart, and the shackles he broke in pieces," does not mean "and," but rather "but." It betrays the Semitic waw with this meaning.[16]
4) "Through the entire night and day" in v 5 betrays the Semitic reckoning of the new day as of sundown. "Day and night" would have been proper Greek.
5) The expression φωνῇ μεγάλῃ in v 7 reflects the Hebrew בְּקוֹל גָּדוֹל or its Aramaic equivalent.

---

[13] Cf. E. Lohmeyer, *Das Evangelium des Markus* 94: "es spricht ein Erzähler zu Hörern über eine vertraute Umgebung." See also J. Gnilka, *Das Evangelium nach Markus (Mk 1 - 8,26)* 207: "Die Vertrautheit mit der örtlichen Lage läßt Galiläa als Ursprungsort der Geschichte vermuten."
[14] But not *Hellenistic* Jewish Christian circles in Galilee. Against Pesch, *Der Besessene von Gerasa* 41 and 44.
[15] BDB 89, III. 1.; BDF § 219,4 (p. 118): "*with* an unclean spirit."
[16] BDB 252, 1. e.; Jastrow 371.

6) The phrase τί ἐμοὶ καὶ σοί in v 7 reflects the Hebrew מַה־לִּי וָלָךְ or its Aramaic equivalent. It is an expression which occurs numerous times in the MT and here probably means: "What do you want from me?"[17] Another possible translation is, "What have you against me?"[18]
7) The verb ἔλεγεν in v 8, lit. "He said," reflects the Semitic אָמַר in the sense of "to command."[19]
8) The word order of ἀγέλη χοίρων μεγάλη in v 11 is probably Semitic.[20]
9) The Semitic behind "for we are 'many' (πολλοί)" in v 9 is רַבִּים . This may be a wordplay with what immediately follows in v 10: "And he besought him 'much' (πολλά)." The latter could be רַב or הַרְבֵּה .[21]
10) If the narrative was originally in Hebrew (and later probably translated into Aramaic, from which the Greek derived), there was a wordplay between רָאָה , "to see," in vv 14 (ἰδεῖν), 15 (θεωροῦσιν) and 16 (οἱ ἰδόντες) and יָרֵא , "to fear," in v 15 (ἐφοβήθησαν).
11) Verse 17 has "they began" (ἤρξαντο) with the infinitive, as does v 20, "he began" (ἤρξατο). This reflects the Semitic הֵחֵל לְ .[22] While the expression "He began to..." also occurs in Greek, its very frequent usage in the Gospels betrays their Semitic origin. In the Gospel of Mark, for

---

[17] Cf. BDB 552, 1. (c), as well as the numerous passages cited in Str-B 2.401 on John 2:4. Above I proposed that the original narrator of Mark 5:1-20 borrowed this expression from the pre-Markan, Semitic form of 1:24, available to him, and slightly modified it.
[18] Cf. 1 Kgs 17:18, where a widow says this with the phrase "O man of God" (Elijah).
[19] BDB 56,4. Cf. also M. Black, *Die Muttersprache Jesu* (BWANT 15; Stuttgart: Kohlhammer, 1982) 301.
[20] Cf. E. Maloney, *Semitic Interference in Marcan Syntax* (SBLDS 51; Chico, CAL: Scholars Press, 1981) 57. For other observations on 5:1-20, see his pp. 69, 182, and 249-250.
[21] Cf. BDB 913, Jastrow 1438 on רַב .
[22] BDB 320, hiphil 2. of חלל ; Jastrow 469. On ἄρχομαι with the infinitive, cf. BAGD 113, 2. a. α.

example, ἤρξατο / ἤρξαντο plus the infinitive occurs twenty-six times.

Of these, six are with λέγειν (10:28, 32, 47; 13:5; 14:19, 69), and one with λαλεῖν (12:1): He / they began to say / speak. Several minor MSS in 5:9 read for λέγει : ἀπεκρίθη λέγων. This may reflect the Hebrew / Aramaic עני, to begin to speak, to answer,[23] or a fuller form עני ואמר (ודבר), "he answered and said." The expression הֵיחֵל לוֹמַר / לְדַבֵּר, "he began to speak," is also possible here.

12) Finally, the Greek verb θαυμάζω in v 20 may have been chosen by the Greek translator because of a similar-sounding Semitic original תמה.[24]

Other commentators also point to Semitic usages in 5:1-20.[25] The above twelve observations, plus the reasons cited in *1.*, make it most probable that the original narrative of the Gerasene demoniac was formulated in a Semitic language. While Hebrew should not be excluded, Aramaic, the common spoken language of the people, seems more probable. Or an originally Hebrew narrative was very soon translated into Aramaic. Bilingual Greek-speaking Jewish Christians from a different area (Syria?) and thus not acquainted with the relatively small fishing village or town of Kursi on the east shore of the Sea of Galilee, then translated it into their native tongue. At this point the puzzling Greek expression "district of the Gerasenes" arose. Later the Greek form of the narrative was included with others to form the unit Mark 4:35 - 5:43, which the Evangelist Mark appears to have appropriated much as it was.

---

[23] Jastrow 1093.
[24] Cf. Jastrow 1675 for the Hebrew and Aramaic forms. Mark 1:27 instead employs the passive of the verb θαμβέω.
[25] Cf. E. Klostermann, *Das Markusevangelium* 50; E. Lohmeyer, *Das Evangelium des Markus* 94; R. Fuller, *Die Wunder Jesu in Exegese und Verkündigung* (Düsseldorf: Patmos, 1967) 41; and M. Black, *Die Muttersprache Jesu* 107 and 128.

3. Date

Most commentators consider the Gospel of Mark to have been completed shortly before or after the end of the Jewish-Roman War (70 CE).[26] Since the Evangelist appears to have found the narrative of the Gerasene demoniac incorporated in what is now 4:35 – 5:43, already in Greek, and the original Semitic anecdote first had to circulate before it was translated into Greek, some time was needed for these processes. A date in the late forties or sometime in the fifties thus seems most probable for the original Semitic narrative.

VI. Form and Historicity

1. Form

Mark 5:1-20 is in broad terms a miracle, more explicitly one of healing by means of exorcism.[27] It exhibits most of the characteristics of an exorcism,[28] which is logical because the narrator knew of the exorcism in 1:21-28 in a pre-Markan, Semitic form and borrowed terms and structural elements from it for his own account. Thus the narrative in 5:1-20 belongs to the other exorcisms in Mark in 1:21-28; 7:24-30; and 9:14-29.

Yet formally the narrative is a "tale," what M. Dibelius in German labeled a "Novelle."[29] With its twenty verses it is the longest anecdote in the Gospel. The death of John the Baptist in

---

[26] Cf. the arguments cited in J. Marcus, *Mark 1 - 8*, 37-39.

[27] Cf. for example R. Pesch, *Der Besessene* 21; and J. Gnilka, *Das Evangelium nach Markus (Mk 1 - 8,26)* 202: "In der Form ist die Perikope als Exorcizmusgeschichte zu bestimmen"; on p. 200 he labels it a miracle story.

[28] Bultmann in *The History* 210 lists them, and he is followed and modified by most others. Unfortunately, E. Sorensen in his *Possession and Exorcism in the New Testament and Early Christianity* (WUNT, 2.157; Tübingen: Mohr/Siebeck, 2002) 129-131 does not add to the discussion of this pericope. The same is true for G. Twelftree, *Jesus the Exorcist. A Contribution to the Study of the Historical Jesus* (WUNT, 2.54; Tübingen: Mohr/Siebeck, 1993) 72-87.

[29] *From Tradition to Gospel* 71.

6:14-29 for example only has sixteen verses, the exorcism of an unclean spirit in a boy in 9:14-29 also sixteen, and the feeding of the five thousand in 6:30-44 only fifteen.[30] Tales are characterized by the great breadth displayed in 5:1-20. Their narrators "understand their art and love to exercise it," they have "a certain pleasure in the narrative itself."[31] This phenomenon has led M. Hooker to state in regard to 5:1-20, "There is ... an embarrassing amount of detail."[32] The description of the Gerasene madman in vv 3-5 is indeed very broad. The number "about two thousand" in v 13 for the swine in the herd is a detail also typical of tales. Even the statements which seem repetitious to modern readers (vv 2b and 6, 14 and 16) or to be parenthetical (v 8) should not be attributed to two originally separate anecdotes later woven into one, or to a later editor, such as the Evangelist Mark. Rather, they are characteristic of oral, popular story telling. The same is true for the antecedents of "he" in vv 9 and 19, "they" in vv 12 and 14b, and "him" in v 17. The originally oral narrative of Samson in Judges 13-16, upon which, in Judaic tradition, much of Mark 5:1-20 is based, displays exactly such characteristics.

2. Historicity

M. Dibelius considered Mark 5:1-20 to have been originally related regarding a Jewish exorcist,[33] thus it is not historical in regard to Jesus. R. Bultmann thought at least the section dealing with the swine was "a popular jest [later] applied to Jesus."[34] F. C. Grant stated flatly: "The story is legendary."[35] J. Gnilka thought that because of the symbolic content of the narrative, "a concrete historical memory" is not very probable.[36]

---

[30] For an analysis of this narrative, cf. my *Water into Wine and the Beheading of John the Baptist* (Brown Judaic Studies 150; Atlanta: Scholars Press, 1988) 39-74.
[31] Dibelius, *From Tradition to Gospel* 76 and 70.
[32] *The Gospel According to Mark* 141.
[33] *From Tradition to Gospel* 101.
[34] "The Gospel According to St. Mark" 712.
[35] Cf. his *The History* 210, in part dependent on O. Bauernfeind.
[36] *Das Evangelium nach Markus (Mk 1 - 8,26)* 207.

The opposite view is taken by V. Taylor, who maintains that 5:1-20 is Petrine in origin and close to "the record of an eyewitness."[37] R. Gundry concurs: "The many vivid details, given from the standpoint of external observation, may derive from eyewitness reporting by a disciple and from descriptions of the demoniac's earlier behavior by locals."[38]

Others such as E. Haenchen believe there may have been a true core to the narrative of the Gerasene demoniac.[39] J. Marcus also thinks "there is probably some sort of historical event at the root of this story...."[40] In his monograph F. Annen agrees, but does not attempt a more exact description of the historical core.[41]

Yet even a small historical core cannot be retained in 5:1-20. As I have pointed out above, the Palestinian Jewish Christian narrator borrowed some terminology and structural elements from 1:21-28, an exorcism by Jesus known to him in a pre-Markan, Semitic form. He combined these with Judaic haggadic traditions on Samson, including the term "legion" and the Egyptians' rushing down steep cliffs in pursuit of the Israelites, only to drown in the Reed Sea (Exod 15:4). The only survivor in Judaic tradition, Pharaoh, then did not return to his home city in Egypt, but as a "convert" who had now observed the Lord's miraculous power went off to the large city of Nineveh to become its king, an example of repentance. He was purposely left alive to proclaim the Lord's name through the whole earth / country (Exod 9:16). This is exactly what happens to the healed Gerasene demoniac, who goes off to proclaim in the Decapolis (Hippos / Susitha nearby) what (the Lord) Jesus had done for him.

Like the narrative of Jesus' stilling the storm, to which it was attached at an early period, the anecdote of the Gerasene

---

[37] *The Gospel According to St Mark* 277-278.
[38] *Mark* 255. See also W. Lane, *The Gospel According to Mark* 180.
[39] Cf. *Der Weg Jesu* 203. See also J. Weiss, *Das älteste Evangelium* (Göttingen: Vandenhoeck & Ruprecht, 1903) 190. J. Derrett in his various studies on Mark 5:1-20 also has this view.
[40] *Mark 1 - 8*, 348.
[41] *Heil für die Heiden* 91. See his whole section (79-101) on the question of historicity.

demoniac is not historical.[42] It was composed with specific purposes in mind. To these I now turn.

VII. The Purposes of the Narrative

The narrative now found in Mark 5:1-20 was not originally related with only one purpose in mind. Several intentions were present from the outset.

1. *Jesus Is Lord of the Unclean Spirits / Demons*

The unclean spirits, so many they are called "Legion" (v 9), beg Jesus earnestly not to send them out of the country (v 10), but into a large herd of swine nearby (v 12). Only when Jesus gives them permission to do so (v 13), do they enter the swine. In this narrative Jesus is presented as being in charge from the very outset. The unclean spirit(s) in the Gerasene demoniac force him to run, bow down before Jesus just as the latter arrives by boat at the shore, and to shout at the top of his voice, Jesus should not torment him. I.e., the unclean spirit(s) acknowledges from the very beginning Jesus' superiority, his ability to command it to leave its victim, to be tortured or tormented, even to be destroyed.

This superiority is emphasized by the fantastic number of the unclean spirits / demons in the one victim. The man in Mark 1:21-28 has only one unclean spirit in him, although it speaks in the plural (v 24) to include generically its fellow unclean spirits. The unclean spirit / demon in 7:24-30 is also singular, as is true for its counterpart in 9:14-29. Elsewhere it is related that Jesus had cured one of his female followers, Mary Magdalene, of seven demons / evil spirits (Luke 8:2). Yet directly across the Sea of Galilee from Magdala, in the region of Kursi, Jesus exorcized a man of a "legion" of unclean spirits, i.e. of up to 6,000, the size of a full Roman legion. This explains why they enter a herd of swine which numbers about 2,000.

Jesus in Mark 5:1-20 is presented as lord not only of individual unclean spirits / demons, or of several. He has

---

[42] Cf. my *The Stilling of the Storm* 74-75.

authority even over thousands of them, so great is his power. Scribes from Jerusalem had earlier maintained in the Gospel of Mark that Jesus "had" Beelzebul (was "mad") and cast out demons by the ruler of the demons (3:22). Yet by "tying up" the strong man (Satan, or Beelzebul the ruler of the demons – 3:27), Jesus demonstrates his authority and his power. The narrative of 5:1-20 illustrates this most vividly.

2. Jesus as the Son of the Most High God Is Stronger Than the Strongest Human

The first hearers of this narrative, originally in Aramaic (or possibly Hebrew), were Palestinian Jewish Christians. In contrast to today's readers, they would immediately have recognized that the Gerasene demoniac is described by the narrator in terms of the strongest man in Judaic folklore, Samson, who at first could break all the hand- and foot-chains by which he was bound. They also would have noted that the demoniac's living in a rock cave, the motif of uncleanness, swearing not to torment or injure someone, and phrases like "What is your name?" derive from the Samson account in Judaic tradition.

Jesus is stronger than the strongest known human, Samson, or a madman described in terms of him, because he is the Son of "the Most High God." The latter phrase was employed daily by Palestinian Jews when reciting the *Shema'* with its benedictions and the *Shemoneh 'Esreh* or Eighteen Prayer. More importantly, it formed the beginning and end of the "Song of Those Afflicted (by Madness)," Ps 91:1 and 9. This Song was recited in the Jerusalem Temple up to 70 CE in order to ward off demons or to heal madness. Since the Gerasene demoniac is described with characteristics typical of madness in Judaic tradition, the phrase "Son of 'the Most High God'" employed by the unclean spirit in Mark 5:7 suits the context very well.

As "the Most High God" was called upon to ward off demons from someone suspected of madness, or to cure him, so the "Son" of the Most High God is described in 5:1-20 as being capable of doing exactly the same thing his Father can. This emphasizes that Jesus is God's "Son." While many human contemporaries do not yet recognize him as such, the unclean spirits / demons already do so (5:7; 3:11; cf. 1:24 with "the Holy One of God"). In the Gospel of Mark it is a (Roman, pagan) centurion who witnesses the prodigia at the time of Jesus' death on the Cross and then is the first human to proclaim: "Truly this man was God's Son!" (15:39). This description of a Gentile is in part to shame those who did not or could not recognize Jesus as such already during his lifetime, his fellow Jews. It is the Gospel writer's hope that through such "shaming," Jesus' own people will also come to acknowledge him as the Son of God.

3. Ridicule of the Unclean and Idolaters

From a typically Palestinian Jewish perspective, the narrator of the original account directed satire against someone who had become thoroughly "unclean." The Gerasene demoniac has an "unclean" spirit (5:2) and lives (in a rock cave) among tombs (v 3), i.e. he has direct contact with the dead, making him "unclean." The unclean spirit adjures Jesus "by God" (v 7), which is ridiculous. The opposite would rather be the normal case: the exorcist Jesus would adjure the unclean spirit to come out of the man (v 8). Jesus could even be expected to adjure it by an incantational formula: "by God."

If the unclean spirit knows Jesus' name and that he is the Son of the Most High God (v 7), the first hearers of the narrative will also have smiled when it is stated that Jesus then asks the unclean spirit its name (v 9). The opposite should have been the case here too.

Swine were unclean animals for Jews, and the description of an unimaginably large herd numbering about 2,000 (v 13) was intended to ridicule its non-Jewish owners. Gentiles were considered by first-century Palestinian Jews to be idolaters. While not expressly mentioned in the text, it may be justly assumed that the owners of the swine were thought to eat the unclean animals, and perhaps even to employ them as religious offerings.[43] When the swine all rush down the steep bank into

---

[43] Cf. F. Annen, *Heil für die Heiden* 164 for pigs offered among others to Vulcan, and R. Gundry, *Mark* 252, referring to E. S. Johnson, Jr. Yet to maintain the tombs in which the Gerasene demonic lived were a site

the Sea of Galilee and drown (v 13), the first Palestinian Jewish Christian hearers will have felt "Schadenfreude." Unclean spirits, a whole legion of them, died within unclean animals, swine, and idolaters could no longer use these as offerings to false gods.

Several centuries later the Roman emperor Diocletian was described as having been a swineherd near Tiberias, also on the Sea of Galilee. This was Jewish scorn at, and ridicule of, the Romans as swine, partly because the wild boar was represented on the insignia of the Tenth Roman Legion stationed at the latest in 6 BCE in nearby Syria, and thus in part also responsible for the region around Hippos, including Kursi. The wild boar's "ravaging" (Ps 80:14), employing violence and taking what doesn't belong to it, recalled how the occupying power Rome oppressed Palestinian Jews in may ways.[44]

Judaic haggadah also labeled Pharaoh a swineherd and the Egyptian army, which rushed down cliffs to pursue the fleeing Israelites and then drowned in the Reed Sea, swine. This became the "Vorlage" for the herd of about 2,000 swine rushing down a steep bank into the Sea of Galilee and drowning there (Mark 5:13), and for the immediate mention of swineherds (v 14). Here too the Palestinian Jewish Christian narrator of 5:1-20 indirectly ridicules non-Jews as unclean swine. His first hearers would have understood this allusion to the Exodus event, especially as described in Judaic tradition, and they would have considered the death through drowning of unclean spirits in unclean animals to be completely appropriate. The fate of the unclean swine in the Sea of Galilee was just like the fate of the unclean, pagan Egyptians in the Reed Sea, also labeled swine and considered idolaters.[45]

---

used for sacrifices and meals is far-fetched. There may have been, however, such an offering site in nearby Hippos.

[44] Cf. the rabbinic sources cited in Str-B 1.449-450.

[45] Cf. for example Baal-Zephon as an idol to which Pharaoh sacrificed, offered incense and libations, and prostrated himself in *Mek. R. Ish.* Beshallaḥ 3 on Exod 14:9 (Lauterbach 1.205). See also the references to the idols of the Egyptians in Ginzberg, *The Legends* 2.78, 114, 334, 349; 3.86; 4.128; and 5.395, 432 and 435.

4. The Beginning of a Christian Mission in the Decapolis

When the Gerasene demoniac, now exorcized of his unclean spirits and again in his right mind, begged Jesus that he might be with him, i.e. become his disciple and follow him (5:18), Jesus refused his request. Rather, he should go to his home (in nearby Kursi), to his relatives and friends and "proclaim" to them the things the Lord (God) had done to him and how He had had mercy on him (v 19). The verb ἀπαγγέλλω here is characteristic of later Christian proclamation (of the Gospel, the εὐαγγέλιον).

Yet the cured Gerasene demoniac did not obey Jesus' command. Instead, he departed and began to "proclaim" in the Decapolis, i.e. in nearby Hippos, the things Jesus had done for him, which produced general amazement (v 20). The verb κηρύσσω here means the proclamation of a preacher, a herald who proclaims a message, the Gospel.

The original Palestinian Jewish Christian hearers would have thought here of Pharaoh. In Judaic tradition he too was the only Egyptian of a whole army to survive drowning in the Reed Sea. Convinced of the Lord's doing miracles for the Israelites there (Exod 15:11), he too did not return to his native city and his family in Egypt, but went off to the large city of Nineveh to become their king and an example of repentance. Therefore Exod 9:16 was then applied to him: The Lord let him live to show His power and "to proclaim (MT סַפֵּר / LXX διαγγελῇ) His name in all the land."

The narrative now found in Mark 5:1-20 was thus also originally intended in part to "legitimate" a later Jewish Christian missionizing of the (primarily Gentile) Decapolis after the death and Resurrection of Jesus. In the account, although Jesus did not plan it, a man healed by him proclaims in (nearby Hippos), a city of the Decapolis, what Jesus, the Lord, had done to him. This event thus now precedes in the Gospel of Mark the healing of a deaf and dumb man by Jesus in the region of the Decapolis in 7:31. Already in 5:20 a mission to the Gentiles had begun, although not carried out by one of Jesus' twelve disciples.

* * *

These were originally the four main reason[s why Mark?] 5:1-20 created his account. By way of contrast[, ...is] not true of the narrative. A brief listing of the[se?] original intentions of the narrator into a proper [...]

1) Mark 5:1-20 is not a "Christian midrash" based [on Ps] (68): 7 LXX and especially Isa 65:3-4 LXX, as maintained by numerous commentators.[46] Nor is it based in part on the LXX of Exod 14:1 - 15:22.[47] It is rather the Hebrew text of the Samson narrative, with Judaic tradition on it and the Exodus event, which has primarily influenced the narrative.

2) There is no concern with private property in the account, i.e. the great loss to the owners of the ca. 2,000 swine which drown.[48] Nor does the narrative emphasize that one healed person is of more value than the possession of an entire herd.[49] The purposes of the narrative are rather the four enumerated above. Everything else is only of minor importance.

3) The unclean spirits are not considered to be "the souls of warriors who had died violent deaths in battle, a notion surviving from primitive times," as suggested by F.C. Grant.[50] Nor is Jesus' exorcism of the unclean spirits in the Gerasene demoniac "a saving act of holy war."[51] Neither is even hinted at in the narrative.

---

[46] Cf. for example W. Grundmann, *Das Evangelium nach Markus* 141; H. Sahlin, "Die Perikope vom gerasenischen Besessenen und der Plan des Markusevangeliums" in *ST* 18 (1964) 160 for Isa 65:1-5; and J. Craghan, "The Gerasene Demoniac" in *CBQ* 30 (1968) 522-536.

[47] Against J. Marcus, *Mark 1 - 8*, 349.

[48] Against B. Weiß, *Die Evangelien des Markus und Lukas* (Göttingen: Vandenhoeck & Ruprecht, 1901⁶) 79-80, and W. Grundmann, *Das Evangelium des Markus* 146. Correctly seen by W. Schmithals, *Das Evangelium nach Markus. Kapitel 1 - 9,1*, 279, and D. Juel, *Mark* (Minneapolis: Augsburg, 1991) 80.

[49] Against J. Schniewind, *Das Evangelium nach Markus* 53-54. He may have been thinking of Jesus' parable in Luke 15:3-7.

[50] "The Gospel According to St. Mark" 712.

[51] Against J. Marcus, *Mark 1 - 8*, 344. He also speaks of "the overall Markan concept of the Messiah as God's holy warrior" (352).

P. Carrington maintains that the Gerasene demoniac's "mania dated from some encounter with the Roman armies."⁵² No indication is given in the account that it is expressly anti-Roman. This sentiment can at the most be felt in the background and muted, as an allusion.

5) The motif of impurity in the narrative does not point to Jesus as the messianic high priest.⁵³ It rather has to do with a typical characteristic of a mad person in Palestinian Judaic tradition, and with the Samson account.

6) The Gerasene demoniac's bowing down before Jesus in Mark 5:6 does not represent the latter as a *theios anēr*, as maintained by R. Pesch.⁵⁴ Rather, he is the Jewish Messiah, the conquerer of the ruler of the demons (Mark 3:22-27),⁵⁵ the unclean spirits to be removed from the land in the eschatological period (Zech 13:2).

7) Mark 5:1-20 does not represent the Gerasene demoniac as "a worshiper of demons, an eater of pork."⁵⁶ Rather, the unclean spirits / demons are described as having taken possession of the (innocent) man, making him mad. Swine appear in the narrative, but he himself eats no pork. This is reading Isa 65:3-4, with the eating of swine's flesh (cf. also 66:17), into the text.

8) The unclean spirits' wish in 5:12 to "enter" the nearby herd of swine also does not mean to include "commerce" with them, i.e. intercourse, as maintained by J. Derrett,⁵⁷ and taken up by J. Marcus.⁵⁸ The first Palestinian Jewish Christian hearers of the narrative would not have had this association, but would simply have thought of the common

---

⁵² Cf. his *According to Mark* 118.
⁵³ Against W. Grundmann, *Das Evangelium des Markus* 142.
⁵⁴ Cf. his *Der Besessene* 24, with n. 34.
⁵⁵ On this, see also O. Betz, "The Concept of the So-called 'Divine Man' in Mark's Christology" 237-239.
⁵⁶ Against R. Pesch, *Der Besessene* 45.
⁵⁷ Cf. his "Spirit-Possession" 290, where he states that "Roman and Greek schoolboys knew that 'pig' means the *pudendum muliebre*...."
⁵⁸ Cf. his *Mark 1 - 8*, p. 345.

motif of a demon's wish, when exorcized, to go into another object or person.
9) Mark 5:12-13 does not deal with "tricking the devil," as maintained by O. Bauernfeind.[59] According to the text, Jesus would have been satisfied with the unclean spirits' simply entering the large herd of swine on the nearby hillside. They themselves do not reckon with the reaction of panic leading to their immediate destruction.
10) There is no emphasis in the narrative on Jesus' now being rejected by Gentiles just as he had already been rejected by his fellow Jews.[60] Rather, the episode legitimates the beginning of a Christian mission in the Decapolis, as noted above in 4.

These ten negative statements could be supplemented by many others found in the main text of the above essay. Yet they suffice to describe the narrative of the Gerasene demoniac by showing what it is not. The colors black and gray help one to appreciate what is white.

* * *

The narrative of the Gerasene demoniac does not lack the "Gospel ethos," as M. Dibelius maintained. Indeed, it demonstrates with suspense and very many vivid details how Jesus, God's Son, has complete authority and power over the unclean spirits / demons. The account conveys that the eschatological period, with Jesus' now conquering the forces of Satan, the ruler of the demons, has in fact begun. This joyful message of the Lord (God's) mercy should now be proclaimed not only to His own people, the Jews, but to Gentiles as well, such as those in (Hippos, a city of) the Decapolis. God's mercy, mediated through His Son Jesus, is for all, both those who are mad and those who are of sound mind, both Jew and Gentile.

---

[59] Cf. his *Die Worte der Dämonen im Markus-Evangelium* 37. See 43 on the demons: "Nicht als betrogene Teufel, sondern als betrügende Teufel handeln sie."
[60] Against F. Annen, *Heil für die Heiden* 200.

Chapter Two

Catchword Connections and Day of Atonement Imagery in Luke 4:16-30

Introduction

Luke's version of Jesus' rejection at Nazareth in 4:16-30 is one of the most commented on passages in the NT. A research report by C. Schreck on the secondary literature regarding the narrative, dealing only with the period 1973-1988, alone lists 309 titles. He correctly notes that "there are as many competing interpretations of its meaning as there are of the whole of Luke's two-volume work."[1]

C. F. Evans called the rejection narrative found in Luke "perhaps the most dramatically elaborated story in his Gospel," "far more artistic and impressive" than Mark's version in 6:1-6a.[2]

---

[1] Cf. his "The Nazareth Pericope. Luke 4,16-30 in Recent Study" in *L'Evangile de Luc, The Gospel of Luke,* ed. C. Schreck and F. Neirynck (BETL 32; Leuven: Leuven University, 1989) 399-471, bibliography on pp. 456-471, quotation p. 400. See also the secondary literature cited by F. Bovon, *Das Evangelium nach Lukas* (EKKNT 3/1; Zurich / Düsseldorf: Benziger; Neukirchen Vluyn: Neukirchener, 1989) 204-206; J. Nolland, *Luke 1 – 9:20* (WBC 35A; Dallas: Word Books, 1989) 188-190; and F. Neirynck, "Luke 4, 16-30 and the Unity of Luke-Acts" in *The Unity of Luke-Acts,* ed. J. Verheyden (BETL 142; Leuven: Leuven University, 1999) 357-395, esp. 380-384.

[2] Cf. his *Saint Luke* (London: SCM Press; Philadelphia: Trinity Press International, 1990) 266.

Yet A. R. C. Leaney in contrast maintains that "Luke, in his desire to combine the narrative of a triumphant visit with a rejection, has given us an impossible story...."[3]

There are indeed many still unsolved difficulties and open questions in 4:16-30. Several of them are the following. Why does the narrative differ so greatly from Mark 6:1-6a (and Matt 13:54 - 58)? Does it derive entirely or in part from the Third Evangelist, or from Special Luke? (I propose the latter and attempt to confirm this throughout this essay.) How can one explain the strange citation of Isa 58:6 between Isa 61:1 and 2 in Luke 4:18-19? How can the apparently abrupt change of mood, beginning in v 22, be accounted for? Does the author of v 29 have poor knowledge of the geographical site Nazareth, or is some other influence at work here? Does the same verse imply stoning, or something else? What was the original language of the pericope: Greek, or one of the two Semitic languages Aramaic or Hebrew? Is the account historical, and if not, what are its purposes or religious truths?

The following study addresses the above and other questions relevant to 4:16-30 in new ways. Section I. deals with catchword connections such as "synagogue" and "all," yet primarily "acceptable," within the original Semitic narrative. Section II. describes Day of Atonement imagery as reflected in the episode, including the High Priest's reading aloud publicly; Isa 58:6 as part of the prophetic reading for the Day of Atonement; the Jubilee year, the Day of Atonement, the Messiah and Isa 61:1-2; and an extensive analysis of Jesus as the scapegoat in Luke 4:29, including the crescendoing development toward this in the previous verses. Section III. deals with the original language, provenance and date of the narrative, section IV. with the question of its historicity, and in conclusion section V. with the purposes of the narrative.

---

[3] Cf. his *A Commentary on the Gospel According to St. Luke* (Black's; London: Black, 1958) 52.

I. Catchword Connections

In Luke 4:16-30 two terms are repeated at least three times, providing inner connections within the pericope, and a third forms the basis for the development of the major scene in the Nazareth synagogue in regard to the choice of the Scriptural texts employed. Since I propose throughout that this entire episode is from Special Luke,[4] which originated in Palestinian Jewish Christianity in a Semitic language and was later translated into Greek by a Hellenistic Jewish Christian, only then becoming available to the Third Evangelist, I also cite here the probable Semitic equivalents to the present Greek terms.

1. *Synagogue*

In Luke 4:16 Jesus is described as going to the *synagogue* on the Sabbath, as was his custom. Verse 20 then states that "the eyes of all in the *synagogue* were fixed on him." Finally, v 28 notes that at the end of Jesus' remarks "all in the *synagogue* were filled with rage."[5] The term "synagogue" thus helps to hold the entire unit together.

The Greek for "synagogue" in all these occurrences is συναγωγή. The Semitic equivalent is [בֵּית הַ]כְּנֶסֶת .[6]

2. *All*

Luke 4:20 notes that after Jesus' reading of the Scripture, "the eyes of *all* in the synagogue were fixed on him." Verse 22 states that "*all* spoke well of him and were amazed at the gracious words that came from his mouth" (NRSV). Verse 23 then has the Nazarites tell Jesus: "Whatever / *all the things* (ὅσα) we heard

---

[4] Cf. also W. Grundmann, *Das Evangelium nach Lukas* (THKNT 3; Berlin: Evangelische Verlagsanstalt, 1984) 119 on the episode as basically from Special Luke (his "SLk").
[5] Cf. also Luke's own general statement in 4:15, that Jesus taught "in their *synagogues* and was esteemed by all." This is an expansion of Mark 6:2, "On the Sabbath he began to teach in the *synagogue*, and many who heard him were astounded...."
[6] Jastrow 650. Cf. the Hebrew New Testaments of Delitzsch (107-108) and the United Bible Societies (155-157; forgotten at v 20).

were done in Capernaum, do here too in your hometown." The Semitic behind ὅσα here could be something like the Hebrew כָּל־אֲשֶׁר.[7] Finally, v 28 relates that when those in the Nazarite site of religious assembly heard Jesus' remarks in vv 23-27, "*all* in the synagogue were filled with rage."[8] Here too through repetition the term "all" helps to hold the pericope together.

The Greek for "all" in 4:20, 22 and 28 is πάντες (as πάντων in v 20). Its Semitic equivalent, as in v 23, is כָּל in its various forms.[9]

3. Acceptable

The most important catchword connection in Luke 4:16-30, however, is "acceptable." The citations of Isa 61:1-2 and 58:6 in verses 18-19 are dependent on the use of this term in the proverb of v 24, and it probably lies behind the "words of 'grace'" in v 22.

3.1 The Proverb in Luke 4:24

When his fellow Nazarites were offended at him in Mark 6:4, Jesus said to them: "A prophet is not *without honor* except in his hometown and among his relatives and in his (own) home." The expression "without honor" is ἄτιμος in Greek. It is ultimately modeled after the statement in 1 Sam 9:6 regarding the prophet Samuel: "Behold, there is a man of God in this city, and he is a

---

[7] Cf. the Hebrew New Testament of Delitzsch (108). The United Bible Societies (156) have : כָּל הַדְּבָרִים שֶׁ, "all the things that...."
[8] Cf. again 4:15, where Luke himself in his generalization changes the "many" of Mark 6:2 into "all." This is probably due to his appropriating the latter term from the unit he inserts at this point. The expression πάντως in 4:23, "doubtless, certainly, probably" (BAGD 609), may be from Luke himself (see also Acts 21:22; 28:4; and 18:21 [D]), or the Hellenistic Jewish Christian translator of the original Semitic expression. It could have been something like the Hebrew בְּלִי סָפֵק. The United Bible Societies Hebrew New Testament has אֵין סָפֵק שֶׁ (156). It thus has nothing to do with the term "all."
[9] Jastrow 638. Cf. the Hebrew New Testament of Delitzsch (108) for כָּל אֲשֶׁר and כֻּלָּם, as well as that of the United Bible Societies (156-157).

man 'held in honor'" (Heb. נִכְבָּד , LXX ἔνδοξος).¹⁰ Matthew at 13:57 employs Mark's ἄτιμος. The Semitic original of the saying, however, developed slightly differently before it was appropriated by the Fourth Evangelist, perhaps already in Greek. In 4:44 he has Jesus testify that "a prophet *has no honor* in his own country."¹¹ The italicized expression is τιμὴν οὐκ ἔχει, which could be לֹא נִכְבָּד in Hebrew, similar to the verbal form found in 1 Sam 9:6 cited above.¹²

Special Luke or the Palestinian Jewish Christian community from which he came modified the basic Semitic form of Jesus' saying which is still found in the other three Evangelists, in its earliest and fullest form in Mark. In the course of transmission and adaptation there, it became: "No prophet is *acceptable* in his hometown" (Luke 4:24). The Greek for "acceptable" is δεκτός.¹³ With only one exception, the Hebrew verb רָצָה and the noun רָצוֹן lie behind the twenty-six occurrences of δεκτός in the LXX.¹⁴ The Hebrew verb basically means to be pleased with, to

---

¹⁰ Cf. my study "Jesus' Rejection at Nazareth (Mark 6:1-6a par.), and Samuel's Anointing Saul as King (1 Samuel 10)" in *Samuel, Saul and Jesus. Three Early Palestinian Jewish Christian Gospel Haggadoth* (SFSHJ 105; Atlanta: Scholars Press, 1994) 65-107, especially 78-80.
¹¹ The noun πατρίς occurs eight times in the NT, seven of which deal with Jesus' saying. In John 4:44 the πατρίς refers to the Galilee of v 43. Cf. BAGD 637 for the noun as meaning both homeland and hometown. The same is true for the Aramaic מדינתא and the Hebrew מדינה, which can also refer either to one's hometown or district, country. See Jastrow 734, as well as my "Jesus' Rejection" 70 for twenty-two cities called πατρίς by Josephus and meant as "hometown."
¹² Cf. the Hebrew New Testament of Delitzsch (171).
¹³ As will now be shown, J. Fitzmyer wrongly asserts that the Evangelist Luke, in light of the δεκτός of Isa 61:2 in Luke 4:19, "almost certainly" changes the Markan ἄτιμος to δεκτός in v 24. See his *The Gospel According to Luke (I-IX)* (AB 28; Garden City, New York: Doubleday, 1981) 528.
¹⁴ Cf. Hatch-Redpath 289.

accept favorably,[15] and the noun goodwill, favor, acceptance, will.[16]

If the proverb of Luke 4:24 was originally in Hebrew, it could have been: אֵין נָבִיא רָצוּי בִּמְדִינָתוֹ.[17] The qal passive participle רָצוּי means favored, "acceptable to."[18] This could also be expressed by the niphal, נִרְצָה, to be accepted.[19] Both translate into English as: "A prophet is not 'accepted / favored' in his hometown." If the saying was originally in Aramaic, it could have been: לָאו אִתְרְעֵי נָבִיא בִּמְדִינְתָּאה.[20]

I suggest that when Special Luke (or already his Jewish Christian community) reworked and modified the Semitic original of the Markan scene of Jesus' rejection at Nazareth, he did so partly in light of Jesus' baptism, known to all Palestinian Christians. The earliest form of it relates that when the (Holy) Spirit descended upon Jesus like a dove, a voice from heaven spoke: "You are My beloved Son; with you *I am well pleased*" (Mark 1:11 par.).[21] This is in Greek: σὺ εἶ ὁ υἱός μου ὁ ἀγαπητός, ἐν σοὶ εὐδόκησα. It is clearly modeled on Isa 42:1, where God states: "Here is My servant, whom I uphold, My chosen, in whom My soul *delights*; I have put My spirit upon him...."[22] *Targum Jonathan* modifies the latter to: "I will set My

---

[15] BDB 953; cf. also Jastrow 1493-1494.
[16] BDB 953; Jastrow 1492.
[17] Both Delitzsch (108) and the United Bible Societies (156) also have רָצוּי at this point. They differ, however, in the noun for "hometown."
[18] BDB 953,1.
[19] BDB 953; Jastrow 1493,1).
[20] Cf. Jastrow 1486 on רעי, רעא, ithpe. 1) to be pleasing, acceptable.
[21] Luke appropriates this literally from Mark at 3:22; Matthew in 3:17 no longer has God address Jesus, but the bystanders: "This is...."
[22] Matthew also quotes this at 12:18. The Isaiah verse also lies behind God's words at the transfiguration in Mark 9:7. Matthew makes this even clearer in 17:5. The Lukan variant in 9:35, "My chosen one," ὁ ἐκλελεγμένος, is due to a different Greek translation of the Hebrew בְּחִירִי.

holy spirit upon him."[23] The Hebrew behind the Markan εὐδόκησα, "I am well pleased," is the רָצְתָה from Isa 42:1 of God's soul and thus in the third person singular.[24] The root רצה, employed of God's favoring or "accepting" His Son Jesus, was thus used for the latter in a well-known scene from the opening of his public ministry. It appears also to have influenced the choice of "accepted" in Jesus' prophet saying at Nazareth. God had already "accepted" Jesus at his baptism. The Nazarites, in contrast, rejected him whom God had accepted. Therefore the prophet Jesus could state that he was not "accepted" (רָצוּי) in his hometown.

3.2   Isa 61:1-2 in Luke 4:18-19

In Luke 4:18 the LXX version of Isa 61:1 is quoted, with the exception of the omitted phrase "to heal the broken in heart."[25] After a phrase from Isa 58:6 (see section 3.3 below), Luke 4:19 continues with the first phrase of Isa 61:2, καλέσαι ἐνιαυτὸν κυρίου δεκτόν, only changing the καλέσαι into κηρύξαι : "to proclaim the *acceptable* year of the Lord."

The Greek for "acceptable" here is δεκτός, as in Jesus' prophet saying in Luke 4:24. The Hellenistic Jewish Christian who translated the Semitic original of the Nazareth rejection episode easily recognized the quotation of Isa 61:1-2 and correctly quoted it according to the LXX. Jesus, however, is presented as reading out loud from the *Hebrew* version of Isaiah. It has at Isa 61:2a: לִקְרֹא שְׁנַת־רָצוֹן לַיהוה , "to proclaim the year of the Lord's *acceptance* / favor." Here the noun רָצוֹן ,

---

[23] Stenning 140-141. Luke 3:22 also has the "Holy" Spirit at Jesus' baptism, lacking in Mark 1:10 and called the "Spirit of God" in Matt 3:16.
[24] *Targum Jonathan* has: "in whom My memra 'is well pleased' (אתרעי)": Stenning 140-141.
[25] Several less important MSS, however, include it; see the apparatus of Nestle-Aland.[26]

acceptance, favor, goodwill is employed, for which *Targum Jonathan* has the similar רַעֲוָא.[26]

The catchword רָצוֹן in Isa 61:2a is the main reason the author of the original Semitic narrative of Jesus' rejection at Nazareth (Special Luke) thought of quoting Isa 61:1-2 at this point. He was reminded of it because of the term רָצוּי, "acceptable," in Jesus' prophet saying. It derives from the same root. This is corroborated by the use of Isa 58:6 at this point.

3.3 Isa 58:6 in Luke 4:18

The phrase ἀποστεῖλαι τεθραυσμένους ἐν ἀφέσει ("to let the oppressed go free") at the end of Luke 4:18 interrupts the quotation of Isa 61:1 in v 18 and Isa 61:2a in v 19. It derives from LXX Isa 58:6, with one modification. The verbal form ἀπέστελλε of the LXX, first aorist singular imperative, has been changed to the first aorist infinitive ἀποστεῖλαι in order to be parallel to the preceding infinitive κηρύξαι ("to proclaim").

Up to now no satisfactory explanation has been offered for the insertion of a phrase from Isa 58:6 into the quotation of Isa 61:1-2, a highly unusual procedure. This too, however, is due to the catchword רָצוֹן in the preceding verse in the Hebrew original, which is emphasized by repetition in *Targum Jonathan* on vv 5-6. The immediate context is thus very important for interpreting v 6.

In Isa 58:5 God asks the Israelites who are fasting before Him:

a) Is such the fast that I choose,
b) a day to humble oneself?
c) Is it to bow down the head like a bulrush,
d) and to lie down in sackcloth and ashes?
e) Will you call [this a] fast,
f) a day acceptable to the Lord? (NRSV)

Targum Jonathan changes "that I choose" in 58:5a, אֶבְחָרֵהוּ, into "wherein I take pleasure," דרעינא בה, with the verb רעא, רעי, equivalent to the Hebrew רצה: to desire, take

---

[26] Stenning 204-205. On the Aramaic noun, see Jastrow 1486: will, pleasure. The Vulgate has at Luke 4:19 *annum Domini "acceptum."*

delight in.[27] The Hebrew of v 5f, "a day *acceptable* to the Lord," is וְיוֹם רָצוֹן לַיהוה , literally "a day of *acceptance / favor* to the Lord." This is also rendered דרעוא ביה in the *Targum*.[28]

This emphasis on רָצוֹן once in the Hebrew and twice in the Aramaic of Isa 58:5 helps one to understand the use of the next verse, 58:6, within the quotation of Isa 61:1-2 in Luke 4:18-19. The Hebrew of Isa 58:6 reads in English (NRSV):

a) Is this not the fast that I choose:
b) to loose the bonds of injustice,
c) to undo the thongs of the yoke,
d) to let the oppressed go free,
e) and to break every yoke?

Isa 58:6a almost literally repeats the Lord's question from v 5a: "Is this not the fast that I choose?" Again, *Targum Jonathan* transforms "that I choose," אֶבְחָרֵהוּ , into "wherein I take pleasure / which I consider acceptable," דרעינא בה .[29] Thus, Isa 58:6 is also connected in Judaic tradition by the catchword רְעִי , and by the Hebrew רָצוֹן and the Aramaic רְעִי in v 5, to the Hebrew רָצוֹן and the Aramaic רעוא of Isa 61:2a. It should also be noted that the "acceptable day" of Isa 58:5 and the "acceptable year" of Isa 61:2 contain two of the only fifteen occurrences of רָצוֹן in the MT which express God's goodwill, favor, acceptance.[30] This method of catchword connection helps to account for the otherwise unexplainable quotation of Isa 58:6d between Isa 61:1 and 2a in Luke 4:18-19.

Finally, the insertion of Isa 58:6d between Isa 61:1 and 2 is a clear indication that the entire narrative of Jesus' rejection in Nazareth, as now found in Luke 4:16-30, is a literary creation. No scroll of Isaiah in a Palestinian synagogue could have had

---

[27] Jastrow 1486.
[28] Stenning 194-195.
[29] *Ibid.*
[30] Cf. BDB 953, l.a.

such a reading.³¹ It is rather a part of the narrative artistry of Special Luke to have made such a catchword connection.

* * *

It should also be noted that Isa 58:6 is employed in the earliest extant Judaic public fasting ritual designed to induce God to let it finally rain again. The Mishnah at *Ta'anith* (affliction, fast)³² 2:1 describes how the ark (with the Torah scrolls inside) was brought out into the public plaza of a town, wood ashes were placed both on it and on everyone's head, and the oldest man present spoke admonitions to penitence.³³ According to the Tannaitic Tosefta at this point (1:8), part of his address included the assertion that (innocent) children should not suffer from famine (due to lack of rain). To buttress this, first Isa 58:3 and 4-5 are quoted. Then the question is asked on the part of God: "But which is the fast *which I find acceptable* / in which I find favor?" The latter is the Hebrew שאני רוצה בו . This paraphrase of Isa 58:6a employs רצה , like the *Targum*'s רעי . Then v 6b, followed by "etc.," is quoted.³⁴

While the Mishnah and Tosefta descriptions of a public fast for rain cannot be dated with certainty to the first half of the first century CE, they are definitely Tannaitic and may even go back to a very early period. Drought, leading to famine in Palestine, occurred from earliest times on, as shown in Gen 12:10 for Abraham and 41:57 – 42:2 for Jacob. Some sort of public fasting ritual very probably developed at a quite early date. If Isa 58:6 was part of it, which is indeed possible, the paraphrase of v 6a

---

[31] According to *m. Meg.* 4:4, verses could be left out in the reading from the prophets, but not in the Torah (Albeck 2.366; Danby 206; Neusner 322-323). Yet this did not allow inserting part of a verse from an earlier chapter into the middle of two adjacent verses from a later chapter.
[32] Jastrow 1684.
[33] Albeck 2.333; Danby 195; Neusner 308-309. Here Jonah 3:10 is quoted, part of the reading from the prophets in the afternoon service of the Day of Atonement. Cf. below, section II.2.
[34] Cf. the Hebrew in S. Lieberman, *The Tosefta*. The Order of Mo'ed 326; Zuckermandel / Liebermann 215; and an English translation in Neusner 2.265-266.

with רצה as now found in the Tosefta version cited above, may have been known to a majority of first century Palestinian Jews, including Special Luke.[35] If so, it too could have encouraged him to employ Isa 58:6d within a quotation of Isa 61:1-2 in Luke 4:18-19 because of the catchword root רצה , associated with the beginning of Isa 58:6, as in the Aramaic of the *Targum*. Unfortunately, more certainty cannot be reached.

(On Isaiah 58 as a reading from the prophets on the Day of Atonement, see below, section II.2).)

3.4 The Benediction Spoken Before the Reading from the Prophets

Luke 4:16-20 describes Jesus' role in the Sabbath synagogue service of his hometown, Nazareth. Very few details are given, partly because the first Palestinian Jewish Christian hearers of this Special Lukan narrative knew them anyway, and secondly because the narrator wished only to emphasize what was most important to him: Jesus as the central, active figure.

One detail of the synagogue service not mentioned before Jesus begins to read from the scroll of Isaiah in Luke 4:16-17 is the benediction spoken before the reading from the prophets. In the form now found in the extra-canonical tractate *Soferim* at 13:9, 40a the wording is:

> Blessed art Thou, O Lord our God, King of the universe,
> Who hast chosen good prophets,
> *and hast found pleasure* in their words which were spoken in truth.
> Blessed art Thou, O Lord, who hast chosen the Torah
> and Moses Thy servant, and Israel Thy people,
> and the prophets of truth and righteousness.[36]

The italicized expression above, "and hast found pleasure," is ורצה in Hebrew.[37] If at least this part of the benediction (simply assumed as spoken before the synagogue reading from the

---

[35] In connection with this theme it should be noted that Special Luke has Jesus mention "a great famine in all the earth," due to lack of rain, in Luke 4:25.
[36] English by I. Slotki in the Soncino edition of *The Minor Tractates of the Talmud* 1.273.
[37] Cf. M. Higger, מסכת סופרים 244 as 13:7.

prophets in Nazareth) was already included in Palestine in the first century CE,[38] it would be another piece of evidence that the catchword root רצה informed the narrative of Luke 4:16-30 in a very major way.

In addition, the above benediction spoken before the reading from the prophets emphasizes that God finds pleasure / favor in the prophets' words which were spoken "in truth" (באמת), and that God has chosen the prophets "of truth" (האמת) and righteousness.[39] If this double emphasis on "truth" in the benediction also prevailed in the first century CE, it may in part account for the expression ἐπ' ἀληθείας in Luke 4:25, which in Hebrew could also be בֶּאֱמֶת.[40]

3.5 Words of "Grace"

Finally, the expression τοῖς λόγοις τῆς χάριτος, "words of 'grace,'" in Luke 4:22 probably also reflects the Hebrew רָצוֹן or the Aramaic רַעֲוָא. While χάρις in the LXX usually translates the Hebrew חֵן,[41] at Prov 10:32; 11:27; and 12:2 it renders רָצוֹן. The first passage is of relevance to Jesus' words of "grace" which emanated from his mouth: "The lips of the righteous (sing.) know 'what is acceptable' (רָצוֹן), but the mouth of the wicked (pl.) what is perverse" (NRSV).[42] Here the LXX translator intentionally rendered "what is acceptable/ favorable" as "grace," χάρις.[43] "Words of grace" in Luke 4:22 could then be

---

[38] While the final compilation of *Soferim* may have occurred only in the eighth century CE (Slotki in his Introduction to the tractate, v; Strack and Stemberger, *Introduction* 248), this says nothing about the original date of individual components. As is well-known, liturgical forms usually change very slowly.
[39] Higger 244-245.
[40] Jastrow 79, also in connection with אמר , to say.
[41] In 60 of 71 occurrences with a Hebrew background; another three correspond to חֶסֶד . See Hatch-Redpath 1455.
[42] Cf. also Prov 16:13, "Righteous lips are 'the delight' of a king...."
[43] Cf. the words often spoken by pastors before beginning a sermon: "May *the words of my mouth* and the meditation of my heart *be acceptable* to You, O Lord, my rock and my redeemer" (Ps 19:15, Eng. 14).

in Hebrew מִילַיָא דְרַעֲוָא (אִמְרֵי דִּבְרֵי רָצוֹן), or in Aramaic
(alternatively מֵימְרַיָא דְרְעוּתָא).[44]

* * *

The above analysis of six instances of the Hebrew catchwords
רצה and רצון, with their Aramaic equivalents, speaks
cumulatively for this Semitic root as playing a major role in the
narrative now found in Luke 4:16-30. It also argues very
strongly for the incident as being originally composed in either
Aramaic or Hebrew, and in Palestine. Only later did a Hellenistic
Jewish Christian translate the episode into Greek, in which form
it became available to the Evangelist Luke. Also recognizing the
quotations from the Hebrew of Isa 61:1-2 and 58:6, the translator
correctly employed their LXX equivalents.

II. Day of Atonement Imagery

The Lukan narrative of Jesus' rejection in Nazareth is not only
connected inwardly by various catchwords. It also has been
influenced by Day of Atonement imagery from beginning to
end.[45] This includes 1) the High Priest as reading aloud; 2) Isa

---

Interestingly, Martínez and Tigchelaar in their *The Dead Sea Scrolls Study
Edition* 2.1206-1207 render שנת הרצון in 11Q Melch, line 9, as the
"year of grace." It derives from Isa 61:2, as cited in Luke 4:19.

[44] After finishing my own research on this section, I was happy to see
that B. Violet in "Zum rechten Verständnis der Nazareth-Perikope
Lc 4,16-30" in *ZNW* 37 (1938) 251-271 proposed basically the same
Aramaic. See especially pp. 263-267. The second alternative is from
him (p. 268). Violet does not consider the possibility of a Hebrew
original. Indeed, he thinks the Evangelist Luke knew Aramaic and got
this incident from someone who was in Nazareth at that time and later
reported it to him in Aramaic. The person recalled only that which was
most striking to him (p. 270). On God's "finding pleasure" (רצה) in
the "words" of good prophets, see the benediction spoken before the
reading from the prophets analyzed above.

[45] Cf. in general the art. "Day of Atonement" in *EJ* (1971) 5.1376-1384 by
M. Herr, who states: "It is certain that during the time of the Second
Temple the Day of Atonement was already considered the greatest of

58:6 as part of the prophetic reading for the Day of Atonement; 3) the Jubilee year, the Day of Atonement, the Messiah, and Isa 61:1-2; and 4) Jesus as the scapegoat in Luke 4:29.

1. The High Priest as Reading Aloud

Special Luke borrowed the general setting of Jesus' reading from Scripture in the Nazareth synagogue from a procedure related of the High Priest on the Day of Atonement in the Jerusalem Temple. It is still found in *m. Yoma* 7:1[46] and definitely goes back to the time before the Temple was destroyed in 70 CE. It should be recalled that the High Priest was also thought of as being "anointed" (Lev 16:32), as Jesus labels himself in the words of Isa 61:1 in Luke 4:18. The following seven similarities occur.

a) The High Priest came (to the Women's Court[47]) "to read" (לִקְרוֹת) sections from Scripture. This corresponds to the ἀναγνῶναι, "to read," in Luke 4:16.

b) If the High Priest "wanted" (רָצָה) to read in linen garments, he did so; if not, he read in his own white vestment. The catchword רצה may have helped the author of Luke 4:16-30 to think of the Day of Atonement ritual which later entered the Mishnah at *Yoma* 7:1.

c) - e) The "sexton / superintendent" (חַזָּן)[48] of the "synagogue" ([בֵּית הַ]כְּנֶסֶת) took a "scroll" (סֵפֶר) of the Torah

---

the festivals" (1377). See also the "Day of Atonement as Annual Purgation in Temple Times" by J. Milgrom, 1384-1387, and his commentary *Leviticus 1-16* (AB 3; New York: Doubleday, 1991) 1009-1084 on Leviticus 16. See also the art. "Azazel" in *EJ* (1971) 3.999-1002 by S. Ahituv. For Qumran, see J. Baumgarten, "Yom Kippur in the Qumran Scrolls and Second Temple Sources" in *Dead Sea Discoveries* 6 (1999) 184-191.

[46] Albeck 2.242-243; Danby 170; Neusner 276. The same text is found in *m. Soṭ.* 7:7 (Albeck 3.251; Danby 301; Neusner 458-459).

[47] Cf. *b. Yoma* 69a (Soncino 326).

[48] Jastrow 444. Neusner has "beadle."

and gave it to the head of the synagogue; the head of the synagogue gave it to the prefect (of the priests); and the prefect gave it to the High Priest to read.

The above three terms are also found in Luke 4:16-30. The c) חַזָּן is translated by ὁ ὑπηρέτης [49] in v 20. The d) בְּנֶסֶת [50] is the συναγωγή of vv 16, 20 and 28. And the scroll, e), סֵפֶר, literally (a biblical) "book,"[51] is the βιβλίον of vv 17 (twice) and 20.

f) The sexton / superintendent of the synagogue "gave" (נתן) the scroll of the Torah (Leviticus) via others to the High Priest, who then read from it chapter 16 and 23:26-32 regarding the Day of Atonement. Commenting on this passage, *y. Yoma* 7:1, 44a states: "In all circumstances people go to the Torah in the synagogue in order to read it publicly. But here you say that they bring the Torah to them. But because they are important men, the Torah is exalted through them."[52]

It should be noted that when Jesus rose to read in the synagogue of Nazareth, the scroll of the prophet Isaiah "was given" (ἐπεδόθη) to him (by the sexton / superintendent) in Luke 4:17. After unrolling and reading from it, Jesus "gave it back" (ἀποδούς) to him in v 20. This was highly unusual procedure, for normally one was not handed a scroll from which to read. Instead, one read from the appropriate passage for the particular Sabbath (especially if it was also a festival), already unrolled by the sexton to that spot. The sexton's "giving" Jesus the scroll of Isaiah is a clear borrowing from the procedure connected with the High Priest on the Day of Atonement, who was also "given" the scroll of Leviticus, from which he then read aloud chapter 16 and 23:26-32. The Palestinian Talmud as cited above shows how unusual this particular procedure was. It also

---

[49] BAGD 842; only here of a synagogue attendant.
[50] Albeck in 2.242, note with references, says the Ḥazan was the attendant of the בית־הכנסת which was on the Temple Mount. Cf. also A. Cohen in *b. Soṭ.* 40b (Soncino 198, n.4).
[51] Jastrow 1017-1018.
[52] Neusner 14.191-192.

points to Jesus as the High Priest, an "important man" connected with the Day of Atonement.

g) After the High Priest read aloud Leviticus 16 and 23:26-32, he "rolled up" (גּוֹלֵל) [53] the Torah book / scroll. This Hebrew term is taken up in Luke 4:20, where Jesus "rolled up" (πτύξας)[54] the scroll of Isaiah, gave it back to the sexton, and sat down again.

* * *

While one could maintain that several of the above seven points would appear in any description of a synagogue reading scene, the cumulative argument is strong that Special Luke borrowed them from Palestinian Judaic traditions on the High Priest's reading publicly on the Day of Atonement in the Jerusalem Temple. These traditions then later entered the Mishnah at *Yoma* 7:1. It is also significant that just before this (*Yoma* 6) a description is given of how the scapegoat was killed on the Day of Atonement by pushing it down a steep precipice. The latter imagery informs Luke 4:29, as will be shown in section 4. below. Special Luke thus drew upon Palestinian Judaic traditions which later entered the Mishnah back to back (*Yoma* 6 and 7:1), for *they were already connected beforehand.*

Special Luke's description of Jesus' reading from the scroll of the prophet Isaiah, and the following episode, are his own narrative creation. He deliberately changed the setting from the Jerusalem Temple to the synagogue of Nazareth, something known to him from the Semitic original which later became Mark 6:1-6a. He also changed the content of the scroll which was read aloud from Leviticus to Isaiah, for he wanted to portray Jesus as fulfilling the prophecy from Isaiah of the Jubilee year (see below, 3.). The creation of such a scene was typical of Judaic haggadah, one of the elements of which was "imaginative

---

[53] Jastrow 249,1). It can mean both to roll or unfold, and to roll up a scroll.
[54] Cf. BAGD 727 on πτύσσω, only here in the NT. The same is true for ἀναπτύσσω in 4:17 (BAGD 60).

dramatization," as J. Goldin remarks.⁵⁵ Luke 4:16-30 is a good example of such imaginative dramatization.

While Jesus is portrayed as the scapegoat of the Day of Atonement in Luke 4:29 (see below), in the scene within the Nazareth synagogue he is described in terms of the High Priest. This may be due to Hellenistic Jewish influence upon Palestinian, particularly Jerusalem thought.

Philo of Alexandria, who was born ca. 20 BCE,⁵⁶ could describe the High Priest as having a nature on the borderline between the divine and the human. This allows men to have a mediator, and God a servitor (*Spec. Leg.* 1.116).⁵⁷ The High Priest for the Alexandrian is a divine Word (λόγος), whose father is God (*Fug.* 108).⁵⁸ Especially when he enters the Holy of Holies in the Jerusalem Temple on the Day of Atonement, he is "less than God, (but) superior to man," as Philo interprets LXX Lev 16:17 in *Som.* 2.188 and 231.⁵⁹ There he pours as a libation the blood of the soul (*Leg. All.* 2.56); there the truly great High Priest "pours that potent undiluted draught, the libation of 'himself'" (ἑαυτόν ; *Som.* 2.183). Indeed, he is "none other than the draught which he pours" (2.249).⁶⁰

There was not only a synagogue of the Alexandrians in Jerusalem (Acts 6:9).⁶¹ Various craftsmen were also summoned from the Egyptian city to practice their expertise in the Temple.⁶²

---

⁵⁵ Cf. his *The Song at the Sea* (Philadelphia and New York: The Jewish Publication Society, 1990; original New Haven: Yale University Press, 1971) 27. Goldin also mentions word plays and free association, also found in Luke 4:16-30.
⁵⁶ Cf. the LCL edition of Philo, I.ix.
⁵⁷ Cf. *Mos.* 2.135 and *Som.* 2.231-232 for the latter, and *Quaes. Exod.* 2.118 (the divine Logos as mediator) for the former.
⁵⁸ On the first, cf. also 110 and 117.
⁵⁹ Cf. also *Her.* 84.
⁶⁰ I employ here the English translations of F. Colson and G. Whitaker in the LCL edition.
⁶¹ Cf. the sources on this cited by Str-B 2.663-665.
⁶² Cf. *t. Yoma* 2:5-6 (Neusner 2.193-194) and *b. Yoma* 38a (Soncino 176). For the Alexandrians' treatment of the scapegoat on the way to its death, see *m. Yoma* 6:4 (Albeck 2.240; Danby 169; Neusner 275). For the

M. Hengel has even estimated that between 10-15% of the Jerusalem population at the time of Paul (and thus also of Special Luke) consisted of Greek-speaking Jews.[63] Certainly much more theological dialogue between Palestinian and Hellenistic Jews took place in Jerusalem than was earlier thought. For this reason it is quite possible that the Palestinian Jewish Christian behind "Special Luke" could also have been influenced by Hellenistic Jewish, especially Alexandrian thought in regard to the High Priest, who on the Day of Atonement "pours out the libation of himself." If so, this was one more reason for his borrowing imagery from the scene of the High Priest's public reading of Scripture in the Temple on the Day of Atonement. For him too Jesus as the High Priest shed / poured out his blood as a sacrifice for the atonement of all on the Cross.[64]

2. Isa 58:6 as Part of the Prophetic Reading on the Day of Atonement

As pointed out in I.3.3 above, Isa 58:6d is cited in Luke 4:18 within a quotation of Isa 61:1-2. There I noted its catchword connection to Isa 61:1-2 and to Jesus' saying regarding a prophet as not being "acceptable" in his hometown. There was another reason, however, for Special Luke to have thought of precisely this verse from Isaiah and to have inserted it at this point.

The reading from the Torah for the morning service on the Day of Atonement was Leviticus 16, itself dealing with the Day. The *haftarah* or reading from the prophets was Isa 57:15 – 58:14

"Babylonians" of the text as a derogatory term for Alexandrians, see Danby 509, n. 2. See also *y. Yoma* 6:4, 43d (Neusner 14.178), and *b. Yoma* 66b (Soncino 312, with n. 4).

[63] Cf. his *The Pre-Christian Paul*, in collaboration with Roland Deines (London: SCM, 1991) 55.

[64] I basically borrow the above two paragraphs from my *The Wicked Tenants and Gethsemane. Isaiah in the Wicked Tenants' Vineyard, and Moses and the High Priest in Gethsemane: Judaic Traditions in Mark 12:1-9 and 14:32-42* (ISFCJ 4; Atlanta: Scholars Press, 1996) 109-110. There I describe nine other uses of High Priest and Day of Atonement imagery in the passion narratives of the Gospels (111-134).

(the end of the chapter), as indicated in *b. Meg.* 31a.⁶⁵ The latter text was particularly appropriate for the Day of Atonement because of its theme of fasting, required of all on that day (Lev 16:29 and 31; 23:27, 29 and 32). Indeed, the Day of Atonement was often simply called "the Fast."⁶⁶ False and true fasting are especially contrasted in Isa 58:3-6, which expressly employ the term צוֹם.⁶⁷ It was then natural for Special Luke to cite part of a verse from just this section, 58:6d. *Tanḥ.* B Bereshith 28 on Gen 5:1, for example, says regarding "one" of the days in Ps 139:16 that it was the Day of Atonement. To buttress this, Isa 58:6 is cited.⁶⁸ Liturgical usage of Isa 57:15 – 58:14 on the Day of

---

⁶⁵ Cf. Soncino 188. The text states that at the afternoon *(minḥah)* service Leviticus 18 and the Book of Jonah were read. See also the art. "Day of Atonement" by M. Herr in *EJ* (1971) 5.1379, and A. Büchler, art. "Hafṭarah" in *JE* (1904) 6.136-137, table. See already his "The Reading of the Law and Prophets in a Triennial Cycle" in *JQR* 6 (1894) 23, where he believes Isa 57:15 (–58:14) was read all three years of the triennial cycle on the Day of Atonement. While some prophetic readings in the Palestinian triennial cycle cannot be ascertained with certainty (cf. the art. "Triennial Cycle" by the editors in *EJ* [1971] 15.1386-1389, and the art. "Triennial Cycle" by J. Jacobs in *JE* [1906] 12.254-257), L. Crocket in "Luke iv.16-30 and the Jewish Lectionary Cycle: A Word of Caution" in *JJS* 17 (1966) 13-46 correctly notes that "lections for *feast days* and *special sabbaths* were fixed relatively early..." (17; see also 26, n. 43). This included, of course, the Day of Atonement, the most solemn festival day of the year. A Tannaitic connection of Isa 57:15 and Isa 61:1 on the basis of the terms "spirit" and "humble" is also found in *Mek.* Baḥodesh 9 on Exod 20:21 (Lauterbach 2.273).

⁶⁶ It is called "the great fast" in *Gen. Rab.* Bereshit 11/4 (Soncino 1.83), *Lam. Rab.* 3:17 § 6 (Soncino 7.197), and *Eccl. Rab.* 11:2 § 1 (Soncino 8.291). Josephus calls it "the day of the Fast" in *Ant.* 14.66 and "the festival of the Fast" in 487; for fasting on the Day of Atonement, see 3.240. Philo speaks of "the fast" in *Spec. Leg.* 1.186, which is a festival (2.193), the greatest of the festivals, a Sabbath of Sabbaths (2.194), a fast on the tenth day (2.200).

⁶⁷ Cf. the verb and noun in BDB 847.

⁶⁸ Buber 1.21; Bietenhard 1.31. In a similar tradition in *Pesiq. R.* 23/1 on Exod 20:8 and Ps 139:16 (Friedmann 115a; Braude 473), Isa 58:5 is cited. Here the author is R. Levi, a third generation Palestinian Amora (Strack and Stemberger, *Introduction* 98).

Atonement also caused the motifs of repentance and forgiveness to be inserted into this section of *Targum Jonathan*.[69]

3. The Jubilee Year, the Day of Atonement, the Messiah, and Isa 61:1-2

Jesus states in Luke 4:21, "Today this Scripture has been fulfilled in your hearing." He refers to Isa 61:1-2, which he has just read out loud in the Nazareth synagogue (4:18-19). The last phrase from Isaiah is interpreted to mean that the Lord has sent Jesus "to proclaim the year of the Lord's favor." As has been frequently noted,[70] the Jubilee year is meant here.[71]

It was to take place at the end of seven septennates, i.e. in the fiftieth year (Lev 25:8). It began with the sounding of the trumpet (שׁוֹפָר) on the tenth day of the seventh month (Tishri), on the Day of Atonement (v 9).[72] God instructs the Israelites:

---

[69] Cf. *Targ.* Isa 57:18 and 19 in Stenning 192-193.

[70] Cf. for example A. Strobel, "Die Ausrufung des Jubeljahres in der Nazarethpredigt Jesu. Zur apokalyptischen Tradition Lc 4,16-30" in *Jesus in Nazareth*, ed. W. Eltester (BZNW 40; Berlin: de Gruyter, 1972) 38-50, and R. Sloan, Jr., *The Favorable Year of the Lord. A Study of Jubilary Theology in the Gospel of Luke* (Austin, Texas: Schola Press, 1977).

[71] On this, cf. the articles by J. Eisenstein, "Sabbatical Year and Jubilee" in *JE* (1905) 10.605-608; and "Sabbatical Year and Jubilee" by D. Lieber in *EJ* (1971) 14.574-577, "Ancient Near East Background" by M. Greenberg, 577-578, "Jubilee in the Second Temple Period" by S. Safrai, 578-582, and "Sabbatical Year in Post-Biblical Times" by A. Rothkopf, 582-585. See also J. Safren, "Jubilee and the Day of Atonement" in *The Bible and its World* (Jerusalem: World Union of Jewish Studies, 1999) 107-113.

[72] Cf. *b. 'Arak.* 12a: "Now which is the year the beginning of which falls on the tenth of Tishri? Say: This is the jubilee year " (Soncino 68, with n.2). See also *b. Roš. Haš.* 8b (Soncino 32). In the "Eighteen Prayer" spoken daily, the tenth petition reads regarding God: "Sound the great horn [trumpet] for our freedom, and lift up the ensign to gather our exiles, 'and proclaim liberty' (וקרא דרור) ...." The latter may refer to Isa 61:1. See D. Hedegård, *Seder R. Amram Gaon* (Lund: Lindstedts Universitetsbokhandel, 1951) 1.91-92, where he maintains this section is from before 70 CE, and the Hebrew at p. 36. Much of this petition is repeated in the prayer employed in the present Musaf service at Roš

"Proclaim liberty (קְרָאתֶם דְּרוֹר) throughout the land to all its inhabitants" (v 10). Jesus is represented as doing exactly this when he quotes Isa 61:1 in the Nazareth synagogue in Luke 4:18. The Lord has sent him, Jesus, "'to proclaim liberty' (לִקְרֹא ... דְּרוֹר) to the captives and release to the prisoners." Finally, in the Jubilee year each person was to return to his property and family (Lev 25:10), which may have influenced Special Luke to have Jesus return to Nazareth and quote Isa 61:1-2 of himself there, and not in Capernaum or at another site.[73]

When Special Luke has Jesus state that the Isaianic prophecy concerning the Jubilee year has been fulfilled in himself, he also portrays Jesus as the Messiah. It is related for example in *b. Sanh.* 98a: "Our Rabbis taught: In the seven year cycle at the end of which the son of David will come...; at the conclusion of the septennate the son of David will come."[74] The son of David is the Messiah, here represented as coming precisely in the fiftieth year (of the last jubilee).[75] I suggest that this is the reason the Synoptic Gospels telescope Jesus' entire public ministry into (less than) one year, although there are several signs that it may have lasted longer.[76] This was to indicate that it was the final or fiftieth year of the world's last jubilee period, when the Messiah was expected to come. This is also the reason why the

---

Haššana. See *Service of the Synagogue. A New Edition of the Festival Prayers...*, ed. H. Adler (London: Routledge & Sons, n. d.[11]) 161-162. I thank Rabbi E. Stein of Berlin for making this available to me. On it, see also the remark by J. Rabbinowitz in the Soncino edition of *b. Ta'an.* 15a (p. 68, n. 8).

[73] He knew from the Semitic account which later entered Mark at 6:1-6a that at least Jesus' sisters still lived in Nazareth (v 3).

[74] Soncino 654. The "messianic woes" mentioned inbetween, including war and famine, recall Mark 13:7 and Matt 24:7 // Luke 21:11.

[75] Cf. *b. Sanh.* 97b (Soncino 658) for Elijah's telling a rabbi that "in the last jubilee the son of David will come."

[76] While the chronology of the Fourth Gospel must be treated with great scepsis, remnants of a longer ministry could possibly be reflected in it. See John 6:4 and 11:55 on other Passover celebrations; 7:14 on Booths; 10:22 on Hanukkah; and 5:1 on an unknown festival also celebrated in Jerusalem.

Evangelist Luke placed Jesus' rejection in Nazareth at the very beginning of his ministry. The "year of the Lord's favor" (Isa 61:2 in Luke 4:19) now began, just before he as the Messiah would perform healings and miracles.

It is also important to note that 11Q Melchizedek first quotes Lev 25:13 and Deut 15:2, interpreting the "release" in the latter "for the last days" in light of Isa 61:1, "to proclaim liberty to the captives." It is not the Messiah or son of David, however, who will here liberate them from all their iniquities, but the heavenly figure Melchizedek. This will take place 7) "in the first week of the jubilee which follows the ni[ne] jubilees. And the d[ay of atonem]ent is the e[nd of] the tenth [ju]bilee 8) in which atonement shall be made for all the sons of [light and] for the men [of] the lot of Mel[chi]zedek," i.e. the Qumranites. Melchizedek will here carry out the "vengeance" of God's judgments, probably an allusion to Isa 61:2, "to proclaim the year of the Lord's favor, and 'the vengeance' of our God." (It should be noted that the latter is intentionally omitted when Jesus quotes this verse in Luke 4:19.) Isa 61:2-3 are then cited, and the unit ends as it began, with a quotation of Leviticus 25 (now verse 9).[77]

Here the angelic figure Melchizedek will liberate the captives of Isa 61:1 precisely on the Day of Atonement, since for the Qumranites it also begins the fiftieth or final year of the last (here tenth) jubilee. The passage is thus remarkable in its similarities to the description of Jesus in terms of Isa 61:1-2 in Luke 4:16-30,[78] where much Day of Atonement imagery also occurs.

---

[77] For the Hebrew and an English translation with bibliography, see *The Dead Sea Scrolls Study Edition* by F. Martínez and E. Tigchelaar, 2.1206-1209, as well as the identification of the verses Isa 61:1-3 in Martínez, *The Dead Sea Scrolls Translated* 139-140, with relevant literature on p. 512, bottom.

[78] Cf. also the studies by M. Miller, "The Function of Isa 61:1-2 in 11Q Melchizedek" in *JBL* 88 (1969) 467-469, and J. A. Sanders, "From Isaiah 61 to Luke 4" in *Christianity, Judaism and Other Graeco-Roman Cults*, Morton Smith Festschrift, ed. J. Neusner (SJLA 12; Leiden: Brill, 1975) 1.75-106.

Finally, it is also possible that Isa 61:1-2 was connected to Leviticus 16, which deals with the Day of Atonement, in the early Palestinian triennial lectionary system. Deut 15:1-18 deals with the sabbatical year of remission or release. As shown in 11Q Melchizedek, this chapter was logically connected to Leviticus 25, which also deals in vv 1-7 with the sabbatical year, and then from v 8 to the end of the chapter with the Jubilee year.

In the Palestinian triennial lectionary system, on the fourth Sabbath of the month Ḥeshwan in the third year, the Torah reading was Deut 15:7 (-18) and the *hafṭarah* Isa 61:1-2, which helps to explain the association of these two texts in 11Q Melchizedek. Exactly on the fourth Sabbath of the month Ḥeshwan in the second year, the Torah reading was Leviticus 16.[79] That is, during the consecutive Sabbath reading of the Torah (and thus not on the Day of Atonement, which had its own specific *hafṭarah*, Isa 57:15 – 58:14), Isa 61:1-2 was the *hafṭarah* for the particular Sabbath on which Leviticus 16 was read precisely one year earlier. If at least these readings from the triennial lectionary system already prevailed in the first century CE, it would be another reason for the association of Isa 61:1-2 with Leviticus 16, also read on the Day of Atonement.

4. *Jesus as the Scapegoat in Luke 4:29*

Before discussing the Nazarites' attempt to hurl Jesus over the cliff to his death and the similar fate of the scapegoat on the Day of Atonement, I would first like to call attention to four factors in Luke 4:16-30 which in crescendo form rapidly led the Nazarites to this drastic behavior.

---

[79] Cf. the art. by J. Jacobs, "Triennial Cycle" in *JE* (1906) 12, chart between pp. 256-257, and the art. "Triennial Cycle" in *EJ* (1971) 15.1386. The prophetic reading associated with Leviticus 16 is Ezekiel 44. The authors are dependent on the Cairo Genizah, listings by Yannai, and the homiletical midrashim for their associations of particular Torah and *hafṭarah* passages. Except for the midrashim, I cannot verify these in regard to Isa 61:1-2.

4.1 The Negative Connotations in Luke 4:22a

Jesus' address or sermonette (דְּרָשָׁה / דְּרָשָׁא) [80] on the mixed citation from Isa 61:1-2 and 58:6 in the Nazareth synagogue is not related in detail. Instead, it is telescoped into the words "Today this Scripture is fulfilled in your ears" (Luke 4:21). Usually v 22a is then translated as positively as in the NRSV: "All spoke well of him and were amazed at the gracious words that came from his mouth." Yet the question immediately following in v 22b already has a negative connotation: "Is not this Joseph's son," (our hometown boy? How could someone who grew up in our midst be the longed for Messiah, expected by all of us when the final Jubilee arrives? Who could possibly believe in Jesus if, as the Lord's anointed prophet, he only makes verbal claims about himself and refuses to verify them by means of signs / miracles, as in Capernaum)?

If v 22a is so positive as it is usually translated, Jesus' very provocative sentences from v 23 to v 27 are inexplicable. Rather than assuming the use of a new source or tradition as of v 22b, one should rather consider whether v 22a has been adequately translated. Building on the insights of K. Bornhäuser,[81] B. Violet very plausibly proposed that ἐμαρτύρουν αὐτῷ should mean in the context: "they bore witness against him" in the sense of "they accused / reproached him."[82] The Semitic original would have been a form of עוּד , "to testify, bear witness" against someone, as in 1 Kgs 21:10 and 13.[83]

The phrase ἐθαύμαζον etc. in v 22a should also be rendered: "and they wondered about / were astonished at...." The

---

[80] Jastrow 325.
[81] Cf. his *Studien zum Sondergut des Lukas* (Gütersloh: Bertelsmann, 1934) 24-25 and 30.
[82] "Zum rechten Verständnis" 256-258. He notes this sense in John 7:7; 18:23; and Sus 41. Cf. also J. Jeremias, *Jesus' Promise to the Nations* (London: SCM, 1958) 44-46, especially 44, n. 2.
[83] Cf. BDB 730, hiphil 1. The meaning "protest" in 3. may also be relevant here. See also Jastrow 1048,4) with the sense of "warn." Both Delitzsch (108) and the United Bible Societies (156) have the hiphil of עוּד at this point in their Hebrew New Testaments.

Hellenistic Jewish Christian who translated 4:16-30 into Greek may have thought of the verb θαυμάζω here because of the similar sounding Semitic original, תָּמַהּ,[84] תָּמַהּ.[85]

That is, the Nazarites now testified against / reproached Jesus, wondering about the words of grace which had just come out of *his* mouth. How could that be? The words of "grace" (רָצוֹן , suggested above in section I.3.5), refer back to the Jubilee year of רָצוֹן just cited by Jesus from Isa 61:2 in Luke 4:19 and not, as usually understood, to Jesus' later "sermonette."[86]

This "negative" interpretation of v 22a, based on a Semitic original, makes it logically a much better preparation for the Nazarites' question in v 22b, also with a negative connotation, and for Jesus' then becoming so provocative in vv 23-27. There is thus no great change of mood on the part of the Nazarites. They react negatively from the outset, already in v 22a.

4.2 The Proverb "Physician, Heal Yourself!"

In Luke 4:22b the Nazarites ask: "Is not this Joseph's son?" Special Luke knew of the Semitic narrative behind what is now found in Mark 6:1-6a, which has at v 3: "'Is this not the carpenter, the son of Mary and brother of James and Joses and Judas and Simon, and are not his sisters here with us?' And they took offense at him." He then inserted into his own account at Luke 4:24 a variant of Jesus' "prophet" saying (as now found in Mark 6:4) and emphasized its negative character by prefacing it in v 23 with the proverb "Physician, heal yourself!" (ἰατρέ, θεράπευσον σεαυτόν). Jesus tells his former fellow citizens they will doubtless quote him this proverb and ask him to do in his hometown the things they have heard he did in Capernaum. This presupposes previous activity on the part of Jesus in Capernaum, related, however, only later in the Gospel of Luke,

---

[84] BDB 1069: be astounded, dumbfounded, bewildered, stupified.
[85] Jastrow 1675, with an example of men wondering and saying: Is such a thing possible?
[86] I follow Violet here in his "Zum rechten Verständnis" 255-256, himself dependent on Bornhäuser. Similarly Grundmann, *Das Evangelium nach Lukas* 121.

for example in 4:31-41. Then come Jesus' two examples from the careers of the prophets Elijah and Elisha.

The "Physician, heal yourself!" proverb thus opens a four-pronged crescendoing defence of his prophetic mission on the part of Jesus. The closest Judaic parallel to it emphasizes its very negative character.

Tanḥuma Bereshith 11 on Gen 4:15 relates that after blind (!) Lamech mistakenly killed Cain while hunting, he returned home and told his wives to get up onto their beds. Rebuffed because they do not want to conceive children for destruction, Lamech suggests they all go to Adam's court for arbitration. When at the end Adam tells the wives to go off and obey their husband, they tell the first human: "Healer, heal your own wound / frailty (first) (אָסְיָא אַסֵי חִגַּרְתָּךְ) ! You kept away from your bed for 130 years, and you would teach us!"[87]

This is a thorough rebuke, showing the depth of the reproach Jesus attributes to the Nazarites when he says they will doubtless tell him something very similar: "Physician, heal yourself!" He presumes they will demand that he should heal in their midst the deaf, blind, lame and speechless,[88] which cures / signs / miracles would then attest him as the Messiah. He refuses to do so, however, as in the Q episode of the sign of Jonah (Matt 12:38-42 // Luke 11:29-32). Instead, Jesus cites other examples of prophets who were not accepted by their own people and thus healed others. This provokes them even more.

4.3 The Widow of Zaraphath and Elijah

In Luke 4:25 Jesus states that "there were many widows in Israel in the time of Elijah, when the heaven was shut up three years and six months, and there was a severe famine over all the

---

[87] Eshkol 1.20; Singermann 31. A parallel with variants is found in *Gen. Rab.* Bereshit 23/4 on Gen 4:23 (Theodor and Albeck 1.225; Soncino 1.195). Only the latter is noted in Str-B 2.156. J. Nolland cites it (as Hebrew) in his art. "Classical and Rabbinical Parallels to 'Physician, Heal Yourself' (Lk. IV 23)" in *NovT* 21 (1979) 205; he was not aware of the *Tanḥuma* passage.

[88] Cf. Isa 29:18-19 and 35:5-6, as well as Matt 11:4-5 // Luke 7:21-22. Isa 61:1 may also be in the background here.

land / earth." This refers to 1 Kgs 17:1 regarding Elijah's causing dew and rain (from heaven) to cease "these years." 1 Kgs 18:1 then notes that after "many days" the Lord told Elijah "in the third year" that He would send rain on the face of "the earth." Verse 2 adds that "the famine was severe" (הָרָעָב חָזָק) in Samaria.

Judaic tradition on these verses explains the puzzling "three years and six months" instead of three years, and the great famine's being over "all the land / earth" in Jesus' remarks. In the official chronology of early Judaism, *Seder 'Olam*, chapter 17 states that "In the thirteenth year of Ahab there was 'a great famine' (רעב גדול) in Samaria three years...." The Oxford MS has at this point, however, "three years 'and a half'" (ומחצה),[89] agreeing with Jesus' statement. The extra six months derive from haggadic interpretation of the "many days" (יָמִים רַבִּים) of 1 Kgs 18:1. The latter verse is cited in *Esth. Rab.* 2/2 on Esth 1:4, "for many days, one hundred and eighty in all."[90] That is, as "many days" in Esth 1:4 specifically means 180 days or six months of thirty days each, so the "many days" of 1 Kgs 18:1 mean six months, added to the three years of the text to make three years and six months, as in *Seder 'Olam* 17, MS Oxford, on the "great famine's" lasting three and a half years.[91]

"The earth" (הָאֲדָמָה) in 1 Kgs 18:1 was also interpreted in Judaic tradition as "the world." *Eliyyahu Zuṭa* 8 has Elijah relate to Ahab the contents of 1 Kgs 17:1. "Then Elijah took the key to rain and went away. 'And there was a great famine in the entire world' until God said to Elijah" 1 Kgs 18:1. The latter sentence in single quotation marks is: 92. והיה רעב גדול בכול העולם כולו

---

[89] Milikowsky 323 and 497. The MS is described on pp. 47-48.
[90] Cf. Wilna 9 or 5a; Soncino 9.34. These were days of grief / trouble (צער - Jastrow 1295).
[91] Thus the number in Luke 4:25 has nothing at all to do with *apocalyptic* persecution and distress. Cf. also J. Jeremias, art. Ἠλ(ε)ίας in *TDNT* 2.934, with n. 52. Against Nolland, *Luke 1 - 9:20*, p. 194, dependent on others at this point.
[92] Friedmann 185-186; cf. the paraphrastic translation of Braude and Kapstein 436.

This corresponds almost exactly to Luke 4:25, ἐγένετο λιμὸς μέγας ἐπὶ πᾶσαν τὴν γῆν, whereby γῆ means "world"[93] and not "land," as in the Hebrew "Vorlage."

Yet why did Jesus emphasize to the Nazarites Elijah's being sent (the divine passive) not to one of the many widows in Israel, but to a widow in Zaraphath of Sidon (4:26)? 1 Kgs 16:31 notes that King Ahab married Jezebel, daughter of King Ethbaal of the "Sidonians," and worshiped her pagan god Baal. The widow of Zaraphath[94] was thus also a pagan in the middle of Baal country. However, in contrast to the Nazarites' behavior imputed to them by Jesus, Judaic tradition emphasizes that the pagan widow of Zaraphath received the prophet with great hospitality, even sharing everything she had with him (1 Kgs 17:15). *Pirq. R. El.* 33 notes that she "received him with great honor."[95] *Cant. Rab.* 2:5 § 3 states that the widow "gave him a good welcome and waited on him."[96] *Exod. Rab.* Shemoth 4/2 on Exod 4:18 relates regarding Elijah's reception by the widow: "a man must respect one by whom he is hospitably received, even more than his father or mother."[97]

The latter may have been behind Special Luke's having Jesus note in Luke 4:26 that God sent the prophet to a pagan foreigner and not to an Israelite widow. The woman from Zaraphath received Elijah hospitably (in contrast to Elijah's reception in Israel, for he had to flee east of the Jordan – 1 Kgs 17:5). Because he was received so well, Elijah could then perform the miracle of restoring the widow's dead son to life. This in turn led her to acknowledge him as a prophet of the Lord,[98] in whom God was truly active (17:24). Yet the Nazarites' lack of trust in their

---

[93] Cf. BAGD 157, 5.b.
[94] Josephus in *Ant.* 8.320 says the site lay between Sidon and Tyre. His haggadic additions to the entire account in 319-337 betray very early Judaic interpretation of the narrative.
[95] Eshkol 113; Friedlander 240.
[96] Donsqi 62; Soncino 9.110.
[97] Mirqin 5.85; Soncino 3.78.
[98] Cf. the Targum of 1 Kgs 17:24 (Sperber 2.256; Harrington and Saldarini 250).

"hometown boy" as a prophet prevented him from doing any signs / miracles / healings there.[99]

Jesus' allusion to the pagan widow of Zaraphath thus was the third stage in the crescendo leading to the Nazarites' later attempt to hurl him to his death from a cliff. The fourth and final stage in this crescendo also deals with a pagan foreigner.

4.4 The Healing of the Leper Naaman the Syrian and Elisha

Luke 4:27 has Jesus tell his former fellow citizens in the synagogue of Nazareth: "There were also many lepers in Israel in the time of the prophet Elisha, and none of them was cleansed except Naaman the Syrian."

This narrative is related in 2 Kings 5. Naaman was commander of the army of the king of Aram (Syria), in high favor with his master because the Lord had given victory (over Israel) to Aram through him, a mighty warrior (2 Kgs 5:1). The narrative is related in Judaic tradition to Elijah's telling the Israelite King *Ahab* there would be a drought (during which period he brought the son of the widow of Zaraphath back to life [1 Kgs 17:1 and 18:1-2, with 17:8-24]). Naaman the Syrian is then the "certain man" who drew his bow, shot his arrow and fatally wounded King *Ahab* in battle (1 Kgs 22:34).[100]

Here Naaman, like the widow of Zaraphath, was a pagan when Elisha "healed" him.[101] *Tanh.* B Meṣorʿa 4 on Lev 14:1-2 states for example that he and the King of Syria were "idolaters."[102] Only after Elisha cured him did he state: "Now I

---

[99] Special Luke certainly knew of the Semitic narrative behind Mark 6:1-6a, including the relevant statements in vv 5-6a.

[100] Cf. *Midr. Pss.* 78/11 on Ps 78:45 (Buber 350; Braude 2.31). It is related by Rabbi (Yehuda ha-Nasi), a fourth generation Tanna (Strack and Stemberger, *Introduction* 89-90).

[101] *Deut. Rab.* Ha'azinu 10/3 (Mirqin 11.143; Soncino 7.166) relates that just as God heals without bandages, so Elisha, being one of the righteous who have power over the same things as God, "healed" (רפא) Naaman without a bandage / plaster / compress.

[102] Buber 43 or 22a; Bietenhard 2.71. Later he was thought to only partly acknowledge idols, as in *Deut. Rab.* Vaethchanan 2/26-27 (Soncino 7.56); to be a Noachide (*b. Sanh.* 74b-75a in Soncino 505); or a

know that there is no God in all the earth except in Israel." Then he took Israelite earth home to Syria and asked in advance to be pardoned for accompanying the Syrian king into the pagan temple of Rimmon (2 Kgs 5:15-19).

When Jesus states in Luke 4:27 that the (pagan) leper Naaman the Syrian was cleansed in the days of Elisha the prophet, while there were plenty of other lepers in Israel, he particularly incensed his fellow Jews in Nazareth. This in part was because pagans / Gentiles were considered "sinners." A good example of this attitude is found in the statement of the converted Jewish Christian Paul in Gal 2:15, "We ourselves are Jews by birth and not Gentile sinners." The Syrians (like Naaman) of 167 BCE are also described as "a sinful people" in 1 Macc 1:34, and the Romans as such in 63 BCE in *Pss. Sol.* 1:1 and 2:1-2. Romans are also meant when Jesus says he will now be betrayed into the hands of "sinners" in the Garden of Gethsemane (Mark 14:41). Finally, a Jewish tax collector, looked down upon by his fellow citizens because of collaboration with the occupational power Rome and because of his own avarice, is classified with a (Jewish) sinner in Luke 7:34 and 15:1, but with a Gentile in Matt 18:17.

These examples suffice to point out how pagans / Gentiles were considered by Palestinian Jews in the first century CE to be "sinners." When Jesus cited God's sending the prophets Elijah and Elisha to just such persons, and not to them, God's own chosen people, the children of Abraham, this not only angered them, it thoroughly incensed them.[103] This had immediate consequences.

---

resident alien (*b. Sanh.* 96b in Soncino 652, with n. 2, and *b. Giṭ.* 57b in Soncino 265, with n. 7). *Mek.* Amalek 3 on Exod 18:11 (Lauterbach 2.176) praises Naaman in contrast to Jethro, quoting 2 Kgs 5:15.

[103] Related to this theme is Jesus' making a Samaritan the hero of his parable in Luke 10:30-37, and in 17:11-19, as well as rabbinic praise of two Gentiles in order to denounce their fellow Jews' behavior. Cf. the sources I cite in *Weihnachtsgeschichte, Barmherziger Samariter, Verlorener Sohn. Studien zu ihrem jüdischen Hintergrund* (ANTZ 2; Berlin: Institut Kirche und Judentum, 1988) 123. See also Jesus' statement in Matt 8:10

Catchword Connections

Now "all (the Nazarites) in the synagogue were filled with rage when they heard these things" (Luke 4:28). Then they proceeded to try to kill Jesus (vv 29-30).

"They were filled with rage" is the Greek ἐπλήσθησαν ... θυμοῦ. In the LXX, θυμός is employed seventy-eight times for חֵמָה, which is literally "heat," then "burning anger, rage."[104] Dan 3:19 has the similar Aramaic phrase הִתְמְלִי חֱמָא, "he was filled with rage."[105] *Num. Rab.* 20/21 on Num 24:3 relates for example concerning a husband's reaction to his wife's behavior: "He was filled with rage towards her and killed her." The first half is the Aramaic: נִתְמַלִי עָלֶיהָ חֵמָה.[106] The result of such heated anger or rage is here the same as the Nazarites' behavior in Luke 4:29. It is thus very probable that precisely this terminology lies behind the Greek expression of v 28, "filled with rage."[107]

I suggest that Special Luke borrowed this "rage" imagery from the story of Naaman in 2 Kings 5, to which he had just alluded. Verse 11 states that when Elisha told him via a messenger to wash in the Jordan seven times, "Naaman 'became angry' and went away...." The first verb is וַיִּקְצֹף,[108] for which the LXX has ἐθυμώθη. The next verse, 12, relates that Naaman then "turned and went away in a 'rage.'" The latter noun is חֵמָה, burning anger, rage, as noted above. The LXX has θυμός, as in Luke 4:28.

Here Naaman "becomes angry" and departs in a "rage." He thinks the prophet Elisha, who at his home had told Naaman via a messenger how the cure of his leprosy was to take place at the

---

// Luke 7:9 regarding the centurion in Capernaum, as well as the role of Tyre and Sidon in Matt 11:21-23 // Luke 10:13-15.
[104] BDB 404,2; cf. Jastrow 475.
[105] On מלא, cf. BDB 569-570 and 1100, as well as Jastrow 785, to be filled / full.
[106] Mirqin 10.269; Soncino 6.817, which translates freely: "He flew into a passion...."
[107] Cf. the Hebrew New Testaments of Delitzsch (108), and the United Bible Societies (157, however with כַּעַס).
[108] On קָצַף, cf. BDB 893. The hithpael means "put oneself in a rage."

Jordan River, should rather come out himself and perform the cure (5:11). The inhabitants of Nazareth also expect that the prophet Jesus should perform a cure / healing or another such miracle / sign in their midst and not elsewhere, such as in Capernaum. His refusal to do so and his castigation of them by means of the prophet proverb and the examples of the pagan foreigners, the widow of Zaraphath and Naaman the Syrian, incense them so much that in their burning rage they decide to murder Jesus. The crescendo has now reached its climax.

4.5 Jesus as the Scapegoat

Burning with anger, those in the Nazareth synagogue "rose, drove [Jesus] out of town and led him to the brow / edge of the hill on which their town was built in order to throw / hurl him headlong down. Yet he passed through their midst and went his way" (Luke 4:29-30).

Jesus' simply passing through the midst of the Nazarites and going his own way (v 30) suggests the miraculous.[109] It recalls passages in the Gospel of John such as 7:30 ("his hour had not yet come"), 44-46; 8:59; and 10:39. Irony is probably involved here. He who refused to perform a miracle / sign in order to confirm his being a true prophet now miraculously escapes their attempt to murder him. His countrymen's striving to kill Jesus will not be successful at the beginning, but only at the very end of his ministry, at Golgotha.

The "brow / edge" (ὀφρῦς) of a hill in Luke 4:29 occurs only here in the NT,[110] which is also true for "to throw / hurl headlong down" (κατακρημνίζω).[111] Special Luke borrowed this imagery from the place where the scapegoat was hurled down from a precipice to its death on the Day of Atonement, as I shall point out below.

---

[109] Cf. S. MacLean Gilmour in "The Gospel According to St. Luke" in *IB* (1952) 8.95, and C. F. Evans, *Saint Luke* 275.
[110] BAGD 600.
[111] LSJ 896: throw down a precipice; generally, throw down headlong; BAGD 412.

C. Kopp correctly notes that Judaic legal procedure is unaware of killing someone by hurling him down from a steep precipice to be smashed to death.[112] The death penalty was rather administered either by burning, beheading, strangling or stoning someone (*m. Sanh.* 7:1).[113] Various commentators have attempted to recognize the procedure of stoning in Luke 4:29. The Mishnah describes the place of stoning in *Sanh.* 6:4 as "twice the height of a man." One of the witnesses first "knocked him down" (דּוֹחֲפוֹ) onto his loins (probably by throwing a stone onto him).[114] If the victim survived this and turned over onto his heart (stomach), the first witness turned him onto his back (and stoned him again). If he was still alive, the second witness stoned him from the heart side. If the victim survived even this, all joined in stoning him.[115]

Stoning cannot be meant in Luke 4:29, however. First, hurling someone headlong down the brow of a hill implies a much greater distance than twice the height of a man. Secondly, no mention whatsoever is made in the text of "stoning." If the careful Greek stylist Luke had wanted to imply it, he would have changed the verb κατακρημνίζω in the Special Lukan material at his disposal here to his own term, λιθοβολέω,[116] as in the stoning of Stephen in Acts 7:58. His not doing so shows that something else was involved, which he chose to preserve as it was in his source. Thirdly, Jesus could only have been stoned as a blasphemer here (*m. Sanh.* 7:4). Yet since he is not described

---

[112] Cf. his *Die heiligen Stätten der Evangelien* (Regensburg: Pustet, 1959) 122.
[113] Albeck 4.189; Danby 391; Neusner 595-596.
[114] Jastrow 293 on דָּחַף : to push, thrust, knock down. The verb is employed interchangeably with דָּחָה. A stone was most probably already used at this first stage, for a fall from such a short height would seldom kill someone.
[115] Cf. n. 113. Neusner's "pushing him over" is misleading, for stoning ("knocking him down") is most probably meant from the outset.
[116] BAGD 474.

as pronouncing the divine name, this possibility is excluded (7:5).[117]

Luke 4:29 says the Nazarites led Jesus out of town to the brow of the hill on which their town was built in order to throw Jesus headlong down from it. No precipitous site can be located anywhere close to ancient Nazareth, which rather lay on a slope. Thus Christian tradition later invented such a site, ca. 2.5 kilometers southeast of the town, which was thought to correspond to Luke's description.[118]

J. Fitzmyer considers the above problem "probably only another instance of Luke's vague awareness of Palestinian geography."[119] Yet the incident is not from the Third Evangelist, but from Special Luke, who described the site of Nazareth in the terms of 4:29 for theological reasons, to be outlined below. The Third Evangelist appropriated the imagery as he found it in his source.

Finally, the scene of v 29 does not portray a "lynching" justified by Zealotic behavior as described in *m. Sanh.* 9:6[120] and

---

[117] Cf. Deut 13:10, often cited in this respect. It deals, however, with idolatry, clearly not the case with Jesus in Nazareth. K. Rengstorf in *Das Evangelium des Lukas* (NTD 3; Göttingen: Vandenhoeck & Ruprecht, 1958⁸) 68 incorrectly advocates blasphemy here.

[118] Cf. Kopp, *Die heiligen Stätten* 124-125, as well as pictures 11 and 12 of the mountains from which and to which Jesus ostensibly leaped. See already G. Dalman, *Orte und Wege Jesu* (Gütersloh: Bertelsmann, 1924³) 70 and 83-84.

[119] Cf. his *The Gospel According to Luke (I-IX)* 538. See also S. Lachs, *A Rabbinic Commentary on the New Testament. The Gospels of Matthew, Mark and Luke* (Hoboken, New Jersey: KTAV, 1987) 57. G. Schneider in *Das Evangelium nach Lukas, Kapitel 1-10* (ÖTKNT 3/1; Gütersloh: Mohn; Würzburg: Echter, 1977) 110 also asserts that "the Evangelist did not know that Nazareth did not lie on a mountain (at the most 'next to' a mountain)."

[120] Albeck 4.201; Danby 396-397; Neusner 604. Correctly seen already by P. Billerbeck in Str-B 2.157, who may be dependent here on J. Lightfoot, *A Commentary on the New Testament from the Talmud and Hebraica* (Peabody, MASS: Hendrickson, 1989; original Oxford University Press, 1859) 3.76.

which forms for example the background of the story of the adulteress "caught in the act" in John 7:53 – 8:11.[121]

Rather, Jesus is portrayed in Luke 4:29 as the scapegoat, killed on the Day of Atonement by being hurled down a steep precipice. Based on the description of Leviticus 16, *m. Yoma* 6 gives the procedure as practiced up until the destruction of the Temple in Jerusalem in 70 CE. There is no reason to doubt its basic historicity. The following six points of similarity can be ascertained between this ritual and the description found in Luke 4:29.

a) Jesus' Appearing Alone in Nazareth

In Mark 6:1-6a, known in an earlier Semitic form to Special Luke, Jesus went to his hometown, "and his disciples followed him" (v 1). That is, they are represented as being with him during his entire stay in Nazareth.

This is strikingly not the case in Special Luke's version of Jesus' rejection there in what is now found in Luke 4:16-30. Jesus is alone from the very beginning. First, this enables the narrator to concentrate all the attention on Jesus. The eyes of "all" in the synagogue are fixed on him (v 20). More importantly, however, when the Nazarites seek to kill Jesus by hurling him off the cliff of the hill on which the town was built, his disciples are not present in order to object or physically to defend him. Nor do they flee, as is later the case in the Garden of Gethsemane when Jesus is arrested (Mark 14:50 par.). They are simply not present at all in Nazareth.

Jesus is represented by Special Luke as being alone in his hometown because he describes him in terms of the scapegoat. On the Day of Atonement it is also led out of the city (Jerusalem) to the precipice of a hill, from which it is hurled down to its death – alone (*m. Yoma* 6:6).[122]

---

[121] Cf. my essay "'Caught in the Act' – With Whom, and By Whom? The Judaic Background of the Incident of the Adulteress in John 7:53 – 8:11" in *"Caught in the Act," Walking on the Sea, and the Release of Barabbas Revisited* 1-48.
[122] Albeck 2.241; Danby 170; Neusner 275.

b) The Scapegoat as Sent Out of the City

The Mishnah at *Yoma* 4:2 already states that the High Priest "bound a thread of crimson wool on the head of the scapegoat 'to be sent off' (הַמִּשְׁתַּלֵּחַ) and turned it towards the way by which it was to be sent out (בֵּית שִׁלּוּחוֹ) (of the Temple, the Temple Mount, and the city of Jerusalem to the wilderness)."[123] This "being sent" probably lies behind the verb ἐκβάλλω employed of the Nazarites' driving or sending Jesus out of their town in Luke 4:28.[124]

c) "Leading Away" the Scapegoat to the Site of its Being Killed

Yoma 6:2-3 states that after the High Priest placed his hands on the scapegoat, praying to God that it bear the "iniquities, transgressions and sins" of all Israel, they delivered it "to the individual who was to lead it away" (לְמִי שֶׁהָיָה מוֹלִיכוֹ - 6:3).[125] The hiphil of הלך is employed here, meaning to lead away / out.[126] It forms the background of the verb ἄγω in the aorist form ἤγαγον in Luke 4:29, "*they led* him *away / out* to the brow of the hill...."

Yoma 6:4 then relates that a "causeway" or a kind of narrow bridge or ramp (כֶּבֶשׁ)[127] was made for the scapegoat because of the Alexandrians, who before its construction used to pull the scapegoat's hair and shout: "Bear [our sins] and depart, bear [our sins] and depart!"[128] S. Safrai and M. Avi-Yonah report that this causeway "extended from the southern end of the Eastern Wall toward the desert. Remains of it have been found close to

---

[123] Albeck 2.233; Danby 166, whose translation I cite here; Neusner 270.
[124] Cf. BAGD 237,2.: send out, send away, lead out.
[125] Albeck 2.240; Danby 169; Neusner 275. The hiphil is then repeated three times. For the complete MS tradition of *Yoma* 6, see J. Meinhold, *Joma* 58-65.
[126] BDB 236,2., and Jastrow 353.
[127] Jastrow 611.
[128] Albeck 2.240. I slightly modify Danby's translation on p. 169.

the southeastern corner of the Temple Mount...."[129] Archaeology thus supports the statement of the Mishnah at this point.[130]

d) *Jerusalem's Eminent Citizens Accompany the Scapegoat*

Yoma 6:4 continues by stating that "the eminent people" (יַקִּירֵי) of Jerusalem[131] used to accompany him (the individual who led the scapegoat away) to the first of ten booths located between Jerusalem and the צוֹק (see e) below). Others according to 6:5 went with him to the tenth booth. There "they stood at a distance and beheld what he did."[132]

Special Luke appropriated the first motif by having those in the synagogue of Nazareth (where the leadership of the town would all be gathered to worship on the Sabbath) rise, drive / send Jesus out of their city, and lead him to the place where they wanted to hurl him to his death (4:29).

e) *The Steep Precipice (צוֹק), a Hill / Mountain*

Yoma 6:4-5 then describes how the individual sent off with the scapegoat led it from Jerusalem to its death in the wilderness (Lev 16:10, 21-22) at the צוֹק . This is not a "ravine," as Danby and Neusner translate, since that term emphasizes what is below, not a site much higher than the present level. From the

---

[129] Cf. their art. "Temple" in *EJ* (1971) 15.964. This causeway is also mentioned in *m. Šeq.* 4:2 and should be differentiated from that for the red heifer.

[130] There is thus no need to ask whether an attempted murder of Jesus is borrowed from another geographical site and inserted at Nazareth. On this suggestion, see L. Brun, "Der Besuch Jesu in Nazareth nach Lukas" in *Serta Rudbergiana*, ed. H. Holst and H. Mørland (Oslo: Brøgger, 1931) 15.

[131] Meinhold, *Joma* 61 and 59, with variants on p. 79 for יקירי ; Albeck 2.240 has מִיקִירֵי , "some of the eminent people." On the noun, see Jastrow 591.

[132] Albeck 2.241; Danby 170; Neusner 275. Literally "one stands...," but all those accompanying are meant, as in Danby. This imagery is behind Mark 15:40, where at Jesus' death on the Cross, women (stood and) "looked on from afar." Cf. my *The Wicked Tenants and Gethsemane* 121-122 for a more detailed analysis of this.

root "to be narrow," צוֹק means a "narrow point, peak, precipice."[133] *Yoma* 6:6 also describes it as located at the top of a הַר, a hill or mountain.[134]

These two expressions lie behind the "brow of the hill / mountain" (ὀφρὺς τοῦ ὄρους) on which Nazareth was built in Luke 4:29. Employing artistic freedom, Special Luke transferred specific terminology from the wilderness site at which the scapegoat was hurled to its death to Jesus' hometown, Nazareth, outside of which he was to be hurled down to his own death.

f) Pushing the Scapegoat Headlong Down to its Death

Yoma 6:6 says that after the individual entrusted with leading the scapegoat from Jerusalem to the *ṣoq* in the wilderness divided the thread of crimson wool, tying half to the rock (סֶלַע - at the top of the *ṣoq*) and half between its horns (see again *Yoma* 4:2), he "pushed it from behind" (וּדְחָפוֹ לַאֲחוֹרָיו). It therefore rolled and went down (מִתְגַּלְגֵּל וְיוֹרֵד), and it did not reach the middle of the hill / mountain before it broke into pieces. The same section speaks of "pushing it from the *ṣoq*" (דְּחִיָתוֹ לַצּוֹק).[135] If the scapegoat somehow survived this ordeal, the accompanying person went down after it and killed it, according to *t. Yoma* 3:14.[136] This was due to the principle: without blood, no atonement (Lev 17:11).

The verb דָּחַף is first employed above for "pushing" the scapegoat to its death, and then in the same section the verb דְּחִי. They are used interchangeably as to push, thrust, knock

---

[133] Jastrow 1270; see also Levy 4.180. Cf. the statement by L. Jung in the Soncino edition of *b. Yoma* (312, n. 6): "Lit., 'the peak,' the mountain top from which the scapegoat was precipitated. Also used to denote the precipice itself." See also 316, n. 2.

[134] Cf. also *Sifra* Aḥare Mot, Pereq 2, § 177 on Lev 16:7-10, where it is described as "a steep / rough [קשה] place in the hills / mountains" (Weiss 81a; Neusner 3.16).

[135] Albeck 2.241; Danby 170; Neusner 275. Here one could also translate "into the ravine," meaning down the side of the *ṣoq*.

[136] Zuckermandel / Liebermann 188; Neusner 2.203.

down.¹³⁷ They lie behind the rare κατακρημνίζω in Luke 4:29, found only here in the NT. The Greek verb means to throw down a precipice, to throw down headlong, to throw someone down from a cliff.¹³⁸

Josephus employs the verb κατακρημνίζω eight times, two of them (*Bell.* 1.57 and *Ant.* 13.231) describing how when John Hyrcanus in 135/134 BCE besieged the fortress Dagon above Jericho, Ptolemy tortured his relatives directly before Hyrcanus below. He also threatened to "hurl them down headlong" over the battlement (to their certain death) if he did not abandon the siege. This is the "little stronghold" Dok (Δωκ) mentioned in 1 Macc 16:15, and called דוק in the Copper Scroll of Qumran, 3Q 15, col. 7.11.¹³⁹ Its peak is more than 500 meters above the surrounding area, with a very good view of the Mount of Olives to the west.¹⁴⁰ It is tempting not only to consider this to be the "Mount of Temptation," the "very high mountain" of Matt 4:8 // Luke 4:5, but also the ṣoq, the site from which the scapegoat

---

¹³⁷ Cf. Jastrow 293 and 291, respectively. In *b. Yoma* 67b on *m.*6:6 (Soncino 317), R. Simeon employs the less frequently found verb זרק (Jastrow 415: to cast, throw) for flinging the scapegoat down headlong. See the similar statement in *Sifra* Aḥare Mot, Parasha 5 § 184 on Lev 16:26-28 (Weiss 82b; Neusner 3.38).

¹³⁸ LSJ 896; BAGD 412. Such situations are described in 2 Chr 25:12 and 4 Macc 4:25. See also Philo, *Spec. Leg.* 3.149. In *Post.* 72 the Alexandrian employs in a metaphorical sense the verbs ἀνατρέπω and καταβάλλω (LSJ 124 and 884) for "overthrowing" and "casting down" diseases and sicknesses as referred to in the second goat of Lev 16:8 and 10. He thus also knew of the scapegoat's being "thrown down" from a precipice. It is incomprehensible to me how U. Busse in *Das Nazareth-Manifest. Eine Einführung in das lukanische Jesusbild nach Lk 4,16-30* (SBS 91; Stuttgart: Katholisches Bibelwerk, 1978) 45, n. 59, can state: "idiomatisch sind die Begriffe 'an den Rand des Berges' und 'hinabstürzen.'" What do these "idioms" mean for him, and where do they come from?

¹³⁹ Cf. J. Milik on it in *DJD* 3.265, and Martínez and Ligchelaar, *The Dead Sea Scrolls Study Edition* 1.236. A good overview of the site is given in O. Keel and M. Küchler, *Orte und Landschaften der Bibel* (Zurich: Benziger; Göttingen: Vandenhoeck & Ruprecht, 1982) 2.550-554.

¹⁴⁰ Cf. Keel and Küchler, 550 and 554.

was hurled down to its death.[141] Its distance from Jerusalem corresponds to the twelve Roman miles indicated in *Yoma* 6:4. More, unfortunately, cannot be said.

By employing the Semitic original behind κατακρημνίζω, either דחף or דחא, דחה, דחי, Special Luke conclusively betrays his dependence on terminology employed of the scapegoat's being "pushed down" to its death from the precipice of a hill / mountain on the Day of Atonement. This tradition later entered the Mishnah at *Yoma* 6, back to back with the description of the High Priest publicly reading from Scripture in *Yoma* 7:1, pointed out above in section II.1) as the background of Jesus' reading Scripture out loud in the Nazareth synagogue.

The body and blood of the scapegoat were considered to make atonement / expiation. Lev 16:9-10 for example reads: "Aaron shall present the goat on which the lot fell for the Lord, and offer it as a sin offering; 10) but the goat on which the lot fell for Azazel shall be presented alive before the Lord to make atonement over it, that it may be sent away [lit. 'to send it away'] into the wilderness to Azazel" (NRSV).

Sifra, the Tannaitic commentary on Leviticus, notes at Aḥare Mot, Pereq 2 § 177, that R. Simeon (b. Yoḥai, a third generation Tanna)[142] explains the phrase "to make atonement over it" (לכפר עליו) regarding the scapegoat in Lev 16:10, as "atonement / expiation which takes place via its body" (כפרה שהיא בגופו).[143] That is, only when the "body"

---

[141] Cf. the older commentaries mentioned in Meinhold, *Joma* 63. It should also be noted that the devil challenges Jesus to "throw himself down" from the pinnacle of the Jerusalem Temple (Matt 4:6 // Luke 4:9), most probably the SE corner, from which the scapegoat was also led out into the wilderness.
[142] Strack and Stemberger, *Introduction* 84.
[143] Weiss 81a; cf. the English translation of Neusner in 3.16, and the German of Winter at 454.

(גּוּף)¹⁴⁴ is hurled down to its death from the precipice ṣoq in the wilderness does atonement / expiation (כַּפָּרָה) ¹⁴⁵ come about.

The midrash continues by citing the following phrase "to send it away" in Lev 16:10. It comments: "That, when the blood was shed / poured out (נִשְׁפַּךְ), the [goat] which is sent away [must] die. [When] the [goat] which is sent away is to die, the blood is to be shed / poured out (יִשָּׁפֵךְ)." ¹⁴⁶   The niphal of שָׁפַךְ , to pour out, / shed,¹⁴⁷ is employed here of the scapegoat's blood. It must be shed in order to effect atonement / expiation for all the iniquities, transgressions and sins of the people of Israel, which it bears upon itself (Lev 16:21-22).

As is well-known, similar imagery is employed by Jesus at the "Lord's Supper," when he labels the bread his "body" and the wine in the Passover cup the "blood" of his covenant, "poured out / shed" for many (Mark 14:22-24; Matt 26:28 adds to the latter "for the forgiveness of sins"). This anticipated his death on the Cross the next day, Jesus' own "Day of Atonement" for others. From the very outset, his followers interpreted Jesus' giving his body and shedding his blood on the Cross as his making atonement / expiation for them. There is even good reason to believe that the place-name "Golgotha" (Γολγοθᾶ, Aramaic גּוּלְגַּלְתָּא , Mark 15:22 par.) may derive from imagery connected with the ṣoq, where the scapegoat was killed.¹⁴⁸   After being pushed down headlong, it "rolls" (מִתְגַּלְגֵּל) and descends, not getting halfway down the hill before it breaks into

---

¹⁴⁴ Jastrow 225.
¹⁴⁵ Jastrow 662. The piel of the cognate verb כָּפַר means to forgive, atone, procure forgiveness (661-662).
¹⁴⁶ Weiss 81a; cf. the German translation of Winter on p. 454. Neusner at 3.16 interprets differently.
¹⁴⁷ Jastrow 1616-1617.
¹⁴⁸ Numerous commentators, for example, connect Luke 4:29 with the later crucifixion of Jesus. Cf. J. Fitzmyer, *The Gospel According to Luke (I-IX)* 538: "This crucial statement in Luke's account foreshadows the locale of the crucifixion itself (23:26)." See also E. Ellis, *The Gospel of Luke* (NCB; London: Oliphants, 1977) 98, and J. Green, *The Gospel of Luke* (NICNT 3; Grand Rapids, Michigan: Eerdmans, 1997) 218-219.

pieces (*m. Yoma* 6:6).[149] As remarked above, the women's standing and "looking on from afar" at Jesus' crucifixion in Mark 15:40 par. also derives from imagery connected with watching the death of the scapegoat.[150]

* * *

The analysis of the above six motifs and expressions from the known Judaic procedure for killing the scapegoat by hurling it headlong down to its death from the precipice of a hill / mountain, makes it almost certain that Special Luke employed this Day of Atonement imagery for Jesus in what is now found in Luke 4:29. When coupled with sections 1. – 4. above, this analysis of v 29 provides a strong cumulative argument for Special Luke's casting his entire narrative of Jesus' rejection in Nazareth in light of imagery from the Day of Atonement, which has been basically unrecognized up to now.[151]

III. The Original Language, Provenance and Date

1. *The Original Language*

Throughout this essay I have argued for a Semitic background to Special Luke's account of Jesus' rejection in

---

[149] Cf. the detailed discussion of this I offer in *The Wicked Tenants and Gethsemane* 122-127.
[150] Cf. n. 132.
[151] The only exception is C. Perrot. In his "Luc 4, 16-30 et la lecture biblique de l'ancienne synagogue" in *RevScRel* 47 (1973) 324-340, he also noted that Isa 57:15 – 58:14 is read on the Day of Atonement, the Jubilee year begins on the same day (332), and the most favorable time for the incident's taking place is Tishri (336). See also his *La Lecture de la Bible dans la Synagogue. Les anciennes lectures palestiniennes du Shabbat et des fêtes* (Hildesheim: Gerstenberg, 1973), 195-204 on Luke 4:16-30. Perrot thinks the homily of Luke 4:21-27 may in reality be the echo of a Christian homily from the diaspora, in Greek (195, n. 31; 197). The opposite is the case. It is from the Palestinian Jewish Christian Special Luke, who composed it in a Semitic language, as shown above. Nor does later Christian tradition attempt to legitimate the reading of the Bible in Christian services through Jesus' example here (p. 204).

Catchword Connections

Nazareth. While the Third Evangelist later appropriated this anecdote and undoubtedly modified some of the original terminology (available to him in a Hellenistic Jewish Christian's Greek translation), as he did with the Gospel of Mark in general,[152] numerous features from the Semitic original are still observable.

a) Verse 16 has Ναζαρά for Nazareth.[153] Luke himself employs Ναζαρέθ in 1:26; 2:4, 39 and 51; and Acts 10:38.

b) The term βιβλίον, (a biblical) book or scroll, in vv 17 and 20 is סֵפֶר or סִפְרָא, betraying a Semitic source. The Third Evangelist would have employed βίβλος, as in 3:4; 20:42; Acts 1:20; 7:42; (and 19:19). The verb ἀναπλήσσω in Luke 4:17 and πλήσσω in v 20 for "unrolling" and "rolling up" a scroll or biblical book, occur only here in the NT, and both translate the Semitic גלל. The noun ὑπηρέτης in v 20 is also only found here in the NT of a synagogue "attendant." It is the Semitic חַזָּן.

In combination the above terms, now Greek but peculiar to this earliest description of a Palestinian synagogue service, also point to a Semitic background to the account.

c) The catchword רָצוֹן / רָצָה lying behind the quotations of Isa 61:1-2 and 58:6 in Luke 4:18-19; words of "grace" in v 22; and a prophet as "acceptable" in v 24, is Semitic. It was properly cited as, and later translated into, δεκτός in vv 19 and 24. (The apparent catchword ἄφεσις in LXX Isa 61:1 and 58:6 cited in

---

[152] For an excellent stylistic analysis of 4:16-30 in regard to what is from tradition and what is typically Lukan, cf. J. Jeremias, *Die Sprache des Lukasevangeliums. Redaktion und Tradition im Nicht-Markusstoff des dritten Evangeliums* (Kritisch-exegetischer Kommentar zum Neuen Testament, Sonderband; Göttingen: Vandenhoeck & Ruprecht, 1980) 119-128. U. Busse's assertion that Luke incorporated stylistic elements from Hellenistic historiography falls apart if the narrative is basically from Special Luke. See his *Das Nazareth-Manifest* 55-62 and 115-116.

[153] In his art. "Ναζαρέθ / Ναζαρά Ναζαρηνός / Ναζωραῖος" in *ZNW* 72 (1981) 257-263, H. Rüger notes that some Palestinian place-names have the variant feminine endings תָ and תָ. He suggests this for the Semitic forms of Nazareth (259).

Luke 4:18 is not found in the Hebrew original as a catchword and is purely accidental here.)

d) "He began to say" (ἤρξατο δὲ λέγειν) in v 21 is Semitic; in Hebrew it could be וְהִתְחִיל לְדַבֵּר . B. Violet suggests the Aramaic שְׁרִי for "beginning."[154]

e) The closest parallel to the proverb "Physician, heal yourself (first)!" in v 23 is found in Aramaic, as pointed out in section II.4.2 above.

f) The term ἀμήν in v 24 is the Semitic אָמֵן.[155]

g) The expression ἐπ' ἀληθείας in v 25, "in truth," "truly," is the Semitic בֶּאֱמֶת , as described in section I.3.4 above.

h) The phrases "three years and six months" and "a great famine over all the land / earth" in v 25 derive from Judaic interpretation of 1 Kgs 18:1-2, only found in Palestinian Semitic sources.

i) J. Wellhausen argued that the Greek εἰ μή in v 26 derives from the Semitic אֶלָּא (אֶלָא) : except, but, only.[156] He also maintained that the expression γυναῖκα χήραν, "a widow woman," at the end of the verse is a translation error from the Aramaic אַרְמְלָא , "widow,"[157] read as אַרְמָאי , "Syrian."[158] This would not be possible in Hebrew, where "widow" is אַלְמָנָה.[159]

j) The very rare term ὀφρῦς, "brow" of the hill / mountain on which Nazareth was built in v 29, only occurs here in the NT, and in the LXX as the plural "(eye-)brows" (Lev 14:9), where it translates the Hebrew גַּב .[160] In rabbinic Hebrew (and Aramaic)

---

[154] Jastrow 1630,3: trnsf. to start, begin; Violet, "Zum rechten Verständnis" 259-260.
[155] Jastrow 77.
[156] Jastrow 66.
[157] Jastrow 123.
[158] Jastrow 122. See his *Das Evangelium Lucae* (Berlin: Georg Reimer, 1904) 10-11.
[159] Jastrow 72. Cf. the אִשָּׁה אַלְמָנָה of the "widow woman" of Zaraphath in 1 Kgs 17:9-10.
[160] BDB 146,5.

the latter can mean the "upper part" of a thing,[161] so it could be behind the ὀφρῦς of v 29.[162] Yet רֹאשׁ or רֵישָׁא , "head" as "top," is just as possible for a hill / mountain.[163] The scene of 2 Chr 25:12, very similar to that of Luke 4:29, favors the latter term. It speaks of the "top" (רֹאשׁ) of a "cliff" (סֶלַע) from which thousands of captives are also thrown down to their death.

Whether גב or רֹאשׁ / רֵישָׁא is behind ὀφρῦς is immaterial; both point to a Semitic background to this very rare term.

k) The verb κατακρημνίζω, to throw down headlong, in v 29 is found only here in the NT, and in the LXX only four times, including 2 Chr 25:12, just cited in j). There it translates the hiphil of שָׁלַךְ as to throw, fling, cast. Yet because the Day of Atonement ritual with "hurling down" the scapegoat from the precipice of a hill / mountain in the wilderness is clearly behind this imagery in Luke 4:29, the term דְּחַף or דְּחִי as still found in *m. Yoma* 6:6 is much more probable.

* * *

Although I have pointed out other examples of possible Semitisms in the body of the text above, the latter eleven terms cumulatively speak very strongly for a Semitic background to the entire pericope,[164] not just to individual sections, as maintained by several commentators. If Violet's and Wellhausen's second suggestion in j) is accepted, the incident will originally have been in Aramaic, except of course for the Hebrew quotation of Isa 61:1-2 and 58:6 in slightly modified form in Luke 4:18-19, and probably also the prophet saying on being "accepted" in v 24. If the narrative was originally related

---

[161] Jastrow 203,1).

[162] It is employed at this point for example in the Hebrew New Testaments of both Delitzsch (108) and the United Bible Societies (157).

[163] Jastrow 1437 and 1477-1478. See the biblical examples with a mountain, הַר , in BDB 910,2.a.

[164] Cf. also other expressions considered Semitic by B. Violet in "Zum rechten Verständnis" 259-261, as well as A. Schlatter, *Das Evangelium des Lukas* (Stuttgart: Calwer, 1960²) 225-228, and J. Jeremias, *Jesus' Promise to the Nations* 44-45.

in Hebrew, it would nevertheless have been translated very soon into Aramaic, the language of the common people. My main point is simply that it was originally composed in one of these two Semitic languages. From there it was translated into Greek by a Hellenistic Jewish Christian, who clearly recognized the biblical passages and employed the LXX for them. Only then did the anecdote become available to the Evangelist Luke, who appropriated it almost intact and fashioned an introduction for it in 4:14-15. While he may have made some minor stylistic changes in it, he did not even bother to omit the reference to the things (miracles / signs / healings) already done by Jesus in Capernaum in v 23, although Jesus' activity in Capernaum only begins in 4:31. This also argues for his taking over the narrative basically as it became available to him. The Evangelist Luke's own major contribution consisted in transferring the narrative of Jesus' rejection in Nazareth, originally located after roughly one third of Jesus' public ministry, to a time at the beginning, after his baptism and temptation. Luke thereby made it "programmatic" for Jesus' entire ministry (see section V. below).

2. *The Provenance*

The Semitic background of Jesus' rejection in Nazareth strongly argues for Palestine as its place of composition. The narrator / author clearly knew not only the procedures involved in a Palestinian synagogue worship service. He was also well acquainted with the ritual of the High Priest's reading publicly on the Day of Atonement, Isa 58:6 as part of the prophetic reading for that day, and the scapegoat's being led out of the city (Jerusalem) to be thrown headlong down to its death from the precipice of a hill / mountain.

Acts 6:8 states that "a great many of the priests [in Jerusalem] became obedient to the faith." While this is a typically Lukan summary statement, there is no reason to doubt its basic validity. The narrator / author of what is now found in Luke 4:16-30 may have been such a priest, either from Jerusalem or Judea. He was not unaware of the topographical setting of Nazareth, as so often maintained. Rather, for theological reasons he creatively transferred a scene from the scapegoat's being hurled down from a precipice in Judea to that Galilean town. This was artistic freedom, characteristic of Judaic haggadah.

Elsewhere I have analyzed six other narratives in Special Luke: 2:1-20;[165] 2:41-52;[166] 10:30-37;[167] 15:11-32;[168] 23:39-43;[169] and 24:13-35.[170] All of them show excellent knowledge of, and acquaintance with, Palestinian customs and geography, and of Judaic exegetical traditions now only found in Palestinian sources such as the Lives of the Prophets, Pseudo-Philo, Josephus, the Mishnah, Tosefta, the Palestinian Talmud (and the Palestinian traditions within the Babylonian Talmud), as well as the halakhic and haggadic midrashim. The narrator / author, and collector of genuine Jesus materials, was definitely a Semitic-speaking Palestinian, probably a Judean, and possibly even a resident of Jerusalem.

The narrative of Jesus' rejection in Nazareth, also from Special Luke, thus with great certainty can also be said to have arisen in Palestine.

3. The Date

I proposed above that Special Luke knew of the Semitic form of the rejection of Jesus in Nazareth before it was translated into Greek and inserted by Mark into his Gospel at 6:1-6a. Either Special Luke or the Palestinian Jewish Christian community in which he lived then modified it by a) adding a dramatic scene with the contents of Jesus' teaching in the synagogue (6:2 in Luke 4:16-22); b) adding a new proverb regarding a physician's first healing himself (4:23); c) rewording the "prophet" saying (6:4 in Luke 4:24); and d) extensively dramatizing the statement

---

[165] *Weihnachtsgeschichte, Barmherziger Samariter, Verlorener Sohn* 11-57.
[166] *Samuel, Saul and Jesus* 1-64.
[167] *Weihnachtsgeschichte, Barmherziger Samariter, Verlorener Sohn* 59-125.
[168] *Ibid.*, 126-173.
[169] *Samuel, Saul and Jesus* 158-173.
[170] Chapter three, "The Road to Emmaus (Luke 24:13-35)" in *The Stilling of the Storm. Studies in Early Palestinian Judaic Traditions* (International Studies in Formative Christianity and Judaism; Binghamton, NY: Global Publications, 2000) 137-229.

in Mark 6:3 that "they took offense at / stumbled over him" in Luke 4:25-30.

All of these modifications and additions must have taken time to develop. Then, like the other Special Lukan material, the narrative of Jesus' rejection in Nazareth was translated by a Hellenistic Jewish Christian into Greek. Only then did it become available to Luke, who incorporated it into his own Gospel. The latter, dependent in part on Mark, is often dated between 80-90 CE.[171] Allowing roughly ten years for the translation of the Semitic original into Greek and its then becoming available to Luke, one could thus posit a period between 40 and 75 CE for the origin of the original Semitic version. A date somewhere in the middle of this period seems most probable.

IV. The Question of Historicity

Before the advent of the historical-critical method, the historicity of Luke 4:16-30 was not questioned. Even today there are some scholars who advocate its basic historicity, while conceding that its portrayal of Nazareth's topography for example is problematical. Yet they can do this only by maintaining that the Lukan form is a different episode from that described in Mark 6:1-6a, known to the Third Evangelist from his copy of Mark, but intentionally not employed by him at this point (contrast Matthew at 13:54-58).[172] One way out of this is to propose, as I. Marshall does, that since it "is difficult to see why anyone should have invented the conclusion of Luke's story, ... it is more probable that Mark's tradition has abbreviated the story."[173] Yet I have pointed out above precisely the way Special Luke expanded or dramatized the words "and they took

---

[171] Cf. for example W. Wiefel, *Das Evangelium nach Lukas* (THNT 3; Berlin: Evangelische Verlagsanstalt, 1988) 5 on 85-90 CE; F. Bovon, *Das Evangelium des Lukas* 1.23; as well as J. Fitzmyer, *The Gospel According to Luke (I-IX)* 57 on 80-85 CE as "the best solution."
[172] Cf. A. Edersheim, *The Life and Times of Jesus the Messiah* (Grand Rapids, Michigan: Eerdmans, 1942; original Oxford, 1883) 1.457, n. 1.
[173] Cf. his *Commentary on Luke* (NIGTC; Grand Rapids, Michigan: Eerdmans, 1978/1992) 180.

offense at / stumbled over him" in what is now Mark 6:3 in the provocative remarks of Jesus in Luke 4:23-27, resulting in the Nazarites' attempting to murder him in vv 28-30. This expansion, as well as that of the "synagogue" scene in vv 16b-22a, make the account now found in Luke over twice as long as that in Mark (fifteen as opposed to six verses).

The rejection episode in its present Markan form in 6:1-6a is thus not an abbreviation of Luke 4:16-30. The opposite is rather the case. For theological reasons Special Luke modified and expanded the Semitic form of the Markan narrative as known to him to produce the account now basically found in Luke 4:16-30. It is thus not historical, yet it has its own "theological truths." To these I now turn.

V. The Purposes of the Narrative

There is not one single purpose to Special Luke's version of Jesus' rejection in Nazareth, now incorporated in 4:16-30. Instead, six interconnected purposes can be ascertained.

1. The original pre-70 CE Palestinian Jewish (and Jewish Christian) hearers of this narrative in a Semitic language would have reacted to Jesus' standing up and being handed (4:17) a scroll of the Scriptures, from which he then read, by thinking of the High Priest's public reading from Scripture in the Jerusalem Temple on the Day of Atonement. Only he was treated with such honor. The original hearers of the incident understood this allusion, and it set the tone for further Day of Atonement imagery in the narrative. Jesus is thus not only the scapegoat, he is also the High Priest.

2. When Special Luke has Jesus maintain in 4:21 that Isa 61:1-2 and 58:6 are fulfilled in him today, he presents Jesus as a prophet. The Lord God's spirit has come upon him, the Lord has anointed him. He is probably also portrayed here as the "servant" of Isa 42:1, words spoken by God to Jesus at his baptism in Luke 3:22 (the OT texts cited above connected by the catchword רצון / רצה , as shown in section I.). As a prophet,

Jesus in his later public ministry was not only to bring "good news" to the oppressed, proclaim liberty to the captives, let the oppressed go free, etc. (MT Isa 61:1-2 and 58:6 in the original Semitic version of Luke 4:18-19). He was also to suffer a prophet's fate such as that of the servant in Isaiah 53, who is wounded and killed for the transgressions of all (v 5). Special Luke probably also knew of the Q saying now found in Luke 13:34 // Matt 23:37 : Jerusalem is "the city that kills the prophets and stones those who are sent to it" (Luke adds in v 33: "it is impossible for a prophet to be killed outside of Jerusalem"). For this reason Jesus, who expressly labels himself a prophet in 4:24, survives the attempt to kill him in v 29. Before meeting that fate in Jerusalem, he must first "proceed" (v 30)[174] to carry out the contents of Isa 61:1-2 and 58:6 in his public ministry.

3. Special Luke's portrayal of Jesus' proclaiming the year of the Lord's favor (Isa 61:2 in Luke 4:19) means that *the long awaited eschatological Jubilee has now arrived.* In its fiftieth year the son of David / the Messiah was expected to come, and Jesus is that Messiah. The Jubilee was to commence on the Day of Atonement. The latter fact was known to the original Palestinian Jewish (and Jewish Christian) hearers, who thus perceived further Day of Atonement imagery here. The motif of the Jubilee year probably also caused Jesus' public ministry, in all likelihood considerably longer, to be telescoped into only one year – in all the Synoptic traditions.

4. In spite of initial acceptance of Jesus in their synagogue, the Nazarites' asking whether Jesus is not just their "hometown boy," the son of Joseph (v 22b), already expresses disbelief in his ability to be the prophet who publicly maintains he himself "fulfills" the Scriptures. Special Luke intentionally portrays Jesus as being so provoked by this negative response that,

---

[174] Well stated by F. Bovon in *Das Evangelium nach Lukas* 1.216: " Πορεύομαι ist 'theologisches' Verbum für die Reise Jesu von Galiläa nach Jerusalem und für seinen heilsgeschichtlichen Lebenslauf (vgl. 9,51 und 13,22)."

miraculously reading their minds, he in turn provokes them with two examples of popular Israelite prophets as sent by God's will (the divine passive ἐπέμφθη in v 26, applicable by implication also to Elisha) to foreigners / idolaters / sinners, but not to His own people.

Special Luke's argumentation here is first of all intramural, taking place within the Palestinian Jewish (Christian) community. It was similar to Jesus' own very provocative use of a Samaritan as the hero of his parable now found in 10:30-37; his remarks regarding the pagan centurion in Capernaum, whose servant he had just healed: "Truly I tell you, in no one in Israel have I found such faith" (Luke 7:9 // Matt 8:10); and elsewhere. Himself provoked, Jesus is represented in Luke 4:23-27 as then intentionally provoking his former fellow citizens as a prophet so much that they spontaneously decide to murder him, a prophet's fate.

Yet Special Luke lived at a time when Gentiles had already become members of the Christian churches. Thus his having Jesus cite the prophets Elijah and Elisha as sent by God not to Israel but to Gentiles / idolaters / sinners foretold *in nuce* Jewish Christian missionaries' spreading the Christian faith to Gentiles after Jesus' death and Resurrection, especially after large sections of Israel could not accept a crucified Jesus as the Messiah. As the Nazarites now rejected Jesus, so many of his fellow Jews would later reject the "good news" of Christian missionaries, opening a way to bring this message to the Gentiles.

5. Alone in contrast to being accompanied by his disciples to Nazareth in Mark 6:1, Jesus is portrayed by Special Luke in 4:29 in terms of the scapegoat of the Day of Atonement. It too was to be hurled down headlong from the precipice of a hill / mountain to its death after being led out of the city (Jerusalem). Special Luke would not have chosen this specific imagery unless he knew it would be known and would appeal to his own Palestinian Jewish Christian community, probably in Judea, perhaps even in Jerusalem itself.

Jesus is already at this point represented as he who bears upon himself all the iniquities, transgressions and sins of the whole people: the scapegoat of the Day of Atonement in

Leviticus 16. The scene is thus partly designed to adumbrate his later suffering and death on the Cross at Golgotha, where by giving his body and shedding his blood like the scapegoat, he was to atone for / expiate the sins of all.

By including Special Luke's version of Jesus' rejection at Nazareth and not that of Mark 6:1-6a which was also known to him, the Evangelist Luke showed that he very probably understood and appreciated the expiation imagery it contained. This incident should thus be included in future discussions of Luke's theology of atonement.[175] Unfortunately, recognition of the scapegoat and Day of Atonement imagery in 4:16-30 became lost when the Third Gospel was read and appropriated primarily by Gentile Christians. Thus it has remained unrecognized even up to now.

6. Finally, by deliberately changing the original setting of the narrative regarding Jesus' rejection in Nazareth from roughly after the first third of Jesus' public ministry (Mark 6:1-6a, after activity in Capernaum, alluded to in Luke 4:23) to its very outset (Luke 4, directly after the baptism and temptation), the Third Evangelist provided it with programmatic character. That which Jesus cited from the prophet Isaiah in 4:18-19 would now take place within his own ministry. E. Ellis has appropriately called this the "'inaugural address' of the Galilean mission."[176] The fiftieth year of the eschatological Jubilee has now arrived, and the Messiah expected at that time now stands directly before the Nazarites. A period of "grace" (v 22) will now take place. Yet it is already overshadowed by the attempt of some of his fellow Jews, who cannot accept him as the Messiah, to cause his death – both as a prophet and as the scapegoat of Israel. For the moment, Jesus miraculously can still avoid such a fate (v 30),

---

[175] A recent discussion of this is found in D. Buckwalter, *The Character and Purpose of Luke's Christology* (SNTSMS 89; Cambridge: Cambridge University Press, 1996), especially in his chapter 11, "Jesus and Servanthood" 231-272. Cf. his statement on p. 234: "The only substantial references to Jesus' death as atoning in Luke-Acts occur in Luke 22:19-20 and Acts 20:28...."

[176] Cf. his *The Gospel of Luke* 96.

perhaps an adumbration of the Resurrection after his death at Golgotha.

* * *

The narrative of Jesus' rejection at Nazareth in Luke 4:16-30 is thus not an "impossible story," but one full of deep theological significance, especially in terms of Jesus' being portrayed as the scapegoat of the Day of Atonement, who bears the sins of all.

Chapter Three

The Name Judas "Iscariot" and Ahithophel in Judaic Tradition

Introduction

The figure called Judas "Iscariot" is one of the most elusive in the Gospels. One of the twelve disciples of Jesus, for unknown reasons he handed over his own teacher to the authorities in Jerusalem, resulting in Pontius Pilate's condemning the prophet from Nazareth to death. Partly because Judas Iscariot was and still is such a mysterious person, a large secondary literature has arisen concerning him, in recent years often pleading for a more positive or at least neutral understanding of the role he played in the Gospel accounts.[1]

---

[1] Cf. W. Klassen, *Judas. Betrayer or Friend of Jesus?* (Minneapolis: Fortress, 1996), with bibliography on pp. 209-225; B. Dieckmann, *Judas als Sündenbock. Eine verhängnisvolle Geschichte von Angst und Vergeltung* (Munich: Kösel, 1991), especially on the period from the Middle Ages to the present; H.-J. Klauck, *Judas – ein Jünger des Herrn* (QD 111; Freiburg: Herder, 1987), bibliography 148-154; W. Vogler, *Judas Iskarioth* (Theologische Arbeiten 42; Berlin: Evangelische Verlagsanstalt, 1983); M. S. Enslin, "How the Story Grew: Judas in Fact and Fiction" in *Festschrift to Honor Felix Wilbur Gingrich*, ed. E. Barth and R. Cocroft (Leiden: Brill, 1972) 123-141, dealing with Judas traditions between the New Testament and the Middle Ages; E. Blair, art. "Judas," 7. "Judas Iscariot" in *IDB* (1962) 2.1006-1008; K. Lüthi, *Judas Iskariot in der Geschichte der Auslegung von der Reformation bis zur Gegenwart* (Zurich: Zwingli-Verlag, 1955), and his art. "Judas Iskariot" in *TRE* 17.296-304. H. Goldschmidt offers a Jewish perspective in 17.304-307.

Ever since at least the end of the seventeenth century it has been recognized that Ahithophel, who betrayed David in Jerusalem (2 Samuel 16-17), has influenced the depiction of Judas in the Gospels, who betrayed Jesus in Jerusalem.[2] This is primarily because Jesus as the Messiah was considered "the Son of David."[3] References to him as such in the earliest Gospel, that of Mark, are found in 10:47-48, implied in 11:10, and in 12:35-37 on the question of David's son. In 12:35 Jesus quotes the scribes as saying that "the Messiah is the son of David." In his letter to the Romans the Apostle Paul also states in 1:3 that Jesus "was descended from David according to the flesh," something never questioned by contemporary Jews. From Palestine and the middle of the first century BCE, *Pss. Sol.* 17:21 already speaks of the Jews' future "king, the son of David...."[4]

In Judaic tradition David, like Jesus much later, is depicted as a great scholar and a teacher of the Torah, also with his own disciples. The following passages exemplify this.

---

[2] Cf. the references to P. Limborchs (1633-1712), C. Heumann, J. von Hofmann and P. Jensen in Lüthi, *Judas Iskarioth* 61, 64, 106 and 130 respectively, for early scholars who maintained this connection. Ahithophel, mentioned only in 2 Samuel 15-17; 23:34; and 1 Chr 27:33-34 in the MT, is described in Judaic sources by K. Kohler and L. Ginzberg, art. "Ahithophel" in *JE* (1901) 1.292-293; L. Ginzberg, *The Legends of the Jews* 4.94-97 and 6.256-258; M. Guttmann, art. "Achitofel" in *Encyclopaedia Judaica* (Berlin: Eschkol, 1928) 1.733-734; and the art. "Ahithophel" in *EJ* (1971) 2.465-466. See also the fine study by B. Gärtner, *Die rätselhaften Termini Nazoräer und Iskariot* (Horae Soederblomianae IV; Uppsala: Gleerup, 1957) 60-68, who also calls attention to several passages I analyze below. In *The Sage in Jewish Society of Late Antiquity* (London / New York: Routledge, 1999) 101-109, R. Kalmin plausibly explains why some Amoraic Palestinian sources treat Ahithophel favorably as a sage, while Tanaaitic and Babylonian sources view him very negatively.

[3] Cf. Str-B 1.525; E. Lohse, art. υἱὸς Δαυίδ in *TDNT* 8.478-488; and C. Burger, *Jesus als Davidssohn. Eine traditionsgeschichtliche Untersuchung* (FRLANT 98; Göttingen: Vandenhoeck & Ruprecht, 1970).

[4] Cf. *OTP* 2.667, and 641-642 for R. Wright on this dating, and the provenance in Jerusalem.

Lev. Rab. Behukkothai 35/1 on Lev 26:3 has David say: "Every day I used to plan and decide that I would go to a particular place or to a particular dwelling-house, but my feet always brought me to Synagogues and Houses of Study."[5] In *b. Šabb.* 30b it is related that "every Sabbath day he would sit and study all day."[6] David even rose at midnight in order to study the Torah,[7] at times pondering it until the break of dawn.[8] *Exod. Rab.* Bo 15/22 on Exod 12:2 notes that David clarified many things in the Torah which Moses wrote without explaining them.[9] In contrast to Saul, he made his studies accessible.[10] According to *Eliyyahu Rabbah* 3, David, seated on the bare ground, taught Torah in Heaven's name to the multitudes.[11] Since he humbled himself by not sitting on comfortable cushions, God told him that he would be like Him in being able to annul His decrees.[12] Because of his superiority in knowledge

---

[5] Mirqin 8.179, Soncino 4.446. Cf. *Midr. Pss.* 25/4 on Ps 25:1 (Buber 211, Braude 1.349).

[6] Soncino 134.

[7] Cf. for example *Midr. Pss.* 57/4 on Ps 57:9 (Buber 298, Braude 1.502), with parallels in 22/8 on Ps 22:1 (Buber 185, Braude 1.305), *Pesiq. R.* 17/3 on Ps 119:62 (Friedmann 86a, Braude 363), 49/2 on Exod 12:29 (Friedmann 196a, Braude 831-832), and *Pesiq. Rav Kah.* 7/4 on Exod 12:29 (Mandelbaum 124, Braude and Kapstein 141-142.)

[8] Cf. *b. Ber.* 3b (Soncino 9).

[9] Mirqin 5.187-191, Soncino 3.187-193. Cf. *b. Ber.* 4a (Soncino 11), where David deals extensively with detailed questions of the Torah before making a decision.

[10] Cf. *b. 'Erub.* 53a (Soncino 371). David wanted statements to be repeated in his name after his death: *b. Yebam.* 96b-97b (Soncino 661).

[11] Friedmann 15, Braude and Kapstein 72-73. This is on haggadic development of 2 Sam 23:8. In the parallel in *b. Mo'ed Qatan* 16b, Soncino 104 has for "the multitudes" (ברבים, after referring to "the people" - העם) "the Rabbis" (לרבנן), which should be corrected accordingly.

[12] *Eliyyahu Rabbah* 3 (Braude and Kapstein 73, with n. 24; here God also addresses David as "My son" [בני] - see also 74, Friedmann 16). In the parallel in *b. Mo'ed Qatan* 16b (Soncino 105) this is in the name of Rab, a first generation Babylonian Amora (Strack and Stemberger, *Introduction* 93). It is haggadic interpretation of the term "Tahchemonite" in 2 Sam 23:8. Was Jesus' special authority (ἐξουσία /

and ability to make deductions, the Torah followed his decisions.[13] David even had his own "disciples," תַּלְמִידִים.[14] The latter is important in regard to Ahithophel as a disciple of David (see section I. below.)

The above short sketch includes Amoraic sources. Nevertheless, it is quite probable that already in the first century CE the main lines of this portrait were already drawn. That is, David was not only revered in Palestinian Judaism as a great warrior, king and poet-musician, but also as a great teacher of the Torah, with his own disciples. In the latter respect Jesus was also the "Son of David."

The following sections deal with sixteen similarities between Ahithophel in Judaic tradition, who betrayed David, and Judas Iscariot, who betrayed Jesus the Son of David. They all serve cumulatively to argue for the expression "Iscariot" as also deriving from Judaic tradition on Ahithophel (section XVII).

I. Ahithophel as a Disciple of David, and Judas as a Disciple of Jesus, the Son of David

Ahithophel the Gilonite was David's counselor (2 Sam 15:12, 23; 1 Chr 27:33). Yet he changed sides and advised David's son

---

רְשׁוּת) in interpreting the Torah attributed to his being the Son of David?

[13] Cf. *Ruth Rab.* 4/3 on Ruth 2:1 (Soncino 8.51). An example of David's halakhic ruling in regard to eating the shewbread of 1 Samuel 21 is found in *b. Menaḥ.* 95b (Soncino 585), important for the background of his dispute in Mark 2:23-28 par. Here Jesus is not only the "Son of man" (v 28), but also "the Son of David." An inclusive statement on David's Torah superiority is found in *Targ.* 1 Chr 11:11. It states that "when he sat down to give instruction in the Law, the correct decision came to his mind; ... skilled in wisdom, intelligent in counsel, mighty in strength, head of the academy..." (Déaut and Robert 2.38; English in McIvor 86).

[14] *Midr. Pss.* 41/7 on Ps 41:10 (Buber 261, Braude 1.439) with "my disciples." See also *Eliyyahu Zuṭa* 5 (Friedmann 181, Braude and Kapstein 427, with n. 6), and *Targ.* Ps 140:10 (Merino 186 and 318).

Absalom, rebelling against his own father, how he could immediately cause David's death (2 Sam 17:1-3).

In Judaic tradition Ahithophel is also labeled David's "disciple" (תַּלְמִיד).[15] R. Yohanan, a second generation Palestinian Amora,[16] relates in *b. Sanh.* 106b: "At first David called Ahithophel his teacher, then his companion [colleague], and finally his disciple (תלמידו)." The latter term is explained by reference to Ps 41:10 – "Even my bosom friend in whom I trusted [107a], who ate of my bread, has lifted the heel against me."[17]

The parallel tradition in *Midr. Pss.* 41/7 on Ps 49:10 (Eng. 9) elucidates the latter. After David quotes this Psalm verse, it has him continue: "'Even my disciples (תלמידיי) turned on me / took cruel advantage of me[18] at the end. How so? When they entered the house of study, they entered my presence gentle as kids. Yet when they left my presence they became like goats goring with their horns.' (Here) 'bread' can only mean words of Torah, as in the verse, 'Come, eat of my bread' (Prov 9:5)."[19]

David is pictured here as the head of the house of study, the master or rabbi whose disciples eat of his "bread," which means

---

[15] Jastrow 1673.

[16] Strack and Stemberger, *Introduction* 94-95; he was active in Sepphoris and Tiberias and died in 279 CE.

[17] Soncino 729; I employ the NRSV. Instead of תלמידו, the variant איש for Ahithophel is also found. See the discussion of 2 Sam 16:23 in section XVII 3) below. On "bread of deceit" (לחם שקר) contrasted to "bread of truth," see *Gen. Rab.* Vayesheb 85/1 on Gen 38:1 (Theodor and Albeck 1029, Soncino 2.787), *Ruth Rab.* 2:5 § 3 (Soncino 9.108-109), and *y. Sanh.* 11:5, 30c (Neusner 31.385).

[18] Cf. BDB 784 on עָקֵב, where the phrase "make great the heel against me" is rendered as "taken some cruel advantage of me." See also the adjective as "insidious, deceitful."

[19] Buber 261; I modify Braude in 1.439. In the Proverbs passage it is wisdom which calls this out. Ps 49:10 is employed of internal enemies at Qumran in 1QH 5:23-24 (Martínez and Tigchelaar 1.72-73).

his interpretation of the Torah.[20] It is one of his disciples, Ahithophel, who cruelly turns against him "at the end."[21]

This Judaic tradition formed the basis for Judas, the "disciple" (μαθητής) of Jesus, the Son of David, who also cruelly turned against his teacher at the end.

II. Ahithophel Eats of David's Bread and Betrays Him, and Judas Eats of Jesus' Bread and Betrays Him

In *b. Sanh.* 106b–107a and *Midr. Pss.* 41/7 on Ps 49:10 it is David's disciple Ahithophel who, though eating his teacher David's "bread" (his interpretation of the Torah), turned on him / took cruel advantage of him at the end. That is, Ahithophel betrayed David to his son Absalom.

In the Gospel tradition this imagery is applied to Judas, the disciple who betrays his teacher Jesus. It is alluded to in A) the Synoptics, and B) stated explicitly in the Gospel of John.

A) Mark 14:10 relates that Judas went to the chief priests in Jerusalem in order to betray Jesus to them. After meeting with them, he sought a concrete opportunity to do so (v 11).

On the evening of the first day of Unleavened Bread, when the Passover lamb is sacrificed, Jesus announced to his disciples who were eating with him: "Truly I tell you, one of you will betray me, 'one who is eating with me' (εἷς... ὁ ἐσθίων μετ' ἐμοῦ)" – v 18.[22] When the disciples then became distressed and began to ask Jesus, "Surely, not I?" (v 19),[23] he replied: "It is one

---

[20] Cf. also the passages cited in Str-B 2.483-484 "c" with the bread of the Torah and Prov 9:5.

[21] Braude forgot to translate the Hebrew בסוף.

[22] It should be noted that the usual expression for "to eat" or "to have a meal" in Hebrew and Aramaic is "to eat bread." Cf. the references in Str-B 1.704-705 and 2.6-7.

[23] On μήτι ἐγώ, cf. the expression וכי דילטור אני, "Am I an informer?" in *b. Sanh.* 11a (Soncino 45) and 43b (Soncino 284). The term derives from the Latin *dēlātor*, "an informer, denouncer" (Chambers Murray 184) and is used elsewhere of Ahithophel; see below, section XII.

of the twelve, one who is dipping (ὁ ἐμβαπτόμενος) [bread] into the bowl with me (v 20). For the Son of Man goes as it is written of him, but woe to that one by whom the Son of Man is betrayed! It would have been better for that one not to have been born" (v 21).

The verb ἐμβάπτω is rare, occurring in the LXX and the NT only here and in the parallels in Matt 26:23 and John 13:26 v.l.[24] Yet the NRSV is correct in adding "bread" at this point, for the Palestinian Jewish Christian author of this incident probably not only had Ps 41:10 in mind here, but also Ruth 2:14. There Boaz tells Ruth, "eat some of this 'bread,' and 'dip' your morsel in the sour wine."[25] In *Ruth Rab.* 5/6 R. Jonathan, either a third generation Tanna or a first generation Palestinian Amora,[26] first interprets the above phrases of David. His bread is the bread of royalty, and the sour wine / vinegar is his sufferings (incurred when Absalom rebelled against him). Since Jesus as the Messiah was the Son of David and the whole scene of betrayal is clothed in terminology from the incident of Absalom's rebellion against David, the original (pre-Markan) Palestinian Jewish Christian author of Mark 14:18-21 could for this reason have borrowed imagery from Ruth 2:14 at this point. Another, messianic interpretation of the verse, however, may have aided him in doing so, if it was early. It refers the whole verse to the Messiah, the bread to the bread of royalty, and dipping the morsel in sour wine / vinegar to the Messiah's sufferings, for which Isa 53:5 is cited.[27] The author then employed imagery from Ruth 2:14 at this point because he believed Jesus was the Messiah, about to suffer through his betrayal, trial and crucifixion.

Yet Ps 41:10 is probably primarily alluded to by "one who is dipping [bread] into the bowl with me" in Mark 14:20, for the

---

[24] Cf. BAGD 254, LSJ 539: dip (in, into).
[25] The LXX has the simple βάψεις for the latter verb.
[26] Cf. Strack and Stemberger, *Introduction* 83 and 92, respectively.
[27] Soncino 8.61-62 (cf. also R. Huna's statement) and 64, respectively. Since "the rabbis" call the Messiah "the leper scholar" on the basis of Isa 53:4 in *b. Sanh.* 98b (Soncino 668), I doubt that the association of this chapter on the Suffering Servant was a later Jewish reaction to Christian teaching.

following phrase ("the Son of Man [= I, Jesus] goes away[28] [to his death] as it is written of him") refers to his betrayal by his disciple Judas (v 21b). The scriptural passage closest to this situation as described is Ps 41:10 in Judaic tradition.[29] It was Ahithophel, the bosom friend in whom David trusted, who ate of his bread (= was one of his closest companions) and turned on him / took cruel advantage of him at the end. That Ahithophel as described in such terms was the model for Judas is shown clearly in the Gospel of John.

B) John 13:21-30 is the Johannine equivalent of the Synoptic scene in Mark 14:18-21. After Jesus announces that one of his disciples will betray him, the disciple whom Jesus loved asks him who this person is. Jesus then answers by saying, "'It is the one to whom I give this piece of bread when I have dipped it in the dish.' So when he had dipped the piece of bread, he gave it to Judas..." (v 26). Then after receiving the piece of bread, Judas went out (to betray him) – v 30.

This betrayal had already been announced in 13:2, which states that "the devil had already put it into the heart of Judas... to betray him." The term διάβολος employed here actually means "the slanderer."[30] It may have been chosen by the author at his point in part because Ahithophel was known in Judaic tradition as "the slanderer" (see section XIV. below). The irony would then be that the Slanderer inspired Judas, modeled on the slanderer Ahithophel, to betray Jesus.

During the supper Jesus washed his disciples' feet (13:2-12), indicating that not all of them were clean, "for he knew who was to betray him" (v 11). Having returned to the table, Jesus

---

[28] Cf. BAGD 836 on ὑπάγω as "going away." Here it is meant as exiting from his life.
[29] Numerous commentators favor Ps 41:10 here. Cf. for example W. Grundmann, *Das Evangelium nach Markus* (THNT 2; Berlin: Evangelische Verlagsanstalt, 1977⁷) 384, with n. 16; W. Schmithals, *Das Evangelium nach Markus, Kapitel 9, 2-16* (ÖTKNT 2/2; Gütersloh: Mohn; Würzburg: Echter Verlag, 1979) 609; and D. Juel, *Mark* (Augsburg Commentary on the New Testament; Minneapolis: Augsburg, 1991) 191-192.
[30] BAGD 182.

interprets the foot washing. Yet he does not speak of all the disciples; he knows whom he has chosen (the eleven, without Judas) – v 18a. Jesus then states, "But it is to fulfill the Scripture, 'The one who ate my bread has lifted his heel against me'" (v 18b). Jesus tells this to the disciples now before it takes place so that when it does occur, they may believe "that I am he" (v 19).

The Nestle-Aland Greek New Testament[26] in its margin identifies this scripture as Ps 41:10, as do the commentators. This is a major reason why it is also most probably alluded to in the similar passage Mark 14:18, 20–21, cited above in A).

The citation of Ps 41:10 in John 13:18 differs greatly from the LXX, which clearly has not influenced the text here. The *Targum* at this point refers the text to Ahithophel: "strengthening himself through my meal (= eating with me), yet he claimed superiority over me in wisdom."[31] The Johannine version of the Ps 41:10 text must be viewed as an independent modification of the Hebrew, i.e. a kind of targumizing it. This points to a Semitic-speaking Palestinian Jewish Christian community in which the reference to Ps 41:10, only alluded to at this point in the Synoptic tradition cited above (Mark 14 par.), was further developed by making it explicit, i.e. clearly identifiable as a citation. This Semitic-speaking Palestinian Jewish Christian community knew that the verse was referred to the traitor Ahithophel in Judaic tradition, and therefore employed it of the traitor / betrayer Judas. The Evangelist John then appropriated it from this community, perhaps already in Greek, and included it in the scene of the foot-washing.

---

[31] Merino 107 and 227. Cf. Jastrow 192 on the afel of ברי, ברא, and 1446 on רברב. On Ahithophel's exceptional wisdom and power of persuasion, see for example 2 Sam 16:23; 17:14; and *Midr. Pss.* 55/5 (Buber 293, Braude 1.495). In *Tanḥ.* B. Maṭṭot 8 (Buber 2.160, Bietenhard 2.397) with a parallel in *Tanḥ.* Maṭṭot 5 (Eshkol 828), Ahithophel is one of the two wise persons in the world, Balaam for the Gentiles and he for Israel. In *Midr. Pss.* 119/67 on Ps 119:135, David weeps for Ahithophel as one of the two "renowned men" who drew away from the Torah (Buber 502, Braude 2.284). The other is Doeg.

III. The General Setting of Ahithophel's Betrayal of David, and the General Setting of Judas' Betrayal of Jesus

Three similarities exist in this regard. They are the following.

1) Jerusalem

Ahithophel makes his offer to betray David in Jerusalem (2 Sam 16:15; 17:1-4).

Judas also makes his offer to betray Jesus in Jerusalem (Mark 14:10-11).

2) Night

Ahithophel proposes to capture (thus betraying) David during the night (2 Sam 17:1).

Judas betrays Jesus after all the disciples eat the Passover meal with him in the evening (Mark 14:17). Then the others go out with Jesus to the Garden of Gethsemane, and after some time there Judas arrives to betray him (vv 42-43). It is also night.[32]

3) The Mount of Olives

David leaves Jerusalem and first goes to the Mount of Olives, where he is told that Ahithophel is among the conspirators (2 Sam 15:30-31). Then at its summit he expresses the hope that Ahithophel's counsel will be defeated (vv 32, 34).

After celebrating the Passover with his disciples, Jesus goes out with them (without Judas) to the Mount of Olives, to a place called Gethsemane, where Judas shortly thereafter betrays him (Mark 14:26, 32, 41-43).[33]

---

[32] Cf. also John 13:30, "And it was night," and 1 Cor 11:23, "on the night when he was betrayed."

[33] On the above three sections, cf. T. Glasson, "Davidic Links with the Betrayal of Jesus" in *ExpTim* 85 (1973-1974) 118-119; L. Trudinger, "Davidic Links with the Betrayal of Jesus: Some Further Observations" in *ExpTim* 86 (1974-1975) 278-279; and R. Brown, *The Death of the Messiah* (ABRL; New York: Doubleday, 1994) 1.125-126.

IV. David Betrayed by Ahithophel When Weary and Discouraged, and Jesus Betrayed by Judas When Weary and Discouraged

In 2 Sam 17:2 Ahithophel plans to capture / betray David, coming upon him "while he is weary and discouraged."

According to Mark 14:33-34, Jesus in the Garden of Gethsemane "began to be distressed and agitated" (v 33), telling three of his disciples, "I am deeply grieved, even to death" (v 34). This shows his being weary and discouraged.

V. Ahithophel's Plan When He Captures / Betrays David That All Those with Him Will Flee, and the Flight of Jesus' Disciples When Judas Betrays Him

Ahithophel states in 2 Sam 17:2 that when he captures / betrays David, "all the people who are with him will flee."

After Judas betrays Jesus to a crowd coming from the chief priests, scribes and elders (Mark 14:43), "All of them (the eleven disciples) deserted him and fled" (v 50).[34]

VI. Ahithophel's Plan When He Captures / Betrays David That Only David Will Be Killed, and Judas' Betrayal Only of Jesus, Who Is Killed

In 2 Sam 17:2 Ahithophel says that when he captures / betrays David, "I will strike down only the king." David is the only one sought (v 3).

In Mark 14:10 Judas goes to the chief priests only to betray one person, Jesus. After the betrayal in the Garden of Gethsemane, only Jesus is interrogated and crucified (15:21-39).

---

[34] This general situation evoked a suitable verse from Scripture; Zech 13:7 is thus quoted by Jesus prophetically in Mark 14:27.

VII. Get Up!

When David heard that most of the Israelites had gone after his rebellious son Absalom, he said to all his "servants" who were with him in Jerusalem: "Get up! Let us flee..." (2 Sam 15:14). The first expression is the Hebrew and Aramaic קוּמוּ, the second the Hebrew וְנִבְרָחָה , Aramaic וּנערוק.[35]

At the end of his prayers in Gethsemane, Jesus tells his disciples in Mark 14:14-42: "The hour has come; the Son of Man is betrayed into the hands of sinners (v 41). 'Get up, let us be going.' See, my betrayer is at hand" (v 42). Here "Get up" is the Greek ἐγείρεσθε. In Hebrew and Aramaic it too would be קוּמוּ.[36] The second expression in 2 Sam 15:14, "let us flee," directly after "Get up!", could also have inspired the original Semitic behind the Greek ἄγωμεν, "Let us be going / go!" in Mark 14:42.

It cannot be emphasized enough how strange these two Greek expressions are in their present context. They only make sense if originally Jesus was pictured as attempting to flee from Judas. Yet it was too late, for the betrayer was already too close, together with a crowd. Jesus could no longer flee and was caught. This would explain why terminology from 2 Sam 15:14 was originally employed at this point: David (successfully) attempts to flee from Absalom, who wishes to have him killed. Jesus (unsuccessfully) attempts to flee from Judas, who wants him to be arrested (and killed). As Mark 14:42 now stands, Jesus is strangely represented as stoically awaiting his fate or "hour." He and the eleven disciples do not attempt to "go off" or flee; it is rather Judas who approaches him (v 45).

---

[35] For the Aramaic, cf. Sperber 2.186. On ערק as to flee, run, see Jastrow 1123.
[36] Cf. the Hebrew New Testaments of Delitzsch (93) and the United Bible Societies (135); the Aramaic is the same as the targum of 2 Sam 15:14.

VIII. Elders, Chief Priests and the Sanhedrin

Mark 14:10 states that Judas went to the chief priests (ἀρχιερεῖς) in order to betray Jesus to them. When he arrived in the Garden of Gethsemane at the Mount of Olives to do so, there was with him a crowd with swords and clubs, "from the chief priests, the scribes, and 'the elders'" (οἱ πρεσβύτεροι – v 43). These then laid hands on Jesus and arrested him (v 46), taking him to the high priest, where "all the chief priests, the elders, and the scribes were assembled" (v 53). This assemblage was the whole "council" (συνέδριον) – v 55.[37]

The elders, chief priests and the Sanhedrin also play major roles in the context of the betrayal of David by Ahithophel in biblical and Judaic tradition.

1) The Elders

After Ahithophel proposed to Absalom how he intended to capture / betray David in 2 Sam 17:1-3, "the advice pleased Absalom and all the elders (זְקֵנִים, LXX οἱ πρεσβύτεροι) of Israel" (v 4). Verse 15 repeats that Ahithophel had so counseled Absalom and "the elders of Israel."[38] In *b. Sanh.* 102b the phrase "all the elders of Israel" in 2 Sam 17:4 is associated with the phrase סבי דבהתא, "elders of shame," i.e. evil elders.[39]

Here Ahithophel's willingness to capture / betray David pleased the elders of Israel, just as Judas' betrayal of Jesus pleased the whole Sanhedrin, which included elders.

---

[37] Cf. also 15:1 and John 11:47. On the high council or Sanhedrin, see BAGD 786, 2., and סַנְהֶדְרִין in Jastrow 1005.
[38] On the elders of Israel, cf. also 3:17, and on the elders of Judah 19:12 (Eng. 11).
[39] Soncino 696. Cf. Jastrow 143 on בַּהְתָא, shame, disgrace. He refers to the same expression in *Gen. Rab.* Vayera 49/9 on Gen 18:25 (Theodor and Albeck 510, apparatus; Soncino 1.429). 2 Sam 17:1-4 are also cited in *Midr. Pss.* 55/5 on Ps 55:22 in regard to Ahithophel's words to Absalom, "so persuasive that everyone heeded him" (Buber 293, Braude 1.495).

2) The Chief Priests

In 2 Sam 17:15 Hushai relates that Ahithophel had counseled Absalom and the elders how to capture / betray David in the manner described in vv 1-3. This he tells "the priests Zadok and Abiathar."[40] Josephus, a native of Jerusalem whose mother tongue was Aramaic, wrote in his retelling of the David story in his *Antiquities*, at the end of the first century CE,[41] that the two were high or chief priests (ἀρχιερεῖς).[42] Jesus himself refers to Abiathar as high priest at the time of David in Mark 2:26, and the oldest Jewish chronology, *Seder 'Olam*, notes in 14 that Zadok became high priest after Abiathar when David fled Jerusalem and went up the ascent of the Mount of Olives.[43]

In early Judaic tradition, there were thus already high or chief priests present in Jerusalem when Ahithophel intended to capture / betray David, just as there were high or chief priests in the same city when Judas betrayed Jesus.

3) The Sanhedrin

Rabbinic tradition attributed a Sanhedrin to Jerusalem already in the time of David. *Midr. Pss.* 49/2 on Ps 49:3 states that Doeg and Ahithophel were "heads of the Sanhedrin" (ראשי סנהדראות).[44] David was closely associated with it.[45]

---

[40] Cf. their names also in 8:17, 15:24 and 27 (Abiathar conjectured here), 35-36.

[41] He completed them in 93/94 CE, when he was 56 years old (*Ant.* 20.267). For Jerusalem and Aramaic, cf. *Vita* 7 and *Bell.* 1.3.

[42] Cf. his *Ant.* 7.200, 222-223, 225, 260 and 262.

[43] Cf. Milikowsky 302 and 488. *Targ.* 1 Chr 27:34 also labels Abiathar the high priest (Déaut and Robert 2.74; McIvor 134).

[44] The plural can also mean the singular (Jastrow 1005); Buber 278, Braude 1.465. Cf. *Targ. Ps* 140:10 for Ahithophel as the head of the Sanhedrin of David's disciples (Merino 108 and 318). See also *Midr. Pss.* 3/4 on Ps 3:2b for Doeg as "chief of the high court" (Buber 38, Braude 1.57).

[45] Cf. *Gen. Rab.* Vayetze 74/15 on Gen 31:52 (Theodor and Albeck 873, Soncino 2.687); *Ruth Rab.* 2/2 (Soncino 8.25); *Midr. Pss.* 55/4 on Ps 55:19 and the counsel of Ahithophel (Buber 292, Braude 1.494); and *b. Yoma* 22b (Soncino 102).

Elsewhere Joab can also be labeled the head of the Sanhedrin,[46] as well as Jehoiada son of Benaiah.[47] In one tradition, Jerusalemites who are members of the Sanhedrin proclaim that if David falls into their hands, they will have no mercy on him.[48]

In Judaic sources there was thus already in David's time a Sanhedrin in Jerusalem, and it was intimately connected with Ahithophel and his plan to capture / betray David and have him alone killed. The latter was the "Vorlage" for Judas' betraying the Son of David, Jesus, to the Sanhedrin in Jerusalem, consisting also of elders and chief priests (together with scribes, not mentioned for the time of David).

IX. Judas as a Guide, and Ahithophel as a Guide

In Acts 1:16 Peter in Jerusalem addresses the assembled adherents of Jesus with the words: "Friends (lit. 'men, brothers'), the Scripture had to be fulfilled, which the Holy Spirit through David foretold concerning Judas, who became a 'guide' for those who arrested Jesus...." The term for "guide" here is ὁδηγός, one of its only four occurrences in the NT.[49]

The scriptural passage from the Psalms ("David") mentioned here cannot refer to Ps 69:25 (Eng. 26) and 109:8 in v 20, for they refer Judas' "homestead" to the field he bought in 1:18-19, and "another" to the necessity of someone else taking over his

---

[46] Cf. *Pesiq. R.* 11/3 (Friedmann 43b, Braude 1.204).
[47] He is mentioned in 1 Chr 27:34 after Ahithophel and before Abiathar. Cf. also Benaiah son of Jehoiada in 18:17 (= 2 Sam 20:23), who was over the Cherethites and the Pelethites. For the latter as meaning the Sanhedrin, see *b. Ber.* 4a (Soncino 10), connected to 1 Chr 27:34. The names were easily mixed up. See also *Targ.* 1 Chr 27:34 (Déaut and Robert 2.74, McIvor 133-134).
[48] Cf. *y. Soṭah* 1:8, 17b (Neusner 27.45-46) and *Num. Rab.* Naso 9/24 (Mirqin 9.200, Soncino 5.290, with n. 5).
[49] BAGD 553. Cf. also Matt 15:14; 23:16; and Rom 2:19, all connected to the blind. In Luke 22:47 the Evangelist employs προέρχομαι of Judas: *to go before* as forerunner or "leader" (BAGD 705).

position among the Twelve.⁵⁰ I suggest instead that the Psalm passage alluded to is 55:14.

Judaic tradition maintains that all of Psalm 55, dealing with the betrayal of a friend, refers to Ahithophel's betrayal of David.⁵¹ It is he who "laid hands on his friend and violated his covenant" with him (v 21, Eng. 20). Verse 14 can be translated: "But it was you, a man according to my order, my guide, and my familiar friend" (who betrayed me).⁵² R. Yehoshua b. Levi, a first generation Palestinian Amora,⁵³ in *Midr. Pss.* 55/1 on this verse interprets David to mean: "'Ahithophel was my orderer, that is to say, it was he who arranged laws in their proper order.' By the words 'my guide' David meant: 'Ahithophel was my master (רבי) who instructed me in Torah,' for the next verse says, 'We took sweet counsel together' (v 15)."⁵⁴

Here the term אַלּוּפִי, "my friend / intimate,"⁵⁵ is interpreted as "my guide" in the sense of Ahithophel's "teaching"⁵⁶ David Torah. Several Judaic sources emphasize this in connection with Ps 55:14.⁵⁷

Finally, it should be pointed out that R. Yoḥanan in *b. Sanh.* 106b-107a, discussed above in section II., cites Ps 55:14 to maintain that David first called Ahithophel "his teacher" (רבו), based on the expression אַלּוּפִי, then his companion, and finally

---

⁵⁰ Against E. Haenchen, *Die Apostelgeschichte* (Meyer; Göttingen: Vandenhoeck & Ruprecht, 1961¹³) 124, with n. 6.
⁵¹ Cf. the many statements found in *Midrash Psalms* on this chapter (Buber 290-293, Braude 1.491-495).
⁵² Cf. Braude's translation in 1.491-492. The NRSV has: "But it is you, my equal, my companion, my familiar friend...."
⁵³ Strack and Stemberger, *Introduction* 92.
⁵⁴ Buber 291, Braude 1.492. The *Targum* also refers the verse to Ahithophel (Merino 117 and 239).
⁵⁵ BDB 48, 2.
⁵⁶ Cf. BDB 48 on אלף as to learn, piel to teach; Jastrow 72; and the *Targum*'s דאליפתא לי.
⁵⁷ Cf. *m. 'Avot* 6:3 (Albeck 4.383, Danby 459); *Kallah Rabbati* 8:3, 54a (*Minor Tractates* 492, see also 504-505); *Eliyyyahu Zuṭa* 17 (Friedmann S18, Braude and Kapstein 484); and *Num. Rab. Korach* 18/17 on Num 16:1 (Mirqin 10.204, Soncino 6.728).

his disciple. For the latter Yoḥanan cites Ps 41:10. It is thus possible that not only Judaic tradition on Ahithophel as the betrayer of David in Ps 55:14 stands behind the allusion to Scripture (David, the Psalms) in Acts 1:16. If Ps 55:14 and 41:10 were already connected at an early time in the above way, the reference to the latter psalm in the margin of the Nestle-Aland Greek New Testament[26] at this point would be appropriate.

While Ahithophel was David's "guide" in matters of the Torah, yet later betrayed him, so Judas, first a faithful disciple of Jesus, in the end "guided" a crowd with swords and clubs from the chief priests, scribes and elders to arrest Jesus in Gethsemane (Mark 14:43 par.), thus betraying the Son of David. For this reason Luke can label Judas a "guide" in Acts 1:16.

X. Judas and a Crowd with Swords and Clubs, and Ahithophel's Band, Swords and Clubs

A) After Jesus said to his disciples in Gethsemane "The hour has come; the Son of Man is betrayed into the hands of sinners" (Mark 14:41), Judas arrived. "With him there was a crowd with swords and clubs, from the chief priests, the scribes and the elders" (v 43). After they arrested Jesus, one (of the disciples) "drew his sword and struck the servant / slave (δοῦλος) of the high priest, cutting off his ear" (v 47). Then Jesus asked those who arrested him: "Have you come out 'with swords and clubs' (μετὰ μαχαιρῶν καὶ ξύλων) to arrest me, as though I were a bandit?" (v 48).[58] He had been with them daily in the Temple, teaching, but they had not arrested him. "But let the Scriptures be fulfilled" (v 49).

The term for "crowd" here is ὄχλος. Luke repeats this in 22:47, while Matthew increases it to a "large (πολύς) crowd" in

---

[58] Matthew repeats this at 26:55, as does Luke at 22:52. The Third Evangelist has Jesus address this question to the chief priests, the captains of the Temple (police) (BAGD 770 on στρατηγοί) and the elders (22:52; cf. v 4).

26:47. John 18:3 instead has Judas bring a military unit (σπεῖρα)[59] and servants / slaves (ὑπηρέται)[60] from the high priests and Pharisees. They had with them lanterns, torches and "weapons" (ὅπλα).[61] With his own sword (μάχαιρα) Peter first cut off the right ear of the high priest's servant / slave (δοῦλος – v 10), yet Jesus told him to put it back into its sheath (v 11). Then the military unit, their commander (χιλίαρχος)[62] and the servants / slaves (οἱ ὑπηρέται) of the Jews arrested Jesus and bound him (v 12).

The expression "clubs" in Mark 14:43 and 48 par. is the plural of ξύλον, literally "wood," but also employed of a "pole," and here as "club, cudgel."[63] These instruments recall the means employed by the high priests in Jerusalem to exact tithes "by force" (בִּזְרוֹעַ)[64] before 70 CE. In *t. Menaḥ.* 13:21 it is stated: "Woe is me because of the House of Boethus. Woe is me because of 'their staves' (אלחן)." In regard to this and other families of the high priests it continues: "For they are high priests, and their sons, treasurers, sons-in-law, supervisors, and 'their servants' (עבדיהון) come and beat us with 'staves' (מקלות)."[65] Josephus castigates the high priests' "shamelessness and effrontery" in this regard, stating that "they actually were so brazen as to send slaves (δούλους) to the threshing floors to receive the tithes that were due to the priests, with the result that the poorer priests starved to death."[66]

---

[59] BAGD 761. If it corresponded to the tenth part of a Roman legion, there could have been up to 600 men in it. Here it probably simply means a large unit of soldiers.
[60] Cf. BAGD 842. This is against the NRSV's "police."
[61] BAGD 575, 2.
[62] BAGD 881, literally the leader of 1000 soldiers.
[63] BAGD 549, 2.b.
[64] Jastrow 412. Cf. the "violent men" in *t. Menaḥ.* 13:19 (see the next note).
[65] Zuckermandel / Liebermann 533, Neusner 5.161-162. A parallel is found in *b. Pesaḥ.* 57a (Soncino 284-285).
[66] Cf. L. Feldman's translation in the LCL edition of *Ant.* 20.181. Josephus also speaks of the "violence" (βία) of the contending parties.

An עֶבֶד can be either a slave or servant.⁶⁷ The same is true for Josephus' δοῦλος, employed also of the slave / servant of the high priest in the Gethsemane account. John, as noted above, employs ὑπηρέτης for the servants of the high priests (and Pharisees). Both Greek nouns most probably derive from the Semitic *'ebed*.

The Tosefta here employs two different Hebrew terms for "staves." The first, אַלָּה, means "lance, fork," a pointed pole.⁶⁸ Danby translates it by "club" in *m. Šabb*. 6:4.⁶⁹ The second, מַקֵּל, usually means a walking stick or staff, yet it could also be used for defensive purposes.⁷⁰ In *m. Roš Haš*. 1:9, for example, it is stated regarding those traveling: "if any lie in wait for them (to rob them), they may take 'staves' in their hands."⁷¹

The Mishnah passage *Šabb*. 6:4 is important in this regard. It states that "A man may not go out (on the Sabbath) with a 'sword' (סַיִף)⁷² or a bow or a shield or a 'club' (אַלָּה) or a spear."⁷³ Here sword and club are found together, as in Mark 14:43 and 48 par. The Jerusalem Talmud remarks at this point: "This teaches that they were armed with five different types of 'weapons.'"⁷⁴ The term for "weapons" here is זַיִן, meaning "weapons" in a collective sense.⁷⁵ It very probably lies behind the "weapons" of John 18:3, for the Evangelist omits the Synoptics' "swords and clubs," only attributing a sword to Peter (vv 10–11).

In a baraitha found in *b. Šabb*. 63a the Sages ask R. Eliezer (ben Hyrcanus), an early second generation Tanna,⁷⁶ why, if the five weapons of *m. Šabb*. 6:4 are considered by him to be

---

⁶⁷ Jastrow 1035.
⁶⁸ Jastrow 66. In *y. Šabb*. 6:4, 8b (Neusner 11.202) it is explained by דייקרן, probably from the Greek δίκρανον, "pitchfork" (LSJ 430).
⁶⁹ *The Mishnah* 105; Neusner has the same on p. 186.
⁷⁰ Jastrow 831.
⁷¹ Albeck 2.313, Danby 189.
⁷² Jastrow 978. It is equivalent to the biblical חֶרֶב (BDB 352).
⁷³ Albeck 2-31, Danby 105. Str-B also calls attention to it in 1.995.
⁷⁴ Cf. *Šabb*. 6:4, 8b (Neusner 11.202).
⁷⁵ Jastrow 393.
⁷⁶ Strack and Stemberger, *Introduction* 77.

ornaments for a man, they should cease in the days of the Messiah. To this he replies: "Because they will not be required," as in Isa 2:4, "nation shall not lift up sword against nation."[77] If this tradition is even earlier, it would be ironic that sword and club, thought to disappear in the days of the Messiah, should be employed to arrest Jesus of Nazareth, the Messiah, in Gethsemane.

A "crowd," "sword" and "club" are also found in Judaic tradition on Ahithophel and probably influenced the scene of Jesus' arrest in a major way.

B)

1) A Band

In Judaic tradition Psalm 55, dealing with the betrayal of a friend, is related to Ahithophel's betrayal of David. In *Midr. Pss.* 55/5 on v 20 (Eng. 19), "such as have no changes" is taken to allude to "Ahithophel and 'his band' (סייעתו), in whose hearts the inclination to evil underwent no change." They put forth their hands "against men who were at peace with them," referring to v 21 (Eng. 20).[78] In 55/6 the phrase "men of blood and deceit" in v 24 (Eng. 23)[79] is also applied to Ahithophel and "his band" (סייעתו), who "will not live out half their days."[80]

The term סִיעָה means "troop," "party," "company," "followers,"[81] or as Braude translates, a "band." I suggest that Ahithophel's troop or band of followers was the model for the "crowd" which followed Judas, who betrayed Jesus.

2) Swords

Midr. Pss. 55/5 comments on v 22a (Eng. 21a), "The words of his mouth were more slippery than butter," that these refer to Ahithophel's words. The next part of the verse, "His words were softer than oil, for they were 'suave,'" means that

---

[77] Soncino 295.
[78] Buber 292; Braude 1.494-495, which I slightly modify.
[79] The NRSV has "the bloodthirsty and treacherous."
[80] Buber 293, Braude 1.495.
[81] Jastrow 984, also true of סיעתא.

Ahithophel's words "were so 'persuasive' that everyone heeded him," resulting in the elders of Israel following his counsel (2 Sam 17:1, 2, 4) in betraying David.[82]

The Hebrew term Braude translates as "suave" is פְּתִיחוֹת, open or "drawn swords."[83] The word "persuasive" is פְּתוּחִין, the pass. part. pl. of פָּתַח, to open, here in the sense of "explained, spoken plainly."[84] The *Targum* on v 22 renders "but they were drawn swords" as "but they were spears / lances / poles of death."[85]

Here Ahithophel, the betrayer of David, is closely associated with "swords," for his persuasive words against David were like "drawn swords."

3) A Club

In a series of seven, beginning "There was a man who used to say...," and "Another man used to say...," *b. Sanh.* 7a states: "Another man used to say: 'The man in whom I trusted raised 'his club' (גְּזִיזֵיה) and rose up against me.' Samuel[86] said to Rab Yehudah[87]: This is alluded to in the verse, 'Even my bosom friend in whom I trusted, who ate of my bread, has lifted the heel against me' (Ps 41:10)."[88] A גְּזִיזָא is a branch or "club."[89]

---

[82] Buber 293, Braude 1.495.
[83] On the noun, cf. BDB 836; it is only found here in the MT. Cf. Braude 2.476, n. 7, for the meaning "pleasing" or "suave."
[84] Cf. Jastrow 1251, 2). See also פִּתּוּי as "persuasion" (1173).
[85] Merino 118 and 239. The term מוֹרְנִיתָא, lance, pole, is employed here (Jastrow 750). On tongues as sharp swords, cf. also Ps 57:5 (Eng. 4) and 59:8 (Eng. 7).
[86] Probably Mar Samuel, a first generation Babylonian Amora (Strack and Stemberger, *Introduction* 94).
[87] Probably a second generation Babylonian Amora (Strack and Stemberger, *Introduction* 96).
[88] Soncino 26, with n. 9, which I slightly modify. Goldschmidt (7.21) translates: "Ein Mann, auf den ich vertraut habe, schwang seinen Kolben und stellte sich gegen mich."
[89] Jastrow 229-230. He translates here: "lifted up his club and stood (against me)." The verb אֲזִי (16) means to swing, throw, pitch.

If the association of raising one's "club" and rising against someone, and Ps 41:10, elsewhere related to the betrayer Ahithophel, was earlier than this Amoraic example, it would be a confirmation of this psalm verse as not only lying beyond terminology in Jesus' Passover meal with the disciples (Judas, who eats Jesus' bread, betrays him), but also the scene of Jesus' arrest. After Jesus in Gethsemane asks the crowd armed with swords and clubs, coming from the chief priests, scribes and elders, whether they have come out with these instruments to arrest him as if he were a bandit, although they didn't arrest him while he daily taught in the Temple, he says: "But let the Scriptures be fulfilled" (Mark 14:49). If this is not a general reference to the necessity of his suffering and dying, it may here also allude to Ps 41:10. The latter verse, as shown above, is referred in Judaic tradition to David's disciple Ahithophel, who betrays him.

* * *

Ahithophel's "band" of followers, his swords (and possibly his club) appear to have influenced in a major way the imagery of Jesus' betrayal by Judas and the "crowd" who followed him with swords and clubs in Gethsemane. If this is indeed the case, it is legitimate to ask how historical these Gospel details are. There seems to have occurred an interweaving of historical tradition (Judas' betrayal of the Son of David, Jesus, by identifying him to the Temple authorities) and details from haggadic tradition on Ahithophel's betrayal of David, also in Jerusalem.

XI. Rabbi and Friend

A) Judas had given the "crowd" from the chief priests, scribes and elders (thus the Sanhedrin) a sign by which they could recognize Jesus at night in Gethsemane in order to arrest him: "The one I will kiss is the man" (Mark 14:44). "So when (Judas) came, he went up to (Jesus) at once and said, 'Rabbi!' and kissed him" (v 45). This led to the crowd's laying hands on Jesus and arresting him (v 46). The term "Rabbi" (ῥαββί) here means "my teacher, my master."[90]

The Evangelist Matthew expands the Markan incident by having Judas say to Jesus: "Greetings, Rabbi!" (χαῖρε, ῥαββί - 26:49). Jesus then addresses his disciple as "Friend" (ἑταῖρε). The latter term ἑταῖρος means "comrade, companion, friend."[91]

The above two expressions "Rabbi" and "Friend" probably also derive from Judaic tradition on Ahithophel.

B)
a) As indicated in section I. above, according to *b. Sanh.* 106b "at the end" David called Ahithophel his "disciple." This means that for the latter David was his teacher or "rabbi," as David was for his many other disciples according to Judaic tradition.

b) In *Midr. Pss.* 55/1 R. Judah bar Isaac[92] teaches: "David had no greater 'friend' than Ahithophel, whom David made chief of his prosecutors, and who was his counselor in all affairs," for which 1 Chr 27:33 is cited.[93] The term "friend" here is אוֹהֵב, literally "lover," but meant as "friend."[94]

Later in the same section of the midrash R. Nahman[95] has David state that Ahithophel was not an "enemy" from the nations of the earth. Rather, "he is my own kind" (זה כיוצא בו הוא),[96] that is, one of his closest associates. It was Ahithophel whom David meant by Ps 55:14 (Eng. 13): "But it is you, my equal, my companion, 'my familiar friend'" (who

---

[90] Jastrow 1442.
[91] BAGD 314, who note that Socrates also employs the expression of his pupils. It is found elsewhere in the NT only in Matt 11:16; 20:13; and 22:12.
[92] A rabbi of an unknown period.
[93] Buber 290, Braude 1.491.
[94] Cf. BDB 13, 4. (b) for biblical examples of the participle אֹהֵב as "friend." See also the passages listed at the end of 1. for "love of friend to friend."
[95] Probably a third, possibly a fourth generation Babylonian Amora (Strack and Stemberger, *Introduction* 101 and 105).
[96] Buber 291, Braude 1.491.

betrayed me).⁹⁷ The latter is the Hebrew מְיֻדָּעִי , the pual participle of ידע : "known," as a substitute "acquaintance,"⁹⁸ yet here certainly in the sense of the NRSV translation given above. Verse 21 (Eng. 20) notes that (the traitor) "laid hands on 'his friend' (שְׁלֹמָיו) and violated his covenant (with me)." The Hebrew noun שָׁלוֹם here means "peace, friendship," and someone שְׁלֹמִי is a person "of my friendship" = a friend.⁹⁹ Here too David and Ahithophel are considered "friends."

Yet the strongest influence on Jesus, the Son of David, as addressing Judas in Gethsemane as "friend" probably is Ps 41:10 (Eng. 9), shown above to be so important in the Passover meal scene and probably elsewhere. After commenting on Ahithophel as David's teacher and companion on the basis of Ps 55:14-15, R. Yohanan in *b. Sanh.* 106b-107a bases Ahithophel as "his (David's) disciple" on Ps 41:10 (Eng. 9) - "Even 'my bosom friend' in whom I trusted, who ate of my bread, has lifted the heel against me."¹⁰⁰ Here, the expression "my bosom friend" is the Hebrew אִישׁ שְׁלֹמִי. As pointed out in the previous paragraph, a person "of my peace, friendship" = a "friend."¹⁰¹

In Judaic tradition on the above scriptural passages, David expresses his extreme disappointment over his betrayal by Ahithophel, one of his own, one of his disciples, whom he labels an intimate "friend." This is the same great irony involved when the Son of David, the Messiah Jesus, is represented by the Jewish Christian Evangelist Matthew (or by a tradition he received from

---

⁹⁷ The *Targum* expressly mentions Ahithophel here (Merino 117, 239).
⁹⁸ BDB 394.
⁹⁹ BDB 1023, 5.a., not the interpretation given in 7 (the NRSV also renders it in the singular). Cf. שׁוֹלְמִי in Ps 7:5 as "my ally, friend," from the verb שׁלם (1023, qal).
¹⁰⁰ Soncino 729. Cf. also *Midr. Pss.* 41/7 (Buber 261; Braude 1.439) with the pl. "disciples."
¹⁰¹ The LXX does not have ἑταῖρος in any of the passages cited above. The Greek translator of the Semitic original for "friend" may have employed *hetairos* because he thought of its use for David's (main) friend Hushai five times in 2 Kgdms 15:32, 37; and 16:16-17. David employed Hushai to defeat the counsel of Ahithophel (15:34).

his own Christian community) as addressing his betrayer in Gethsemane as "friend."

XII. Judas and Ahithophel as Informers / Betrayers

A) Mark 14:10 states that Judas went to the chief priests in order to "betray" (παραδίδωμι) Jesus to them. The same Greek verb is employed similarly in 3:19, in the passion predictions of 9:31 and 10:33, and again explicitly of Judas in 14:11, 18, 21 and 41, and Judas is labeled "the betrayer" of Jesus (ὁ παραδιδούς με / αὐτόν) in vv 42 and 44.[102] Luke explicitly describes Judas as "a betrayer / traitor" (προδότης) in 6:16.[103]

Some recent writers on the figure of Judas have attempted to exonerate him on the basis of passages such as Matt 26:50 ("Friend, do what you are here to do")[104] and John 13:27 ("Do quickly what you are going to do"). They think that Jesus even encouraged Judas to hand him over to the Jewish religious officials, a part of the divine plan of salvation.[105] This may in part be true of the *later* tradition as found in the above two passages, yet in the earliest Gospel, that of Mark, there is no trace yet of such "theologizing." Judas does not innocently "hand over" Jesus, hoping that he will be kept "safe"[106] by the Jewish authorities until the Passover festival is past and the Roman Pilate, wary of any possible messianic pretender who could challenge Rome's rule, had returned to Caesarea on the Mediterranean Sea. Judas at the earliest level of the Gospel tradition intentionally "betrayed" Jesus to the chief priests, scribes and elders, i.e. to the Sanhedrin, and he certainly knew that they and others sought to get rid of the popular prophet

---

[102] It is used of "handing over" Jesus to others in 15:1, 10 and 15. On *paradidōmi* in regard to Judas' betrayal of Jesus, cf. BAGD 614, 1.b.
[103] LSJ 1475, BAGD 704.
[104] The NRSV; the Greek expression is very difficult.
[105] Cf. especially the first two works mentioned in n.1.
[106] The ἀσφαλῶς of Mark 14:44 could be construed so. The RSV has "lead him away 'safely,'" while the NRSV more probably renders: "lead him away under guard" (so that he cannot escape).

from Nazareth (already in Galilee in Mark 3:6; then in Jerusalem in 11:18; 12:12-13; and 14:1).

One major influence on early Palestinian Jewish Christians' characterization of Judas as the betrayer of Jesus, the Son of David, was Judaic tradition on Ahithophel as an informer / denouncer of David.

B) The Latin term *dēlātor* means an "informer, denouncer."[107] It was taken over at an early time into Hebrew and Aramaic[108] and also employed to describe the situation of David in 2 Samuel 15-17. At 15:12 Ahithophel is presented as participating in this "conspiracy" (קֶשֶׁר).[109] In v 31 David is told he is among the "conspirators" (קֹשְׁרִים).[110] The latter two passages probably contributed to Ahithophel's being considered an "informer / denouncer / betrayer" of David where the term דילטור is employed.

Pesiq. Rav Kah. 4/2 has R. Levi, a third generation Palestinian Amora,[111] state that children who lived in the time of David had superior learning. Despite this (reservoir of merits), "when the men of the generation of David's time went into battle, they perished. Whenever they went into battle, they perished because there were 'informers' (דילטורין) among them. David

---

[107] Chambers Murray 184, b. The related noun *dēlātio* means informing, denunciation. Cf. the Greek δηλητήρ, destroyer (LSJ 384).

[108] Cf. Jastrow 299 on דִּילָטוֹר, דלטור and דילטורא, דל׳. The noun for "informing against" is דילטוריא , דל׳. Yehudah b. Ilai, a third generation Tanna (Strack and Stemberger, *Introduction* 84-85), employs the first term in *Deut. Rab.* Shofeṭim 5/10 on Deut 17:14 (Mirqin 11.91, Soncino 7.111), and Simeon b. Yoḥai, also a third generation Tanna (*Introduction* 84) the second term in *y. Ber.* 1:2, 3b (Neusner / Zahavy 1.35).

[109] BDB 905.

[110] This is the active participle of the verb קָשַׁר, bind, league together, conspire (BDB 905). The *Targum* employs מרדא, "rebellion," and מרודיא, "rebels," here (Jastrow 837-838; Sperber 2.186-187).

[111] Strack and Stemberger, *Introduction* 98; he was a student of R. Yoḥanan bar Nappaḥa, a second generation Palestinian Amora who taught in Sepphoris and Tiberias until his death in 279 CE (*ibid.*, 94-95).

meant this when he said: 'My soul is among lions; I lie down among those who would lap up; their teeth are spears and arrows, their tongue a sharp sword' (Ps 57:5, Eng. 4).[112] 'My soul is among lions' refers to Abner and Amasa who were like lions in the Torah. 'I lie down among those who would lap up' refers to Doeg and Ahithophel, for they delighted in lapping up 'slander' (לשון הרע) (and passing it on)."[113]

In regard to the latter, W. Braude remarks that "Doeg informed on David and Nob the city of priests (1 Sam 22:9). As for Ahithophel, even though his being an informer is not mentioned in Scripture, the Rabbis apparently had a tradition that he also was one."[114] I suggest that this was due to his being part of the "conspiracy," one of the "conspirators" against David mentioned above in 2 Sam 15:12 and 31.

R. Levi continues his exposition of Ps 57:5 by saying: "their teeth are spears and arrows" refers to the men of Keilah. Of them it is written, "Will the men of Keilah 'deliver up' me and my men (into the hand of Saul? The Lord said, 'They will deliver you up')" (1 Sam 23:12). "And their tongue a sharp sword" refers to the Ziphites, of whom it is written, "they went and told Saul, 'David is hiding among us'" (Ps 54:2, Eng. superscription). David then requests God for this reason to remove His presence from the earth back to heaven, as Ps 57:6a (Eng. 5a) is interpreted. In contrast to them, the generation of Ahab consisted entirely of idolaters, yet there were no "informers" (דילטורין) among them. Thus when they went forth to battle, they were victorious.[115]

The above exposition is found in numerous sources, showing its popularity.[116] It should be noted that "informers" in David's

---

[112] I cite the whole verse here; in the text the first part ends with "etc."
[113] Mandelbaum 1.56-57; I slightly modify Braude and Kapstein at 61.
[114] *Pesikta de-Rav Kahana* 61, n. 18.
[115] Mandelbaum 1.57, Braude and Kapstein 61-62.
[116] Cf. *y. Peah* 1:1, 16a (Neusner / Brooks 2.67-68); *Lev. Rab.* 'Emor 26/2 on Lev 21:1 (Mirqin 8.76, Soncino 4.326); *Deut. Rab.* Shofeṭim 5/10 on Deut 17:14 (Mirqin 11.91, Soncino 7.111); *Num. Rab.* Ḥukkath 19/2 on Num 19:2 (Mirqin 10.220, Soncino 6.746); *Tanḥ.* Ḥukkat 4 (Eshkol 759-

generation are closely associated with those who "deliver up" David "into the hand of" the ruling power, at that time King Saul. Both the men of Keilah (1 Sam 23:12) and the Ziphites (v 20; here Ps 54:2) are thus willing to betray David. The Hebrew verb employed in 1 Sam 23:11-12 and 20 for "to deliver up" is סגר, which in the piel and hiphil has this meaning.[117] In the LXX versions of Origen and Lucian it is translated by παραδίδωμι at 1 Kgdms 23:12, as well as in Deut 23:15; 32:30; and Ps 77(78):48. Job 16:11 also reads: παρέδωκεν γάρ με ὁ κύριος εἰς χεῖρας ἀδίκου / ἀδίκων, "The Lord delivered me up into the hands of an unrighteous person / unrighteous persons." It is thus quite probable that the Semitic original of Judas' "betraying / delivering up" (παραδίδωμι) Jesus into the hands of the Jerusalem authorities was the piel or hiphil of סגר, if the narrative was originally in Hebrew. All twenty-three occurrences of this verb in the piel and hiphil in the MT are translated in the targums by מסר,[118] making this term most probable if the original was Aramaic. It means to hand over or deliver, especially to deliver a person to the authorities, to inform against.[119] M. Jastrow notes its occurrence in *Sifre* Ha'azinu § 323 on the הִסְגִּירָם of Deut 32:30 - "I shall not 'deliver' (מסגיר) you into the hands (of the enemy) Myself, but via the hands of others (who will betray you). It once happened that flies 'delivered' them 'up' (מסרון) in Judea."[120] The cognate noun מָסוֹר means "informer, traitor (delivering Jews into the hands of the Roman government),"[121] and probably stands

---

760); *Tanh*. B Ḥukkat 7 (Buber 106, Bietenhard 2.334-335); and *Midr. Pss*. 7/7 on Ps 7:8 (Buber 67, Braude 1.107-108).
[117] Cf. BDB 689, and Jastrow 956: to bind over, hand over, deliver.
[118] The passages are listed under the piel and hiphil of סגר in BDB 689. Only Obad 14 has מסרתהא, yet it is also meant in the sense of "delivering up." For Deut 23:16 and 32:30 I consulted Onqelos.
[119] Jastrow 810. While the verb does not appear to be employed in the MT, cf. BDB 588 on the Aramaic: to deliver up, denounce, betray.
[120] Cf. Jastrow's beginning translation in 956, supplemented by that of Hammer (335; Finkelstein 373, with the note on line 4).
[121] Jastrow 805. Cf. also M. Kayserling, art. "Moser" in *JE* (1905) 9.42-44, who calls attention to the synonyms *masor*, *delator* and *malshin*, and the

behind the προδότης of Luke 6:16 employed of Judas, if there was a Semitic original here.[122]

Ahithophel, together with Doeg, as noted above was considered an informer / betrayer of David in Judaic tradition, connected to wanting to deliver him up to death.[123] This was a major reason early Palestinian Jewish Christians employed Ahithophel as a model for their depiction of Judas' betraying / delivering up Jesus to the Jewish (and later Roman) authorities. It also means that the verb παραδίδωμι employed of Judas in the Gospels does not imply a neutral "handing over" of someone, with no evil intent. The opposite is the case. Judas' "delivering up" Jesus meant surrendering him to his death, intended from the outset.

XIII. Ahithophel's Motivation for Betraying David, and Judas' Motivation for Betraying Jesus

Ahithophel's motivation for betraying David is not noted in the biblical text. Basically three possible explanations exist for his behavior.

1) According to 2 Sam 11:3, Bathsheba was the daughter of Eliam. He in turn was identified as the son of Ahithophel (23:34). Since Bathsheba was married to Uriah the Hittite, when David lay with her (11:3-4) he debauched a married woman. His closest counselor, Ahithophel (15:12; 16:23; 1 Chr 27:33), thus may have sought an opportunity to revenge this

---

art. "Informers" in *EJ* (1971) 8.1364-1373. The verb קָרַץ can also mean to inform against (Jastrow 1425, III). See also *b. Sanh.* 97a (Soncino 656), where "the son of David (= the Messiah) will not come until 'denunciators' are in abundance."
[122] Cf. the Hebrew New Testament of Delitzsch (p. 112) for מוֹסֵר.
[123] This treacherous, unforgivable deed led to their being considered two of the four commoners who have no share in the world to come. Cf. *m. Sanh.* 10:2 in Albeck 4.202, Danby 397.

dishonoring of his granddaughter to restore the family's reputation.[124]

2) *'Avot R. Nat.* A 41 states that Ahithophel was one of the six people who "had a hankering for greatness."[125] *Eliyyahu Rabba* 31 notes that he had an "overweening pride."[126] An example of his being greatly offended by David was when the latter appointed 90,000 elders on the occasion of his bringing up the ark to Jerusalem. Yet Ahithophel was not included.[127] This may have inspired him to attempt to remove the cause of this insult.

Interestingly, the Evangelist Luke does not have the disciples' dispute about greatness in a position similar to Mark 10:41–45, but in 22:24–30 after the institution of the "Lord's Supper." That concludes by Jesus' saying of the Son of Man: "woe to that one by whom he is betrayed" (v 22). Judas is obviously meant, and the dispute on greatness precisely at this point may be based on David's disciple Ahithophel, who craved this.

3) In *t. Soṭa* 4:19 it is stated that Ahithophel is one of those who "set their eyes on what they did not have coming to them. What they wanted was not given to them, and what they had in hand was taken away from them."[128] This refers to ruling or becoming

---

[124] For Bathsheba as Ahithophel's (grand-)daughter, cf. *b. Sanh.* 101a (Soncino 689, with n. 3) and 107a (Soncino 731). The latter passage deals with David's adultery with her (730-731). For Ahithophel's reproach of David for seizing an ewe-lamb (Bathsheba) and murdering her shepherd (Uriah), see *Pesiq. Rav Kah.* 2/1 on Ps 3:3 (Mandelbaum 1.16, Braude and Kapstein 22, with n. 4) and *Midr. Pss.* 3/5-6 on Ps 3:3 (Buber 38, Braude 1.57). On Ahithophel's possibly wanting to revenge David's misusing his granddaughter, see H. Hertzberg, *I & II Samuel* (Philadelphia: Westminster Press, 1964) 337 and 350.
[125] Schechter 133, Goldin 173.
[126] Friedmann 157-158, Braude and Kapstein 382-384.
[127] Cf. *y. Sanh.* 10:2, 29a (Neusner 31.344) and *Num. Rab.* Bemidbar 4/20 (Mirqin 9.86 and 88, Soncino 5.122, 124). For Ahithophel's reproach of David on the occasion of the ark, see *Sifre* § 46 on Num 7:9 (Horovitz 51, Neusner 1.210).
[128] Zuckermandel / Liebermann 301, Neusner 3.166. It is also found in *b. Soṭa* 9b (Soncino 40-41), and for the most part in *Gen. Rab.* Bereshith

king, as the preceding discussion of a snake shows. In *Midr. Pss.* 4/8 on Ps 4:3 David says Ahithophel (and Doeg) maintain that God has abandoned him, has forgotten him, has taken His presence away from him, and from now on kingship (המלכות) will never return to him.[129] This probably refers to the following period, when David was smitten with leprosy after his sin of adultery with Bathsheba.

In *b. Sanh.* 101a "our Rabbis taught" that Ahithophel was one of the three who beheld, but did not see. He beheld leprosy breaking out on his penis and thought that this meant he himself would reign as king. Yet it was not so. Rather, it referred to his (grand-)daughter Bathsheba, from whom came (King) Solomon.[130]

On another occasion according to *y. Sanh.* 10:2, 29a, David wanted to dig the foundations of the future Temple. Finally he found a clay pot, which told him he should not remove it because it covered the great deep. David nevertheless did so, and "the great deep surged upward to flood the world. Ahithophel was standing there. He said, 'Thus will David be strangled (choked to death in the flood) and 'I shall be king' (ואנא מליך)."[131]

All the above passages agree in attributing to Ahithophel the desire to become king instead of David.

* * *

In summary, one must conclude that neither Ahithophel's possible desire to revenge David's debauching his

---

20/5 on Gen 3:15 (Theodor and Albeck 187-188, Soncino 1.163, which forgot Ahithophel). Absalom is also one of the ten in this list.
[129] Buber 45; Braude 1.71, who correctly supplies the names. The parallel in *Pesiq. Rav Kah.* 18/1 has them (Mandelbaum 1.293; Braude and Kapstein 316).
[130] Soncino 689, which explains the significance of the leprosy in n. 2. In 107a (Soncino 733) David is smitten with leprosy for six months after his debauching Bathsheba. On this, see also *b. Yoma* 22b (Soncino 102).
[131] Neusner 31.345. In *b. Sukk.* 53a-b, R. Ḥisda relates a similar narrative he heard elsewhere ("it was stated thus" – Soncino 255), yet without the remark of Ahithophel's wanting to become king.

granddaughter, nor his being offended at not being appointed an elder together with others, nor his desire to become king himself, offers a possible model for Judas' motivation in betraying Jesus.

In the biblical text, there is no reason given for Ahithophel's betrayal of David. This is similar to the earliest recoverable layer of the Judas tradition. No motivation on his part is ascertainable. In Mark 14:11 it is only *after* Judas goes to the chief priests and offers to betray Jesus that they promise to give him money. The text implies he did not seek it from the outset. The motif of avarice on his part is only a further development of the tradition,[132] as legends later developed to explain why Ahithophel betrayed David.

XIV. Falsehood / Betrayal

The term שֶׁקֶר is also important in regard to Ahithophel and Judas "Iscariot." It means "deception, what deceives, disappoints, and betrays one."[133] *Gen. Rab.* Noach 38/1 on Gen 11:1 has "the Rabbis" relate Ps 59:12 (Eng. 11) to Doeg and Ahithophel. The next verse, "For the sin of their mouths, the words of their lips" (v 13, Eng. 12), is taken to refer to their permitting incest and bloodshed. The latter for Ahithophel was his plan to have David killed (2 Sam 18:2).[134] The motif of bloodshed is also found in Judaic interpretation of Ps 55:24 (Eng. 23), "'the bloodthirsty and treacherous' (אנשי דמים ומרמה) shall not live out half their days." This is related in *b. Sanh.* 69b and 106b to Doeg and Ahithophel, the latter passage as a baraitha.[135] *Midr. Pss.* 55/6 relates it to "Ahithophel and his

---

[132] Cf. Matt 26:15, "What will you give me if I betray him to you?" John 12:6 maintains that Judas kept the common purse. He was a thief "and used to steal what was put into it." *Cant. Rab.* 2:5 § 3 states that when David saw a certain man's "love of money, he put him in control of his treasury" (Soncino 9.108). Yet this was not Ahithophel.

[133] BDB 1055,1., Jastrow 1628. It occurs 112 times in the MT. The cognate verb is also שָׁקַר.

[134] Theodor and Albeck 351, Soncino 1.302.

[135] Soncino 470-471 and 729, respectively.

band."¹³⁶ B. Gärtner correctly points out that the *Targum* inserts שְׁקַר three times into this "Ahithophel" psalm.¹³⁷

The term מִרְמָה, "deceit, treachery,"¹³⁸ is a synonym of שֶׁקֶר in Jer 9:4-5 (Eng. 5-6); Amos 8:5; Ps 109:2; and Prov 12:17. The related noun רְמִיָּה,¹³⁹ is a synonym of שֶׁקֶר in Mic 6:12; Ps 101:7; and 120:2. In *Midr. Pss.* 119/50 on Ps 119:118, for example, "for their deceit is falsehood" (כי שקר תרמיתם) means that Doeg and Ahithophel taught the Torah "with falsehood and deceit" (בשקר וברמיות).¹⁴⁰

Finally, *Midr. Pss.* 5/8 on 5:6b (Eng. 5b), "workers of iniquity," refers this to Doeg and Ahithophel, who "perverted the truth into 'falsehood' (שֶׁקֶר)." "Those who speak lies, a man of blood and 'deceit' (מרמה)" (v 7, Eng. 6), is then related in the following section to Doeg and Ahithophel, who have no portion in the world to come.¹⁴¹ The latter tradition is also found in *Gen. Rab.* Noach 32/1 on Gen 7:1.¹⁴²

Because of the deceitful, treacherous deed of seeking to betray David by having him killed, Ahithophel is labeled in Judaic sources a man of שֶׁקֶר. In Hebrew this could be אִישׁ שֶׁקֶר. A number of scholars favor the latter as the derivation of Judas "Iscariot."¹⁴³ While I propose a different solution below, the first Palestinian Jewish Christians who heard the betrayer of Jesus, Judas, designated "Iscariot" (אִישׁ קְרִיּוֹת) certainly also recognized that he was modeled on Ahithophel, closely

---

¹³⁶ Buber 293, Braude 1.495.
¹³⁷ Cf. his "Die rätselhaften Termini Nazoräer und Iskariot" 65, n. 73, and Merino 117.
¹³⁸ BDB 941.
¹³⁹ *Ibid.*
¹⁴⁰ Buber 500, Braude 2.278.
¹⁴¹ Buber 55, Braude 1.89-90.
¹⁴² Theodor and Albeck 288-289, Soncino 1.249.
¹⁴³ Cf. E. Hengstenberg, *Das Evangelium des heiligen Johannes* (Berlin: Schlawitz, 1861) 1.419; C. Torrey, "The Name 'Iscariot'" in *HTR* 36 (1943) 59-61, and his "Studies in the Aramaic of the First Century A.D." in *ZAW* 65 (1953) 246-247; and B. Gärtner, "Die rätselhaften Termini" 65.

connected to שֶׁקֶר. He was a "deceitful, treacherous" person. They would have appreciated this wordplay.

XV. Ahithophel's Suicide, and Judas' Suicide

A. In *b. Sanh.* 106b, R. Yohanan, a second generation Palestinian Amora,[144] maintains that along with Doeg, Ahithophel did not live out half his days. A baraitha is then cited regarding them: "'Bloody and deceitful men shall not live out half their days' (Ps 55:24): Doeg's entire lifetime amounted to only thirty-four years, and Ahithophel's to thirty-three."[145] This tradition is also found in 69b,[146] and in *Midr. Pss.* 55/6 on Ps 55:24 in regard to "Ahithophel and his band."[147] It is based on Ps 90:10, "The days of our life are seventy years...." Half of this is thirty-five, which Ahithophel did not reach.

According to 2 Sam 17:23, when Ahithophel saw that his counsel (to have David captured and killed) was not followed, he went home "and hanged himself" (וַיֵּחָנַק). The verb חנק means to strangle, the niphal here as Ahithophel's strangling, i.e. hanging himself.[148] Josephus in *Ant.* 7.229 notes that Ahithophel "went into the innermost part of his house and 'hanged himself' (ἀνήρτησεν ἑαυτόν)."[149]

As remarked above, *m. Sanh.* 10:2 notes that Ahithophel is one of the four commoners who will have no share in the world to come. The Jerusalem Talmud at this point relates four anecdotes about Ahithophel. In the first he refuses to help

---

[144] Strack and Stemberger, *Introduction* 94-95.
[145] Soncino 729. Earlier the same psalm verse is applied to Balaam, who according to "Balaam's Chronicle" was "thirty years old when Phinehas the Robber killed him" (Soncino 725). Jesus, a Gospel, and Pontius Pilate may be meant here.
[146] Soncino 470-471.
[147] Buber 293, Braude 1.495.
[148] BDB 338. The *Targum* employs the same verb (Sperber 2.191, Harrington and Saldarini 191), with the same meaning (Jastrow 485).
[149] He does not follow the LXX here, which has ἀπήγξατο. This verb is ἀπάγχω, to strangle, throttle, in the midd. and pass. "hang oneself, to be hanged" (LSJ 174).

David stabilize the ark's strange conduct. David then tells him: "One who knows how to make the ark stop and does not do so in the end 'will commit suicide / hang himself' (מִתְחַנְּקָא)."[150] In the second incident David digs very deep in order to lay the foundations for the Temple. When he finds a clay pot and wants to remove it, it informs him that it is the cover over the great deep. Nevertheless David removes it, and the great deep surges up to flood the world. Standing next to David, Ahithophel believes David will be "choked" to death (מתחנק – in the flood), and he will become king. At this point David rebukes him by stating: "He who is a sage, knowing how to stop up the matter, and does not stop it, will in the end 'hang himself / commit suicide' (מתחנקא)." Then Ahithophel pronounces an incantation and stops up (the flood). Nevertheless, "in the end 'he hanged himself' (מתחנקה)."[151]

The former passage is also found in *b. Makk.* 11a,[152] and the latter in *Midr. Samuel* 26/2, including comment by R. Simeon b. Gamaliel, a third generation Tanna.[153] In *Eliyyahu Rabbah* 31 it is also related that since Ahithophel held back the halakhah in his throat and did not speak it to the multitudes, he died by "strangulation" (חֲנִיקָה),[154] for which 2 Sam 17:23 is cited.[155]

The above passages show how important the betrayer Ahithophel's death by hanging / strangling himself was in Judaic haggadic tradition. In the MT only two other figures commit suicide: Saul in 1 Sam 31:4, and Zimri in 1 Kgs 16:18. This makes it all the more probable that Ahithophel's hanging himself became the model for the only suicide in the NT, that of Judas.

---

[150] This is 10:2, 29a (Neusner 31.344 has: "is going to be put to death through strangulation," which wrongly implies by another person). Cf. Jastrow 485, ithpa. of חנק as "to hang oneself," citing this passage and *Targ.* 2 Sam 17:23.
[151] Neusner 31.345-346, whom I modify as above.
[152] Soncino 74.
[153] Buber 125; Wünsche, *Aus Israels Lehrhallen* 5.144-145.
[154] Jastrow 483 and 485.
[155] Friedmann 157, Braude and Kapstein 383.

B. The earliest Gospel, that of Mark, does not relate what became of Judas after he betrayed Jesus in the Garden of Gethsemane. Luke relates one later tradition in Acts 1:16-19. The Evangelist Matthew, however, was acquainted with another later tradition, which depended on the Ahithophel haggada. In 27:5 he notes that when Judas repented of betraying Jesus, having thrown down the money given him by the chief priests and elders in the Temple, "he departed and 'hanged himself' (ἀπήγξατο)." The latter verb is exactly the same as that employed in the LXX of Ahithophel's "hanging himself" in 2 Sam 17:23. It only occurs here in the NT.[156] This makes it very probable that Judas' death in Matt 27:5 was based on that of him who betrayed David, Ahithophel.

XVI. Ahithophel's Remorse / Repentance, and Judas' Remorse / Repentance

A) 2 Sam 17:23 states that "when Ahithophel saw that his counsel was not followed, he saddled his ass and went home to his own city. 'He set his house in order,' and hanged himself." The phrase "He set his house in order" is וַיְצַו אֶל ~ בֵּיתוֹ. The verb is the piel of צוה, lay charge (upon), give charge (to), charge, command, order.[157]

The latter phrase is the basis for comment in *y. Sanh.* 10:2, 29a. After asking how Ahithophel "removed himself" (from this life), it cites 2 Sam 17:23 and states in this fourth unit on Ahithophel: "Three things did Ahithophel command his sons, saying to them: 1) 'Do not rebel against the royal house of David, for we shall find that the Holy One, blessed be He, shows favor to them even in public. 2) And do not have business dealings with someone on whom the hour smiles. 3) And if the day of Pentecost is bright, sow the best quality of wheat.'"

The first thing Ahithophel commands his son before hanging himself is in regard to his own betrayal of David (2 Sam 17:1-3).

---

[156] Elsewhere in the LXX it is only found in Tob 3:10.
[157] BDB 845. Cf. 2 Kgs 20:1 (= Isa 38:1) for Hezekiah's also setting his house in order before dying.

In Judaic tradition he regrets having done so, even advising his sons not to do the same. Similar traditions are found in *b. B. Bat.* 147a[158] and *Eliyyahu Rabbah* 31.[159]

Ahithophel's regret is most probably also a haggadic development of the verb וַיֵּחָנַק in 2 Sam 17:23, "and he hanged himself." The niphal of חנק in rabbinic Hebrew also means to feel like choking, "to be sorry."[160] Ahithophel's hanging himself was thus also thought to be due to his regret in betraying David. The same is true for Judas, who betrayed the Son of David, Jesus.

B) Matt 27:3 states that when Judas, Jesus' betrayer, saw that he was condemned, he "regretted" it or "repented" (μεταμέλομαι).[161] He realized that he had sinned by betraying innocent blood (v 4). Therefore he threw down in the Temple the thirty pieces of silver he had received from the chief priests and elders, departed and "hanged himself" (v 5). If the Evangelist Matthew appropriated this special material from a Semitic source within his own (bilingual) Christian community, Judas' regret / repentance could also have originally been a wordplay with his "hanging himself." It was at any rate closely modeled on Ahithophel's regret shown before he hanged himself.

XVII. Ahithophel and the Name Judas "Iscariot"

The above sixteen sections may be questioned individually. Cumulatively, however, they argue very strongly for Ahithophel, especially in Palestinian Judaic tradition, as the

---

[158] Soncino 635.
[159] Friedmann 157, Braude and Kaptstein 383.
[160] Jastrow 485, with examples of "grieving" and dying "in despair." He cites a section of *y. Sanh.* 10:2, 29a with the ithpael מִתְחַנֵּק, "now David will die in despair." Cf. also *Tanh.* B Mesora' 1 on Lev 14:1-2 (Buber 2.43, Bietenhard 2.70), where Ahithophel in connection with 2 Sam 17:23 is "troubled" or "agitated" (נטרד; Jastrow 550 on טרד, niphal). A parallel is found in *Tanh.* Mesora' 1 (Eshkol 553). See also the connection of hanging oneself, grief and distress in Tob 3:10.
[161] BAGD 511.

"Vorlage" for many aspects of the description of Judas in the Gospels. I suggest that this is also true for the name "Iscariot." The latter in the Gospels is the Greek 'Ισκαριώτης, and in Mark 3:19, 14:10, and Luke 6:16 'Ισκαριώθ, perhaps because a rough breathing follows (ὅς, ὁ).[162] The core of the designation is 'Ισκαριώτ. The following remarks propose that this is based on Judaic tradition regarding the betrayer of David, Ahithophel.

1) The Name "Ahithophel" as a Distortion, with Slander and Denunciation

The personal name Ahithophel, אֲחִיתֹפֶל was certainly not original, perhaps later distorted from Ahiphelet.[163] The root טפל, to "plaster,"[164] is associated in Job 13:4 and Ps 119:69 with שֶׁקֶר. In rabbinic Hebrew תָּפַל means not only to "paste," but also to "denounce, slander,"[165] and the Aramaic טְפַל, together with שְׁקָרָא, to "charge falsely, calumniate."[166] "Ahithophel" as "brother of slander / denunciation" fits his role in the conspiracy against David very well. It is known that other Hebrew names are similar distortions.[167] The distorted name Ahithophel may thus be one reason Judas was later given the surname "Iscariot," which as אִישׁ שְׁקַר יוח also recalled to Semitic-speaking Palestinian Jews the term שֶׁקֶר, employed of Ahithophel in Judaic tradition. Indeed, he and Doeg were considered the two great slanderers / denouncers.

2) Ahithophel from the Unknown Judean City of Giloh, and Judas from the Unknown Judean City of Qeriyyot

2 Sam 15:12 states that when Absalom began his conspiracy against his father David, he sent for "Ahithophel the Gilonite, David's counselor, 'from his city Giloh.'" The latter phrase is

---

[162] The one exception is Matt 10:4, where -ēs is followed by ho.
[163] Cf. Hertzberg, I & II Samuel 338, followed by others.
[164] BDB 381 : smear or plaster (over), stick, glue.
[165] Jastrow 1686.
[166] Jastrow 547-548.
[167] Cf. for example אִישׁ ~ בֹּשֶׁת, "man of shame" in 2 Sam 2:8 for אֶשְׁבַּעַל in 1 Chr 8:33 and 9:39, and BDB 102 on בֹּשֶׁת.

literally "from his city, from Giloh" (מֵעִיר מִגִּלֹה). From "his city" in turn in the *Targum* is קְרִתֵיה,[168] which I suggest was one factor which helped to cause a Palestinian Jewish Christian to invent the surname אִישׁ קְרִיּוֹת ~ for Judas: "an inhabitant of (the city) Qeriyyot." The Aramaic קְרִיָּה, קְרָיָּא corresponds to the Hebrew קִרְיָה, town, city.[169]

According to Josh 15:51 Giloh was one of the eleven towns in the hill country of Judah. Its exact location is now unknown, and it is not mentioned in rabbinical writings.[170] The latter is true also for the site קְרִיּוֹת (v 25), located somewhere in Judah, "in the extreme south, toward the boundary of Edom" (v 21).[171] Making Judas into an inhabitant of Qeriyyot somewhere in Judah appears in part to have been modeled on the "Vorlage" of Ahithophel, who also came from an unknown town in Judah.

The latter is important to note, for because of the place-name Qeriyyot many scholars maintain Judas was the only Judean, i.e. non-Galilean disciple of Jesus.[172] This is, however, highly

---

[168] Sperber 2.186, Harrington and Saldarini 187.

[169] Cf. Jastrow 1420 and 1419. Interestingly, the other denunciator with whom Ahithophel is closely associated in Judaic sources, Doeg, is always labeled "the Edomite." In the postexilic period Edom became Idumea, part of southern Judah. *Midr. Pss.* 52/4 on 52:2 (Buber 284, Braude 1.478) states that Doeg was called "the Edomite," "and he was called by the name of 'his city' (עִירוֹ)."

[170] Cf. V. Gold, art. "Giloh" in *IDB* 2.399, and the lack of its occurrence in G. Reeg, *Die Ortsnamen Israels nach der rabbinischen Literatur* (Beihefte zum Tübinger Atlas des Vorderen Orients, B 51; Wiesbaden: Reichert, 1989).

[171] Cf. BDB 901, 1., which notes Judas אִישׁ קְרִיּוֹת, and Reeg, *Die Ortsnamen*. In the MT it is a separate place (with no ~). It may be Khirbet el-Qaryatein / Quryatē. Cf. R. Boling and G. Wright, *Joshua* (AB 6; Garden City, New York: Doubleday, 1982) 382, and V. Fritz, *Das Buch Josua* (HAT I/7; Tübingen: Mohr/Siebeck, 1994) 165. In The Survey of Israel, 1979, "Israel 1:250,000, South" there is a Tel Qeriyyot in section J22. It is ca. 21 km (13 m) south of Hebron, and 8 km (5 m) southeast of Sammu' (Eshtemoa'). See also the *Tübingen Bible Atlas*, B IV 6, southern part: 1616.0839.

[172] Cf. for example J. Klausner, *Jesus von Nazareth* (Berlin: Jüdischer Verlag, 1934; Jerusalem: The Jewish Publishing House, 1952³) 446;

improbable. Everywhere else in the Gospels Jesus is represented as calling his twelve disciples in Galilee, especially near the Sea of Galilee. The epithet "Iscariot" was given to Judas *after* he betrayed Jesus and was in part based on his biblical "model," for Ahithophel also came from a Judean locality. To imply that Judas was from the (now unknown) southern Judean town of Qeriyyot may also have been a conscious effort on the part of post-Resurrection Galilean Christians in the north to distance themselves as far as possible from him who betrayed their Lord: "He was certainly not one of us!"[173]

3) Ahithophel and קרי איש, and Judas as a "Man from Qeriyyot"

In *b. Ned.* 37b R. Isaac (probably II., a third generation Palestinian Amora[174]) states that "The textual reading, as transmitted by the Soferim, their stylistic embellishments, [words] read [in the text] but not written, and words written but omitted in the reading, are all *halachah* from Moses at Sinai."[175] That is, as part of the oral Torah they are to be considered on the same level as the written Torah and to be just as ancient.

Seven examples of words read in the text, but not written, are then given, including 2 Sam 16:23 – "[the word] man (איש) in

---

W. Vogler, *Judas Iskarioth* 23; and H.-J. Klauck, *Judas – ein Jünger des Herrn* 137. G. Schwarz in *Jesus und Judas. Aramaistische Untersuchungen zur Jesus-Judas Überlieferung der Evangelien und der Apostelgeschichte* (BWANT 123; Stuttgart: Kohlhammer, 1988) 10 maintains Judas was from Jerusalem. W. Klassen in *Judas. Betrayer or Friend of Jesus?* 38 says he "possibly" was.

[173] Cf. the similar phenomenon of their placing the birth of Jesus not in Nazareth, where his parents were at home (Mark 1:9; 6:1; Luke 1:26; 2:4, 39), but in Bethlehem in Judea in order to fulfill Mic 5:1 (Eng. 2), as in Matt 2:6. The Messiah had to be born in Bethlehem. See also *Targ.* 2 Sam 20:26, which purposely changes Ira from Jair in Gilead to Tekoa in Judah (Sperber 2.200, Harrington and Saldarini 198, with n. 32; see also 23:26), and θεκωνει in B⁺ of 2 Kgdms 15:12.

[174] Strack and Stemberger, *Introduction* 98.

[175] Soncino 116. Cf. 290 on the explanation of "Soferim" (scribes): "title of the pre-Tannaitic treachers, beginning with Ezra (v. Ezra VII, 11)."

'the counsel that Ahithophel gave was as if a [man - אִישׁ] consulted (~ יִשְׁאַל) the oracle of God.'"[176]

This is also found in the minor tractate of the Babylonian Talmud, *Soferim* 6:8, 38a, which lists the above seven plus three more passages. Yet only the words actually read are enumerated here. The reader of this tractate was expected to know that "man" (אִישׁ) was inserted at 2 Sam 16:23.[177]

The above is the reason the Masoretic text of the Hebrew Bible has in the margin of 2 Sam 16:23, אִישׁ קְרֵי וְלֹא כְּתִיב ("'Man' is read, but not written"). Haggadic tradition embellished this passage.

Midr. Pss. 3/4 on Ps 3:2b, "How great are they that rise up against me," notes that along with Doeg, Ahithophel was great in learning. 2 Sam 16:23, with אִישׁ inserted after ישאל, is first cited. Then follows אִישׁ קרי ולא כתיב, which is explained as "for he was not like a 'man,' but like an angel." The passage concludes with a citation from the "Ahithophel" psalm, 55:12-14.[178]

In the third of the four sections regarding Ahithophel at *y. Sanh.* 10:2, 29a, the Jerusalem Talmud also relates:

> When someone came to him for advice, he would say to him, "Go and do thus and so, and if you don't believe me, then go and ask the Urim and Thummim."[179] And the man would go and ask and find out that this was how matters were. This is in line with that which is written in Scripture: "Now in those days the counsel which Ahithophel gave was as if one consulted [the oracle of God; so was the counsel of Ahithophel esteemed, both by David and by Absalom" - 2 Sam 16:23]. "Man" is read but not written

---

[176] Soncino 117. On the expression *Qere we-lo' ketiv*, cf. A. Dotan, art. "Masorah" in *EJ* (1971) 16.1420.
[177] English in *The Minor Tractates of the Talmud* 240.
[178] Buber 38, with n. 66; Braude 1.57, with n. 37 on p. 2.409.
[179] Oracular media thought to be on the "breastplate" of the high priest. Cf. the art. "Urim and Thummim" by I. Mendelsohn in *IDB* 4.739-740.

(אִישׁ קְרִי וְלֹא כְתִיב). The Scriptures could not "call him a man" (לִקְרוֹתוֹ אִישׁ).[180]

I suggest that the Palestinian Jewish Christian who first coined the epithet "Iscariot" (אִישׁ קְרִיּוֹת) derived it primarily from the first part of this well-known scribal instruction regarding Ahithophel at 2 Sam 16:23 - אִישׁ קְרִי. He then only very slightly expanded this reading by adding וֹת to make Judas into an אִישׁ קְרִיּוֹת ("man from Qeriyyot") in Judah, as noted above in section 2). As Ahithophel, the betrayer of David, was from the unknown site Giloh in Judah, so Judas, the betrayer of the Son of David, the Messiah Jesus, was made into an inhabitant of the unknown site Qeriyyot in Judah, far away from Galilee. This is certainly the reason several MSS have ἀπὸ Καρυώτου in John 6:71; 12:4; 13:26; and 14:22.

The expression "... אִישׁ," "a man from / an inhabitant of...," is found very frequently in early Judaic sources. To this I now turn.

JUDAS ISCARIOT AS A MAN FROM / INHABITANT OF QERIYYOT

The noun אִישׁ followed by a place-name is a well-known Hebrew way of expressing "a man from / an inhabitant of...." Yet it is also found in Aramaic writings.[181] This explains why, although of Hebrew origin, אִישׁ קְרִיּוֹת as an epithet for Judas was not only understood but also further employed by Aramaic-speaking Palestinian Jewish Christians.

The following alphabetical table, although not meant to be exhaustive, lists a large number of occurrences of a personal name, together with אִישׁ followed by a place-name, in the Mishnah, Tosefta, the Jerusalem and Babylonian Talmuds, and Tannaitic midrashim. It shows how typical Judas plus אִישׁ קְרִיּוֹת was for early Judaic sources.

---

[180] Neusner 31.346, which I slightly modify.
[181] Cf. the sources cited by G. Schwarz, *Jesus und Judas* 9, n. 5. For the expression, see also Jastrow 60.

א

איש אונו

R. Ḥanina *of Ono*
a) *m. Giṭ.* 6:7 (Albeck 3.292, Danby 315).
b) *t. Sanh.* 2:13 (Zuckermandel / Liebermann 417 as Ḥananya, Neusner 4.200). The *t.* passage is quoted in *y. Ned.* 6:8, 4a (Neusner 23.124) and *y. Sanh.* 1:2, 18d (Neusner 31.38).
c) *b. Giṭ.* 67a (Soncino 317).
d) *b. Sanh.* 11b (Soncino 50).

איש איבליים

R. 'Eleazar b. Yehudah *of Eiblayyim*
a) *t. Ma'as. Š.* 1:9 (Zuckermandel / Liebermann 87, Neusner 1.295).
b) *t. Zebaḥ.* 2:3 (Zuckermandel / Liebermann 481, Neusner 5.8).
c) *b. Zebaḥ.* 28a (Soncino 139).
d) *b. Ḥull.* 55b (Soncino 305).
e) *b. Ḥull.* 122b (Soncino 682).

ב

איש הבירה

Yo'ezer *of the Birah*
a) *m. 'Orlah* 2:12 (Albeck 1.299, Danby 91; 140, n. 3: it refers to the Temple Mount; Jastrow 165: to the Temple or the whole Temple Mount).

איש ביריא

Eliezer *of Biria*
a) *b. 'Erub.* 55b (Soncino 391).

איש בית דלי

Neḥemya *of Beth Deli*
a) *m. Yebam.* 16:7 (Albeck 3.73, Danby 244).
b) *m. 'Ed.* 8:5 (Albeck 4.316, Danby 436).

איש בקעת בית חורתן

R. Neḥunya *of the Plain of Beth Ḥawartan / Hauran*
a) *b. Sukk.* 44a (Soncino 202-203).
b) *b. Ta'an.* 3a (Soncino 7).
c) *b. M.Q.* 3b (Soncino 14).
d) *b. Zebaḥ.* 110b (Soncino 543).

איש ברתותא
R. Eleazar b. Yehudah *of Bartotha*
a)   *m. 'Orlah* 1:4 (Albeck 1.294, Danby 89).
b)   *m. Beṣa* 3:5 (Albeck 6.466, Danby 777).
c)   *t. Bekh.* 7:6 (Zuckermandel / Liebermann 542, Neusner 5.186).
d)   *t. Zabim* 1:5 (Zuckermandel / Liebermann 676, Neusner 6.314).
Cf. כפר תותא in *Mek. R. Ish.* Beshallaḥ 4 on Exod 14:15 (Lauterbach 1.220).
e)   *y. Dem.* 5:1, 24c (Neusner / Sarason, 3.154).
f)   *y. Ḥall.* 2:1, 58c (Neusner 9.63).
g)   *b. Pesaḥ.* 13a (Soncino 57-58).
See also R. Eleazar of Bartotha
a)   *m. 'Abot* 3:7 (Albeck 4.365, Danby 451, with n. 2).

ג

איש גופתה אריח
Menaḥem *of Gufta Ariaḥ*
a)   *y. Sanh.* 10:2, 28d (Neusner 31.339).
איש גינוסר
Yonathan b. Ḥersha *of Ginnosar*
a)   *t. Kel. B. B.* 5:6 (Zuckermandel / Liebermann 595, Neusner 6.73).
b)   *y. Ma'as.* 1:2, 48d (Neusner / Jaffee 7.47)
איש גליא
R. Menaḥem *of Galia*
a)   *t. 'Erub.* 8:9 (11:10) (Zuckermandel / Liebermann 153, Neusner 2.111).
b)   *b. Keth.* 60a (Soncino 358).
איש גמזו
Naḥum *of Gimzo*
a)   *t. Šebu.* 1:7 (Zuckermandel / Liebermann 446, Neusner 4.272).
b)   *y. Pe'ah* 8:9, 21b (Neusner/Brooks 2.335).
c)   *y. Šeq.* 5:4, 49b (Neusner 15.112).
d)   *b. Ber.* 22a (Soncino 132).
e)   *b. Ta'an.* 21a (Soncino 104-105).
f)   *b. Ḥag.* 12a (Soncino 67).
g)   *b. Sanh.* 108b-109a (Soncino 747).
h)   *b. Šebu.* 26a (Soncino 138).

ד

איש הדרום

R. Eliezer b. Isaac *of the South*
a) *Sifre* Num. Naso § 8 on Num 5:15 (Horovitz 15, Neusner 1.95).
b) *b. Soṭa* 20b (Soncino 105):
איש כפר דרום (see under כ below).

ה

איש הדר

R. Yaqim *of Haddar*
a) *m. 'Ed.* 7:5 (Albeck 4.312, Danby 434).

איש הוצא / חוצי

Yehudah *of Hoṣa / Hoṣi*
a) *y. Šebi.* 8:5, 38b (Neusner / Avery-Peck 5.279).
b) *y. Ned.* 11:1, 42c (Neusner 23.199).

איש הוצל

Yose / Yosef *of Huṣal*
a) *b. Pesaḥ.* 113b (Soncino 585).
b) *b. Yoma* 52a-b (Soncino 243-244).

ח

איש חבתא

Pinḥas *of Ḥabbata*
a) *t. Yoma* 1:6 (Zuckermandel / Liebermann 180, Neusner 2.186).

ט

איש טבעון

Abba Yose Ḥoliqofri *of Ṭib'on*
a) *m. Makš.* 1:3 (Albeck 6.416, Danby 758).

איש טורייא / טרייא

Abba Hoshaiah *of Ṭurya*
a) *y. B. Qam.* 10:10, 7c (Neusner 28.224).
b) *y. B. Meṣ.* 2:5, 8c (Neusner 29.48).

איש טיבעין
R. Ḥanina *of Ṭibʿin* a) *Sifre* Deut. Ha'azinu § 323 on Deut 32:30 (Finkelstein 373, Hammer 335).
איש טיריאה
Isaiah *of Ṭiriah* a) *t. B. Qam.* (Zuckermandel / Liebermann 371, Neusner 4.71).

י

איש יאני
Abba Yose b. Ḥanin *of Yani* a) *t. Kil.* 2:1, 4 (Zuckermandel / Liebermann 75, Neusner 1.254-255).
איש יבנה
Levitas *of Yabneh* a) *m. 'Abot* 4:4 (Albeck 4.469, Danby 453).
איש ינוח
Abba Yose b. Ḥanan *of Yanoaḥ* a) *Sifre* Deut. Debarim § 2 on Deut 1:2 (Finkelstein 9, Hammer 28). b) *y. Kil.* 2:4, 28a (Neusner / Mandelbaum 4.76 as Yoḥanan).
איש ירושלים
1) Yose / Yosef b. Yoḥanan *of Jerusalem* a) *m. Soṭa* 9:9 (Albeck 3.259, Danby 305). b) *m. 'Abot* 1:4, 5 (Albeck 4.354, Danby 446). c) *t. B. Q.* 8:13 (Zuckermandel / Liebermann 362, Neusner 4.47). d) *y. Šabb.* 1:4, 3d (Neusner 11.66). e) *y. Pesaḥ.* 1:6, 27d (Neusner 13.33). f) *y. Soṭa* 9:10, 24a (Neusner 27.252). g) *y. Keth.* 8:11, 32c (Neusner 22.264). h) *b. Šabb.* 14b (Soncino 59). i) *b. Šabb.* 15a (Soncino 62-63). j) *b. Tem.* 15b (Soncino 107). 2) Abba Yose b. Yoḥanan *of Jerusalem* a) *t. Menaḥ.* 13:21 (Zuckermandel / Liebermann 533, Neusner 5.161). b) *b. Yebam.* 53b (Soncino 354). 3) Shebna *of Jerusalem* a) *b. Šabb.* 12b (Soncino 47).

כ

איש כפר אבוס / אמוס / עיכוס

R. Simeon b. Yehudah *of Kefar 'Ibbus / 'Immus / 'Ikus*
a) *y. Soṭa* 7:4, 21c (Neusner 27.185).
b) *y. Sanh.* 10:5, 29c (Neusner 31.358).
c) *b. Zebaḥ.* 28a (Soncino 305).
d) *b. Zebaḥ.* 122b (Soncino 682).

איש כפר אובלין

R. Eleazar b. Yehudah *of Kefar 'Ublin*
a) *t. Nidd.* 9:18 (Zuckermandel / Liebermann 652, Neusner 6.234).

איש כפר הבבלי

1) R. Neḥunya b. 'Elinathan *of Kefar ha-Babli*
a) *m. 'Ed.* 6:2 (Albeck 4.308, Danby 433).

2) R. Yose b. Yehudah *of Kefar ha-Babli*
a) *m. 'Abot* 4:20 (Albeck 4.372, Danby 455).

איש כפר ברקאי

Issachar *of Kefar Barkai*
a) *b. Pesaḥ.* 57a-b (Soncino 285).
b) *b. Ker.* 28b (Soncino 220).

איש כפר ברתותא

R. Eleazar b. Yehudah *of Kefar Bartotha*
a) *b. Bekh.* 57a (Soncino 390).

איש כפר גבוריא / גבירא / גבור / נפור חיל

R. Yehudah *of Kefar Gibboraya / Gibbor Ḥayil*
a) *b. Meg.* 18a (Soncino 109).
b) *b. Keth.* 65a (Soncino 391).

איש כפר דרום

R. Eleazar b. Isaac *of Kefar Darom*
a) *b. Soṭa* 20b (Soncino 105).

איש כפר חיטיא

R. Ya'aqob *of Kefar Ḥiṭaya*
a) *b. Ḥag.* 5b (Soncino 24).

איש כפר חנניה

R. Ḥalafta [b. Dosa] *of Kefar Ḥananyah*
a) *m. 'Abot* 3:6 (Albeck 4.364, Danby 450).
b) *t. Kel. B. Qam.* 4:17 (Zuckermandel / Liebermann 574, Neusner 6.15).

Cf. Abba Ḥalafta *of Kefar Ḥananyah*
a) *b. B. Meṣ.* 94a (Soncino 542).

איש כפר ימא / דימא

Ishmael *of Kefar Yama / Dima*
a) *b. Ned.* 57d (Soncino 181).

איש כפר יתמה

Dositheus *of Kefar Yatmah*
a) *m. 'Orlah* (Albeck 1.298, Danby 91).

איש כפר נבוריא

Yaʻaqob *of Kefar Niborayya*
a) *y. Bekh.* 3:3, 65d (Neusner 10.202).
b) *y. Šabb.* 19:5, 17d (Neusner 11.472).
c) *y. Yebam.* 2:6, 4a (Neusner 21.82).
d) *y. Qidd.* 3:12, 64d (Neusner 26.209).

איש כפר סכנין

Yaʻaqob *of Kefar Sikhnin*
a) *t. Ḥull.* 2:24 (Zuckermandel / Liebermann 503, Neusner 5.75).
b) *b. 'Aboda Zara* 17a (Soncino 85).
c) *b. 'Aboda Zara* 27b (Soncino 137).

איש כפר סמא

Yaʻaqob *of Kefar Sama*
a) *t. Ḥull.* 2:22 (Zuckermandel / Liebermann 503, Neusner 5.74).
b) *y. Šabb.* 14:4, 14d (Neusner 11.398).
c) *y. 'Aboda Zara* 2:2, 40d (Neusner 33.66).

איש כפר עותני

Shemaʻiah *of Kefar 'Otenai*
a) *t. Para* 10:2 (Zuckermandel / Liebermann 638, Neusner 6.195).

איש כפר עכו

1) R. Ḥiyya *of Kefar Akko*
a) *b. Ber.* 63b (Soncino 400).

2) R. Yehudah b. Agra *of Kefar Akko*

a)	*t. Kil.* 1:12 (Zuckermandel / Liebermann 74, Neusner 1.252).
3)	R. Yehudah b. Gamda *of Kefar Akko*
a)	*b. Soṭa* 43b (Soncino 218).
4)	R. Simeon b. Yehudah *of Kefar Akko*
a)	*t. Soṭa* 8:11 (Zuckermandel / Liebermann 311, Neusner 3.188).
b)	*t. B. Bat.* 7:10 (Zuckermandel / Liebermann 408, Neusner 4.175).
c)	*t. Sanh.* 13:12 (Zuckermandel / Liebermann 435, Neusner 4.241).
d)	*t. Zebaḥ.* 2:3 (Zuckermandel / Liebermann 481, Neusner 5.8).
e)	*t. Neg.* 6:1 (Zuckermandel / Liebermann 625, Neusner 6.156).
f)	*b. Soṭa* 37b (Soncino 185).
g)	*b. Sanh.* 110b (Soncino 759).
h)	*b. Nidd.* 52b (Soncino 362).
i)	*Mek. R. Ish.* Beshallaḥ 7 on Exod 20:11 (Lauterbach 2.256).
Cf.	R. Simeon *of Kefar Akko*
a)	*b. Sanh.* 71a (Soncino 484).
5)	R. Isaac *of Kefar Akko*
a)	*b. ʽAboda Zara* 7b (Soncino 32).
b)	*b. Bekh.* 31a (Soncino 196).
6)	R. Tanḥum *of Kefar Akko*
a)	*b. Taʽan.* 7b (Soncino 28).
Cf.	R. Tanḥum b. R. Ḥama *of Kefar Akko*
a)	*b. Moʽed Qaṭ.* 16b (Soncino 105).
Cf.	R. Tanḥum b. R. Ḥiyya *of Kefar Akko*
a)	*b. Yebam.* 45a (Soncino 292).
b)	*b. Bekh.* 57b–58a (Soncino 393).

איש כפר שערים

R. Menaḥem *of Kefar Sheʽarim / Beth Sheʽarim*
a)   *b. Nidd.* 27a (Soncino 184).

איש כפר תמרתא

Shila *of Kefar Temarta*
a)   *b. Meg.* 16a-b (Soncino 94, 99).
b)   *b. Soṭa* 35a (Soncino 173).
c)   *b. Nidd.* 26a (Soncino 179).

מ

איש המדי

Naḥum *of Media*
a)   *y. Naz.* 5:3, 54a (Neusner 24.123).

איש המצפה

R. Simeon *of Miṣpah*
a) *m. Pe'ah* 2:6 (Albeck 1.45, Danby 12).
b) *t. Yoma* 1:13 (Zuckermandel / Liebermann 182, Neusner 2.189).
c) *t. Zebaḥ.* 6:13 (Zuckermandel / Liebermann 488, Neusner 5.28).
d) *y. Yoma* 2:2, 39d (Neusner 14.63).
e) *b. Yoma* 14b (Soncino 65).
f) *b. Yoma* 15a (Soncino 68).

ס

איש סוכו

Antigonos *of Sokho*
a) *m. 'Abot* 1:3 (Albeck 4.353, Danby 446).

ע

איש עוזא

Yehoshuʻa *of ʻUzza*
a) *b. Ned.* 38b (Soncino 122).

צ

איש צידן

Abba Gorion *of Ṣaidon*
a) *m. Qidd.* 4:14 (Albeck 3.329, Danby 329).

איש צידן

Abba Yudan *of Ṣidon*
a) *t. Yebam.* 14:7 (Zuckermandel / Liebermann 259, Neusner 3.56).
b) *t. ʻOhal.* 18:7 (Zuckermandel / Liebermann 616, Neusner 6.131).

איש צרדה

Yose / Yosef b. Yoʻezer *of Ṣeredah*
a) *m. Soṭa* 9:9 (Albeck 3.259, Danby 305).
b) *m. ʻEd.* 8:4 (Albeck 4.315, Danby 436).
c) *m. 'Abot* 1:4 (Albeck 4.354, Danby 446).
d) *t. B. Q.* 8:13 (Zuckermandel / Liebermann 362, Neusner 4.47).
e) *y. Šabb.* 1:4, 3d (Neusner 11.66).
f) *y. Pesaḥ.* 1:6, 27d (Neusner 13.33).
g) *y. Soṭa* 9:10, 24a (Neusner 27.252).
h) *y. Keth.* 8:11, 32c (Neusner 22.264).

i)	*b. Šabb.* 14b–15a (Soncino 59, 62-63).
j)	*b. Pesaḥ.* 16a-b (Soncino 71, 74).
k)	*b. Pesaḥ.* 17b (Soncino 78).
l)	*b. Tem.* 15b (Soncino 107).

ק

איש קטרון

Simeon *of Qiṭron*

a) *Mek. R. Ish.* Beshallaḥ 4 on Exod 14:15 (Lauterbach 1.220).

ר

איש רומי

Todos (Theudas, Thaddeus) *of Rome*

a) *t. Beṣa* 2:15 (Zuckermandel / Liebermann 204, Neusner 2.239).
b) *y. Pesaḥ.* 7:1, 34a (Neusner / Bokser 13.304).
c) *y. Beṣa* 2:7, 61c (Neusner 18.70).
d) *y. Moʻed Qaṭan* 3:1, 81d (Neusner 20.175).
e) *b. Ber.* 19a (Soncino 115).
f) *b. Pesaḥ.* 53a-b (Soncino 260-261).
g) *b. Beṣa* 23a (Soncino 118-119).

ש

איש שיחין

Neḥemiah *of Shiḥin*

a) *y. Peʼah* 8:9, 21b (Neusner / Brooks 2.335).
b) *y. Šeq.* 5:4, 49b (Neusner 15.112).
c) *y. Soṭa* 2:5, 18b (Neusner 27.78).

ת

איש תקוע

Nittai *of Tekoaʻ*

a) *m. Ḥall.* (Albeck 1.287, Danby 88).

The above table demonstrates how widespread the designation "So and so, ... אִישׁ" was in early Judaic sources. Most of the persons cited are Tannaitic. At least six of them, like אִישׁ קְרִיוֹת, predate the destruction of the Second Temple in 70 CE, or coincide with it: Antigonos of Sokho, Yose b. Yo'ezer of Ṣereda, Yose / Yosef b. Yoḥanan of Jerusalem, Issachar of Kefar Barkai, Naḥum of Media, Pinḥas of Ḥabbata, and perhaps also Naḥum of Gimzo.[182]

As pointed out above, Judas אִישׁ קְרִיוֹת has in the past been most frequently interpreted as "a man of / an inhabitant of Qeriyyoth." My proposed solution to the epithet, based on early Judaic tradition regarding the betrayer of David, Ahithophel, corroborates that interpretation, although for different reasons.

This means that other proposed explanations of Ἰσκαριώτ / Ἰσκαριώθ miss the mark. The expression does not derive, for example, from סוֹכֵר or סִיכַר, the Samaritan city of Sychar; סְקַר, to paint red;[183] סִיקְרָא,[184] a Jewish Zealot or assassin (sicarius) with a dagger (sica); סכר, meaning to shut up, stop up, yet in Isa 19:4 as "I will 'deliver' the Egyptians into the hand of...";[185] שָׂכַר, to hire;[186] a man of the tribe of "Issachar" (יִשָּׂשכָר);[187] or אִישׁ קִרְיָתָא, "the man from the city

---

[182] Interestingly, an early adherent of Jesus who related one of his teachings to R. Eliezer b. Hyrcanus, an older second generation Tanna (Strack and Stemberger, *Introduction* 77), and who wanted to heal someone (in the name of Jesus) of an otherwise fatal snake bite, was named Yaʻaqob "of Kefar Sikhnin" (אִישׁ כְּפַר סִכְנִין) or "of Kefar Sama" (אִישׁ כְּפַר סָמָא). Cf. the references in the above table, as well as *Eccl. Rab.* 1:8 § 3 (Soncino 8.27-28). On the two place-names, see Jastrow 998 and 992.
[183] Jastrow 1021, 2).
[184] Jastrow 986, III, and סִיקָרִין, *sicarii*, "murderers, robbers."
[185] BDB 698, piel.
[186] Jastrow 1575-1576, in the sense of "the hired one"; yet this would be שָׂכוּר, which is improbable.
[187] BDB 441; it may be related to the verb שכר. Cf. the אִישׁ יִשָּׂשכָר in Judg 10:1.

(i.e. Jerusalem)."[188] Finally, Iscariot(h) is not based on the verb שָׁקַר, to be false, deceitful or faithless, or on the noun שֶׁקֶר, deception, what deceives and betrays one, or שִׁקְרָא, שִׁקְרָא, liar or faithless, false person.[189] Nevertheless, as remarked above, when a Palestinian Jewish Christian heard the Semitic expression אִישׁ קְרִיּוֹת of Judas, "a man from Qeriyyoth," the consonants שׁקר also reminded him of Judas' deceit in betraying his teacher Jesus.

Summary

The above study points to how creative early Palestinian Jewish Christians were. They invented an epithet for Judas, the betrayer of the Son of David, the Messiah Jesus, on the basis of Judaic tradition (אִישׁ קְרִי) concerning the betrayer of David, Ahithophel. As the latter was from an unknown Judean city (Aramaic קרתה, קרתא), Giloh, so Judas, a Galilean disciple of Jesus, was made into an inhabitant of a no longer known city in southern Judea, Qeriyyoth. For post-Resurrection Galilean Jewish Christians, the betrayer of Jesus could not be placed far enough away. He was certainly not one of them! Therefore they labeled him "a man / inhabitant of Qeriyyot," the solution to the epithet "Iscariōt(h)" favored – albeit for different reasons – by the majority of interpreters throughout the centuries. Judas may originally have been known as "the son of Simon"

---

[188] This is the solution favored by G. Schwarz, *Jesus und Judas* 8-10. Yet this is found nowhere else in the sense of a particular city. In contrast, "so and so, a man of Jerusalem" is indeed attested, as shown in the above table. For references to those who have made the other proposals, as well as other very improbable ones, cf. his p. 7, as well as E. Blair, art. "Judas Iscariot" in *IDB* 2 (1962) 1006; R. Brown, *The Death of the Messiah* 1413-1416; D. Haugg, *Judas Iskarioth in den neutestamentlichen Berichten* (Freiburg im Breisgau: Herder, 1930) 74-78; and J. Derrett, "The Iscariot, M^e^sira, and the Redemption" in *JSNT* 8 (1980) 9-10, including his own suggestion of a business friend.
[189] This has been favored for example by C. Torrey, "The Name 'Iscariot'" in *HTR* 36 (1943) 59-61, and B. Gärtner, *Die rätselhaften Termini* 42, 63-65.

(Σίμωνος), as found in John 6:71; 13:2 and 26. Yet after he betrayed his teacher to the Jewish authorities in Jerusalem, although knowing in advance their wish to get rid of (= kill) the popular prophet from Galilee, Judas was instead given the epithet "man from / inhabitant of Qeriyyoth." Semitic-speaking Palestinian Jewish Christians also recognized and appreciated the connotation of deceit, treachery, betrayal (שקר) in this epithet. It reminded them of the betrayal of David by Ahithophel, and the "Judas legend" then began to develop, based primarily on Judaic traditions regarding Ahithophel.

Chapter Four

Jesus' Weeping over the Destruction of Jerusalem in Luke 19:41-44, and David's Weeping over the Destruction of Jerusalem in Judaic Tradition

Introduction

Jesus' weeping over the future destruction of Jerusalem when he sees it from the top of the Mount of Olives, after having come from Jericho,[1] is a short narrative of only four verses (Luke 19:41-44). Nevertheless, its "profound pathos"[2] makes it into a very moving anecdote.[3] It is not just a "petit morceau

---

[1] Cf. the lovely present-day Franciscan chapel called "Dominus Flevit," "The Lord Weeps," halfway up the western slope of the Mount of Olives. The site of commemoration, however, should actually be at the summit, from which Jesus first beheld the city, coming from the east. For secondary literature on the narrative, see the most recent commentaries, as well as J. Nolland, *Luke 18:35-24:53* (WBC 35c; Dallas, Texas: Word Books, 1993) 929, and J. Fitzmyer, *The Gospel According to Luke X-XXIV* (AB 28A; Garden City, New York: Doubleday, 1985) 1256-1260.

[2] D. Tiede, *Luke* (Augsburg Commentary on the New Testament; Minneapolis: Augsburg, 1988) 331. Cf. also "the power and pathos of the oracle" in J. Green, *The Gospel of Luke* (NICNT 3; Grand Rapids, Michigan: Eerdmans, 1997) 689.

[3] Cf. J. Kremer in his *Lukasevangelium* (Die Neue Echter Bibel 3; Würzburg: Echter Verlag, 1988) 188: "dieses kleinen, durch die Notiz über Jesu Weinen ergreifenden Abschnitts...."

sentimental."[4] Rather, it is an account borrowed by the Evangelist from his source, "Special Luke," which has Jesus prophetically see Jerusalem "borne as a mill-stream to its doom."[5] The syntax is broken in v 42, and vv 43-44 heap up one expression after another, all of them related to the city's being besieged by "enemies." It must be asked whether these descriptive terms derive exclusively or primarily from the Roman siege of Jerusalem, culminating in the destruction of the city in 70 CE, as mirrored in Josephus' description of these events and in rabbinic sources, or whether they rather go back to scriptural and Judaic traditions on the destruction of the city under Nebuchadnezzar in 586 BCE. Was there a model in Judaic tradition for Jesus' weeping over Jerusalem? In what language was the original narrative composed, and to what extent has the Evangelist Luke edited it? The following study deals with these and other open questions regarding the incident.

Section I. deals with the narrative's geographical and eschatological setting; section II. with the biblical David's weeping at the Mount of Olives; section III. with David as a prophet, and the Messiah as the Son of David; section IV. with David's weeping over the future destruction of Jerusalem in Judaic tradition; section V. with 2 Sam 17:13; section VI. with the major influence of Isaiah 29 on the pericope; section VII. with the genre, original language and provenance; section VIII. with the question of historicity and the date of the incident; section IX. with Lukan editing; and finally section X. with the four major emphases in the narrative.

I. The Geographical and Eschatological Setting (Zechariah 14)

Luke 19:41 states: "As he [Jesus] came near and saw the city [Jerusalem], he wept over it." Then he spoke vv 42-44 concerning it. It is assumed that Jesus is at the very top of the

---

[4] A. Loisy, *L'Évangile selon Luc* (Paris: 1924; reprint Frankfurt: Minerva, 1971) 472.
[5] W. Manson, *The Gospel of Luke* (Moffatt's; London: Hodder and Stoughton, 1963) 217.

Mount of Olives[6] to the east of Jerusalem, for this is the first point from which one can view the city when coming from the east. The reader of Luke's Gospel knows this, for v 37 has already stated: "As he was now approaching the path down from the Mount of Olives...." That is, Jesus is envisaged as still at the summit, where the path down began.[7]

The Mount of Olives is mentioned explicitly only twice in the Hebrew Bible. While I shall comment on the great importance of 2 Sam 15:30 below in section II., here it should be noted that the second occurrence is found in Zech 14:4 in an eschatological context. "On that day" (v 4), the day of the Lord (v 1), the nations shall attack Jerusalem and take it, looting its houses and raping its women (v 2). Yet the Lord will ultimately prevail, and "there shall no longer be a כְּנַעֲנִי in the house of the Lord of hosts on that day" (v 21).

The "house of the Lord" refers here to the Jerusalem Temple, and the above Hebrew noun does not mean "Canaanite," but "trader" or "merchant,"[8] as in *Targum Jonathan* and the discussion of the passage in *b. Pesaḥ.* 50a.[9] This verse from Zechariah's vision of the end time inspired Jesus to "cleanse" the Temple of the merchants and money-changers within its precincts. While Mark (11:15-19) has this occur on the day after Jesus' "triumphal entry" into Jerusalem (vv 11-12), Luke has it

---

[6] On this site, cf. the art. "Olives, Mount of" by G. Barrois in *IDB* 3.596-599; "Mount of Olives (Olivet)" by J. Braslavi and M. Avi-Yonah in *EJ* (1971) 12.481-485; Str-B 1.840-842; and G. Dalman, *Jerusalem und sein Gelände* (Gütersloh: Mohn, 1930; reprint Hildesheim: Olms, 1972) 39-57.
[7] The small village of Bethphage (Mark 11:1 par.) may have been located at what is now Kafr et-Tur on the second or middle of the Mount of Olive's three summits. The ancient Roman road to Jericho, from where Jesus came (Mark 10:46 par.; Luke 19:1), did not follow the modern route from the southeast and then north up the Kidron Valley, but was located much further north. See the map in *IDB* 3.598.
[8] BDB 489.
[9] Cf. Sperber 3.499, and Cathcart and Gordon 226, with n. 52; and תַּגָּר(א) (Jastrow 1646-1647) as "merchant, vendor" in the talmudic passage (Soncino 240-241).

on the same day (19:45-48), with only Jesus' weeping over the future destruction of Jerusalem in-between (vv 41-44).[10]

During the "triumphal entry" Jesus rode on the colt of a donkey (Luke 19:29-40 par.), deliberately fulfilling Zech 9:9. This verse was treated messianically in Judaic sources,[11] showing Jesus let himself be celebrated as the Messiah, at least by the Galilean followers who had accompanied him.

The Mount of Olives, הַר־הַזֵּיתִים in Zech 14:4, was also called הַר הַמִּשְׁחָה in rabbinic Hebrew.[12] Literally, this is the "mount of 'anointing,'"[13] from the same root as מָשִׁיחַ, Aramaic מְשִׁיחָא, the "anointed one" or Messiah.[14] This symbolism also plays an important role in the Messiah Jesus' being "anointed" by a woman in the house of Simon the leper. The event took place in Bethany, on the "mount of anointing."[15]

The Gospels also relate that Jesus lodged with his disciples in Bethany on the Mount of Olives before entering Jerusalem in order to teach and debate in the Temple (Mark 11:11-12, 19-20, 27; 14:3 par.). In 21:37 Luke states summarily: "Every day he was teaching in the Temple, and at night he would go out and spend the night on the Mount of Olives."

Gethsemane, to which Jesus retired with his disciples after the "Last Supper," was also located on the Mount of Olives (Mark 14:26, 32 par.). The Evangelist John notes in 18:3 that "Jesus often met there with his disciples." Luke 22:39 states that Jesus went to the Mount of Olives (to Gethsemane), "as was his custom." Gethsemane was probably located on the lower part of the slope. Abba Saul (ben Batnit), an older second generation Tanna who frequently relates material about the Temple and the

---

[10] Matt 21:12-16 also has the cleansing on the same day, followed by Jesus' retiring to Bethany in v 17. John 2:13-22 places the cleansing also at Passover, but on an earlier visit to Jerusalem.

[11] Cf. the many sources cited in Str-B 1.842-844. The Evangelist Luke omits the actual entry into Jerusalem.

[12] Cf. the passages cited by Jastrow 851.

[13] Cf. Jastrow 851 on the noun.

[14] Jastrow 852.

[15] Cf. Mark 14:3-9 and Matt 26:6-13. While John 12:1-8 also has this event take place in Bethany, in Luke 7:36-50 it occurs earlier in Galilee.

environs of Jerusalem,[16] states in *b. Šebu.* 16a that there were two בֵּצְעִין on the Mount of Olives, a lower and an upper. A בִּצְעָה is a pond, meant here as a reservoir.[17] At this site both strictly and less strictly observant Jews ate part of their sacrifices and second tithe.[18] It is possible that this was also true for the Passover pilgrims Jesus and his disciples from Galilee because of the convenient source of water in the reservoir.

Luke 19:11 also states that after coming from Jericho, Jesus was near to Jerusalem, that is, only a little east of the Mount of Olives. His disciples then "supposed that the kingdom of God was to appear immediately." This is probably based on Zech 14:9, "And the Lord will become king over all the earth...." *Targum Jonathan* at this point reads: "And the kingdom of the Lord shall be revealed upon all the inhabitants of the earth...."[19]

In Mark 13:2 par., upon leaving the Temple Jesus also tells his disciple(s): "Do you see these great buildings? Not one stone will be left here upon another; all will be thrown down." After this prediction of the destruction of the Temple, he sits down on the Mount of Olives, (exactly) opposite the Temple (v 3 par.),[20] and elucidates in the rest of the chapter when and how this judgment on the city will take place. The Evangelist Luke clearly alludes at this point to the destruction of Jerusalem by the Romans in the Jewish-Roman War of 66-70 CE in 21:20. He has Jesus say: "When you see Jerusalem surrounded by enemies, then know that its desolation is at hand." These will be "days of

---

[16] Cf. Strack and Stemberger, *Introduction* 78.
[17] Jastrow 184. The Soncino translation at 78 incorrectly has two "meadows." The upper reservoir may in part have served the High Priest when he went to the top of the Mount of Olives to slaughter the Red Heifer. He immersed before doing so (*m. Par.* 3:7-8 in Albeck 6.264, Danby 700).
[18] Cf. Soncino 78, with the accompanying notes.
[19] Sperber 3.498, Cathcart and Gordon 224. Cf. also *Targ.* Zech 14:5, "and the Lord my God shall reveal himself, and all his holy ones with him" (Sperber 3.497, Cathcart and Gordon 223). The latter verse influenced Mark 13:13-14 par., but especially Matt 25:31. For the "holy ones" of Zech 14:5 as angels, see *Pesiq. R.* 21/9 (Friedmann 104a, Braude 430) and *Midr. Pss.* 2/4 (Buber 26, Braude 1.38).
[20] Luke omits this place notice in 21:7.

vengeance" (v 22), when this people (the inhabitants of Jerusalem) "will fall by the edge of the sword and be taken away as captives among all nations," when "Jerusalem will be trampled on by the Gentiles" (v 24). Although Luke had the "Synoptic Apocalypse" of Mark before him, he preferred to quote this more specific material at this point, probably also from Special Luke.

During his prediction of the destruction of the Jerusalem Temple, Jesus sits (exactly) opposite it on the (top of the) Mount of Olives because only the eastern wall of the Temple was made intentionally low. According to *m. Midd.* 2:4, this was "because the [High] Priest that burns the [Red] Heifer and stands on the top of the Mount of Olives should be able to look directly into the entrance of the Sanctuary [הֵיכָל] when the blood is sprinkled."[21] This is comment on Num 19:1-10.

Jesus is thus pictured as sitting on the summit of the Mount of Olives and predicting the destruction of the Temple, into which he can see almost to the Holy of Holies. The image is extremely vivid. The Palestinian special source of Luke 19:41-44 probably also thought of exactly the same view westward when it has Jesus predict the destruction of (the Temple and all of) Jerusalem from the top of the Mount of Olives.

The Evangelist Luke also closes his Gospel by having the resurrected Jesus lead his followers out to Bethany on the Mount of Olives, where he is carried up into heaven (24:50-51). In his companion volume, Luke has two angels tell the disciples that Jesus "will come in the same way as you saw him go into heaven" (Acts 1:11). That is, he will return via the Mount of Olives, where the eschatological events of Zechariah 14 are to take place "on that day."

A final observation should be made here in regard to the eschatological significance of the Mount of Olives as envisioned

---

[21] Albeck 5.321-322, Danby 592. A parallel is found in *b. Yoma* 16a (Soncino 71). On the הֵיכָל, see Jastrow 345: "*the Holy*, the hall containing the golden altar, etc." See also the diagram of the Temple in Albeck 5.328, insert, where it contains the golden altar, table and menorah before the Holy of Holies, as well as Josephus, *Bell.* 5.216.

in Zechariah 14. Josephus reports that around 55 CE an Egyptian false prophet collected some 30,000 followers and led them via the wilderness to the Mount of Olives. From there he planned to enter Jerusalem by having the city's walls collapse at his command, to overcome the Roman forces there, and then to rule over the people. However, the Roman procurator, Antonius Felix, quashed the movement with the help of the Jerusalemites. While Felix killed and took many prisoners, the false prophet somehow escaped (*Bell.* 2.261-263; *Ant.* 20.169-172). The incident is alluded to in Acts 21:38.

Another false prophet, Theudas, ca. 44-45 CE convinced many Judeans to follow him to the Jordan River, where at his command the waters would divide and they could easily pass through.[22] In contrast to him, the false prophet at the Mount of Olives most probably considered himself to be the Messiah, fulfilling the eschatological drama of Zechariah 14 from that site.

Before commenting on the only other explicit reference to the Mount of Olives in the Hebrew Bible, I would like to point out that when Jesus weeps over the future destruction of Jerusalem from the summit of the Mount of Olives in Luke 19:41–44, he does so from exactly the same site at which the Tenth Roman Legion (Fretensis) established its camp under Titus at the beginning of 70 CE, having come up to Jerusalem from Jericho (Josephus, *Bell.* 5.69-70). Titus himself with other troops had to repel Jewish sallies up the western slope of the Mount of Olives so that the Tenth Legion could finish building its own camp and fortifications at the top (5.71–97).[23]

The first post-70 CE Palestinian Jewish Christian hearers of the unit now found in Luke 19:41–44, from Special Luke, would have appreciated the great irony involved in this description. They knew that from exactly the same site at which a crack Roman legion encamped at the siege of Jerusalem, leading to the

---

[22] Josephus, *Ant.* 20.97. Since they were to take along their possessions, he too probably intended to rule over them. Cf. Acts 5:36.

[23] G. Dalman in *Jerusalem und sein Gelände* emphasizes that the site of the camp necessarily had to lie at the summit, where Jesus' Ascension also took place. On the Legio X Fretensis, see the art. with this title by Ritterling in PW 24 (1925) 1671-1678.

destruction of the Temple and the city, Jesus is here described as prophesying the destruction of Jerusalem through a siege of enemy troops – from the summit of the Mount of Olives.

II. David's Weeping at the Mount of Olives

The only other explicit reference to the Mount of Olives in the Hebrew Bible, beyond Zechariah 14, is found in 2 Samuel 15. There it is associated with David's weeping.

Some time after David made Jerusalem his capital (2 Sam 5:6-10), his son Absalom led a conspiracy against him, hoping thereby to become king himself (15:1-12). Absalom sought the counsel of Ahithophel in his rebellion (v 12), and much of the Gospels' description of the traitor Judas Iscariot is based on Judaic traditions regarding this person (see the previous chapter).

Informed of Absalom's conspiracy, David tells all his officials in Jerusalem to flee with him. He is afraid that his son (with his army of rebels) will soon overtake them, bring disaster upon them, "and attack the city with the edge of the sword" (v 14). That is, David wants to avoid Jerusalem's being "besieged."[24]

It is in this context that the threefold motif of "weeping" occurs. All the people (of Jerusalem) stopped at the city's last house (v 17). Then David's officials, together with other adherents, passed by him in a kind of parade. Verse 23 states: "The whole country 'wept aloud' (בּוֹכִים קוֹל גָּדוֹל) as all the people passed by; the king crossed the Wadi Kidron, and all the people moved on toward the wilderness." After telling the priests Zadok and Abiathar to carry the ark back to Jerusalem, "David went up the ascent of the Mount of Olives, 'weeping' (וּבוֹכֶה) as he went, with his head covered and walking barefoot; and all the people who were with him covered their heads and went up, 'weeping' (וּבָכֹה) as they went" (v 30).

---

[24] Cf. the remarks by H. Hertzberg, *I & II Samuel* 341: "So the king decides to evacuate the city, not only to save himself and his men, but also so as not to expose Jerusalem to the devastation which would take place were it really besieged and captured."

Soon he reached the summit of the Mount of Olives (v 32), which he then passed (16:1). David then headed with his adherents for the Jordan River (16:14), which they crossed before daybreak (17:22), thus avoiding capture by Absalom's troops.

Here David "weeps" (בָּכָה) [25] as he goes up the "ascent" or "slope" (מַעֲלֵה)[26] of the Mount of Olives. In *Ant.* 7.203 Josephus, probably following Judaic tradition, reserves David's own weeping for the summit. The Septuagint translates the above three occurrences of בכה with κλαίω, the same Greek verb employed of Jesus' "weeping" over the city of Jerusalem in Luke 19:41.

When Jesus weeps over the future fate of Jerusalem, he does so from the summit of the Mount of Olives, having approached it from the east. The Evangelist Luke knew that his material in 19:41-44 from "Special Luke" was related to a specific geographical setting, since he prepared for it in v 36 with his remark: "As [Jesus] was now approaching the 'path down' from the Mount of Olives...." The Greek κατάβασις is literally "descent," then slope, road leading down.[27] It occurs only here in the NT. The reference is to exactly the same "slope" mentioned in 2 Sam 15:30, only it is now viewed from the summit as a "descent" and not from the Wadi Kidron below as an "ascent."

Before I describe David's weeping and his prophesying the future destruction of Jerusalem from the above site in Judaic tradition, it will be helpful to examine texts which view him as a prophet, and the Messiah as the Son of David.

---

[25] BDB 113: weep, bewail.
[26] BDB 751. On this slope, cf. P. McCarter, Jr., *II Samuel* (AB 9; Garden City, New York: Doubleday, 1984) 371.
[27] BAGD 409.

III. David as a Prophet, and the Messiah as the Son of David

1) David as a Prophet

In the Hebrew Bible, Isaiah, Jeremiah, Ezekiel and the twelve minor prophets from Hosea to Malachi are labeled the "latter prophets." The "first" or "former prophets" are the books Joshua through Second Kings. David, whose exploits are described in 1-2 Samuel, was also considered a prophet in Judaic tradition. Examples of this are the following.

The earliest Judaic chronology is the *Seder 'Olam*. In its chapter 20 David is listed as one of the ten prophets about whom "man of God" is said.[28] Both *y. Soṭa* 9:13, 24b [29] and *b. Soṭa* 48b [30] mention David as one of the former prophets.[31] Josephus notes at the end of the first century CE that after Samuel anointed David, the divine spirit removed to him and "he began to prophesy" (*Ant.* 6.166). *Pseudo-Philo*, Palestinian, originally in Hebrew and roughly from the time of Jesus, gives an example of David's prophecy on this occasion.[32]

While other Judaic sources emphasize David's prophesying,[33] very frequently he is described as prophesying through the many psalms he composed. Acts 2:31 is an example outside the

---

[28] Milikowsky 353 and 509. See also Acts 2:30 for David as a prophet.
[29] Neusner 27.259.
[30] Soncino 258.
[31] Cf. also *b. Ta'an.* 27a (Soncino 143).
[32] Cf. OTP 2.372 on 59:4, and 298-300 on the language, date and provenance of *Pseudo-Philo*.
[33] Cf. *Sifre* Deut. Debarim 1 on Deut 1:1 (Finkelstein 2, Hammer 23); *Mek. R. Ish.* Pisḥa 1 (Lauterbach 1.5, where David and Aaron are cited as if they were prophets; 1.10, where David exemplifies the prophets - against Lauterbach, n. 15); *Targ. Jon.* 2 Sam 22:1 and 23:1-2 (Sperber 2.202, 206; Harrington and Saldarini 200, 203); and in the pseudepigrapha *Apoc. Dan.* 14:11 (OTP 1.770); *Apoc. Sedrach* 14:4 (OTP 1.613); *Mart. and Asc. Isa.* 11:2 (OTP 2.174); and *Test. Sol.* 1:1 and 2:1, MS "E" (OTP 1.960).

Gospels.³⁴ In Mark 12:36 Jesus himself says David spoke of the Messiah in Ps 110:1 "through the Holy Spirit," i.e. prophetically. This is explicitly labeled David's prophesying, for example, in *b. Sukk.* 52a;³⁵ *Pesiq. R.* 31/3;³⁶ and *Eccl. Rab.* 10:1 § 2.³⁷

The latter sources aid in understanding how David can be described as prophesying the future destruction of Jerusalem in connection with Psalm 137 (see section IV. 4) a) below).

2) The Messiah as the Son of David

From Jerusalem and originally in Hebrew from about the middle of the first century BCE, the *Psalms of Solomon* in 17:21 speak of Israel's "king, the son of David." In v 32 he is labeled "the Lord Messiah."³⁸ In Mark 12:35 par. Jesus states that the scribes of his day maintained that the Messiah is the son of David. The expression "son of David" is also a standard one for the Messiah in rabbinic writings.³⁹

In the Gospels Jesus is addressed as the "son of David," for example by the blind beggar Bartimaeus upon leaving Jericho (Mark 10:47-48 par.), just before his "triumphal entry" into Jerusalem. The latter in Mark 11:10 mentions "the coming kingdom of our ancestor David," which Matthew in 21:9 reformulates as "the Son of David." Luke in 19:38 adds "king"

---

³⁴ Cf. also 11Q5 (11QPsa) 27.11 (Martínez and Tigchelaar 1178-1179). I thank C. A. Evans for this reference.
³⁵ Soncino 247.
³⁶ Friedmann 143b, Braude 603-604.
³⁷ Soncino 8.261. Cf. David's "foreseeing" something through the Holy Spirit when composing a psalm in *Lev. Rab.* Vayyikra 5/5 on Lev 4:3 (Soncino 4.70-71), and *Midr. Pss.* 102/1 on Ps 102:1 (Buber 429, Braude 2.153). See also Acts 1:16, 20 and 4:25.
³⁸ Cf. *OTP* 2.667, and 640-641 on the language, date and provenance of this writing.
³⁹ Cf. Str-B 1.525 for several examples, some of them Tannaitic. On the entire question, see E. Lohse, art. υἱὸς Δαυίδ in *TDNT* 8.478-488; C. Burger, *Jesus als Davidssohn. Eine traditionsgeschichtliche Untersuchung* (FRLANT 98; Göttingen: Vandenhoeck & Ruprecht, 1970); and K. Pomykala, *The Davidic Dynasty Tradition in Early Judaism: Its History and Significance for Messianism* (Atlanta: Scholars Press, 1995).

here, recalling the very frequent expression "the messianic king" (מֶלֶךְ הַמָּשִׁיחַ).[40]

The earliest Palestinian Jewish Christians considered Jesus to be the Messiah, the Son of David. It is thus very understandable that Special Luke in Luke 19:41-44 can have Jesus, the Son of David, prophesy the destruction of Jerusalem, for his ancestor David had already done so in Judaic tradition. To this I now turn.

IV. David's Weeping over the Future Destruction of Jerusalem in Judaic Tradition

1) *Josephus*

Himself a native of Jerusalem and well acquainted with the topography of the area, Josephus towards the end of the first century CE rephrased 2 Sam 15:30 in *Ant.* 7.203 in the following way: "Now when he [David] reached the summit of the Mount [of Olives], he looked steadily[41] at the city and 'with many tears' (μετὰ πολλῶν δακρύων) ... prayed to God."

2) *Psalm 3*

Judaic tradition asks regarding Ps 3:1 (Eng. superscription), "A Psalm of David, when he fled from his son Absalom": "When did David compose this psalm? When 'he went up the ascent of the Mount of Olives, weeping as he went' (2 Sam 15:30). But if David was 'weeping' (בוכה), how can he have been composing a psalm? And if he was composing a psalm, why was he 'weeping' (בוכה)?" Several answers to this question are then proposed.[42]

---

[40] Cf. Str-B 1.6-7.
[41] The verb ἀποσκοπέω is employed here, LSJ 217: look steadily (at), regard. R. Marcus in the LCL edition has "he gazed."
[42] *Midr. Pss.* 3/3 on Ps 3:1 (Buber 34, Braude 1.50). The midrash continues by commenting on the possible destruction of the city Jerusalem, and by stating that the psalm was composed at the summit of the Mount of Olives. In 3/1, also on Ps 3:1, reference is made to God's destroying His Temple, His house (Buber 33, Braude 1.49). For

3) The Ninth of Ab

The Ninth of Ab was traditionally considered to be the date on which the Babylonian Nebuchadnezzar destroyed the first Temple in Jerusalem in 586 BCE, and the Romans the second Temple in 70 CE.[43] Psalm 79, beginning "O God, the nations have come into Your inheritance; they have defiled Your holy Temple; they have laid Jerusalem in ruins," was one of two psalms read on this annual commemoration of the destruction of the Temple and Jerusalem.[44] *Midr. Pss.* 79/3 on verse one asks whether Asaph (in the superscription) should have here recited a psalm (of praise).[45] Should it not rather have been a "lament" (בְּכִיָּה)?[46] 2 Sam 15:30 and Ps 3:1 are then cited to support the latter.[47] Here the emphasis is again on David's "weeping, lamenting," as found in 2 Sam 15:30, and the weeping, lamenting appropriate to the destruction of the Temple and Jerusalem.

4) Psalm 137

Psalm 137 is also a lament over the destruction of Jerusalem, originally through the Babylonian Nebuchadnezzar in 586 BCE.

---

another combination of 2 Sam 15:30 and David's composing Psalm 3, see *Midr. Pss.* 119/26 on Ps 119:75 (Buber 496, Braude 2.267).

[43] Cf. *m. Ta'an.* 4:6 (Albeck 2.344, Danby 200), which became normative. Josephus in *Bell.* 6.250 and 268 maintains it was the tenth for both. On the Ninth of Ab, see the art. "Ab, Ninth Day of" by M. Landsberg in *JE* (1901) 1.23-24, and the art. "Av, the Ninth" by M. Ydit in *EJ* (1971) 3.936-940.

[44] Cf. *Soferim* 18:3, 42b (*The Minor Tractates of the Talmud* 301). The other psalm is 137, to be discussed below. Both are found in *Eliyyahu Rabbah* 30 (28) on the destruction of the two Temples (Friedmann 147-151, Braude and Kapstein 364-370). For these two psalms in modern-day services on the Ninth of Ab, see the art. "Nine Days" by the editors in *EJ* (1971) 12.1168, as well as I. Elbogen, *Der jüdische Gottesdienst in seiner geschichtlichen Entwicklung* (Frankfurt am Main, 1931³; reprint Hildesheim: Olms, 1962) 128. For Psalm 137 as read on the Ninth of Ab, see also *Pesiq. R.* 28 (Braude 552, with n. 1, to p. 560).

[45] This is the usual meaning of מִזְמוֹר : song, psalm. Cf. Jastrow 755, and BDB 274 on זמר : make music in praise of God.

[46] Jastrow 169: weeping.

[47] Buber 360, Braude 2.44-45.

It was recited on the Ninth of Ab for this reason, and later also to commemorate the destruction of the Temple and the city in 70 CE by Titus.[48] One probable indication of its liturgical usage is found in *Targum Jonathan*, which has a voice from heaven recite v 5, Michael the head of Israel v 7, and Gabriel the head of Zion v 8.[49] The Septuagint (Psalm 136) already adds the superscription Τῷ Δαυιδ, corresponding to the Hebrew לְדָוִד, "a psalm of David," not in the MT. David is thus represented as having also composed this psalm. Verse one reads: "By the rivers of Babylon - there we sat down and also 'wept' (בָּכִינוּ, LXX ἐκλαύσαμεν) when we remembered Zion." David is pictured as "foreseeing" the fate of those exiled from Jerusalem to Babylon hundreds of years after his own time. The attribution of the psalm to David in the pre-Christian LXX period makes it into a prophecy on his part. The catchword "weeping" (בכה) also connected it to David's "weeping" over Jerusalem from the Mount of Olives in 2 Sam 15:30.

a) David's Prophecy of the Destruction of the Two Temples (and Jerusalem)

In *Midr. Pss.* 137/1 on Ps 137:1 Rab, probably a first generation Palestinian Amora,[50] teaches that the Holy One, blessed be He, showed David "the destruction of the first Temple and the destruction of the second Temple" (חרבן בית ראשון וחרבן בית שני)." The first is indicated in v 1, and the second in v 7, "Remember, O Lord, against the

---

[48] Cf. n. 44. This is true both for the triennial Palestinian lectionary system, and for the annual system of Babylonia. The readings for the festivals were the first to become fixed.

[49] Merino 183-184 and 316. The voice from heaven may also be thought of as uttering v 6. Psalm 137 was also part of the "Great Hallel" recited at Passover, making it appropriate as part of the background of Luke 19:41-44, spoken by Jesus during the weeklong Passover festival. On the Great Hallel with psalm 137, see *Midr. Pss.* 136/1 (Buber 519, Braude 2.324) and *b. Pesaḥ.* 118a (Soncino 605-606).

[50] Strack and Stemberger, *Introduction* 93. Properly called Abba Arikha, he was from Babylonia and followed his uncle Ḥiyya to Palestine to study under Rabbi, Judah the Prince. He died in 247 CE.

Edomites the day of Jerusalem, who said: 'Raze it, raze it, even to its foundation!'"[51] Here as in many other rabbinic sources Edom stands for wicked Rome, the fourth or last kingdom, following Greece.[52] Rab asks in regard to the expression "daughter of Babylon" in Ps 137:8 whether Edom was really the daughter of Babylon. Answering the question himself, he replies that "Edom continued doing the very things Babylon had done."[53] That is, just as Babylon destroyed the Temple and Jerusalem and mistreated its inhabitants, so did Rome centuries later in 70 CE.

In *Midr. Pss.* 137/1 David is thus represented as being shown by God the destruction of the first and the second Temples. This is a further illustration of David as a prophet described in section III. 1) above. *Midr. Pss.* 121/3 on 137:7, "Remember, O Lord, against the Edomites the day of Jerusalem [its fall]," specifically states that although Babylon was the first to destroy Jerusalem, "he [David] 'prophesied' (נתנבא) that the Temple would be rebuilt and Edom would destroy it."[54]

The above haggadic interpretation of Psalm 137, recited on the Ninth of Ab commemorating the destruction of the Temple and Jerusalem, in an earlier form was influential in regard to a Palestinian Jewish Christian's description of Jesus on the Mount of Olives. As the Son of David, he weeps like David at the same site and predicts the destruction of the second Temple in Luke 19:41-44. R. Eliezer (ben Hyrcanus), a second generation Tanna, R. Joshua, also a second generation Tanna, and R. Dosa, a fourth generation Tanna, all comment on various aspects of

---

[51] Buber 522, Braude 2.331. A parallel is found in *b. Git.* 57b (Soncino 266).
[52] Cf. for example *Midr. Pss.* 80/5 and 6 (Braude 1.51-52) and 97/1 (Braude 1.141). In 83/3 on Ps 83:7-9 it is related that "through the Holy Spirit David foresaw that wicked Edom in company with ten nations would destroy the Holy Temple" (Buber 369-370, Braude 2.62).
[53] Cf. *Midr. Pss.* 137/11 (Buber 526, Braude 2.339 and 522, n. 16). Cf. also *y. Yebam.* 9:8 (9), 10b (Neusner 21.303), as well as *Num. Rab.* Naso 7/10 on Num 5:4 (Mirqin 9.139, Soncino 5.199) and *Midr. Pss.* 121/3 (Buber 507, Braude 2.298).
[54] Buber 506, Braude 2.296. Cf. the rest of the passage for [Titus'] entering the Temple with his sword, bloodying it and boasting that he had slain God Himself.

Psalm 137.[55] Because of this known early comment, it is quite probable that David was originally represented as having prophesied the destruction of the first Temple, under Nebuchadnezzar, in the period before 70 CE, as indicated in the LXX superscription to the psalm.[56] In light of the events of 70 CE, this was then expanded by Tannaitic commentators to include the destruction of the second Temple by "the Edomites," the Romans.

b) Dashing Children to Pieces

Luke 19:41–44 is also influenced by Judaic tradition on Psalm 137 in another way. Verse 44a reads: καὶ ἐδαφιοῦσίν σε καὶ τὰ τέκνα σου ἐν σοί. The noun ἔδαφος means "bottom, foundation, base" of something, as well as "ground, soil." The cognate verb ἐδαφίζω, only occurring here in the NT, basically means to "beat level and firm like a floor or pavement,"[57] and of a city as in LXX Isa 3:26 to "raze to the ground."[58] Yet it also means to "dash to the ground."[59] In their *Lexicon*, W. Bauer, W. Arndt, F. Gingrich and F. Danker maintain that both meanings are present in Luke 19:44.[60] The KJV preferred the first meaning: "And shall lay thee even with the ground, and thy children within thee." It was followed by the NRSV: "They will crush you to the ground, you and your children within you." The RSV preferred the second meaning: "and dash you to the ground, you and your children within you." Judaic interpretation of Ps 137:9 aids in better understanding the original meaning of the phrase in Luke 19:44a.

---

[55] On the dating of these rabbis, cf. Strack and Stemberger, *Introduction* 77 and 87, and *Midr. Pss.* 137/10, 6 and 7 (Braude 2.338 and 335-337).

[56] Cf. *Pesiq. R.* 6/7 in regard to the Solomonic Temple. Here David prays to God: "Master of the Universe, by the prophetic gift which is mine I foresee that the Temple will be destroyed in the end" (Friedmann 25b, Braude 129).

[57] LSJ 477.

[58] BAGD 217.

[59] Cf. the above two notes. LSJ only cite LXX Ps 136 (137) : 9 and Luke 19:44 for this meaning.

[60] Cf. n. 58.

Jesus' Weeping over the Destruction of Jerusalem

The NRSV of Ps 137:9 reads regarding Babylon, which together with its allies, the Edomites, had besieged Jerusalem and razed it to its foundations (v 7): "Happy shall they be who take your little ones and 'dash' them against the rock!" The verb נָפַץ means to shatter, as a jar or vessel. In the piel, as here, it means to "dash to pieces." In Ps 2:9 God's son, the king, dashes the nations in pieces like a potter's vessel, and both Jer 13:14 and 48:12 have the Lord as the subject.[61] Only in Ps 137:9, however, are "little ones" dashed down and killed as retaliation for an enemy's besieging Jerusalem, the latter the same situation as envisaged in Luke 19:43-44. The Greek τὰ τέκνα σου, "your [Jerusalem's] children," is a good rendering of the Hebrew עֹלָלַיִךְ, "your children."[62] The argument for Ps 137:9 as behind Luke 19:44a is reinforced by the Septuagint's translating נָפַץ at this point by the verb ἐδαφίζω. In the course of this study I propose evidence that Luke 19:41-44 was originally composed in a Semitic language, Hebrew or Aramaic. This would mean that the Semitic verb behind ἐδαφίζω in Luke 19:44a, as in Ps 137:9, was נָפַץ.[63] If so, "dash to pieces," similar to the wording of the RSV, was originally intended and not "lay even with the ground" (KJV) or "crush to the ground" (NRSV). Nor are both meanings intended, as in BAGD *ad verbum*.

Judaic interpretation of Ps 137:9 supports the above translation of "dash to pieces." *Midr. Pss.* 121/3 on Ps 121:4 is an extensive midrash on Ps 137:5-9. Taking the "us" of verse 8 to mean both Israel and God, the midrash states in regard to Edom (Rome) in v 9: "There will come a time when I Myself will 'dash' your little ones against the rock, even as you 'dashed down' My little ones in this world." Acknowledging that while (Rome in

---

[61] Dan 12:7 also speaks of the "shattering" of the power of the holy people, which the Lord will bring to an end.

[62] Cf. BDB 760 on עוֹלֵל, "child," also employed elsewhere of children dashed to pieces (רָטַשׁ, p. 936) in 2 Kgs 8:12, Hos 14:1, Nah 3:10 and Isa 13:16. This means that τέκνα should also be taken literally as "children" and not only to mean the inhabitants of Jerusalem in general, as some commentators maintain.

[63] The *Targum* here has רטש (Merino 184 and 316), which in the pael also means to scatter, to "dash to pieces" (Jastrow 1472).

70 CE) led Israel out in chains, burnt the Temple and ravished women, it did not "dash down" the little ones of Israel, the commentator states: "As Edom has done to others, so I shall do to Edom." Nah 3:10 with children dashed to pieces is then cited. God further states that Edom "dashed to pieces" His little ones who were the first ones to make him king over them. Therefore "Blessed shall he be who pays you [Edom] back for what you have done to us [Israel and God]."[64]

Here the rabbinic commentator, probably with the events of 66-70 CE relatively fresh in mind, applies the "dashing to pieces" of children in Ps 137:9 to the Romans' siege of Jerusalem (and destruction of its Temple), although he acknowledges that this phenomenon did not actually take place.[65] The Palestinian Jewish Christian author of what later became Luke 19:41-44 also employed the same imagery to the destruction of Jerusalem in 70 CE, here prophesied by Jesus, although he most probably knew that the Roman soldiers did not act that way. "Literary freedom" was taken by both authors, and the vengeful language[66] was understandable in light of the severe atrocities of the Jewish-Roman War.

c) *The Necessity of Repentance*

One more motif underlying Luke 19:41-44 derives from Judaic interpretation of Psalm 137. After weeping over the city of Jerusalem, Jesus says in v 42: "If you, even you, had only recognized on this day the things that make for peace!" The

---

[64] Buber 507, Braude 2.298, which I slightly modify. Cf. also *Midr. Pss.* 138/1 on Ps 138:1 (Buber 527, Braude 2.340), and 17A/7 (Braude 1.222-223, with 2.439, n. 1). Interestingly, the prophet Elisha weeps in 2 Kgs 8:11 because he foresees the evil Aram / Syria will later do to Israel, including dashing in pieces (רטש) their little ones (v 12).

[65] Nor does Josephus, personally involved in the conflict, ever mention such behavior on the part of the Romans. While some children were killed in *Bell.* 6.271, this was only in connection with older people, lay people and priests, i.e. with everyone else too. In 5.433, because of the extreme famine in Jerusalem, *Jewish* rebels lifted up children with morsels of food and dashed them to the ground in order to get at it.

[66] Cf. the same imagery applied to Samaria in Hos 14:1 (Eng. 13:16), Babylon in Isa 13:16, and Nineveh in Nah 3:10.

second aorist of γινώσκω, to know, is employed here (ἔγνως), yet meant in the above sense of to perceive or recognize.[67] "On this day" refers to Jesus' entry into Jerusalem. S. Gilmour correctly states regarding this: "Jesus' entry provided the city with a final opportunity for repentance."[68] He then prophesied the destruction of the city "because you did not recognize (ἔγνως) the time of your visitation" (v 44). That is, it did not acknowledge Jesus as God's prophetic messenger, calling it to repentance. The same thought is expressed in 13:33-35.[69] In Luke 19:42-44 the term ἔγνως both begins and concludes Jesus' remarks regarding Jerusalem, a mark of rhetorical / literary artistry.

The motif of Jerusalem's lack of repentance, leading to its destruction, is based on Judaic interpretation of Psalm 137. In *Midr. Pss.* 137/10 on Ps 137:7, R. Eliezer (ben Hyrcanus), a second generation older Tanna,[70] is asked: "Are the later generations more worthy than the early generations?" He replies: "What befell the Temple shrine [in 70 CE] because of your conduct gives the answer. Your forefathers brought it about that the Temple roof was broken away [in 586 BCE], as is said: 'And the covering of Judah was laid bare' (Isa 22:8). But we, we brought it about that the very walls were razed [in 70 CE], as is said: 'Raze it, raze it, even to its foundation!' (Ps 137:7). Thus you learn that when a generation in whose days the Temple is not rebuilt goes by, it is reckoned against the generation as if it had destroyed the Temple. Why is it reckoned so? Because the generation 'did not repent.'"[71] Literally, the

---

[67] Cf. "Would that even today you 'knew' the things that make for peace!" (v 42, RSV).
[68] Cf. "The Gospel According to St. Luke" in *IB* (1952) 8.340-341. See also A. Plummer, *The Gospel According to S. Luke* (ICC; Edingburgh: Clark, 1956 / 1896) 452: "The whole of this period of opportunity, which culminated ἐν τῇ ἡμέρᾳ ταύτῃ, was unnoted and unused."
[69] Cf. also 23:28-31.
[70] Cf. Strack and Stemberger, *Introduction* 77.
[71] Buber 526, Braude 2.338.

latter phrase is: "did not do תְּשׁוּבָה." The Hebrew noun means "returning" to God, or repentance.[72]

Here one of the earliest known Tannaim reproaches his own contemporaries, some of whom had personally experienced the destruction of the Temple and Jerusalem by the Romans in 70 CE, with having caused this through lack of repentance. The same, he says, is true for the Temple's not being rebuilt after this date.

The same motif of lack of repentance as causing the destruction of the Temple and Jerusalem (as well as exile) is found in *Midr. Pss.* 137/2 on Ps 137:1, "By the rivers of Babylon – there we sat down and there we wept when we remembered Zion." The prophet Jeremiah here tells the weeping exiles: "I call upon heaven and earth to witness that if 'you had wept but once' (בכיתם בכיה אחת) while you were still in Zion, you would not now be going into exile."[73] In regard to Ps 137:2, R. Isaac, probably a third generation Palestinian Amora,[74] maintains in *Pesiq. R.* 28/3: "While the children of Israel were in the Land of Israel, Jeremiah used to say: 'Repent (עשו תשובה) before the decree of judgment against you be sealed,' but they would not." Thus they were exiled to Babylon.[75]

In the above examples the prophet Jeremiah is represented as calling the inhabitants of Jerusalem and other Israelites to repentance. Since they rejected it, the city was destroyed by Nebuchadnezzar in 586 BCE, and many of its inhabitants were exiled to Babylon. Because of the very similar situation in Luke

---

[72] Jastrow 1703. A parallel to this incident is found in *y. Yoma* 1:1, 38c (Neusner 14.26). Before this, R. Zeira maintains "The people in the time of the First Temple repented, while those in the time of the Second Temple did not repent" (p. 25).

[73] Buber 522, Braude 2.331. A parallel is found in *Pesiq. R.* 26/6 (Friedmann 131b, Braude 537).

[74] Strack and Stemberger, *Introduction* 98.

[75] Friedmann 136a, Braude 558. For the exiles' repenting in Babylon and God's weeping with them there, cf. *Eliyyahu Rabbah* 30 (28) in Friedmann 154, Braude and Kapstein 375. On the Babylonians' fear of the exiles' repenting ("turning") on the way from Jerusalem to Babylon, see *Midr. Pss.* 137/3 on Ps 137:1 (Buber 522, Braude 2.331).

19:41-44, Jesus may be represented here not only as the Son of David, the successor of the prophet David, but also as a kind of second Jeremiah, who also predicted the destruction of Jerusalem (Jer 26:6) while calling it to repentance.

Finally, *Pesiq. R.* 31/3 has R. Jonathan, perhaps a third generation Tanna but more probably a first generation Palestinian Amora,[76] state in regard to the Jewish-Roman War ending in 70 CE: "During the three and a half years that the [Roman] enemies surrounded Jerusalem, the Divine Presence stood on the Mount of Olives calling every day: 'The voice of the Lord cries to the city ... Hear the rod and who has appointed it' (Mic 6:9), and 'Seek the Lord while He may be found, call upon Him while He is near' (Isa 55:6). Yet the children of Israel did not even try 'to do penance' (לעשות תשובה). Hence God says: Yet you dare to say: 'Why, O Lord, do You stand far off?' (Ps 10:1)."[77]

Here the term "the enemies" (השונאים)[78] occurs, as in Luke 19:43 (οἱ ἐχθροί), as does the term "to surround" (מקיפים ... היו),[79] employed in the same verse (περικυκλώσουσιν). The Roman siege of Jerusalem ending in 70 CE is meant in both cases. The allusion is to the haggadic tradition of the Divine Presence (*Shechinah*) leaving Israel by making ten journeys, originally from the cherubim in the Temple to the wilderness, from which it then ascended to heaven.[80] The

---

[76] Strack and Stemberger, *Introduction* 83 and 92.
[77] Friedmann 143b; Braude 604, whom I modify. The section is based on Isa 49:14, part of the reading on the second Sabbath after the Ninth of Ab (Braude 600, n. 1).
[78] Cf. Jastrow 1537 on שׂוֹנֵא : hater, enemy.
[79] Cf. Jastrow 934 on the hiphil of נקף.
[80] The tradition is related to the destruction of the first Temple, but was later also connected to that of the second Temple. Cf. for example *b. Roš Haš.* 31a (Soncino 147-149, connected to the hope for Israel's repentance); *Lam. Rab.*, proem 25 (Soncino 7.50-52, with 56, n. 4, on the period three and a half years as related to Vespasian's siege of Jerusalem, noted explicitly in 1:5 § 31 on p. 101); *'Avot R. Nat.* A 34 (Schechter 102, Goldin 141; the last of ten descents of the Shechinah will

last station before the wilderness is the Mount of Olives, where the Shechinah now waits three and a half years in vain for the Jerusalemites to repent while the Romans besiege it. It should be noted that it is precisely from this site that Jesus also predicts the destruction of Jerusalem because it did not recognize what would lead to its peace, i.e. it did not repent and acknowledge him as God's final messenger to it.

V. 2 Sam 17:13

Because it referred to David and a besieged city, and was part of the scriptural unit close to 2 Sam 15:30 with David weeping at the Mount of Olives in part over the possibility of Jerusalem's being besieged (v 14), I suggest that Judaic interpretation of the verse 17:13 influenced the Semitic formulation behind Luke 19:44's καὶ οὐκ ἀφήσουσιν λίθον ἐπὶ λίθον ἐν σοί.

Before David and his followers crossed the Jordan River to escape his rebellious son Absalom (2 Sam 17:22), David's friend Hushai had via the sons of Zadok and Abiathar, Jonathan and Ahimaaz, advised the king to do so quickly (vv 15-21). He had persuaded Absalom not to pursue his father immediately, but only after gathering an army from all Israel. Then David and all those accompanying him could be killed (v 12).

At this point Hushai argues concerning David: "If he withdraws into a city, then all Israel will bring ropes to that city, and we shall drag it into the valley, 'until not even a pebble is to be found there'" (v 13). This seemingly good advice is then accepted by Absalom and his followers (v 14), leading Ahithophel to take his own life by hanging himself (v 23 – the model for Judas in Matt 27:5).

The phrase "until not even a pebble is to be found there" is in Hebrew: עַד אֲשֶׁר ~ לֹא ~ נִמְצָא שָׁם גַּם ~ צְרוֹר. The term צְרוֹר, "pebble," is only found here and in Amos 9:9.[81] Here the Septuagint translates it by "stone," λίθος, as does the *Targum*:

---

be to the Mount of Olives, based on Zech 14:4 – *ibid.*); and Ginzberg, *Legends* 6.392-393. See also Ezek 11:23.

[81] BDB 866.

אַבְנָא.⁸² The *Targum* renders the above Hebrew phrase by the active: "until we will not leave there a stone." "We will [not] leave" is וְנִשְׁאַר, the pael of שְׁאַר, meaning "to leave over."⁸³

The *Targum* also employs more siege imagery than in the Hebrew text. It states regarding the city to be besieged: "all Israel will be gatherered against that city and [army] camps will surround it." The stone motif is then emphasized by repetition: "And we will root out / destroy it 'and its stones,' and we will cast it into the wadi until we will not leave there 'a stone.'"⁸⁴ Josephus, whose native tongue was Aramaic, was clearly influenced by the haggadic tradition still found in the *Targum*. He writes in *Ant*. 7.220 in a paraphrase of 2 Sam 17:13: "But if your father [David] shuts himself up to stand a siege, we shall destroy that city through engines of war and underground tunnels / mines."

"Not even a pebble" in the Hebrew (גַּם ~ צְרוֹר) thus became "a stone" in the *Targum* (אַבְנָא), one of the besieged city's "stones." It is called λίθος in the LXX, which has "not even a stone" (μηδὲ λίθος). The term "stone" from 2 Sam 17:13 is most probably behind the λίθον ἐπὶ λίθον in Luke 19:44. This is made even more probable by the verb employed here. The phrase καὶ οὐκ ἀφήσουσιν, "And they will not leave," employs the active form of ἀφίημι⁸⁵ in order to conform to the other preceding verbs in vv 43-44: "your enemies *will set up* ramparts around you and *surround* you and *hem* you *in* on every side and *dash* you and your children *to the ground*." While the Hebrew וְנִמְצָא in 2 Sam 17:13 is niphal / passive, as is the LXX's καταλειφθῇ, ⁸⁶ the *Targum* renders the verb actively, "We will

---

⁸² Sperber 2.190, and Jastrow 7 on אַבְנָא.
⁸³ Jastrow 1509.
⁸⁴ Sperber 2.190, Harrington and Saldarini 190 with modifications.
⁸⁵ Cf. BAGD 126 on ἀφίημι, 3.a., leave.
⁸⁶ This is the aorist passive of καταλείπω, to leave (BAGD 413). The passive form, however, did influence the formulation of Mark 13:2 par.: οὐ μὴ ἀφεθῇ ὧδε λίθος ἐπὶ λίθον ὃς οὐ μὴ καταλυθῇ, "Not one stone *will be left* here upon another; all will be thrown down." On this whole theme, cf. L. Gaston, *No Stone on Another*: Studies in the Significance of

not leave" (see above). The tradition as still found in the *Targum* was then modified by the Palestinian Jewish Christian author of Luke 19:41-44 because of the context to "They will not leave."

Luke 19:44b thus appears to be a conscious modification of a very similar expression in 2 Sam 17:13, especially as found in Judaic tradition.

VI. Isaiah 29

Another scriptural passage which plays a major role in Luke 19:41-44 is chapter 29 of the prophet Isaiah.[87] There God Himself will besiege Jerusalem, called Ariel in vv 1-2 and 7,[88] and the nations will also fight against the city (v 7). It is connected to other texts dealing with David through the mention of him in v 1 ("the city where David encamped")[89] and in the LXX of v 3.[90] Rabbinic texts also relate the chapter to the destruction of the first Temple and the second Temple.[91] Isaiah 29 appears to have influenced Luke 19:41-43 in nine different ways.

---

the Fall of Jerusalem in the Synoptic Gospels (NovTSup 23; Leiden: Brill, 1970), especially 355-360.

[87] The use of Isaiah 29 here has long been recognized. Cf. for example A. Plummer, *The Gospel According to S. Luke* 451, and A. Loisy, *L'Évangile selon Luc* 472. Yet no one up to now has traced the extensive use of imagery from the chapter, and the commentators list many other passages they consider just as influential. See also the margin of the Nestle-Aland *Novum Testamentum Graecum* [26] ad loc.

[88] The term probably signifies the altar hearth (in the Temple). Cf. BDB 72 on אֲרִיאֵל and אֲרִאֵיל, and Ezek 43:15-16.

[89] For David's besieging the Jebusite city Jerusalem and taking it, cf. 2 Sam 5:6-9 and 1 Chr 11:4-8.

[90] The NRSV follows the LXX here. See below for a discussion of this.

[91] Cf. *Lam. Rab.*, proem 26 (Wilna, Ekah 14-15; Soncino 7.52-53) in regard to Isa 29:2, "like the destruction of the first Temple will be the destruction of the second Temple"; *Exod. Rab.* Yithro 29/9 on Exod 20:1 (Mirqin 6.28; Soncino 3.344), *Pesiq. Rav Kah.* 13/15 (Mandelbaum 239, Braude and Kapstein 265), and *Pesiq. R.* 27/28.1 (Friedmann 133b, Braude 548) on Nebuchadnezzar's destruction of the Temple; and *'Avot R. Nat.* A 1 (Schechter 4, Goldin 9) on Titus' challenging God to make war upon him when he and his troops destroy the Temple. He strikes

Jesus' Weeping over the Destruction of Jerusalem 233

1) Luke 19:43b reads: καὶ παρεμβαλοῦσιν ... χάρακά σοι, "and they will throw up a palisade against you." The verb παρεμβάλλω occurs only here in the NT and in this context means to throw up.[92] In the LXX it never occurs with χάραξ. A χάραξ, which also only occurs here in the NT, is a palisade,[93] or a pointed stake, a pale used in fortifying the entrenchments of a military camp.[94]

The above phrase in Luke 19:43b derives from Isa 29:3. The original Semitic was dependent on the Hebrew וְצַרְתִּי עָלַיִךְ מֻצָּב. The verb צוּר with עַל means to besiege (a city), here "you," Jerusalem.[95] The term מֻצָּב, which only occurs here in the MT, means palisade or entrenchment.[96] "I will besiege you with a palisade" was then rendered by the LXX as "I will throw up a palisade around you," βαλῶ περὶ σὲ χάρακα. Yet both Aquila and Theodotion read here παρεμβαλῶ, as in Luke. The Hellenistic Jewish Christian translator of the episode in Luke 19:41–44 recognized the background of the Semitic original in Isa 29:3 and correctly borrowed the corresponding phrase from the LXX, modifying it to the third person plural of παρεμβάλλω and employing the fuller form of the verb, as did

---

its altar, equated with Ariel here. See also b. Ḥag. 5b (Soncino 23, with n. 8). In the NT, Paul quotes Isa 29:10 in Rom 11:8, v 14 in 1 Cor 1:19, and he may allude to v 16 in Rom 9:20-21. Jesus quotes v 13 in Mark 7:6-7 // Matt 15:8-9, and Matt 11:5 // Luke 7:22 may in part allude to vv 18-19.
[92] BAGD 625; LSJ 1335 as to put in beside or between, interpose, insert (troops in a line of battle), place.
[93] BAGD 876, 2.
[94] LSJ 1977. Josephus employs χάραξ with the verb βάλλω in Ant. 15.12; 20:86; and Vita 214 and 395, but never of the Roman siege of Jerusalem. Cf. however the similar term χαράκωμα (LSJ 1977) in Bell. 5.269. For χάραξ in Philo, see Agr. 11. For the Roman use of four immense χώματα, earth-works or mounds (LSJ 2014), at Jerusalem, see for example Josephus, Bell. 5.466-473.
[95] BDB 848, 2.
[96] BDB 663. The Targum (Stenning 92-93) has: "and I will build siege works against you." It employs בְּרָקוֹם, the same as בְּרָכוֹם, siege works (Jastrow 669).

Aquila and Theodotion. Or the fuller form was later added by the Evangelist Luke.

2) Luke 19:43c reads καὶ περικυκλώσουσίν σε, "and they will surround you." The verb περικυκλόω, occurring only here in the NT, means to surround or encircle (a besieged city).[97]

The above phrase also derives from Isa 29:3, where God says of Jerusalem: "I will encamp against you like a circle," i.e., "I will surround you with My military camp(s)." The Hebrew is וְחָנִיתִי כַדּוּר עָלָיִךְ. The verb חָנָה means to encamp, of an army.[98] The noun דּוּר is a circle.[99] The LXX has καὶ κυκλώσω ὡς Δαυιδ ἐπὶ σέ, "and I will surround you, as David (did)." The LXX translators rendered כַּדּוּר, "like a circle," with κυκλόω. Yet even in their time the variant כְּדָוִד, "like David," was apparently preferred by some. Thus they simply rendered both options into Greek: κυκλώσω and ὡς Δαυιδ. They also took some liberty in translating "towers" (πύργους) for the siege works, מְצֻרֹת, of the MT.[100]

The Palestinian Jewish Christian author of Luke 19:41-44 probably borrowed "I will encamp against you like a circle" from the MT of Isa 29:3 and modified it to "they" because of the subject, Jerusalem's enemies (the Romans). When a Hellenistic Jewish Christian translated the Semitic into Greek, he again recognized the origin of the phrase in Isa 29:3 and employed the verb he was acquainted with from the LXX at that point: κυκλόω. Just as he added παρεμ- to βάλλω in the preceding

---

[97] BAGD 648; LSJ 1378: encircle, encompass. Philo in Leg. All. 1.68 employs the verb of "encompassing" a country, where κυκλόω also occurs in the same meaning. Josephus uses κυκλόω in Bell. 5.338 of Roman soldiers within Jerusalem "surrounded" on all sides (πάντοθεν - see Luke 19:43) by enemies. In 496 Titus notes the difficulty involved in the siege of throwing up earthworks and in "encompassing" the city with troops. He therefore decides to throw up a wall around it (499, 508-510).
[98] BDB 333, 2.c.
[99] BDB 189, 1, only here in this meaning. Cf. the verb דּוּר I, 1) in Jastrow 288 : to form a circle or enclosure.
[100] BDB 848 on מְצוּרָה : siege works, rampart.

phrase, however, he also added περι- to κυκλόω here. Apparently he preferred fuller sounding verbs. Or again, the Evangelist Luke may have done this himself.

3) Luke 19:43d reads καὶ συνέξουσίν σε πάντοθεν, "and they will confine you on every side." The verb συνέχω means to hold or keep together, confine, enclose.[101] Siege terminology is again employed here.

The above verb also derives from Isa 29:3. The Hebrew וְצַרְתִּי עָלַיִךְ מֻצָּב can mean "I will besiege you with a palisade," as in 1) above. Yet the basic meaning of the verb צוּר is to confine.[102] It is rendered by συνέχω as here in 1 Kgdms (1 Sam) 23:8, where Saul orders people to confine or besiege David and his men in the city of Keilah. The Palestinian Jewish Christian author of the Semitic original of Luke 19:41–44 already had mentioned a palisade from the same Hebrew phrase in v 43b. Now he employed צוּר in its more frequent meaning, to confine.[103] To make this more explicit, he added "on every side."

* * *

The analysis in 1) – 3) above shows that the original Palestinian Jewish Christian author of the narrative in Luke 19:41–44 took his three main verbs in v 43 all from one source, Isa 29:3. This means that while several of the verbs occur in the LXX and Josephus in similar constellations, the author at this point made no other scriptural allusions or direct references to the Roman siege of Jerusalem as we know it from the Jewish historian. God's own siege of Jerusalem in Isaiah 29 sufficed him as a source for his imagery. Six other aspects of the narrative in

---

[101] LSJ 1714. Their suggestion (5.) of "oppress" here is too far from the basic meaning. BAGD 789, 3., have press hard, crowd. The NRSV has "hem you in." Josephus employs it of troops "blocked" by arrows and thirst during a siege in *Ant.* 13.385; see also 15.111 and *Vita* 213.
[102] BDB 848.
[103] Cf. F. Delitzsch's translation in his *Hebrew New Testament* (148): וְצָרוּ עָלַיִךְ. The United Bible Societies' *Hebrew New Testament* (214) also has וְיָצוּרוּ עָלַיִךְ.

Luke 19:41-44 also appear to have been borrowed from Isaiah 29.

4) Luke 19:43b reads "and 'your enemies' will throw up a palisade against you." The Greek of "your enemies" is οἱ ἐχθροί σου.

This derives from Isa 29:5, which also speaks of Jerusalem's enemies: "But the multitude of 'your enemies' shall be like small dust, and the multitude of tyrants like flying chaff." While the present MT has זָרָיִךְ , "your strangers,"[104] this seems improbable in the context.[105] Rather, the suggestion of *BHS*, צָרַיִךְ , should be preferred, also followed by the NRSV: "your enemies."[106] The noun צַר means adversary, foe, enemy,[107] which is most frequently translated in the LXX by ἐχθρός.

Another argument favors the Palestinian Jewish Christian author of Luke 19:41-44 as employing צָרִיךְ from Isa 29:5 here. Above in 1) I proposed the verb צוּר as behind παρεμβαλοῦσιν in v 43b, and in 3) the same verb as behind συνέξουσιν in v 43d. The use of צוֹר from 2 Sam 17:13 as the ultimate background of λίθος in v 44 was pointed out in section V. That is, the original author of Luke 19:41-44 appears to have made a wordplay with the root צוּר / צרר in at least three expressions. This would have been much appreciated by his original hearers in a Semitic language.

5) The end of Luke 19:44 says of Jerusalem: "because you did not recognize the time of your 'visitation.'"[108] The noun

---

[104] The participle of זוּר is used as a noun : stranger (BDB 266).
[105] The Isaiah Scroll from Qumran has זֵדִיךְ , "your insolent ones" (BDB 267 on זֵד), reflected in the LXX's ἀσεβῶν.
[106] G. Fohrer in *Das Buch Jesaja* (Zurich / Stuttgart: Zwingli, 1962) 2.68, n. 74, for example also argues for this reading.
[107] BDB 865. Cf. its use in 26:11.
[108] The NRSV adds "from God," which is only one possible meaning.

ἐπισκοπή is employed here, meaning a visitation, which can be either pleasant or unpleasant.[109]

I suggest that the Palestinian Jewish Christian author of the originally Semitic account now found in Luke 19:41-44 borrowed the term "visitation" from Isa 29:6. Verse 5c begins the sentence: "And in an instant, suddenly, 6) you [Jerusalem] 'will be visited' by the Lord of hosts with thunder and earthquake and great noise, with whirlwind and tempest, and the flame of a devouring fire." The verb "will be visited" is the Hebrew תִּפָּקֵד, the niphal imperfect of פָּקַד, to attend to, "visit," muster, appoint.[110] The cognate noun פְּקֻדָּה means oversight, mustering, "visitation."[111] The Palestinian Jewish Christian author employed the Semitic noun form here because it better suited his phrase "the time of your..." than the verbal form "the time of your being visited." The Hellenistic Jewish Christian who later translated the phrase into Greek correctly employed here the noun ἐπισκοπή, which is also found in LXX Isa 29:6.

Jerusalem's "visitation" refers here to Jesus' prophetically calling it to repentance (see section IV. 4) c) above). It refuses to recognize, even on the day Jesus enters the city (19:42), what would grant it שָׁלוֹם : peace, security, prosperity, welfare, salvation. By refusing to accept Jesus as the Lord's final (messianic) messenger, the leadership of Jerusalem is represented as condemning itself to the visitation / punishment of the Romans' besieging and capturing the city in vv 43-44. Because the city's religious authorities now reject a visitation of grace, it will later receive one of punishment and destruction.

* * *

The above five expressions stem from adjacent verses in Isaiah twenty-nine: 3, 5 and 6. This makes it even more probable that the original Palestinian Jewish Christian author of Luke

---

[109] BAGD 299 opt for the first here: "your gracious visitation." In LSJ 657 only biblical references are given for this noun. It is also lacking in Philo and Josephus.
[110] BDB 823.
[111] BDB 824.

19:41-44 also employed other expressions from the same Isaianic chapter, yet further away from the above cluster of verses.

6) Luke 19:42b states: "But now 'they are hidden' from your eyes." This refers to the things which make for Jerusalem's peace. "They are hidden" is the Greek ἐκρύβη, the second aorist passive of κρύπτω, to hide.[112] The divine passive is meant here: God Himself has hidden these things from Jerusalem's eyes. It cannot see or recognize them. The expression "from your eyes" is the Greek ἀπὸ ὀφθαλμῶν σου. Both of these phrases also derive from Isaiah 29.

Because Jerusalem's worship is spurious (29:13), the Lord will bring about the following: "The wisdom of their wise shall perish, and the discernment of the discerning 'shall be hidden'" (v 14). Such people even try to "hide" a plan they think is too deep for the Lord (v 15). The Hebrew of both verbs is סתר, to hide, conceal.[113] In the first instance, meant passively[114] as in Luke 19:42b, it is God who causes the Jerusalemites' discernment to be hidden.[115] In Isa 29:14 the Septuagint makes this even clearer by employing the future active: κρύψω, "I [the Lord] will hide...." The Hellenistic Jewish Christian translator of Luke 19:41-44 correctly rendered the Semitic סתר from Isa 29:14 by the passive of κρύπτω, ἐκρύβη, in v 42b.

The phrase "from your [Jerusalem's] eyes" also derives from Isaiah 29. In v 9 the prophet sarcastically tells the inhabitants: "blind yourselves and be blind!" In v 10 he states in regard to their prophets: The Lord "has closed 'your eyes.'" The latter in the MT is עֵינֵיכֶם, for which the LXX has τοὺς ὀφθαλμοὺς αὐτῶν, "their eyes."[116] The Palestinian Jewish Christian author

---

[112] BAGD 454.
[113] BDB 711. The *Targum* employs טמר with the same meaning (Jastrow 540): Stenning 94-95.
[114] The hithpael הִסְתַּתָּר, "shall hide itself carefully / completely," means as in the NRSV "shall be hidden."
[115] The *Targum* emphasizes this motif also in v 10: The Lord "has hidden" from you the prophets, He "has hidden" the scribes and teachers who taught you the instruction of the law (Stenning 92-93).
[116] Only in the future will "the eyes of the blind" see again (v 18).

Jesus' Weeping over the Destruction of Jerusalem 239

of Luke 19:41-44 borrowed the phrase "your [pl.] eyes" from Isa 29:10 and modified it to "from your [sing., Jerusalem's] eyes" in v 42. The things which lead to Jerusalem's peace, security, and welfare have now been hidden from its eyes by God Himself, as in Isaiah 29. It is as if the city were blind.[117]

7) Luke 19:42 has Jesus address Jerusalem with the words: "If 'you had recognized'...." The verb ἔγνως here is from γινώσκω, to know, understand, comprehend, perceive.[118] Verse 44 concludes with the same verb: "because 'you did not recognize' (ἔγνως) the time of your visitation." As remarked above, the verb artistically begins and ends the words of Jesus in the narrative. Here too the term most probably derives from Isaiah 29.

Isa 29:14 notes that the discernment of the discerning shall hide itself completely, i.e. be hidden. The prophet Isaiah continues in v 15 by saying: "Ha / alas![119] You who hide a plan too deep for the Lord, whose deeds are in the dark, and who say, 'Who sees us? Who knows us?'" The latter question is the Hebrew וּמִי יֹדְעֵנוּ. The *Targum* employs the same verb יְדַע , to know, perceive,[120] and the LXX has γινώσκω, as in Luke 19:42 and 44. The proximity of the verb יְדַע in Isa 29:15 to the motif of hiding / being hidden in vv 14-15 makes it probable that the Palestinian Jewish Christian author of Luke 19:41-44 borrowed it

---

[117] Cf. on this motif J. Fitzmyer, *The Gospel According to Luke X-XXIV*, 1258: "Implied is the blindness of its irresponsibility." See also L. Johnson, *The Gospel of Luke* (Sacra Pagina 3; Collegeville, Minnesota: The Liturgical Press, 1991) 298: "The weeping of Jesus is a sign of sorrow over the city's blindness and its future fate...," as well as E. Ellis, *The Gospel of Luke* (NCB 3; London: Oliphants, 1977) 226: "What blind Bartimaeus accepts (18:41), the blind leaders of Jerusalem reject."
[118] BAGD 160-161.
[119] Cf. BDB 222-223 on הוֹי : Ah, alas, ha, especially preparatory to a declaration of judgment. The *Targum* has וַי , "O, oh, *woe!*" (Stenning 94-95: "Woe unto them that..."; Jastrow 576). In this regard one may note that from 62-69 CE Jesus, son of Ananias, proclaimed "Woe to Jerusalem" before he was himself killed in the siege of the city (Josephus, *Bell.* 6.304-308).
[120] BDB 393-395; Jastrow 565; Stenning 95.

from here and employed it in v 42, where it is followed by things "hidden."

The verb יָדַע is employed also in Isa 29:11, 12 (twice) and 24. The latter passage expresses the hope that those who err in spirit "will come to know / perceive" understanding. The *Targum* also employs the verb יָדַע here,[121] and the LXX γινώσκω. This hope was not fulfilled in regard to the city of Jerusalem "because you did not recognize the time of your visitation" (Luke 19:44). The fivefold occurrence of the verb יָדַע in Isaiah 29, especially in v 15, thus most probably influenced the same terminology in Luke 19:42 and 44.

8) Luke 19:42 has Jesus say to Jerusalem: "If you had only recognized 'on this day' the things that make for peace!" "On this day" is the Greek ἐν τῇ ἡμέρᾳ ταύτῃ, which only occurs here in the NT. This expression may also derive from Isaiah 29.

Isa 29:18 states that "'On that day'... the eyes of the blind shall see," referring back to v 9, "blind yourselves and be blind!" and to v 10, where the Lord has closed the prophets' eyes. "On that day" is the Hebrew הַהוּא ~ בַּיּוֹם, translated literally in the LXX: ἐν τῇ ἡμέρᾳ ἐκείνῃ, very similar to the phrase in Luke 19:42.[122]

9) Luke 9:42 has the expression "the things that make for peace," in Greek τὰ πρὸς εἰρήνην. Jesus weeps over the city of Jerusalem because on this day it has not recognized / perceived what would lead to its own peace, welfare, security, prosperity, salvation. The Semitic background of εἰρήνη here is definitely שָׁלוֹם, which has this broad meaning.[123]

Judaic tradition on Isaiah 29 may have influenced the choice of the term "peace" here. Verse 24 states that in the future those

---

[121] Stenning 95.
[122] The *Targum* has "at that time," with עִדָּנָא (Jastrow 1067: period, time). It may have influenced the choice of καιρός, time (BAGD 394-395), in v 44.
[123] BDB 1022-1023; Jastrow 1579, who also translates with "salvation." On the Aramaic, cf. Jastrow 1586.

who err in spirit will "know" (יָדַע - NRSV "come to") understanding, and those who murmur rebelliously will learn instruction. The pre-Christian LXX has for the latter: "will learn to speak 'peace.'" Here εἰρήνη is employed, as in Luke 19:42. It is the hope of the prophet Isaiah, so very early Judaic tradition on Isa 29:24, that Jerusalem and its inhabitants will "know" (יָדַע , LXX γινώσκω) understanding and learn to speak "peace." This is like Jesus' wish in Luke 19:42, "Would that on this day you, even you, had 'known' the things leading to 'peace.'"

In *b. Ḥag.* 5b the "angels of peace" (מלאכי שלום) weep over the destruction of the Temple. Isa 33:7 is cited to buttress this, interpreting the term אראלם as "their 'altar,'" the אריאל of Isa 29:1-2 and 7.[124] If this Judaic tradition is early, it may also help to explain why "the things leading to peace" in Luke 19:42 are said by Jesus in regard to the threatened destruction of Jerusalem (including the Temple).

Finally, the Semitic שָׁלֵם / שְׁלָמָא , "peace," may also be a popular wordplay on the name of the city addressed in Luke 19:41, יְרוּשָׁלַם , Jerusalem. It was considered to consist of יראה שלם , "he will see 'peace.'"[125]

* * *

The above analysis of nine different expressions from Isaiah 29 shows how much the Palestinian Jewish Christian author of the original narrative now found in Luke 19:41-44 borrowed from that chapter, also associated in rabbinic sources with the destruction of the first Temple and the second Temple in Jerusalem. The chapter provided the major source of his imagery.

---

[124] Soncino 23, with n. 8.
[125] Cf. *Gen. Rab.* Vayera 56/10 on Gen 22:14 (Theodor and Albeck 608, Soncino 1.500, in regard to the Salem of 14:18), and *Midr. Pss.* 76/3 on Ps 76:3 (Buber 342, Braude 2.15). See also Josephus, *Bell.* 6.438 on Σόλυμα and Ἱεροσόλυμα. For several pre-Christian Jewish sources with this etymology, see J. Fitzmyer, *The Gospel According to Luke X–XXIV*, 1256. See also Ps 122:6 and 147:12-14.

VII. The Genre, Original Language and Provenance

1) *The Genre*

In Luke 19:41-44 Jesus is represented as weeping over the terrible future fate of Jerusalem. He foresees this as the Son of David. The latter in Judaic tradition also prophetically foresaw the destruction of the first Temple, the second Temple and the city. As such, the narrative may best be described as a prophetic lament of judgment and destruction.[126]

2) *The Original Language*

The model for Jesus' weeping over the future destruction of Jerusalem from the Mount of Olives is a Judaic tradition, now found in Hebrew, concerning David's weeping over the future destruction of the first Temple and the second Temple from the Mount of Olives. The latter is related to the Hebrew text of Psalm 137, as is the "dashing to pieces" of Jerusalem's children in Luke 19:44, and the motif of Jerusalem's refusal to repent, leading to its destruction. Many expressions based on the Hebrew text of Isaiah 29 are also found in vv 42-44.

The above argues very strongly for the original Palestinian Jewish Christian author of Luke 19:41-44 as basing his narrative on the Hebrew text of the Bible and on Judaic tradition

---

[126] Cf. D. Tiede, *Luke* 331, who speaks of "an oracle of destruction," but also of the pericope as a "Prophetic Lament." C. F. Evans in *Saint Luke* (London: SCM Press, 1990) 683 describes it as "a rhythmical prophetic oracle, which is a mixture of doom and lament." He produces no evidence, however, for rhythm in these verses. W. Wiefel in *Das Evangelium nach Lukas* (THKNT 3; Berlin: Evangelische Verlagsanstalt, 1988) 336 notes that the form is that of the Old Testament *lamentatio*. On this, see for example A. Weiser, *The Psalms* (Philadelphia: Westminster Press, 1962) 66-83, including the individual lament with the motifs of judgment and enemies / the wicked. A. Schlatter in *Das Evangelium des Lukas aus seinen Quellen erläutert* (Stuttgart: Calwer, 1931) 410 correctly notes that Jesus laments Jerusalem's destruction when he enters the city (here), and when he leaves it (23:28). The category "pronouncement-story," which J. Fitzmyer prefers in *The Gospel According to Luke X-XXIV* 1254, is not helpful here.

regarding the above scriptural passages, available to him in Hebrew.[127] Thus he may originally have composed his own account also in Hebrew. Yet Aramaic should not be excluded, since the author also appears to be acquainted with traditions still found in the targum to 2 Sam 17:13 and to Isaiah 29. If the original was in Hebrew, it would have been translated very soon into Aramaic, the common language of the people. My main point here is that the author wrote in one of these two Semitic languages.

3) The Provenance

The above linguistic discussion argues very strongly for the narrative now found in Greek in Luke 19:41-44 as originally having been composed in Palestine. In addition, all the Judaic traditions cited above on Psalm 137 and Isaiah 29 are Palestinian (and not for example Babylonian or Alexandrian). The narrative belongs to "Special Luke," and there is good reason to believe this material was originally composed in a Semitic language, probably in Judea.[128]

VIII. The Question of Historicity and the Date of the Narrative

1) The Question of Historicity

A number of commentators consider Luke 19:41-44 to be historical.[129] Others find in it an historical core, which was then

---

[127] Against C. H. Dodd, who analyzes Luke 19:42-44 and 21:20-24 in "The Fall of Jerusalem and the 'Abomination of Desolation'" in *JRS* 37 (1947) 47-54. He maintains that "the whole significant vocabulary of both Lucan passages belongs to the language of the Septuagint..." (p. 50), yet he acknowledges that "the idiom is markedly Semitic at several points" (p. 52). Dodd correctly emphasizes that the author of 19:41-44 borrowed from biblical passages dealing with the destruction of Jerusalem by Nebuchadnezzar in 586 BCE, yet he fails to consider OT passages in Hebrew and Palestinian Judaic traditions on them.
[128] Cf. the remarks on this topic in chapter two, p. 147.
[129] A. Schlatter, *Das Evangelium des Lukas* 411; W. Manson, *The Gospel of Luke* 217; R. Stein, *Luke* (The New American Commentary 24; Nashville: Broadman Press, 1992) 483; and J. Nolland, *Luke 18:35-24:53*, 930.

edited or re-formulated in light of the destruction of Jerusalem in 70 CE.[130] Some, however, reject its historicity completely and view it as a *vaticinium ex eventu*.[131]

It is very probable that like the prophets Jeremiah (26:11) and Micah (3:12) centuries before him, and like Jesus ben Ananias after him in 62-69 CE in Jerusalem itself,[132] Jesus threatened the religious leadership in Jerusalem with the destruction of the Temple and the capital city if they would not repent.[133] Yet the narrative now found in Luke 19:41-44, or even its core, cannot be attributed to the historical Jesus. Its Palestinian Jewish Christian author knew of Jesus' "prophecy" (threat) of the destruction of the Temple (and the city) if its inhabitants, primarily its leaders, did not repent of their ways. He also was acquainted with a Judaic tradition of David's "prophesying" the destruction of the first Temple (and possibly the second too after 70 CE) and Jerusalem from the Mount of Olives, based on 2 Sam 15:30 and

---

[130] Cf. A. Plummer, *The Gospel According to S. Luke* 451; E. Ellis, *The Gospel of Luke* (NCB 3; London: Oliphants, 1977) 226, who speaks of a possible "peshering" of it by Christian prophets; I. Marshall, *The Gospel of Luke* (Grand Rapids, Michigan: Erdmans, 1978) 717; J. Fitzmyer, *The Gospel According to Luke X-XXIV*, 1254-1255; J. Kremer, *Lukasevangelium* 189; and C. F. Evans, *Saint Luke* 685.

[131] Cf. R. Bultmann, *The History of the Synoptic Tradition* (New York and Evanston: Harper & Row, 1963) 36 and 123; G. Schneider, *Das Evangelium nach Lukas, Kapitel 11-24* (ÖTKNT 3/2; Gütersloh: Mohn; Würzburg: Echter Verlag, 1977) 388, who attributes v 41 to the Evangelist and thinks the whole narrative may have been composed by him; D. Tiede, *Prophecy and History in Luke-Acts* (Philadelphia: Fortress, 1980) 80; G. Petzge, *Das Sondergut des Evangeliums nach Lukas* (Zurich: Theologischer Verlag, 1990) 173-174; and K. Paesler, *Das Tempelwort Jesu. Die Traditionen von Tempelzerstörung und Tempelerneuerung im Neuen Testament* (FRLANT 184; Göttingen: Vandenhoeck & Ruprecht, 1999) 230.

[132] Cf. n. 119. See also 1QpHab 9:5-7 in *The Dead Sea Scrolls Study Edition*, ed. F. Martínez and E. Tigchelaar, 1.18-19, where the riches and loot of the last priests of Jerusalem "will be given into the hands of the army of the Kittim" (the Romans). Reference from J. Fitzmyer, *The Gospel According to Luke X-XXIV*, 1258.

[133] Cf. for example Mark 13:2 par. and 14:58a par. in earlier levels of tradition.

Psalm 137, read liturgically on the Ninth of Ab commemorating the destruction of the first Temple in 586 BCE, and later also that of the second Temple in 70 CE on exactly the same day. He also knew that the title "Son of David" was attributed to Jesus during his lifetime according to the pre-Gospel tradition. He then had Jesus as the Son of David prophesy the destruction of (the Temple and all of) Jerusalem from the Mount of Olives just as his forebear had done. In addition to Judaic tradition on Psalm 137, he employed materials regarding Isaiah 29, itself interpreted in Judaic sources of the destruction of the Temple and Jerusalem in 586 BCE, and later in 70 CE. The latter is the reason he included no specific details of the siege of Jerusalem by the Romans, ending in its fall in 70 CE, which he certainly knew of. Imagery from Psalm 137 and Isaiah 29 were traditionally associated with the destruction of the Temple and the city, and he closely followed the traditions with which he was well acquainted.

2) The Date of the Narrative

In Luke 19:41-44 Jesus is represented as prophesying the destruction of Jerusalem in 70 CE by the Romans. The author is thus writing from the perspective of post 70 CE. The *terminus ad quem* is the date of the Gospel of Luke, which many scholars place at the beginning of the eighties.[134] Some time was needed for the narrative's circulation (in Hebrew or Aramaic) in a Palestinian Jewish Christian community(-ies), after which it was translated from Aramaic into Greek by a Hellenistic Jewish Christian. It became available in this language to the Evangelist Luke. A date at the end of the seventies for the original Semitic narrative thus seems most appropriate. This was still quite close to the destruction of the Temple and Jerusalem by the Romans, an event which was also heartbreaking for Palestinian Jewish Christians.

---

[134] Cf. for example D. Tiede, *Luke* 37: "the midpoint in the early 80s may be the most likely," and W. Wiefel, *Das Evangelium des Lukas* 5: not before 75 CE and before Acts, finished ca. 85-90 CE.

IX. Lukan Editing

The Evangelist Luke only very slightly re-formulated the narrative he appropriated from his additional source, "Special Luke." Two expressions are frequently thought to derive from him.

The verb συνέχω in Luke 19:43 is one of six occurrences in the Gospel, supplemented by three in Acts. In the other Gospels it only occurs once, in Matt 4:24. While this seems to argue for its Lukan origin,[135] I have shown above in section VI. 3) that it correctly translates the verb צוּר in Isa 29:3, the model for the image. It was thus already part of the tradition Luke appropriated from Special Luke.

Another expression, however, does appear to be Lukan. The term ἀνθ' ὧν in Luke 19:44 also occurs in Luke 1:20; 12:3; and Acts 12:23, yet only in 2 Thess 2:10 in the rest of the NT. This favors Lukan redaction at this point.[136]

Apart from the latter expression, the pericope Luke 19:41–44 has been basically left as Luke found it in his additional source, Special Luke.[137]

Following the Gospel of Mark, which he had before him, the Evangelist Luke after 19:38 omits Mark's mention of a first short

---

[135] J. Jeremias, *Die Sprache des Lukasevangeliums* 282; J. Fitzmyer, *The Gospel According to Luke X–XXIV*, 1258; and J. Nolland, *Luke 18:35–24:53*, 931-932, all maintain the verb συνέχω here is Lukan.

[136] The Semitic original may have been כִּי in the sense of "because, since" (BDB 473). If the Hellenistic Jewish Christian translator rendered it by ὅτι, the Evangelist may have considered this in the sense of "for" too weak and may have desired a definitely causal relationship through his changing it to ἀνθ' ὧν, "because." The Greek literally means "in return for which" (BAGD 73, 3.), suitable to the retributive tenor of the passage.

[137] Cf. the remarks of J. Jeremias and J. Fitzmyer in the works cited in n. 135. J. Nolland provides no evidence for his assertion that vv 41-42 and the final clause of v 44 are Lukan (see also n. 135). As pointed out above in sections VI. 1) and 2), the Evangelist Luke *may* have added παρεμ - to βαλοῦσιν in 19:43b, and περι- to κυκλώσουσιν in v 43c. Yet the Hellenistic Jewish Christian translator of the Semitic original could just as well have done so.

visit to Jerusalem and the Temple (Mark 11:11) and the cursing of the fig tree (Mark 11:12-14, and later vv 20-25) on the part of Jesus. Instead of Jesus' cleansing of the Temple on the second day, between a first and second encounter with the fig tree as in Mark, Luke first inserts the special material in 19:41-44 and has this immediately followed by the cleansing of the Temple. He thus condenses the Markan framework in regard to time. Coming straight from the Mount of Olives (Zech 14:4-5), Jesus in Luke immediately causes the fulfillment of Zech 14:21, "And there shall no longer be traders in the house of the Lord of hosts in that day." The Evangelist also recognized that part of the background of Luke 19:41-44 derived from 2 Sam 15:30, with David's weeping as he went up the "ascent" of the Mount of Olives. Therefore he prepared for his special material by explicitly mentioning Jesus' approaching the "descent" down the Mount of Olives in 19:37.[138] Finally, the Evangelist Luke does not describe Jesus' actual entry into the city of Jerusalem between 19:44 and 45, in contrast to Mark 11:11a and 15a and Matt 21:10-11. Here too he condenses.

By inserting the narrative of 19:41-44 where he did, the Third Evangelist produced an intense dramatic contrast. Just before this people had even spread their cloaks on the road of the Mount of Olives, hailing Jesus as the messianic king who rides on the colt of an ass (19:36 and 29-35, with Zech 9:9). The whole multitude of the disciples then started to praise God loudly and shouted out Ps 118:26, originally spoken by the priests to festival pilgrims within the sanctuary of the first Temple.[139] At the time of Jesus the verse was part of the "Hallel" (Psalms 113-118) sung by the Levites from a platform in the Temple while the Passover pilgrims slaughtered their lamb offerings there at twilight on the

---

[138] It is unlikely that the mention of the "descent" derived from a pre-Lukan source. A short individual note of this nature would have had no context.

[139] Cf. S. Mowinckel, *The Psalms in Israel's Worship* (New York / Nashville: Abingdon Press, 1962) 1.6, 181; 2.46-47; and A. Weiser, *The Psalms* 724 and 729.

fourteenth of Nisan (Exod 12:6),[140] and by families and fellowship groups such as Jesus and his disciples before and after the "Last Supper."[141]

Luke has the multitude of disciples on the Mount of Olives intentionally insert into Ps 118:26 "king" for Jesus. He is here the messianic king, already adumbrated by Jesus in 13:35, who finally arrives near Jerusalem. He actually should be received here by all the inhabitants as the messianic king, yet Luke knows this will not be the case. Instead, Jesus will be rejected by the religious leadership of his own nation and be handed over by them to the Romans to be killed. The dramatic contrast between the jubilation on the Mount of Olives and Jesus' weeping over the future destruction of the adjacent city of Jerusalem could not be greater. This is a major contribution on the part of the Evangelist Luke to the literary artistry of his Gospel.

X. The Emphases in the Narrative

Luke 19:41-44 does not have one single emphasis, but several. They are the following.

1) *Jesus as a Prophet*

Just before Luke 19:41-44, Jesus has been loudly acclaimed as Israel's and thus also Jerusalem's messianic "king" (v 38). Here, however, he is represented as a prophet. The original Palestinian Jewish Christian author of this incident knew that his hearers would appreciate the depiction of Jesus' already foreseeing the destruction of the city some forty years later, in 70 CE. Jesus here prophesied the destruction of Jerusalem just as David had done centuries before him (in Judaic tradition known also to these hearers). By including this material from Special Luke, the

---

[140] Cf. *m. Pesaḥ.* 5:7 (Albeck 2.158, with note; Danby 142) and *t. Pesaḥ.* 4:11 (Zuckermandel / Liebermann 162, Neusner 2.136).
[141] Cf. Mark 14:26, where ὑμνήσαντες should be translated: "When they had finished singing the [Hallel] psalms" – i.e., ending with Psalm 118. The NRSV incorrectly has "the hymn." See *m. Pesaḥ.* 10:6-7 for the division of the Hallel psalms, the last ones completed over the fourth and last cup of wine (Albeck 2.178-179, Danby 151).

Evangelist emphasized Jesus as a prophet, something he also did in 7:16, 13:33 and 24:19.[142]

2) *Jesus as the Son of David*

Jesus, the Son of David (= Messiah), is represented in Luke 19:41-44 as doing exactly the same thing his forebear David did in Judaic tradition on 2 Sam 15:30 and Psalm 137. On the Mount of Olives, he weeps over (the Temple and) the city, prophesying their destruction. This comparison also would have appealed to the first hearers of the Palestinian Jewish Christian's original narrative. When the Evangelist included this account from Special Luke at this point, he knew that his readers might not only think of 6:3; 18:38-39; and 20:41-44, all from Mark, but also of his own references to David and Jesus' Davidic descent in 1:27, 32, 69; 2:4, 11; and 3:31. For Luke, Jesus is indeed the Son of David, the Messiah.[143]

3) *True Lamentation over the Fate of Jerusalem*

The only other occurrence of Jesus' weeping in the NT is in John 11:35, where Jesus weeps or sheds tears (δακρύω)[144] over the death of Lazarus. This is private and personal, yet Jesus' weeping in Luke 19:41 is public, a wailing or lamenting, a loud expression of sorrow (κλαίω).[145] It should be emphasized that

---

[142] Cf. also 7:39, not in Mark 14:39 // Matt 26:6-13. The references in 9:8 and 19 are from Mark. See also the remark of D. Tiede in his *Luke* 331: "Luke's depiction of Jesus as the prophet-Messiah reaches its peak in this episode."

[143] This means that Jesus is not *primarily* depicted in 19:41-44 as a Jeremiah-type figure, as maintained by numerous commentators. Cf. for example L. Sabourin, *L'Évangile de Luc* (Rome: Editrice Pontificia Università Gregoriana, 1985) 316, and J. Nolland, *Luke 18:35-24:53*, 930 and 932.

[144] BAGD 170, LSJ 367.

[145] BAGD 33, LSJ 955-956. Cf. on this C. F. Evans, *Saint Luke* 683, and A. Plummer, *The Gospel According to S. Luke* 449: "it implies wailing and sobbing." For this reason the English term "Lamentations" is very appropriate for the biblical book of this name, dealing with the Babylonian destruction of Jerusalem in 586 BCE. See also Lam 1:2 and 16 for Jerusalem's weeping, and *Lam. Rab.* 1:17 § 52 (Soncino 7.141) on

Jesus does not weep in self-pity for the fate of crucifixion awaiting him, but rather for the fate of the inhabitants of Jerusalem: being besieged and killed in war with their "enemies," the Romans, culminating in the destruction of the city in 70 CE. As the Son of David he does the same thing his ancestor David did when he predicted the destruction of the Temple and the city of Jerusalem (in Judaic tradition): he wept over it from the Mount of Olives.

In contrast to Luke 19:27 and 21:20-24, for example, vv 41-44 are not vindictive. A. Loisy thought "the sorrowful prediction of the Christ regarding Jerusalem shows that Judaism merited the condemnation by which it was struck in the year 70 [CE]."[146] However, J. Wellhausen correctly maintained that the verses are meant to express Jesus' "deep sorrow over the fall of the city" in 70 CE.[147] A. Plummer noted that "there is deep patriotism in this lamentation."[148]

The Palestinian Jewish Christian who originally composed Luke 19:41-44 deeply regretted not only the Jerusalem religious authorities' rejection of Jesus as the Son of David (= Messiah), but also the tragic fate of his own Temple and capital city in the terrible destruction culminating in 70 CE. He therefore depicted Jesus' weeping over / lamenting the fate of the city. The Evangelist Luke appropriated the episode from Special Luke and also shared this viewpoint. This is shown for example in the very last words of his Gospel. After Jesus' ascension at Bethany on the Mount of Olives, the disciples returned to Jerusalem "and were continually in the Temple blessing God" (24:53). Only someone with a deep love for Israel and the city of Jerusalem could write in such terms.[149]

---

v 16 in regard to the destruction of the Temple in 70 CE: "Now I go up with weeping [to the ruins of Jerusalem] and come down with weeping."

[146] *L'Évangile selon Luc* 471.
[147] Cf. his *Das Evangelium Lucae* 109.
[148] *The Gospel According to S. Luke* 450.
[149] Cf. J. Nolland on 19:41-44 in his *Luke 18:35-24:53*, 933: "This is no more a writing off of the Jews than the Babylonian exile had been centuries before."

4) Jerusalem's Last Opportunity to Repent and to Acknowledge Jesus as the Son of David, the Messianic King

In the "Q" passage of Luke 10:13-15 (// Matt 11:21-23), Jesus castigates ("Woe to you") the towns Chorazin, Bethsaida and Capernaum near and on the Sea of Galilee because they did not repent in spite of the mighty works done in them. The pagan cities Tyre and Sidon would have done so. The pagan inhabitants of the city Nineveh will also condemn this generation (of Jesus' fellow Jews) at the Final Judgment because they repented at the preaching of Jonah (while this generation doesn't): Luke 11:32 (// Matt 12:41).

In regard to the city of Jerusalem, Jesus accuses it in 13:34-35 (// Matt 23:37-38) of killing the prophets and stoning those sent to it. He says: "How often have I desired to gather your children together as a mother bird gathers her brood under her wings, and you were not willing. 35) See, your house [the Temple] is forsaken."[150] Here a threat of the destruction of the Temple (and by implication the rest of Jerusalem) is coupled with Jesus' *repeated* offers of repentance to the inhabitants of Jerusalem. Yet they (primarily the religious leadership) rejected these offers. Even the cleansing of the Temple in 19:45-46, directly after Jesus' weeping over Jerusalem in vv 41-44, is designed to make the religious authorities change their ways, i.e. repent. The same is true for his scathing parable of the wicked tenants (of the Temple) in 20:9-16a, which the scribes and high priests correctly perceived was directed against them (v 19).[151]

Jesus' weeping over the future destruction of Jerusalem and its inhabitants in 19:41-44 should be seen within this context. It derives from Special Luke, which greatly emphasizes the necessity of repentance (cf. 13:3, 5; 15:10, 17; 16:30), as does the Evangelist Luke himself.[152] Yet the motif of the necessity of repentance in 19:41-44 derives from Judaic tradition on Psalm

---

[150] See chapter seven on this passage.
[151] For a thorough analysis of it, see my *The Wicked Tenants and Gethsemane* 1-64.
[152] Cf. 5:32; 15:7; and Acts 2:38; 3:19; 5:31 ("God exalted [Jesus] at His right hand as Leader and Savior that He might give repentance to Israel and forgiveness of sins"); 8:22; 11:18; 17:30; and 26:20.

137, a verse of which is alluded to in Luke 19:44a. As shown above in section IV. 4) c), not only David's prophesying the destruction of the first and second Temples is connected to this psalm in Judaic tradition. The motif of the necessity of repentance, a lack of which will lead to the destruction of the Temple and to exile (by the Babylonians in 586 BCE and by the Romans in 70 CE), is also emphasized.

Thus Jesus can say in 19:42, "If you had only known / recognized / perceived on this day – even you – the things leading to peace / welfare / salvation!" This is a wish, meant positively. He could just as well have said, "If you would only repent today, your last opportunity!" The result of this lack of repentance is the religious leaders'[153] blinding their own eyes to God's final messenger, the prophet Jesus, who is also the Son of David and messianic king.[154] The result of their not wanting to recognize the things leading to peace will be the opposite of peace, the war with the Romans described in vv 43–44. Since the religious establishment refused Jesus' offer of repentance, a visitation of grace, it will in the future receive a visitation of judgment. The threat of Jerusalem's destruction due to lack of repentance is a basic motif in the Hebrew Bible (Jer 26:11, Mic 3:12). Jesus is here depicted as a true son of his people, prophetically calling them, especially their leaders, to repentance.

* * *

These are the four main emphases in Luke 19:41–44, which is indeed a narrative with profound power and pathos.

---

[153] J. Green in *The Gospel of Luke* 690 correctly notes that the "mention of the city relates primarily to the temple system and the leadership that draws its legitimacy from the temple."
[154] Cf. the "hardening" of Pharaoh's heart, leading to one plague after another in Exodus, and the divine passive of ἐκρύβη in Luke 19:42, leading to the destruction of Jerusalem and its inhabitants.

Chapter Five

Abraham's Prophetic Vision of the Messiah: The Judaic Background of John 8:56-58

Introduction

John 8:31-59 is a dialogue between Jesus and those of his fellow Jews who had once believed in him (v 31), but no longer do so. It begins in a rather neutral way, but crescendos to the point where they attempt to stone him to death because of what he claims to be (v 59). The narrative reflects the increasing hostility experienced by Palestinian Jewish Christians in regard to those who sought to expel them from the synagogue(s) for their belief in Jesus as the Messiah.[1] Throughout, the issue of who are the true descendants or children of Abraham is at stake, as well as Jesus' identity, especially in regard to the heavenly Father and father Abraham. The end of the episode has Jesus say (NRSV):

> 56) "Your ancestor Abraham rejoiced that he would see my day; he saw it and was glad."
> 57) Then the Jews said to him: "You are not yet fifty years old, and have you seen Abraham?"
> 58) Jesus said to them, "Very truly, I tell you, before Abraham was, I am."

---

[1] Cf. the remarks in section VII. below.

While these verses have received extensive comment,[2] numerous questions remain open. H. Ridderbos, for example, noted that Jesus' statement regarding Abraham in v 56 is "most remarkable," yet it "is not entirely clear."[3] J. Bernard and A. McNeile labeled v 56b "a strange and mysterious saying."[4] There is indeed no passage in the Abraham narratives of Genesis which refers to the patriarch's seeing the Messiah's day and rejoicing over it. This has led to inquiry about whether Abraham experienced this in a vision during his lifetime according to Judaic tradition, in heaven after his death, or in Sheol / Hades (cf. Luke 16:23), perhaps at Jesus' descent there after his resurrection.[5] Is Abraham's rejoicing connected to the promise of the birth of Isaac, as so often maintained? M.-J. Lagrange also asserted that the number fifty in v 57 is "une difficulté célèbre."[6] What is its significance? Finally, does Jesus' statement in v 58 that before Abraham was, "I am," reflect Judaic belief in the Messiah's so-called "pre-existence"? If so, how is this connected to Abraham's seeing Jesus' day in v 56?

The following study deals with the above and related questions. It is based to a great extent on Palestinian Judaic traditions regarding Genesis 15.

---

[2] Cf. the commentators as well as the Würzburg dissertation of H. Lona, *Abraham in Johannes 8*. Ein Beitrag zur Methodenfrage (Bern: Lang, 1976). Other secondary literature on the pericope is cited below.

[3] *The Gospel of John. A Theological Commentary* (Grand Rapids, Michigan: Eerdmans, 1997) 320.

[4] *The Gospel According to St. John* (ICC; Edinburgh: Clark, 1928/1958) 1. 321.

[5] In "John 8:57B. The Contribution of the Diatessaron of Tatian" in *NovT* 38 (1996) 336-343, T. Baarda argues for the variant reading in v 57, "And has Abraham seen you?" This would agree with Abraham's "having seen" Jesus' day in v 56. Yet the Fourth Evangelist intentionally has Jesus' fellow Jews ask him if he has seen Abraham in order to point out his true age – from before the creation of the world. See section V. below.

[6] *Évangile selon Saint Jean* (Études bibliques; Paris: Gabalda, 1936[5]) 255.

I. Genesis 15

Genesis 15 was a separate *seder* in the triennial lectionary system of the early Palestinian synagogue, read on the third Sabbath in the month Sivan of the first year.[7] This led to expansive comment on the first verse in the Palestinian targums.[8] Because Abram in v 10 "cut in two" (בתר)[9] the animal offerings mentioned in v 9, laying each "piece" (בֶּתֶר)[10] over against the other (v 10); a smoking fire pot and a flaming torch passed "between these 'pieces' (גְזָר , pl.)";[11] and the Lord on that day made a "covenant" (בְּרִית)[12] with Abram (v 18), the whole episode in Judaic tradition is called "the covenant between the pieces."[13] Already in the third century BCE the Septuagint made major changes to it.[14]

Pesiq. R. 47/3 on Lev 16:1 states that because Abram asked "How am I to know that I shall possess it ['this land' of v 7]?" (Gen 15:8), God put him to trial after trial.[15] This is a reference to what is usually labeled the ten trials or temptations of Abraham

---

[7] Cf. the art. "Triennial Cycle" in *EJ* (1971) 15. 1387.
[8] Cf. M. Maher, *Targum Pseudo-Jonathan: Genesis* 59, n. 1; M. McNamara, *Targum Neofiti 1: Genesis* 93, n. 1; and M. Klein, *The Fragment Targums of the Pentateuch* 1. 50, 133–134; 2.12, 97-98.
[9] BDB 144.
[10] *Ibid.* : part, piece.
[11] BDB 160. The term is used in Ps 136:13 of divided portions of the Reed Sea at the Exodus, causing Genesis 15 and the redemption of Israel from Egyptian slavery at the Exodus to be connected in rabbinic comment. In addition, the only reference to the Exodus event in the book of Genesis is found in 15:13–16.
[12] BDB 136–137.
[13] Another form of the covenant, years later, is found in chapter 17.
[14] Cf. "the son of Masek my home-born female slave" for Eliezer "of Damascus" in 15:2; the addition of "immediately" in v 4; the city "Ur" of the Chaldees in v 7 is changed to the "land"; the addition of "upon their divided parts" in v 11; and the addition of "and will afflict them" in v 13. On this early dating of the LXX, see O. Eissfeldt, *The Old Testament. An Introduction* (Oxford: Blackwell, 1966) 605 and 702.
[15] Friedmann 190a, Braude 803.

in Judaic tradition.[16] Two of these are based on texts from Genesis 15. Abraham's second trial was when he was thrown into the "fiery furnace" (כִּבְשָׁן הָאֵשׁ)[17] of the Chaldeans. This is derived from the phrase "'Ur' (אוּר) of the Chaldeans" in v 7, interpreted as "flame."[18] The other is Abraham's ninth trial, when God showed him at the covenant between the pieces the four kingdoms which in the future would enslave his descendants. This is based on several elements of chapter fifteen.[19]

The student of the NT is also well acquainted with the use of Genesis 15 by the converted Jew Paul in his letters. About the middle of the first century CE he quotes (LXX) Gen 15:5 in Rom 4:18, and (LXX) Gen 15:6 ("And [Abraham] believed God, and it was reckoned to him as righteousness") in Gal 3:6 and Rom 4:3, 9 and 22.[20] Both chapters employ Abraham's faith, not his works, as the basis of his justification.

Other Jewish authors, some earlier, some slightly later than the Gospel of John, paraphrase or comment on Genesis 15, showing how important a text it was in early Palestinian

---

[16] Cf. Ginzberg, *The Legends of the Jews* 1. 217 and 5. 218, no. 52, and G. Friedlander's notes to the ten trials enumerated in *Pirq. R. El.* 26-31 (187-230).

[17] Jastrow 611: kiln, furnace, for the first word.

[18] BDB 22, Jastrow 32, I. Cf. the remarks of R. Liezer b. Jacob, a third generation Tanna (Strack and Stemberger, *Introduction* 85) in *Gen. Rab.* Lech Lecha 44/13 on Gen 15:6-7 (Theodor and Albeck 435; Soncino 1. 369, with n. 3), *Pirq. R. El.* 26 (Friedlander 188, with Gen 15:7 and Neh 9:7), and *Targ. Ps.-Jon.* (Rieder 20, Maher 60), *Targ. Neofiti 1* (Díez Macho 79, Mc Namara 95), and *Frag. Targ.* (Klein 1. 134; 2. 98) on Gen 15:7.

[19] Cf. *Gen. Rab.* Lech Lecha 44 (Theodor and Albeck 424-447; Soncino 1. 361-378) and *Pirq. R. El.* 28 (Friedlander 197-202). The numbering of the trials differs. *Midr. Pss.* 18/25 on Ps 18:31b (Buber 152a-b, Braude 1. 255-256) enumerates all ten, also listing as the ninth trial God's showing Abraham between the pieces the four kingdoms which would enslave his descendants.

[20] Cf. also James 2:23. Stephen alludes to Gen 15:13-14 in Acts 7:6-7.

Judaism.[21] After briefly describing these writings, I will list early Tannaitic comment on Genesis 15, showing how the rabbinic commentators stand in a chain of tradition in regard to the biblical narrative. All of this serves to justify my use of rabbinic sources which describe Abraham's seeing the Messiah at the covenant between the pieces.

1) *Jubilees*

Originally written in Hebrew, *Jubilees* is a Palestinian writing most probably from the middle of the second century BCE.[22] In 14:1–20 the author haggadically retells Genesis 15. Among the many details which are changed or added, it is stated that Abram "in the middle of the month" took the offerings of Gen 15:9 when he "was dwelling by the oak of Mamre, which is near Hebron" (v 10).[23] The emphasis on this offering's occurring in the middle of the month is important for the messianic setting, to be described below in section III. 2).

Jub. 14:11 expands the Hebrew text by noting that Abram "built an altar there," and after slaughtering the animals "he poured out their blood upon the altar."[24] Also amplifying Gen 15:11, *Jub.* 14:12 states: "And the birds came down upon the pieces, and Abram kept turning them away, and he did not let the birds touch them."[25] Here a doubling of the latter motif

---

[21] P. Billerbeck noted several of them in a very brief manner in Str-B 2.525-526. H. Lona acknowledged his dependence on Billerbeck in his *Abraham in Johannes 8*, p. 302, n. 242. See also Ginzberg, *Legends*, 1.234-237, with the sources noted in 5.227-230 (in n. 112 Ginzberg correctly calls attention to John 8:56).

[22] Cf. O. Wintermute in *OTP* 2.43-45.

[23] *OTP* 2.85. Cf. "that day" in v 19, "on that day" in v 20, "in that month" in v 20, and "on the first of the third month" in v 1 (2.84). Only Jubilees separates the beginning of the episode from the latter part.

[24] *OTP* 2.85. Verse 19 also adds that Abram offered up the pieces' "(fruit) offering and their libation." This special interest corroborates Wintermute's suggestion that the author was from a priestly family and was much concerned with ritual details (2.45).

[25] *OTP* 2.85. In 11:11 it is Prince Mastema who sends crows and birds to steal farmers' seed from the earth. Abraham developed a reputation for

occurs, showing how Gen 15:11 was already treated in an haggadic way in the second century BCE. This verse later was interpreted messianically (see also section III. 3) below).

Finally, the motif of "rejoicing" occurs in 14:21. After paraphrasing Genesis 15 in *Jub.* 14:1–20, the author states: "And Abram 'rejoiced,' and he told all of these things to Sarai his wife. And he believed that he would have seed...." This motif, lacking in the biblical text, is of direct relevance to Abraham's "rejoicing," his "being glad" in John 8:56 (see section VI. below).

2) *Pseudo-Philo*

Palestinian, this work was also originally written in Hebrew, perhaps at the beginning of the first century CE.[26] Chapter 23 relates that "on the sixteenth day of the third month" (v 2), "the Lord appeared to Joshua in a dream vision" (v 3). Part of the latter vision, vv 5–7 haggadically retell Genesis 15.

Verse 5 notes that the Lord rescued Abraham from "the flame" and took him to Canaan. This is an allusion to "Ur" of the Chaldees in Gen 15:7 treated as a flame of fire or furnace (see above). In Canaan the Lord spoke to him in a vision, referring to Gen 15:1. After Abraham brought the offering mentioned in Gen 15:9, the Lord in *Pseudo-Philo* 23:6 showed him the place of judgment for the wicked and the reward of the just (v 6). These places are to attest to the Lord's granting Abraham offspring (v 7).

The author then interprets the offering of Gen 15:9 to refer to various groups of people, from Abraham himself like the dove, to barren women whom the Lord will help to bear, like a female goat. In conclusion the Lord states: "And these prophecies and this might will be a witness between us, that I will not go against My words" (v 7). [27] This passage is one of the earliest haggadic interpretations of the animals mentioned as offerings in

---

shooing them away (vv 18–22): *OTP* 2.78–79. This may be an aggadic development of Gen 15:11; see 2.40.

[26] Cf. D. Harrington in *OTP* 2.298–300.

[27] *OTP* 2.333. The Latin is found in D. Harrington, *Pseudo-Philon. Les Antiquités Bibliques* (SC 229) 184 and 186.

Gen 15:9. It also labels the explanations "prophecies," a motif also emphasized in rabbinic sources (see section III. 1) below).

3) Philo

This native of Alexandria, who was born ca. 25 BCE and lived until ca. 45-50 CE,[28] wrote exclusively in Greek. He devoted his longest tractate, *Quis Rerum Divinarum Heres* ("Who Is the Heir of Divine Things"), to Genesis 15. In it he is in part dependent on older interpreters.[29] In 106 he interprets the heifer, ram and female goat of Gen 15:9 as soul, speech and sense.[30] In 126-129 he views the turtle dove and pigeon of the same verse as divine and human reason, or divine wisdom and human knowledge.[31] In regard to Gen 15:11 Philo states in 243: "in a figure he [Moses] pictures the enemies of the soul as birds, eager to intertwine and ingraft themselves in bodies and to glut themselves with flesh, and it is to restrain the onsets and inroads of such that the man of worth [ὁ ἀστεῖος][32] is said to sit down in their company like a chairman or president of a council." Here Abraham is presented as seeking to ward off the negative activity of the birds of Gen 15:11.

Philo continues his interpretation of the LXX text by describing Abraham's ecstasy in Gen 15:12 as being of the prophetic kind (249). It shows him to be a prophet (258, which also quotes Gen 20:7 on Abraham as a prophet).[33] In the *Questions and Answers on Genesis*, the Alexandrian also emphasizes Abraham as a prophet in connection with Gen 15:12 and 13-14.[34] This accords with the rabbinic interpretation noted in section III. 1) below.

---

[28] Cf. E. Goodenough, *An Introduction to Philo Judaeus* (Oxford: Blackwell, 1962²) 2, as well as F. Colson and G. Whitaker, *Philo* (LCL, 1. ix).
[29] Cf. 280-281 and 283.
[30] Cf. also 125, 129 and 132.
[31] Cf. also 230.
[32] Translation Colson and Whitaker. LSJ 260 have "refined, elegant, witty," or simply "good" for a "town-bred, polite" person.
[33] Cf. also 266.
[34] Cf. *Philo Supplement* III. 9 (LCL 1.191-192) and III. 10 (LCL 1.192-195).

In III. 7 on Gen 15: 11a, Philo gives a different interpretation of the heifer, female goat and ram. They are now the earth, water and air. The flight of the birds above them "alludes to, and warns against, the attack of enemies."[35] A completely different rendering is found in III. 8 on Gen 15:11b. There the Alexandrian states that "we disciples of Moses... say that by these gathered birds that fly above he [Moses] represents 'the virtuous man,' and symbolically indicates nothing else than that he restrains wrongdoing and greed, and is hostile to quarrels and fights, but loves stability and peace."

If R. Marcus correctly translates the Armenian version of the original Greek at this point, it would mean that the "birds" of Gen 15:11a are here a very positive entity, indeed, a "good" or "excellent" person.[36] This approaches the rabbinic interpretation of the "bird(s)" as the Messiah (see section III. 3) below).[37]

There was a synagogue of the Alexandrians in pre-70 CE Jerusalem.[38] Much more "cross-fertilization" took place between Hellenistic and Palestinian Judaism than was earlier thought, for example in precisely such a synagogue. It is thus possible that Philo's "positive" interpretation of the bird(s) in Gen 15:11a was influenced by the messianic interpretation of the term found in a Palestinian rabbinic tradition to be discussed below. As in other rabbinic sources, this stood side by side with a "negative" interpretation of the passage. Because of the translation of the text from Greek into Armenian, caution must nevertheless be exercised here.

---

[35] LCL *Philo Supplement*, 1.189, in the translation of R. Marcus. See also III. 10 on Gen 15:13-14 (LCL 1.193), where Abraham hindered, drove off, and turned away "in word the flesh-eating birds which were flying over the divided animals, but in deed the afflictions which come upon men."

[36] LSJ 1630 on σπουδαῖος, which Marcus considers to be behind the Armenian. On it, see his remarks in *Philo. Supplement* 1. vii-viii.

[37] In "'Before Abraham Was I Am': Does Philo Explain John 8:56-58?" in *Studia Philonica* 6 (1979-1980) 157-195, L. Urban and P. Henry do not analyze the above passages in Philo, but rather deal with "God's promise of Isaac to Abraham according to Philo's exegesis of Genesis 17 in *De mutatione nominum*" (p. 167).

[38] Cf. Acts 6:9 and the sources cited on this in Str-B 2.663-664.

4) The Genesis Apocryphon of Qumran (1QapGen ar)

The Genesis Apocryphon found at Qumran, written in Aramaic, in its present form definitely dates from before 68 CE and may go back to the second half of the first century BCE.[39] It breaks off in column XXII 27-34 with an haggadic paraphrasing of Gen 15:1-4.[40] Unfortunately the interpretation of the rest of the chapter is missing. Nevertheless, this text shows that one more section of first-century Judaism, that of the community of Qumran on the Dead Sea, interpreted Genesis 15 in an haggadic manner.

5) Josephus

Aramaic-speaking and of priestly descent, Josephus was born in Jerusalem in 37-38 CE and completed his *Jewish Antiquities* in 93-94 CE.[41] In 1.183-185 (3) he paraphrases Genesis 15, introducing it by noting that God commended Abraham's "virtue" (ἀρετή) as shown in 14:22-24. Adding "before the altar was erected" to the sacrifice of Gen 15:9-10, Josephus in 1.185 says that "while 'birds of prey' were flying to the scene lusting for the blood, there came a divine voice announcing" the contents of Gen 15:13-14 and 19-21.

"Birds of prey" here is the plural of οἰωνός, a large bird or "bird of prey."[42] Josephus did not employ the LXX's ὄρνεα here, but remained faithful to the Hebrew text of Gen 15:11. It has עַיִט, derived from the verb עִיט, to scream or shriek.[43] Although singular, it can be used collectively to mean "birds of prey," as the NRSV translates at this point. The noun is the source of the

---

[39] Cf. J. Fitzmyer, *The Genesis Apocryphon of Qumran Cave 1: A Commentary* 12-17.
[40] Cf. the text and an English translation in Martínez and Tigchelaar, *The Dead Sea Scrolls Study Edition* 1.48-49, as well as in Fitzmyer, *The Genesis Apocryphon* 66-67, and his comments on pp. 160-164.
[41] Cf. his *Bell.* 1.3; *Vita* 1, 5; and *Ant.* 20.267.
[42] LSJ 1211. They give examples with the devouring of carcasses, as in the biblical narrative. In *Bell.* 3.123 Josephus notes that the eagle is the king and bravest of all the "birds of prey." See also *Ant.* 2.71.
[43] BDB 743.

messianic interpretation of the verse, to be discussed in section III. 3) below.

6) *The Apocalypse of Abraham*

Composed in a Semitic language, probably Hebrew, most likely in Palestine, and sometime at the end of the first century CE,[44] this apocalypse deals in chapters 9–32 with Genesis 15.

In 13:3 it relates in regard to Gen 15:11 that Abraham said: "And an unclean bird flew down on the carcasses, and I drove it away."[45] Here the עַיִט of the Hebrew text in Genesis is interpreted in the singular. The adjective "unclean" also appears in the *Fragment Targums, Targum Pseudo-Jonathan* and *Targum Neofiti 1* at this point.[46]

Apoc. Abr. 13:4 continues by stating: "And the unclean bird spoke to me...." Amazed, Abraham asks the angel accompanying him who this is. He tells the patriarch in 13:6, "This is disgrace, this is Azazel!" In 13:12 the angel then reproaches Azazel: "Hear, 'counselor,' be shamed by me! You have no permission to tempt all the righteous."[47]

The above term "counselor" for Azazel is derived from the stem of עַיִט, "bird(s) of prey," in Gen 15:11. The verb יָעַט means to counsel, and the noun עֵיטָא is counsel, advice.[48] The "P" manuscript of the *Fragment Targum* on Gen 15:11 expressly interprets the עַיִט of the Hebrew text as the kingdoms of the earth which "take counsel (יעטון עיטא)" against the people of Israel.[49]

---

[44] Cf. R. Rubinkiewicz in *OTP* 1.682-683, with n. 15 on the dating. The text is now only available in an Old Slavonic version.

[45] *OTP* 1.695.

[46] Cf. respectively Klein 1.51 and 134-135, and 2.12-13 and 98; Rieder 20, and Maher English 60; and Díez Macho 81, and McNamara English 95-96.

[47] *OTP* 1.695.

[48] Jastrow 584 and 1068, respectively.

[49] Klein 1.51 and 2.13. While not referring to the *Fragment Targum*, L. Ginzberg in his *Legends* 5.230, n. 114, notes that the עַיִט of Gen 15:11 can mean "counselor" (seducer), "and accordingly, it may safely be

In *Apoc. Abr.* 24:2 God tells Abraham, "And I will explain to you what will be, and everything that will be in the last days." After God's showing him various future events, He tells the patriarch in 29:2, "what you have seen will be until the end of time."[50]

Here in the *Apocalypse of Abraham*, the patriarch has been allowed to see, to have a vision of, what will take place on earth until the end of time, including the later punishment of the wicked and the reward of the just. In 29:8 and 31:1 the liberator of Israel from the heathen in the last days, sent by God, is also described.[51] If this is not a later Christian addition, it points to messianic hope still present among Palestinian Jews after the destruction of the Jerusalem Temple in 70 CE.[52]

The *Apocalypse of Abraham* is singular in representing the עַיִט or bird of prey of Gen 15:11 as an individual, Azazel. Another interpretation of the same bird of prey as an individual is found in section III. 3 below. There it is the Messiah.

7) Fourth Ezra

Originally written in a Semitic language, probably Hebrew, ca. 100 CE in Palestine,[53] this apocalypse in chapter 3 describes Ezra's first vision. Verse 13 states that God chose Abraham. Verse 14 continues: "You loved him and to him only You revealed the end of the times, secretly by night." Verse 15 then remarks: "You made with him an everlasting covenant, and promised that You would never forsake his descendants."[54] B. Metzger correctly calls attention in the margin of his *OTP* translation to Gen 15:5, 12 and 17 at this point.

Here another Palestinian Judaic source, written only some thirty years after the destruction of the Temple and Jerusalem

---

assumed that this pseudepigraph is of Semitic – Hebrew or Aramaic – origin."
[50] *OTP* 1.701 and 703, respectively.
[51] *OTP* 1.703-705.
[52] This hope later flamed up again under Bar Kokhba in 132-135 CE. Cf. Schürer, *The history* 1.542-552.
[53] Cf. B. Metzger in *OTP* 1.519-520.
[54] *OTP* 1.528. For the Latin, see B. Violet, *Die Esra-Apokalypse* 1.8.

(3:1-2) in 70 CE, also emphasizes that God in a night vision secretly revealed to Abraham alone the end of the times. This is based on earlier Judaic interpretation of Genesis 15, known to the author.

8) 2 (Syriac) Baruch

Finally, A. Klijn notes that this apocalypse, in Syriac, is a translation from the Greek, which in turn is a translation of a Hebrew original. It was probably written in Palestine in one of the first two decades of the second century CE.[55]

Chapter four has God reveal to Baruch the new Jerusalem, prepared by Him when He also decided to create Paradise. He first showed it to Adam, but after his sin God removed it from him. Verse 4 then states: "After these things I showed it to My servant Abraham in the night between the portions of the victims."[56] This is a clear reference to Genesis 15. It shows that another Palestinian Jewish author was aware of God's revealing to Abraham in the narrative of Genesis 15 something which already existed before creation, and which would again be revealed at the end of days: the new Jerusalem.

* * *

The above eight Judaic sources, from the middle of the second century BCE to the beginning of the second century CE, and with the exception of Philo of Alexandria from Palestine and in Hebrew or Aramaic,[57] all show haggadic development of the content of Genesis 15. This indicates that the rabbinic interpretation of the same chapter stood in a long chain of tradition. While the present sources in which the rabbinic statements regarding Genesis 15 appear are from a later period,

---

[55] *OTP* 1.615-617.
[56] *OTP* 1.622.
[57] Although the *Biblical Antiquities* are in Greek, Josephus' mother tongue was Aramaic; he reflected Palestinian traditions known to him in his native Jerusalem and from the rest of the country.

there is no reason to doubt the early date of many of these traditions.[58]

Before analyzing the messianic interpretation of Gen 15:11 now found *Pirq. R. El.* 28, which in an earlier form influenced the formulation of John 8:56-58, it will be helpful to note the relatively large number of Tannaitic rabbis who commented on various aspects of Genesis 15. This makes it even more possible, if not probable, that the messianic interpretation I analyze below was also very early.

II. Tannaitic Interpretation of Genesis 15

The following fifteen Tannaim, among the earliest rabbinic commentators known to us, offer interpretations of various aspects of Gen 15:1-21.

1) Shemayah, pre-Tannaitic.[59]
2) Yoḥanan b. Zakkai, a first generation Tanna.[60]
3) Eliezer (b. Hyrcanus), a second generation Tanna.[61]
4) Joshua (b. Ḥananyah), a second generation Tanna.[62]

---

[58] Cf. the view of J. Neusner described in the section "Rabbis' Names as an Aid for Dating" in Strack and Stemberger, *Introduction* 63-64. While Neusner refers to Tannaitic collections, when a rabbi deals with a particular verse there and in a later work (in regard to its final redaction), there is no valid reason not to attribute the latter comment also to him.

[59] He and his contemporary Abtalion were the teachers of Hillel the Elder (Strack and Stemberger, *Introduction* 20 and 71). In *Mek. R. Ish.* Beshallaḥ 4 on Exod 4:15 (Lauterbach 1.220) he comments on Gen 15:6. Abtalion then gives a different interpretation.

[60] *Introduction* 74-75. Cf. *Gen. Rab.* Lech Lecha 44/22 on Gen 15:18 (Soncino 1.376), and *Pirq. R. El.* 48 (Friedlander 374) with Gen 15:18, 3, 8 and 13 (see n. 2 on v 3).

[61] *Introduction* 77. Cf. *b. B. Bat.* 56a (Soncino 227) on Gen 15:19; *Pesiq. R.* 1/7 on Isa 66:23 (Braude 47) with Gen 15:13; and *Pirq. R. El.* 28 (Friedlander 198) on Gen 15:9 (the first editions have R. Aqiba). The reference to the "sons of Ishmael" appears to be due to a redactor in the Islamic period (199, n. 1). See, however, C. Mangan, *The Targum of Job* 7, who maintains that "Ishmael is a substitution for Esau standing for Rome" in the Targum of Job. She relies on a study of E. Epstein (n. 18).

5) Eleazar b. 'Azaryah, a second generation Tanna.[63]
6) Eleazar b. 'Arakh, a second generation Tanna.[64]
7) Ishmael (b. Elisha), a second generation Tanna.[65]
8) Aqiba, a second generation Tanna.[66]
9) Judah (bar Ilai), a third generation Tanna.[67]
10) Meir, a third generation Tanna.[68]
11) Simeon (b. Yoḥai), a third generation Tanna.[69]
12) (E)liezer b. Jacob, a third generation Tanna.[70]

---

[62] *Introduction* 77. Cf. *Gen. Rab.* Lech Lecha 44/21 on Gen 15:17, and 44/22 on Gen 15:18 (Soncino 1.376 and 377); *Eccl. Rab.* 4:3 § 1 (Soncino 8.113) with Gen 15:8; and *Pereq Ha-Shalom* 1:16, 59b (*The Minor Tractates of the Talmud* 601) with Gen 15:15.
[63] *Introduction* 78. Cf. *Pirq. R. El.* 48 (Friedlander 374-375) with Gen 15:13.
[64] *Introduction* 78. Cf. *Pirq. R. El.* 48 (Friedlander 375-376) on Gen 15:13.
[65] *Introduction* 79. Cf. *Tanḥ.* B Lech Lecha 13 on Gen 15:1 (Bietenhard 1.76).
[66] *Introduction* 79. Cf. *m. 'Ed.* 2:9 (Danby 426) with Gen 15:13 and 16, with a parallel in *t. 'Ed.* 1:14 (Neusner 4.300); *Gen. Rab.* Lech Lecha 44/22 on Gen 15:18 (Soncino 1.376); and *Semaḥot* 8:14, 47b (*The Minor Tractates of the Talmud* 1.370-371) with Gen 15:14 and 13.
[67] *Introduction* 84. Cf. *y. Qidd.* 1:8, 61d (Neusner 26.116) with 15:18-21, 10; *Gen. Rab.* Lech Lecha 43/8 on Gen 14:8, dealing with 15:5 (Soncino 1.358); 44/15 on Gen 15:10 (Soncino 1.371); Vayera 53/5 on Gen 21:1, referring to 15:18 and 1 (Soncino 1.465, with n. 1); *Lev. Rab.* Shemini 11/5 on Lev 9:1, commenting on Ps 18:26-27 (Soncino 4.138-140), dealing with Gen 15:2, 4, 8 and 13 (parallel in *Midr. Pss.* 18/22 on Ps 18:26-27, in Braude 1.250-251); and *Cant. Rab.* 2:8 § 1 with Gen 15:13 (Soncino 9.116). Parallels to the latter passage are found in *Pesiq. Rav Kah.* 5/7 on Exod 12:2 (Braude and Kapstein 100), and *Pesiq. R.* 15/7 on Exod 12:2 (Braude 315).
[68] *Introduction* 84. Cf. *b. B. Bat.* 56a (Soncino 227) on Gen 15:19, and *Cant. Rab.* 1:4 § 1 (Soncino 9.41-42) on Gen 15:8.
[69] *Introduction* 84. Cf. *b. Ber.* 7b (Soncino 35) on Gen 15:8; *b. B. Bat.* 56a (Soncino 227) on Gen 15:19; *y. Qidd.* 1:8, 61d (Neusner 26.116) with Gen 15:18-21, 10; *Gen. Rab.* Lech Lecha 44/14 on Gen 15:10 (Soncino 1.370); 44/17 on Gen 15:12 (Soncino 1.373, with Simon); 44/23 on Gen 15:19-21 (Soncino 1.377); *Lev. Rab.* Vayyiqra 3/3 on Lev 2:1 (Soncino 4.38) with Gen 15:10; *Midr. Pss.* 16/7 on Ps 16:7 (Braude 1.200) on Gen 15:17, 9, 17 and 12; and *Tanḥ.* B Lech Lecha 13 on Gen 15:1 (Bietenhard 1.76).

13) Nehemiah, a third generation Tanna.[71]
14) Nathan, a fourth generation Tanna.[72]
15) Rabbi (Judah the Prince), a fourth generation Tanna.[73]

These fifteen Tannaim show that not only the eight authors briefly analyzed in section I. above dealt with Genesis 15 at a relatively early time, but also many of the earliest rabbis known to us.

III. The Messianic Interpretation of Gen 15:11

Before describing this in section 3), it will be helpful first to note two other relevant aspects of the rabbinic interpretation of Genesis 15, in part agreeing with details noted in the eight Judaic sources analyzed in section I. above.[74]

---

[70] *Introduction* 85. Cf. *y. Qidd.* 1:8, 61d (Neusner 26.116) on Gen 15:18-21 and 10; *Gen. Rab.* Lech Lecha 44/13 on Gen 15:6-7 (Soncino 1.369); 44/23 on Gen 15:19-21 (Soncino 1.377); and *Cant. Rab.* 1:12 § 1 (Soncino 9.78) on Gen 15:7.

[71] *Introduction* 85. Cf. *Mek. R. Ish.* Beshallaḥ 7 on Exod 14:31c (Lauterbach 1.253), dealing with Gen 15:6; *Gen. Rab.* Lech Lecha 41/8 on Gen 13:14-15 (Soncino 1.338) with Gen 15:18; 44/15 on Gen 15:10 (Soncino 1.371); and *Exod. Rab.* Bo 18/5 on Exod 12:29 (Soncino 3.220), commenting on Gen 15:7.

[72] *Introduction* 88. Cf. *Mek. R. Ish.* Baḥodesh 9 on Exod 20:18 (Lauterbach 2.268) on Gen 15:17, 9 and 12, and *Exod. Rab.* Mishpaṭim 30/16 on Exod 21:1 (Soncino 3.364), commenting on Gen 15:13.

[73] *Introduction* 89. Cf. *y. Qidd.* 1:8, 61d (Neusner 26.116) with Gen 15:18-21, 10; *Mek. R. Ish.* Pisḥa 14 on Exod 12:40 (Lauterbach 1.111) with Gen 15:16; *Gen. Rab.* Lech Lecha 44/21 on Gen 15:17 (Soncino 1.376); 44/23 on Gen 15:19-21 (Soncino 1.377); and *Pesiq. R.* 49/6 on Exod 12:29 (Braude 836-837) with Gen 15:14.

[74] On other rabbinic sources regarding Genesis 15, cf. M. Kasher, *Encyclopedia of Biblical Interpretation* (New York: American Biblical Encyclopedia Society, 1955), Genesis 2.173-212.

1) Abram's Prophetic Vision

Gen 15:1 states that the word of the Lord came to Abram in a "vision" (מַחֲזֶה).[75] The usually reticent *Targum Onqelos* says that it came to him here "in prophecy."[76] *Targum Neofiti 1* also has "a word of prophecy" at this point,[77] as does MS "V" of the *Fragment Targum*.[78] Commenting on Gen 15:1, *Gen. Rab.* Lech Lecha 44/6 states that prophecy is designated by ten terms, including "vision" and "the flow of speech." Abram's power was great since God spoke with him here in vision and (divine) speech.[79]

Commenting on God's bringing Abram outside and telling him to look toward heaven and count the stars in Gen 15:5, "the rabbis" in *Gen. Rab.* Lech Lecha 44/12 have God reprimand Abram by telling him: "You are a prophet, not an astrologer." To buttress this, they cite Gen 20:7, with Abraham as a "prophet."[80] Before this, two Amoraim maintain that God took him out and "showed him the streets of heaven," or He "lifted him up above the vault of heaven" to do so.[81]

Rab, a first generation Amora,[82] noted that "the torpor of prophecy" is meant by Abram's "deep sleep" in Gen 15:12.[83]

---

[75] BDB 303: vision, in the ecstatic state. This may have influenced the choice of ἔκστασις in the LXX for the "deep sleep" of MT 15:12. The LXX in v 1 has ὅραμα, a "vision" during sleep, a "dream" (LSJ 1244).
[76] Aberbach and Grossfeld 90-91.
[77] Díez Macho 77, English in McNamara 94. See also v 4 (Díez Macho 79, English in McNamara 95).
[78] Klein 1.134 and 2.98.
[79] Cf. the divine passive, "he was spoken to," in Theodor and Albeck 429, Soncino 1.364. Reference is to the "word" of the Lord in a "vision."
[80] Theodor and Albeck 433, Soncino 1.368.
[81] Theodor and Albeck 432, Soncino 1.367-368. Similar traditions are found in Vayera 53/4 on Gen 21:1 (Soncino 1.463); *Exod. Rab.* Tetzaveh 38/6 on Exod 29:1 (Soncino 3.453); *Num. Rab.* Bemidbar 2/12 on Num 2:32 (Soncino 5.42); and *Tanh.* Shophetim 11 (Eshkol 898).
[82] Strack and Stemberger, *Introduction* 93. While Babylonian, he studied under Rabbi in Palestine.
[83] *Gen. Rab.* Bereshith 17/5 on Gen 2:21 (Theodor and Albeck 156, Soncino 1.136).

Abraham's Prophetic Vision of the Messiah

R. Nathan, a fourth generation Tanna,[84] maintained that God "showed" (הֶרְאָה) "our father Abraham" Gehenna, the giving of the Torah [at Sinai] and the division of the Red Sea [at the Exodus] in the words of Gen 15:17. He also showed Abram the Temple with the order of the sacrifices, based on the animals to be offered in v 9. Finally, He also showed him the four kingdoms, Babylon, Media, Greece and wicked Rome, which would oppress his descendants in the future. This is based on an interpretation of nouns in v 12. R. Nathan remarks that other interpreters reverse the latter order, showing other early comment on these verses.[85]

In conclusion, commenting on the phrase "in that day" of Gen 15:18, either R. Yoḥanan b. Zakkai, a first generation Tanna, or R. Aqiba, a second generation Tanna,[86] maintains that when God made a covenant with Abram between the pieces, "He revealed to him both this world and the world to come."[87]

The above passages suffice to show that in early rabbinic tradition on Genesis 15, God showed or revealed to Abram the future. The patriarch saw it prophetically. This included not only events in this world such as the four wicked kingdoms, culminating in Edom / Rome, which would persecute Israel. It also included God's showing the patriarch the world to come, with Gehenna and the final judgment. This makes it very understandable that in another strand of rabbinic tradition Abram also sees the Messiah at the covenant between the pieces.

2) *The Fifteenth of Nisan*

According to Tannaitic tradition, a (divine) decree was made on the fifteenth of Nisan at the covenant between the parts (Genesis 15). This is when God spoke with "our father

---

[84] Cf. n. 72.
[85] Cf. *Mek. R. Ish.* Baḥodesh 9 on Exod 20:18 (Lauterbach 2.268-269). See also *Exod. Rab.* Pequde 51/7 on Exod 38:21 (Soncino 3.568-569). See also my comments on the four kingdoms in regard to Gen 15:11 below.
[86] Cf. notes 60 and 66, respectively.
[87] Cf. *Gen. Rab.* Lech Lecha 44/22 on Gen 15:18 (Theodor and Albeck 444-445; Soncino 1.376, with notes 3-4). See also *Tanḥ.* B Sarah 6 on Gen 24:1 (Buber 119, Bietenhard 1.126), with Str-B 2.525 on it.

Abraham." On the same date the ministering angels later came to bring good news to "our father Abraham," i.e. that "at this season next year" Sarah would bear him a son (Gen 17:21; 18:10). On the same date exactly a year later Isaac was born. And on exactly the same date Israel later left Egypt at the Exodus. This haggadah is based on Exod 12:41, "At the end (מִקֵּץ) of four hundred thirty years, 'on that very day' (בְּעֶצֶם הַיּוֹם הַזֶּה), all the companies of the Lord went out from the land of Egypt."[88] *Pirq. R. El.* 28 refers to this tradition by stating that when God at the covenant between the parts brought Abraham outside (Gen 15:5) and spoke to him, this took place "on the night of Passover," i.e. also on the fifteenth of Nisan.[89]

Commenting on Exod 12:42 ("That was for the Lord a night of vigil, to bring them out of the land of Egypt. That same night is a vigil to be kept for the Lord by all the Israelites 'throughout their generations'"), R. Joshua (b. Ḥananyah), a second generation Tanna,[90] states in *Mek. R. Ish. Pisha* 14: "In that night they were redeemed, and in that night they will be redeemed in the future."[91]

Exod. Rab. Bo 18/12 on the above verse notes that "on that night Messiah and Elijah will appear."[92] That is, the Messiah was expected to appear on the fifteenth of Nisan, the same night in which God made a covenant with Abram between the pieces in Genesis 15. In broader terms this is stated in *Exod. Rab.* Bo

---

[88] Cf. *Mek. R. Ish. Pisha* 14 on the verse (Lauterbach 1.112-113, with n. 3a); *Seder 'Olam* 1 (Milikowsky 210, Eng. 449), 3 (Milikowsky 225, Eng. 455) and the full tradition in 5 (Milikowsky 241-243, Eng. 462). To help explain the difference between 430 years of servitude in Exod 12:41 and only 400 years in Gen 15:13, Abraham's age is considered to be seventy in Genesis 15 and 100 at Isaac's birth (Gen 21:5). See also *Tanḥ.* Bo 9 on Exod 12:37 ff. (Eshkol 1.269), and *Pesiq. R.* 49/5 on Exod 12:29 (Friedmann 196b, Braude 834-835, with Gen 15:5).
[89] Cf. Higger in *Horeb* 10 (1948) 187; Eshkol 89; Friedlander 198, with n. 2.
[90] Cf. n. 62.
[91] Lauterbach 1.115, which I slightly modify.
[92] Mirqin 5.219; Soncino 3.227. I prefer Radal's emendation (n. 7). The text as is has "will be made great."

15/1 on Exod 12:1, where the Messiah, called "first" in regard to Isa 41:27, will come in the "first" month, [i.e. Nisan].[93] In *Cant. Rab.* 2:8 ("The voice of My beloved! Look, he comes") § 3, R. Yose the Galilean and R. Eliezer b. Jacob, both third generation Tannaim,[94] maintain that this is the Messiah. He will tell the Israelites: "In this month [that of Exod 12:2, Nisan] you are to be redeemed."[95]

Finally, it should be noted that the Synoptics portray Jesus as eating the evening Passover meal with his disciples in Jerusalem.[96] On the next afternoon (according to Jewish time reckoning part of the same day, the fifteenth of Nisan), he was crucified. The first Jewish (and other later) Christians considered the death of their Messiah to be redemptive.

The above passages, most of them quite early, show that the Messiah was intimately connected to the fifteenth of Nisan, the same night in which in Judaic tradition God made a covenant with Abram between the pieces in Genesis 15, and in a prophetic vision showed the patriarch what was to take place in this world and in the world to come. This makes the following key passage from *Pirq. R. El.* 28 more understandable.

3) The Messiah as the Bird of Prey of Gen 15:11

When Abram asked God in Gen 15:8 how he was to know that he would inherit / possess the land of Israel, God instructed him to bring Him (as an offering) a three year old heifer, a female goat and a ram, as well as a turtledove and a young pigeon (v 9). Abram obediently cut up the first three, laying them out, but he did not divide the latter two offerings (v 10).

---

[93] Mirqin 5.162; Soncino 3.160.
[94] Strack and Stemberger, *Introduction* 85.
[95] Donsqi 66; Soncino 9.117. A parallel is found in *Pesiq. R.* 15/7 on Cant 2:8 (Friedmann 71b, Braude 316-317). The Song of Songs was associated with Passover, and it is still read as part of the liturgy of that festival. See the art. "Song of Songs" by B. Bayer in *EJ* (1971) 15.147, 149 and 151, and "Song of Songs Rabbah" by M. Herr, 15.154.
[96] Cf. Mark 14:1 and 12. The "evening" of v 17 was already Passover, the fifteenth of Nisan. See J. Jeremias, *The Eucharistic Words of Jesus*, available to me as *Die Abendmahlsworte Jesu* (Göttingen: Vandenhoeck & Ruprecht, 1967⁴) 9-82 on this as a Passover meal.

Verse 11 continues: "And when birds of prey came down on the carcasses [of the offerings], Abram drove them away."

The verb for Abram's "driving away" the large bird(s) is וַיַּשֵּׁב, the hiphil of נָשַׁב.[97] The LXX did no recognize the root, which occurs only three times in the MT, and instead translated: "And he sat together[98] with them [to guard them]." It also adds "upon their divided parts" to the bodies / carcasses, showing very early interpretation of the verse.

A later explanation of Gen 15:11b is given by R. Assi, a third generation Palestinian Amora.[99] According to him Abraham took a hoe[100] and struck the birds, yet they were not wounded (to death). Nevertheless he could drive them away through "repentance."[101] The latter is תְּשׁוּבָה, a wordplay with וַיַּשֵּׁב.

R. Assi apparently understood the birds of prey to be the four kingdoms which seek to plunder Israel. Unable to resist them through pure force, the Israelites / Jews can nevertheless drive them off if they truly repent.[102]

The four kingdoms which severely oppressed Israel during its history (Babylonia, Media, Greece and Edom / Rome) in rabbinic sources are usually thought to be represented by the various nouns of Gen 15:12.[103] Other sources consider them to be the five offerings of v 9, whereby the turtle dove and young

---

[97] BDB 674.
[98] Cf. LSJ 1662 on συγκάθω, intrans. Aquila correctly translated here with the verb ἀποσοβέω, to scare away, as one does birds (LSJ 218). See Sir 22:20, as well as Deut 28:26 and Jer 7:33, where the LXX has this verb for the hiphil of חרד (BDB 353 and Jastrow 498, to frighten [away]).
[99] Strack and Stemberger, Introduction 98. He was a student of R. Yohanan, either at Sepphoris or Tiberias (95).
[100] The noun מַכּוֹשָׁה also can mean "hammer": Jastrow 782.
[101] Gen. Rab. Lech Lecha 44/16 on Gen 15:11 (Theodor and Albeck 438, Soncino 1.371-372).
[102] Cf. H. Freedman's similar explanation in Soncino 1.372, n. 1.
[103] Cf. for example Mek. R. Ish. Bahodesh 9 on Exod 20:18 (Lauterbach 2.268-269); Gen. Rab. Lech Lecha 44/17 on Gen 15:12 (Theodor and Albeck 439-440, Soncino 1.372-373); and Targ. Ps.-Jon. (Rieder 20, Eng. in Maher 60-61) and Targ. Neofiti 1 (Díez Macho 81, Eng. in McNamara 96) on this verse.

pigeon are seen as a unity.¹⁰⁴ The *Fragment Targum* on Gen 15:11 says the birds of prey are the (four) kingdoms of the earth which "take counsel" against the people of Israel, a wordplay with עֵיט.¹⁰⁵ *Targum Neofiti 1* and *Pseudo-Jonathan* are similar.¹⁰⁶ Another rabbinic source associates the four kingdoms with Gen 1:2, of relevance to the "birth" or so-called "pre-existence" of the Messiah (see below, section V.).

The above shows that the motif of the four kingdoms was a "floating tradition," attaching itself to various biblical verses. The occurrence most relevant to John 8:56-58 is found in *Pirq. R. El.* 28, at this point also dealing with Gen 15:11.

THE TEXT

R. Joshua (b. Ḥananyah, a second generation Tanna ¹⁰⁷) stated: Abraham took his sword and divided them (the offerings of Gen 15:9), each into two pieces, as it is written: "He brought Him all these and cut them in two" (v 10a). Now if he had not divided them, the world would not be able to exist. Yet since he did divide them, he weakened their strength. And he placed each piece over against its corresponding piece, as it is written: "laying each half over against the other" (v 10b). However, the young pigeon he left alive, as it is written: "but the bird (הַצִּפֹּר)¹⁰⁸ he did not cut in two" (v 10c). From here you learn that there was no other pigeon¹⁰⁹ there except a young pigeon.¹¹⁰

---

¹⁰⁴ Cf. *Gen. Rab.* Lech Lecha 44/15 on Gen 15:9 (Theodor and Albeck 437-438, Soncino 1.370) and *Pirq. R. El.* 28 (Higger 187; Eshkol 89; Friedlander 198-199 and 200, whereby "the sons of Ishmael" is a later redactor's substitution for Babylonia).
¹⁰⁵ MS "P" in Klein 1.51, Eng. 2.12-13. On the wordplay, see section I. 6) above on *Apoc. Abr.* 13:12.
¹⁰⁶ Cf. Díez Macho 81, Eng. McNamara 95-96, and Rieder 20, English Maher 60, respectively.
¹⁰⁷ Cf. n. 62.
¹⁰⁸ The noun is considered singular here (BDB 861-862); it can also be meant collectively as "birds."
¹⁰⁹ Hebrew גּוֹזָל : brood, chick, esp. pigeon (Jastrow 220).

The bird of prey (הָעַיִט) came down upon them to scatter them and to destroy them. Now this bird of prey is none other than the Son of David, the son of Jesse, who is compared to a bird of prey, as it is written: "My inheritance is to Me [like] 'a speckled bird of prey' (הַעַיִט צָבוּעַ)" (Jer 12:9).[111]

When the sun was emerging from the east, Abraham sat down and waved over them his scarf[112] so that the bird of prey would not prevail over them until evening[113] came.

R. Eleazar b. 'Azaryah (also a second generation Tanna[114]) comments: From here you learn that the rule of these four kingdoms will only be for one day (יוֹם), derived from the day (יוֹם) of the Holy One, blessed be He. R. Eleazar ben 'Arakh (also a second generation Tanna[115]) tells him: It is really like your opinion, for it is stated: "He has left me stunned, faint all day (יוֹם) long" (Lam 1:13) – except for (the last) two thirds of an hour. Know that it is so, come and see. When the sun declines in the west, for two thirds (of an hour) it is weakened and has no splendor. Likewise, while [or although] evening has not yet come, the Son of David will (definitely, in the future) cause the light of Israel to break forth / shine,[116] as it is stated: "at evening (עֶרֶב) time there shall be light" (Zech 14:7).[117]

---

[110] Higger has בֶּן יוֹנָה for "young pigeon" at this point (188), as does Eshkol (90). The latter reads, however: From here you learn that there is no "bird" (צִפּוֹר) in the Torah except a young pigeon.

[111] This is how R. Joshua understands the beginning of the biblical verse here. BDB 840 on צָבוּעַ have "colored, variegated."

[112] The סוּדָר was a scarf wound around the head and hanging down over the neck (Jastrow 962).

[113] So in Eshkol 90; cf. Friedlander 200, n. 5. Some other MSS have הָעוֹרֵב, the raven or crow (Jastrow 1058), yet this is a scribal error which appears to have crept into the text at an early time. The following remarks by R. Eleazar ben 'Azaryah with the "evening" of Zech 14:7, and the contrast between day and "evening," show that "evening" is original.

[114] Cf. n. 63.

[115] Cf. n. 64.

[116] Here I prefer the reading in the Eshkol edition (90) with the verb צָמַח (Jastrow 1287). See also Friedlander 201, n. 3. Higger (188) has יָשַׁמֵּם,

ANALYSIS

Only found in *Pirq. R. El.* 28,[118] this interpretation of the "covenant between the pieces" in Genesis 15 is uniquely messianic and has not been related by NT scholars to John 8:56-58 before. The offerings brought by Abram (called "Abraham" here) represent the four kingdoms which have oppressed Israel in the past (Babylonia, Media and Greece) and continue to do so now (Edom / Rome).[119] If Abram had not divided them, weakening their strength, their (combined) wickedness would have caused the world to end.

The bird of prey is interpreted here as the Son of David, the Messiah, who already now wishes to come down, scatter and destroy the four kingdoms. Abraham's waving his scarf over the offerings temporarily prevents this, however. First "evening" must come, i.e. the very last part of God's "day."[120] Only when

---

"will cause to rejoice." In an oral stage of the tradition, ṣade was heard as sin.

[117] Cf. also Friedlander's translation (200-201, with the notes), which I at times follow. He based it on an unedited MS which belonged to A. Epstein of Vienna. The Hebrew is found in Higger, *Horeb* 10 (1948) 188 and Eshkol 89-90.

[118] From here it was included in the medieval work of collected quotations, *Yalquṭ Shem'oni Lech Lecha* on Genesis 15, section 76 (Kook, Genesis 1.294), as well as in *Midr. Haggadol* on Gen 15:11, by David ben Amram. Cf. *Midrash Haggadol*, Genesis, ed. M. Margulies (Kook, 1.255). For the messianic interpretation of Gen 15:11, see also *Leqaḥ Tob* ad loc. (Buber, Genesis 70). In *Midr. Haggadol* on the chief baker's dream in Gen 40:16-19, the uppermost basket is considered to be the wicked (fourth) kingdom (Rome). "The bird eating them [all sorts of baked food for Pharaoh]" in v 17 is interpreted as the royal Messiah, in keeping with the verse, "And the bird of prey descended upon the carcasses" (Gen 15:11). See Kook, Genesis 1.668.

[119] For Edom as a substitute for Rome, cf. Jastrow 16 on אֱדוֹם.

[120] Cf. Ps 90:4 for God's day as 1000 years. If the author of this interpretation thought this period began in the seventh century BCE with the Babylonian captivity, he may have expected it to end in the fourth century CE. Yet for him that time was still several centuries away, "evening" had not come yet. This accounts for the delay of the Messiah's (first) coming.

the reign of the fourth wicked kingdom, Edom / Rome, is at an end, will the Son of David / the Messiah cause Israel's light to again "break forth" or "shine." The latter verb is צָמַח. It is an overt allusion to another name of the Messiah, צֶמַח, the "sprout" from the Davidic tree.[121]

While most people today may consider the term "bird of prey" (עַיִט) strange for the Messiah, here it fits the context in Genesis 15 very well. As a large raptor, it would have the power to descend and seize the animal offerings laid out by Abram (Gen 15:11). Yet the patriarch prevents its doing so, for the end or "evening" of the fourth wicked kingdom, Rome, has not yet come.

I suggest that the above Judaic tradition, in the present or an earlier, related form, was known to the Evangelist John. Therefore he could maintain in 8:56 that Abraham had "seen" (in the vision of Genesis 15) the Messiah's "day." Indeed, for him Jesus as the Son of David / Messiah had on that occasion "seen" Abraham (John 8:57). If the textual variant, "And has Abraham seen you?" is original, it refers to the same incident from Judaic tradition. There Abraham saw the Son of David / Messiah as a bird of prey and prevented his scattering and destroying the last of the four wicked kingdoms, Rome, for its time had not yet come.

THE DATE

Unfortunately there is no critical edition of the *Pirqe de Rabbi Eliezer*, in which the above messianic passage is found.[122] While the final redaction of this midrashic work probably occurred in the eighth or ninth century CE, it contains much early Tannaitic material.[123] In light of other definitely early Judaic works which

---

[121] Cf. BDB 855, 3 and the biblical passages cited there, as well as Jastrow 1287, and other rabbinic sources noted by Str-B 2.113 on Luke 1:78.

[122] The basis of M. Higger's edition is very limited. For other editions, cf. Strack and Stemberger, *Introduction* 357, and the variants cited in the very extensive notes by Friedlander 200-201.

[123] Cf. *Introduction* 356-357 ("its use of a wealth of older tradition, its knowledge of the pseudepigrapha"), and *Pirq. R. El.* 39 (Friedlander

deal with Genesis 15 (see section I. above) and other known Tannaitic comment on the chapter (see section II. above), there is no valid reason to doubt that the remarks of R. Joshua b. Ḥananyah, R. Eleazar b. 'Azaryah and R. Eleazar b. 'Arakh cited above go back to these second generation Tannaim. That is, the messianic interpretation of the bird of prey at the covenant between the pieces, also taking place on the fifteenth of Nisan, the time of the first and last (messianic) redemption, with great probability existed before the Evangelist John wrote down the incident alluded to in 8:56-58, probably in the last decade of the first century CE.[124] The Evangelist appropriated it from Palestinian Judaism, probably from a Semitic language (most probably Hebrew, possibly Aramaic), or possibly already translated into Greek.[125]

The Palestinian Judaic interpretation of the עַיִט, "bird of prey," as the Messiah is probably ultimately based on a passage in the prophet Isaiah. In 46:11 God is depicted as "calling 'a bird of prey' (עַיִט) from the east." This is a reference to Cyrus of Persia,[126] also labeled "a victor from the east" (41:2), who will swiftly (v 3) conquer Babylonia and allow the Israelite / Jewish refugees there to return to Judea and rebuild Jerusalem. In 45:1 Cyrus is even described as the Lord's "Anointed" or "Messiah" (מָשִׁיחַ). These passages most probably provided the biblical

---

305) on Joseph's "repenting" as part of the background of the prodigal son's "going into himself" in Luke 15:17. On this, see my *Weihnachtsgeschichte, Barmherziger Samariter, Verlorener Sohn. Studien zu ihrem jüdischen Hintergrund* (ANTZ 2; Berlin: Institut Kirche und Judentum, 1988) 140.

[124] On this dating, cf. for example R. Brown, *The Gospel of John, I - XII* (AB 29; Garden City, New York: Doubleday, 1966) LXXXVI.

[125] For his appropriation of other Palestinian Judaic traditions, now available only in Hebrew, cf. my studies of John 2:1-11 in *Water Into Wine and the Beheading of John the Baptist* (BJS 150; Atlanta: Scholars Press, 1988) 1-37; 7:53-8:11 in *"Caught in the Act," Walking on the Sea, and the Release of Barabbas Revisited* (Atlanta: Scholars Press, 1998) 1-48; and 11:45-54 in *Barabbas and Esther and Other Studies in the Judaic Illumination of Earliest Christianity* (Atlanta: Scholars Press, 1992) 29-63.

[126] Cf. for example G. Fohrer, *Das Buch Jesaja* (Zurich: Zwingli Verlag, 1964) 3.101-102.

basis for the later Judaic designation of the Messiah as a "bird of prey."[127]

IV. Jesus' Day

John 8:56 has Jesus tell his fellow Jews: "Your father Abraham rejoiced that he would see 'my day' (τὴν ἡμέραν τὴν ἐμήν); he saw it and was glad."

Rabbinic sources usually speak in the plural of "the days of the Messiah" (יְמוֹת הַמָּשִׁיחַ), for example R. Eliezer (b. Hyrcanus), a second generation Tanna, in *b. Sanh.* 99a.[128] This period is variously calculated,[129] and it is usually differentiated from "the world to come," which follows the days of the Messiah.[130]

In *Pesiq. R.* 36/1 the Messiah speaks of "my days," which is parallel to "the time of redemption."[131] The latter is probably intended when Jesus speaks of his "day" in John 8:56.

---

[127] The magi present at the Messiah Cyrus' birth also provided the background for the magi present at Jesus' birth in Matt 2:1–12. Cf. my essay with the similar title, "The Magi at the Birth of Cyrus, and the Magi at Jesus' Birth in Matt 2:1–12" in the Howard Clark Kee Festschrift *New Perspectives on Ancient Judaism*, ed. J. Neusner et al. (Lanham: University Press of America, 1987) 2.99-114, reprinted in my *Barabbas and Esther and Other Studies in the Judaic Illumination of Earliest Christianity* 95-111.

[128] Cf. n. 61 on him, as well as Soncino 669. See also *Pesiq. R.* 1/7 (Friedmann 4a-b, Braude 47). While Luke 17:22 and 26 have the "days" of the Son of Man, v 30 speaks of "on the day that the Son of Man is revealed," and some MSS of v 24 have "so will the Son of Man be in his day." See also 4 Ezra 13:52 (*OTP* 1.553, with n. "n"), and 1 Enoch 61:5 (*OTP* 1.42).

[129] In *b. Sanh.* 99a, R. Eliezer maintains it will last forty years; R. Eleazar b. 'Azaryah seventy years; Rabbi (Judah the Prince) three generations; and R. Dosa four hundred years, based on Gen 15:13 (Soncino 669).

[130] Cf. the sources mentioned in P. Billerbeck's excursus "Diese Welt, die Tage des Messias u. die zukünftige Welt" in Str-B 4.799-976.

[131] Friedmann 161b; Braude 679, with n. 8. Cf. "the time of your redemption has come" in 36/2 (Friedmann 162a; Braude 682, who has "the day" for the Hebrew זְמָן, "time").

Two Judaic traditions in regard to the covenant with Abram "between the pieces" in Genesis 15 may have contributed to the terminology of the singular "day" in John 8:56. As noted above, in *Gen. Rab.* Lech Lecha 44/22 on Gen 15:18, "In that day...," either R. Yoḥanan b. Zakkai or R. Aqiba maintains that God here revealed to Abram both this world and the next. Either R. Leazar or R. Yose b. R. Ḥanina[132] then comments on the preceding by maintaining regarding God: "He revealed [the future] to him from 'that day' (היום ההוא),"[133] i.e. from the Exodus until the day / time the Messiah will come.[134] As pointed out above, this day in early Judaic tradition was and will be a particular day, the fifteenth of Nisan, when the Messiah is to be revealed and is to redeem his people. The same "day" is meant.

A second possible influence on Jesus' "day" in John 8:56 is found in *Pirq. R. El.* 28 on Genesis 15. Here R. Eleazar b. 'Azaryah maintains that the incident of the bird of prey's not prevailing over the oppressive four kingdoms, including the last one, Rome, until "evening" comes means that the rule of these four kingdoms will last only one "day." He bases this on the "day" of God, (which in Ps 90:4 is 1000 years). R. Eleazar b. 'Arakh agrees with him, cites Lam 1:13 with "the day," and then "evening," including the "evening" of Zech 14:7. That is, the Messiah is here thought to come in the future only on the evening of God's "day," when Rome's wickedness and oppression of Israel are complete and the time of redemption will have arrived. As remarked above, the latter can be equated with the "days of the Messiah."

If the Evangelist John was also acquainted with any of the above Palestinian Judaic traditions on Genesis 15, they probably contributed to his formulation of "my day," i.e. the day of the

---

[132] The first was a third, the second a second generation Palestinian Amora (Strack and Stemberger, *Introduction* 98 and 96).
[133] Theodor and Albeck 445, Soncino 1.376.
[134] So basically Matnoth Kehunah, cited by H. Freedman in Soncino 1.376, n. 4 (see p. xxv).

Messiah Jesus in John 8:56.[135] The rare expression is equivalent to "the time of redemption," as noted above. At the covenant between the pieces Abram saw the bird of prey / Messiah, who descended and wanted to scatter and destroy the four kingdoms, including Edom / Rome. Yet Abram prevented him from doing so because the evening of God's "day," the time of redemption, had not yet arrived. However, it definitely will come in the future, on the fifteenth of Nisan, which then can be thought of as the "day" of the Messiah.

V. Jesus' True Age

After Jesus tells his fellow Jews that their father Abraham saw his day and was glad, they say to him in John 8:57: "You are not yet fifty years old, and have you seen Abraham?" In v 58 Jesus then replies to them, "Very truly, I tell you, before Abraham was, I am." The question is: If Jesus is at the beginning of his thirties,[136] how can he already have seen Abraham, only possible after death?[137]

In spite of Ps 90:10, Palestinian Judaic sources note that sixty is already a ripe old age.[138] R. Judah b. Tema, a fourth generation Tanna,[139] remarks in *m. 'Abot* 5:21, however, that at fifty one is fit for counsel (עֵצָה),[140] that is, still active mentally.

It appears therefore that the Evangelist John, composing this incident, first of all wants to contrast Jesus' present age, when he has not yet become mature enough to become a counselor at

---

[135] Cf. 12:41, where the prophet Isaiah "saw his [Jesus'] glory and spoke about him." This may refer to Isaiah's vision in chapter six.

[136] Cf. Luke 3:23, and the assertion that Jesus was born while Herod the Great still reigned (Matt 2:1). The latter died in 4 BCE.

[137] Cf. Gen 15:15; 25:7-8; and Luke 16:19-31. A vision of the patriarch is not thought of here.

[138] Cf. *Semaḥoth* 3:7, 44b (*Minor Tractates* 337), referring to Job 5:26. A parallel is found in *y. Bik.* 2:1, 64c (Neusner 10.159; on p. 160 it cites Num 8:25 on the Levites retiring at fifty, and Ps 90:10); see also *b. M. Q.* 28a (Soncino 182-183).

[139] Strack and Stemberger, *Introduction* 89.

[140] Albeck 4.380-381, Danby 458. Cf. the remarks on this mature age in *Eliyyahu Rabbah* 5 (6) (Friedmann 27, Braude and Kapstein 102).

fifty, to Abraham's very advanced age at death. The patriarch died at 175 (Gen 25:7) and now is in Sheol (see John 8:52-53).

Secondly, the Fourth Evangelist wants his readers also to contrast Jesus' *true* age with that of Abraham. Therefore he has Jesus say, "Before Abraham was (born – γενέσθαι), I am (ἐγώ εἰμί)."[141] Already in his prologue John had emphasized that the Word (λόγος) was in the beginning (1:1), he / it was in the beginning with God (v 2). Another rabbinic passage aids in understanding the thought of John 8:57-58, connected to that of the prologue.

Pesiq. R. 33/6 notes: You find that at the beginning of the creation of the world the king Messiah "came into being" (נולד), for he ascended in God's thought even before the world was created. The past tense of the verb "came forth" in Isa 11:1 proves this. The midrash continues by stating that at the beginning of the world you find written that it (Scripture) mentions the oppression of the (four) kingdoms, and the redeemer, the king Messiah. Gen 1:1, with "In the beginning," as in John 1:1, is then quoted, and various nouns in Gen 1:2 are interpreted of Babylonia, Media, Greece and Edom / Rome.

The author of the midrash then asks: From where can one state that from the beginning of the creation of the world the king Messiah existed (היה)? From Gen 1:2, "And the spirit of God hovered" – this is the king Messiah. Thus Scripture states, "The spirit of the Lord shall rest on him" (Isa 11:2).[142]

* * *

Although it unfortunately cannot be dated, the above passage from *Pesiqta Rabbati* greatly helps to explain the contents of John 8:57-58. In Palestinian Judaic thought the messianic king / royal

---

[141] On this expression, cf. also 4:36; 6:20; 8:24, 28; 13:19; and 18:5-6. Here it has nothing to do with the divine name in Exod 3:14, but with the Messiah's existence before the creation of the world. See the following.

[142] Friedmann 152b, Braude 641-643. Cf. also 36/1, where the "light" of Gen 1:4 is the light of the Messiah. This shows that God thought of the Messiah and his works before the world was created (Friedmann 161a-b, Braude 677). On this motif of the Messiah's light, see John 1:4-5.

Messiah "came into being" at the beginning of the creation of the world. The niphal form נוֹלַד literally means "to be born, to originate."[143] The second similar assertion is that the royal Messiah "existed" or "was" (הָיָה) from the beginning of the creation of the world. This is buttressed by a messianic interpretation of the "spirit" (רוּחַ) of God as hovering over the face of the waters in Gen 1:2. I have elsewhere analyzed this motif in regard to the Messiah's walking on the Sea of Galilee in Mark 6:45-52 par.[144]

It is possible that the Evangelist John knew not only of the four kingdoms which oppressed and continue to oppress Israel in connection with Genesis 15, the covenant between the pieces with Abram, but also of this floating tradition in connection with Gen 1:1-2. The messianic interpretation of the latter verse then could have aided him in stating that the Messiah Jesus "existed" or "was" from the beginning of the creation of the world. That is, long before the time of Abram / Abraham, Jesus as the Messiah could maintain "I am" (John 8:58).[145]

VI. Abraham's Rejoicing

John 8:56 states that "Abraham your father 'rejoiced' that he would see my day; he saw it and 'was glad.'" The first verb, "rejoiced," is ἠγαλλιάσατο, the first aorist middle of ἀγαλλιάω: exult, be glad, overjoyed. Bauer / Arndt / Gingrich translate here: "he was overjoyed to see."[146] The second verb, "was glad," is ἐχάρη, the second aorist passive of χαίρω: to rejoice, be glad,

---

[143] Jastrow 577 on ילד.
[144] Cf. my "Caught in the Act," Walking on the Sea, and the Release of Barabbas Revisited 110-115.
[145] If the Evangelist was not aware of this tradition, it nevertheless demonstrates a thought pattern very similar to his own, even referring to Gen 1:1, as in John 1:1. It is extremely improbable that the Palestinian Jewish author of Pesiq. R. 33/6 was aware of the Gospel of John and was intentionally copying its thought pattern at this point.
[146] BAGD 3-4. Cf. also LSJ 5.

be delighted.[147] It is also connected to "seeing" someone in John 20:20. The two verbs, ἀγαλλιάομαι and χαίρω, occur in John 8:56 in what is usually labeled Hebrew parallelism.

The Evangelist John probably also borrowed the motif of Abraham's "rejoicing" from Palestinian Judaic tradition, just as he did with other sections of 8:56-58. The Hebrew verb שׂוֹשׂ, שׂישׂ most probably lies behind ἀγαλλιάομαι. It means to exult, rejoice, display joy.[148] It is translated by the Greek verb in Ps 18(19):5; 39(40):16; 69(70):4; and 118(119):162. In Isa 66:10 it is also connected with seeing someone, as in John 8:56.

A cognate noun of ἀγαλλιάομαι is ἀγαλλίασις, exultation, joy, gladness.[149] It translates the cognate noun of שׂוֹשׂ, שׂישׂ in Ps 45:8, שָׂשׂוֹן - exaltation, rejoicing.[150] It is this psalm verse which aids in explaining Abraham's "rejoicing" in John 8:56.

In *Pesiq. Rav Kah.* 16/4, R. Aḥa, a fourth generation Palestinian Amora,[151] says Ps 45:8 alludes to Abraham: "You love righteousness and hate wickedness. Therefore God, your God, has anointed you with the oil of 'gladness' beyond your companions." The first part of the verse refers to "our father Abraham's" arguing with God not to bring another flood to the world and destroy more human lives. The latter part of the verse, especially "beyond your companions," refers to God's telling Abraham: "From the time I spoke to Noah to the time of My speaking to you, I have spoken to no other creature of Mine. But with you I make a new beginning of speaking: 'After these things the word of the Lord came to Abram' (Gen 15:1.)"[152]

---

[147] BAGD 873-874. Cf. also LSJ 1969, rejoice at, take pleasure in, delight in.
[148] BDB 965. Cf. Jastrow 1542. Both Delitzsch (p. 184) and the United Bible Societies (p. 262) employ it at this point in their Hebrew New Testaments.
[149] BAGD 3; LSJ 5 as great joy, exultation.
[150] BDB 965.
[151] Strack and Stemberger, *Introduction* 103.
[152] Mandelbaum 268-269; Braude and Kapstein 291-292, whom I slightly modify. Parallels, without reference to Gen 15:1, are found in *Gen. Rab.* Lech Lecha 39/6 on Gen 12:2 (Soncino 1.315); Vayera 49/9 on Gen 18:25 (Soncino 1.429-430); *Lev. Rab.* Tsav 10/1 on Lev 8:1-4 (Soncino 4.121-

W. Braude and I. Kapstein correctly point out that the oil of "gladness" as applied to Abraham here means words of prophecy.[153] In section III. 1) above I called attention to Gen 15:1 in Judaic tradition as considered Abraham's "prophecy." It is precisely this verse which is cited by R. Aha at the end of his interpretation. If he borrows this motif from an earlier source, as seems probable, it may have provided the Fourth Evangelist with the major background for his maintaining that Abraham (prophetically) saw Jesus' day (in the covenant between the pieces, beginning with Gen 15:1). Therefore he "rejoiced" and "was glad."

Four other factors may also have encouraged the Evangelist to employ the motif of Abraham's "rejoicing" in John 8:56. As noted above in section I. 1), after a paraphrase of Genesis 15 in Jubilees 14:1-20, the author in the middle of the second century BCE notes in 14:21, "And Abram 'rejoiced,' and he told all these things to Sarai his wife."

Secondly, *Exod. Rab.* Bo 18/11 on Exod 12:41 states that on the same day the Israelites descended into Egypt, they departed from there at the Exodus. This night then became one of "rejoicing" (שִׂמְחָה) for all Israel, as in v 42: "That was for the Lord a night of vigil."[154] As noted above in section III. 2), this night was that of the fifteenth of Nisan, the very same night on which God made a covenant with Abram between the pieces in Genesis 15, and in Judaic tradition showed him the future, including the Messiah as a bird of prey.

Thirdly, *Tanh.* B Sarah 3 on Gen 23:1 notes that when God showed Abraham Gehenna, He "announced to him the good news" (בישרה)[155] that none of his children would descend into it. Gen 15:17 is then employed as a prooftext: "See, a smoking

---

122); and *Pesiq. R.* 29/30 A4 (Braude 576). Ps 45:8 is applied to the Son (Jesus) in Heb 1:9.

[153] *Pesikta de-Rab Kahana* 292, n. 24. They call attention to Jer 15:16, where God's words became to the prophet Jeremiah a "joy" (שָׂשׂוֹן) and a "delight" (שִׂמְחָה). For these nouns and the cognate verbs as often in parallelism, cf. the respective entries in BDB.

[154] Mirqin 5.219; Soncino 3.227.

[155] Cf. Jastrow 199 on the piel of בשׂר.

fire pot and a flaming torch" – that is Gehenna.[156] Here too "good news," a form of joy, is associated with Genesis 15.

Fourthly, *Pesiq. R.* 42/7 on Gen 21:1 says the Lord's remembering Sarah (by giving her a child) is to be understood in light of Ps 126:5, "May those who sow in tears reap with 'shouts of joy' (רִנָּה)."[157] "Of such was Abraham, who wept and pleaded before the Holy One, blessed be He: 'Behold, You have given me no offspring' (Gen 15:3). At once 'he was given good tidings' (נִתְבַּסֵּר)[158] in regard to children: 'it is through Isaac that offspring shall be named for you' (21:12). Thus it is said, 'shall reap with shouts of joy.'"[159]

Here Abram's being given good news, a source of joy, is directly connected to Gen 15:3, part of God's covenant with him between the pieces. As noted above in section III. 2), this took place on the fifteenth of Nisan. On the very same day many years later the angels came to give Abram the good news that his wife would bear a child exactly one year later. Thus Isaac was also born on the fifteenth of Nisan, thirty years after the event described in Genesis 15.

Combined with the application of the oil of "gladness" of Ps 45:8 to Abraham in connection with Gen 15:1, the above four Judaic traditions, all related to Genesis 15, may also have aided in the Evangelist John's having Abraham "rejoice" and "be glad" that he saw the day of Jesus, (the Messiah, at the covenant of the pieces in Genesis 15).[160]

---

[156] Buber 119-120; Bietenhard in 1.124 follows a slightly different text.
[157] BDB 943, which lists passages where it is parallel to שִׂמְחָה and שָׂשׂוֹן .
[158] A variant spelling of the niphal of בשׂר : Jastrow 199, to be gladdened, to receive good tidings.
[159] Friedmann 178a, Braude 748-749.
[160] This means that Abraham's "rejoicing" in *Targ. Onq.* Gen 17:17, instead of the "laughing" in the MT, is irrelevant here. It is cited by commentator after commentator as the source of Abraham's rejoicing and being glad in John 8:56. Judaic tradition on Genesis 15 is rather the source of this motif.

VII. Our Father Abraham

Jesus' fellow Jews ask him in John 8:53, "Are you greater than 'our father Abraham' (τοῦ πατρὸς ἡμῶν 'Αβραάμ), who died?" Therefore Jesus can say in v 56 "Abraham your father" (cf. v 41). Verse 39 also has "our father Abraham." This expression in Hebrew is אַבְרָהָם אָבִינוּ. It occurs for example many times in sources dealing with Genesis 15.[161]

Throughout the narrative of John 8:31-59 one of the issues is: Who are the true descendants ("seed") of Abraham, the Jews (vv 33, 37, 39, 53, 56), or those who now believe in Jesus as the Messiah? The hostility between Jews and Jewish Christians at the end of the first century CE had in part become so severe[162] that the Evangelist John here speaks of "*the* Jews" in a derogatory manner (vv 31, 48, 52, 57), as if Jesus were not Jewish himself. The author of the Fourth Gospel even has Jesus maintain that the Jews' real father is the devil (v 44). Just as he

---

[161] Cf. *Mek. R. Ish.* Pisḥa 14 on Exod 12:41 (Lauterbach 1.112); Beshallaḥ 7 on Exod 14:31 (Lauterbach 1.253); Baḥodesh 9 on Exod 20:18 (Lauterbach 2.268); *Seder 'Olam* 1 (Milikowsky 210 and 449), 3 (Milikowsky 225 and 455), 5 (Milikowsky 242 and 462); *'Abot R. Nat.* B 36 (Saldarini 214); *Exod. Rab.* Shemoth 3/11 on Exod 3:21 (Soncino 3.69); Pequde 51/7 on Exod 38:21 (Soncino 3.568); *Lev. Rab.* Vayyiqra 3/3 on Lev 2:1 (Soncino 4.38); *Num. Rab.* Naso 11/7 on Num 6:26 (Soncino 5.441); *Cant. Rab.* 1:12 § 1 (Soncino 9.78); *Pesiq. Rav Kah.* 5/2, 5/7 and 16/4 (Braude and Kapstein 92, 100 and 291); and *Pirq. R. El.* 48 (Friedlander 387).

[162] An expression of this was the formulation of the "Birkat ha-Minim," the benediction regarding heretics, the twelfth part of the so-called "Eighteen Prayer" or Amidah. It was composed by Samuel the Small under Rabban Gamaliel II at Yabneh (*b. Ber.* 28b in Soncino 175). Both were older second generation Tannaim (Strack and Stemberger, *Introduction* 78 and 76). Among other things the benediction effected the complete exclusion of Jewish Christians from the synagogue, where up to then they still could even be prayer leaders. Cf. I. Elbogen, *Der jüdische Gottesdienst in seiner geschichtlichen Entwicklung* 36-39 and 51-52, as well as M. Ydit, art. "Birkat ha-Minim" in *EJ* (1971) 4.1035-1036. In the Fourth Gospel passages such as 9:22; 12:42; 16:2; 19:38; and 20:19 attest this separation and hostility.

was a murderer from the beginning, so they now attempt to kill Jesus, whose father is God (vv 37-38, 40-41, 44, 49, 54, 59).

Instead of being understood as a rough, name-calling, internecine altercation between Jews and Jewish Christians, i.e. a "family quarrel," the above narrative, especially when later read and appropriated by Gentile Christians, became a major source of anti-Semitism. Jews are labeled liars (8:55), the children of the devil (v 44), because they have not accepted Jesus as their Messiah. It has taken almost two thousand years for Christians to recognize what terrible effects passages like John 8:31-59 have had not only on their own view of Judaism at the time of Jesus, but also on their relationships to contemporary Jews throughout the centuries. It is my hope that through my pointing out the Palestinian Judaic background of John 8:56-58, present-day Christians can not only become more appreciative of how the Fourth Evangelist creatively developed this background, but also of how the root of the Jewish people and the Jewish faith supports them (Rom 11:18).

Chapter Six

The Messiah as a Vulture in Matt 24:28 // Luke 17:37b

Introduction

Sitting on the Mount of Olives with Jesus, his disciples ask him when the Temple will be destroyed, "and what will be the sign of your coming and of the end of the age?" (Matt 24:3). Part of the answer he gives them in the so-called "Synoptic Apocalypse" consists of vv 27-28: "as the lightning comes from the east and flashes as far as the west, so will be the coming of the Son of Man. 28) Wherever the corpse is, there the vultures will gather." The latter in Greek is: ὅπου ἐὰν ᾖ τὸ πτῶμα, ἐκεῖ συναχθήσονται οἱ ἀετοί.

The Evangelist Luke splits up these two sayings from Q,[1] citing the first in 17:24, "as the lightning flashes and lights up the sky from one side to the other, so will the Son of Man be in his day." At the conclusion of the discourse Luke has the disciples ask "Where, Lord," (will these things take place)? Jesus then tells them, "Where the corpse is, there the vultures will gather" (v 37b). The latter in Greek is: ὅπου τὸ σῶμα, ἐκεῖ καὶ οἱ ἀετοὶ ἐπισυναχθήσονται.

---

[1] This view is now held by most scholars, who contend that the Third Evangelist intended a climax with the contents of 17:37. Cf. J. Nolland, *Luke 9:21-18:34* (WBC 35B; Dallas, Texas: Word Books, 1993) 862-863; F. Bovon, *Das Evangelium nach Lukas, 3. Lk 15,1-19,27* (EKK III/3; Zurich: Benziger; Neukirchen-Vluyn: Neukirchener Verlag, 2001) 180; and J. Fitzmyer, *The Gospel According to Luke, X-XXIV* (AB 28A; Garden City, New York: Doubleday, 1986) 1173.

Elsewhere in the Gospels Jesus frequently employs bird imagery. The birds of the air are taken care of by God (Matt 6:26 // Luke 12:24); in contrast to the Son of Man they have a home (Matt 8:20 // Luke 9:58); they come and eat up the sower's seed which has fallen on the path (Mark 4:4 par.); they nest in the branches of a mustard seed which has grown into a large bush (Mark 4:32 par.); God even cares for sparrows, sold for a very modest price (Matt 10:29-31 // Luke 12:6-7); Jesus compares himself to a mother bird which would like to gather its brood under its wings (Matt 23:37 // Luke 13:34; see the next chapter); and he predicts Peter's denying him before the cock or rooster crows twice (Mark 14:30, 68, 72 par.; John 13:38 and 18:27).

Yet Matt 24:28 // Luke 17:37b is the only passage in which the prophet from Nazareth makes a comparison with a bird of prey, here the vulture. While ἀετός in classical and Koine Greek is normally an eagle, the NRSV correctly has "vulture" here because the original Semitic behind the saying most probably had the Hebrew עַיִט, which can mean both.[2] The later Hellenistic Christian translators of the Semitic sayings now found in Q could have employed the term γύψ for vulture here.[3] Yet it only occurs six times in the LXX for various birds of prey,[4] whereas the much more common term is ἀετός, which includes both vultures and eagles.[5] They therefore correctly chose ἀετός,

---

[2] Cf. BAGD 19 on *aetos*, and BDB 743 and Jastrow 1068 on *'ayiṭ* as "bird(s) of prey."
[3] LSJ 364.
[4] See the references in the Hatch Redpath concordance, p. 283.
[5] Cf. Hatch Redpath, p. 28. The NRSV has "vulture" for the LXX's *aetos* in Hos 8:1 and Prov 30:17. Yet J. Feliks in his art. "Vultures" in *EJ* (1971) 16.233 correctly labels the birds of prey in Deut 32:11, Mic 1:16, Job 39:27, and Ps 103:5 also vultures. Pliny the Elder, who died in 79 CE at the eruption of Vesuvius, describes in his *Natural History* X. 3-6 eagles, the vulture in 7, and two thought by some to be vultures in 8 (LCL, vol. III). Vultures' flying to *cadavera* is mentioned in 7. The differentiation between eagles and vultures is not entirely clear here, which was already the case for Aristotle (d. 322 BCE) in his *History of Animals*, VIII (IX).xi on vultures and xxxii on eagles. One of the latter kinds, probably a vulture, takes τεθνεῶτα, "dead animals" (cf. LXX Job 39:30 below). The texts are in *History of Animals* (LCL, vol. III).

mistakenly taken by some modern interpreters only to mean "eagle." The "carcass/corpse" in Matt 24:28 // Luke 17:37b also points to a vulture, for this is its normal food. An eagle usually seizes living prey.[6]

The Greek ἀετός, Attic αἰετός,[7] is probably even connected philologically to the Semitic *'ayiṭ* (עַיִט), "bird(s) of prey," which includes both vultures and eagles.[8] In Gen 15:11, analyzed in the previous chapter, vultures are definitely meant by this term. They try to descend on the carcasses of the animals Abram just cut up and readied for sacrifice.

People of the modern Western world usually consider the scene of a vulture sticking its head into a blood-filled cadaver in order to pick out bits of rotting meat to be revolting, and not just the bird's homely appearance per se. Therefore commentators on Jesus' comparison with a vulture in Matt 24:28 // Luke 17:37b can speak here of a "terrible image,"[9] a "grisly image,"[10] its "strangeness,"[11] its being "rather gruesome,"[12] a "hard" depiction,[13] even "widerlich und abstoßend."[14] Yet at the time of Jesus vultures were much more common in Israel / Palestine than they are today, and as scavengers they devoured the flesh

---

[6] Cf. G. R. Driver, "Birds in the Old Testament" in *PEQ* 87 (1955) 9: "Both vultures and eagles live on live or dead prey, the former largely on carrion and the latter on either...."

[7] LSJ 29.

[8] If one removes the typically Greek ending *os* from *aietos*, resulting in *aiet*, the resemblance is striking. Cf. the articles "Eagle" and "Vultures" by J. Feliks in *EJ* (1971) 6. 337-338 and 16. 232-233, respectively. See also G. R. Driver, "Birds in the Old Testament" 5.

[9] J. Schniewind, *Das Evangelium nach Matthäus* (NTD 2; Göttingen: Vandenhoeck & Ruprecht, 1956[8]) 244.

[10] F. W. Beare, *The Gospel according to Matthew* (Oxford: Blackwell, 1981) 470.

[11] J. Gnilka, *Das Matthäusevangelium, II. Teil* (Herders; Freiburg: Herder, 1988) 326.

[12] J. Nolland, *Luke 9:21-18:34*, 863.

[13] W. Grundmann, *Das Evangelium nach Lukas* (THKNT 3; Berlin: Evangelische Verlagsanstalt, 1984[10]) 345.

[14] P. Gaechter, *Das Matthäus Evangelium* (Innsbruck: Tyrolia-Verlag, 1963) 781.

of dead animals, which led to fewer health problems both for humans and domestic animals. Even today the raḥam, "the smallest of Israel vultures..., is found in flocks near garbage heaps where it feeds on carcasses and insects."[15] When Jesus made a comparison with a vulture, his listeners thus did not react negatively as most moderns do. This particular bird of prey was a part of their daily lives, and they appreciated its usefulness.

In 24:28 the Evangelist Matthew has πτῶμα for "corpse." It is literally "that which has fallen," thus a "(dead) body" or "corpse."[16] In codex Vaticanus of LXX Ezek 6:5 it translates the Hebrew פֶּגֶר. In 17:37 the Evangelist Luke instead has σῶμα for "corpse." Literally "body," it is meant here as "(dead) body" or "corpse."[17] It also translates the Hebrew פֶּגֶר in LXX Gen 15:11, 4 Kgdms 19:35 and Isa 37:36. The Hebrew term means "corpse, carcass."[18] The Aramaic is פְּגַר, פִּגְרָא.[19] It is thus quite probable that πτῶμα and σῶμα, both meaning "corpse, carcass," are simply translation variants of the original Aramaic or Hebrew within the Greek traditions of Q obtaining in the communities of Matthew and Luke.[20]

The Hellenistic Jewish Christian translators of the Q saying now found in Matt 24:28 and Luke 17:37b with only slight variants both have the plural οἱ ἀετοί, "vultures." This caused the verb also to become plural: (ἐπι -)συναχθήσονται, "they shall

---

[15] J. Feliks, art. "Vultures" in *EJ* (1971) 16.233. Against G. R. Driver in "Birds in the Old Testament" 16-17, who falsely believes this is the osprey. See also the discussion of *b. Ḥull.* 63a below.

[16] BAGD 727-728; LSJ 1549 II. fallen body, corpse, carcass. One reason for its choice may have been that the Semitic verb נשׁר, with the same letters as the noun "vulture," means to drop or "fall" off (Jastrow 942).

[17] BAGD 799, 1.a., with other NT references; LSJ 1749, I.1.a.

[18] BDB 803, Jastrow 1136.

[19] Jastrow 1136.

[20] There is no pressing reason to believe the Third Evangelist changed the πτῶμα he found in Q to σῶμα for stylistic reasons, as maintained by a number of commentators. However, for stylistic reasons he did probably add ἐπι to the συναχθήσονται he found in Q.

gather."[21] The Hebrew נֶשֶׁר, Aramaic נְשַׁר (later also נִשְׁרָא),[22] always stands behind ἀετός in the LXX. If the Semitic original was the far less common sing. עַיִט, [23] however, it could have meant either the singular, "bird of prey," or the collective plural "birds of prey."[24] Since the Hellenistic Jewish Christian translators behind the Q saying in Matthew and Luke thought the plural was meant, they rendered *'ayiṭ* with οἱ ἀετοί. However, as in the previous chapter dealing with Palestinian Judaic interpretation of the *'ayiṭ* in Gen 15:11 as the Messiah, I suggest that *'ayiṭ* meant as the singular also originally stood in the Semitic of Matt 24:28 and Luke 17:37b and meant the Messiah, here too as a bird of prey, a "vulture." To better understand this, the biblical basis of the saying in Job 39:30b should be examined.

I. Job 39:30b

In Job 38:1-3 the Lord states that He is going to question Job, and he should then answer Him. One of these questions has to do with a vulture, 39:27-30.

27) Is it at your command that the vulture mounts up and makes its nest on high?
28) It lives on the rock and makes its home in the fastness of the rocky crag.
29) From there it spies the prey; its eyes see it from far away.
30) Its young ones suck up blood; and where the slain are, there it is.

---

[21] The future passive of συνάγω is meant here in the reflexive sense, "gather, come together." Cf. BAGD 782. For birds of prey with this verb for "gathering," see LXX Isa 18:6. The niphal of קבץ means to "gather" or assemble (BDB 867, 1.), and birds do so in Isa 34:15 (buzzards) and Ezek 30:17 (birds of prey - עֵיט צִפּוֹר - in v 4).
[22] Jastrow 942.
[23] BDB 743, Jastrow 1068.
[24] On the latter, cf. LXX Gen 15:11's ὄρνεα, pl., for הָעַיִט.

The "vulture" of v 27 is the Hebrew נֶשֶׁר, "griffon vulture," *gyps fulvus*, its wingspread extending up to ten feet (three m).[25] Lest the reader of the LXX think ἀετός meant "eagle" here, the translator (or a later redactor) added "vulture" (γύψ) in v 27.[26]

Verse 30b is of direct relevance to the Q saying in Matt 24:28 and Luke 17:37b. It reads in Hebrew: וּבַאֲשֶׁר חֲלָלִים שָׁם הוּא.

The term חָלָל, literally "pierced," "bored through," means "slain" here.[27] The *Targum* has קְטִילַיָּא, "the killed," from קְטַל, to cut, to kill.[28] The LXX translates with τεθνεῶτες, "the dead," the perf. part. of θνῄσκω.[29] It is important to note that instead of the plural as here, the Q saying of Jesus in Matt 24:28 has τὸ πτῶμα, and in Luke 17:37b τὸ σῶμα, both singular and very probably going back to פֶּגֶר / פִּגְרָא. If Jesus based his saying on Job 39:30b, as seems probable, the singular would show his creative artistry. He deliberately changed the plural, "the slain," to the singular "the corpse/carcass" in order to coincide with his choice of one "bird of prey." One bird of prey would not normally feed on several corpses / carcasses at once.

Job 39:30 states that where the slain are, "there 'it / he' is." The latter is הוּא, referring back to the one vulture mentioned in v 27. The *Targum* also has the sing. הוּא.[30] This was the model

---

[25] BDB 676, and J. Feliks, art. "Vultures" in *EJ* (1971) 16. 232-233, who states that it is "the largest of Israel's carnivorous birds" and feeds on carcasses, as in Job 39:30. One from the Jerusalem Biblical Zoo is pictured on p. 232. Driver in "Birds in the Old Testament" 8 notes the "great wings" of Ezek 17:3. They "attain a span of eight or ten feet across."

[26] Cf. also the addition of the "black eagle" (עוֹזְנָא, Jastrow 1049), also probably a vulture, in 11QtgJob, col. 33, at this point (Martínez and Tigchelaar 2. 1198-1199).

[27] BDB 319, 2.

[28] Cf. Jastrow 1349 on the verb, and the text in Merino, *Targum de Job* 162, and de Lagarde, *Hagiographa Chaldaice* 116.

[29] LSJ 802.

[30] Merino 162, de Lagarde 116. The LXX has: "they are immediately found," referring to the two birds of v 27. Against R. Gundry, *The Use of the Old Testament in St. Matthew's Gospel* (NovTSup 18; Leiden: Brill,

for Jesus' modifying the "he" (the male vulture, נֶשֶׁר) to the עַיִט, a bird of prey, primarily a vulture. As pointed out in the previous chapter, Isa 45:1 has the Lord address the Persian king Cyrus as His "anointed" or "Messiah" (מָשִׁיחַ). He is called a "bird of prey" (עַיִט) in 46:11. This biblical imagery of a Messiah called a bird of prey then developed in Judaic tradition into the Davidic Messiah described as an *'ayiṭ*, as in *Pirq. R. El.* 28, the background of John 8:56-58.

In Palestinian Judaic tradition, the "he" of Job 39:30 was interpreted of the Lord's indwelling, His presence. In *Lev. Rab.* Aḥare Moth 20/4 on Lev 16:1, for example, "and where the slain are, 'there is he'" is rendered by "the Shechinah."[31] Here God is described as present in the Sanctuary of the Jerusalem Temple, where "the slain," Aaron's sons Nadab and Abihu, were killed for offering unholy fire before Him (Lev 10:1-3). *Pesiq. Rab Kah.* 26/4 on Lev 16:1 has a parallel tradition, adding that God's presence is the vulture of Job 39:27 which mounts up and rests upon the Ark in the Temple.[32] *Pesiq. R.* 47/3 on Lev 16:1 also interprets God to be the vulture of Job 39:27, here with reference to Deut 32:11. God is like a vulture which "stirs up its nest, and hovers over its young."[33]

If the Judaic interpretation of the "he" of Job 39:30 as God's "presence," in connection with the Lord thought of as the vulture of v 27, already prevailed in Jesus' time, it may have been one more factor which encouraged the Galilean prophet to substitute *'ayiṭ*, a bird of prey / vulture, for the "he" of v 30. The bird of prey as the Messiah, the Son of David, stood in a very special relationship to the heavenly Father.

1967) 88, who maintains "the carcasses are found by the vultures" in the LXX. He also incorrectly speaks of the plural "vultures" in the Hebrew.

[31] Mirqin 8.15, Soncino 4.257. Cf. also the apparatus of Margulies 457.

[32] Mandelbaum 390-392, Braude and Kapstein 399-401. Cf. also *Tanḥ.* B. Aḥare Moth 4 on Lev 16:1 (Buber 58-60, Bietenhard 2.90-91), and *Tanḥ.* Aḥare Moth 3 on Lev 16:1 (Eshkol 570-572).

[33] Friedmann 190a, Braude 804. This verse is important for the interpretation of Luke 13:34 // Matt 23:37, to be analyzed in the next chapter.

II. The Carrion Vulture in Judaic Tradition

Another vulture tradition has to do with the advent of the Messiah. The carrion vulture (רָחָם) is one of the unclean birds listed in Lev 11:18.[34] In *b. Ḥull.* 63a Rab Judah, probably a first generation Palestinian Amora,[35] states that the *raḥam* is the שְׁרַקְרָק, a vulture.[36] R. Yoḥanan (bar Nappaḥa), a second generation Palestinian Amora,[37] asks why it is called *raḥam*. Answering his own question, he states: "Because when the *raḥam* comes, mercy (*raḥamim*)[38] comes to the world." Another rabbi then notes that this will obtain only if the bird perches upon something and cries *sheraq-raq*.[39] This sound is obviously an imitation of the bird's name, just as the Hebrew *raḥamim* is a play on the name *raḥam*.

At this point in *b. Ḥull.* 63a the statement is made: "There is a tradition that if it (the *raḥam* vulture) settles upon the ground and hisses (שריק), the Messiah will come, for it is said: 'I will hiss (אֶשְׁרְקָה) for them and gather them' (Zech 10:8)."[40] The word "tradition" here is גְּמִירֵי, "they have a tradition, 'it is a well-known maxim.'"[41] The statement thus seems to be quite old. The Messiah appears here to be equated with the *raḥam*

---

[34] Cf. BDB 934; Deut 14:17 has it as רָחָמָה. See also Jastrow 1467, and Feliks, art. "Vultures" in *EJ* (1971) 16.233.
[35] Strack and Stemberger, *Introduction* 92 on Yehudah II, son of Gamaliel III. He was associated with Yoḥanan bar Nappaḥa.
[36] Jastrow 1634. Cf. the *Pal. Targum* on Lev 11:18 (Rieder 159) and Deut 14:17 (Rieder 275), as well as *Neofiti 1* (Díez Macho 3.67 and 5.133) on these verses.
[37] *Introduction* 94.
[38] Cf. BDB 933 on רַחֲמִים, usually of God's compassion to man; Jastrow 1468: love, mercy. This is not rain, as later Jewish commentators maintained, but the Messiah. See the following.
[39] The Munich MS has *sheriq-riq*.
[40] Soncino 343, Goldschmidt 8.1002. See also *Yalquṭ Shem'oni*, Kook 1.537 on Lev 11:18. See also Ginzberg, *Legends* 1.45 and 5.62.
[41] Jastrow 255 on גְּמַר II. 5. end.

vulture, who when he hisses and gathers (the Israelites), will bring "mercy" (*raḥamim*) into the world, i.e. salvation.[42]

Targum Zechariah on the nearby verse 10:4 interprets "the cornerstone" as "their king," and "the tent peg" as "their Anointed One / Messiah."[43] The messianic King or royal Messiah is thus meant here in Palestinian Judaic tradition close to v 8.

The eleventh century CE work *Bereshit Rabbati*[44] combines numerous earlier sources. It interprets "binding his foal to the vine" in Gen 49:11 of the Messiah when he comes to redeem Israel. "And his donkey's colt to the choice vine" of the same verse is related to when (the Messiah) comes to gather Israel. Zech 10:8 is then quoted to buttress this, making the Messiah the one who will hiss and gather (the Israelites). Finally, Zech 9:9 is also quoted of the Messiah's coming as a king, riding on a donkey.[45]

In light of the above materials, the first quite early, the latter quite late in their present form, it seems probable that in another section of Palestinian Judaism the Messiah was also capable of being described as a vulture, though here as the *raḥam* and not the *'ayiṭ*.

III. Gathering

Zech 10:8 is interpreted above to mean that the Messiah will gather (קבץ) the Jewish exiles. This belief is found at the latest already in the first century BCE in Palestine. Psalms of Solomon 17:32 speaks of the people's "king," "the Lord Messiah." Before this v 26 states that "he will gather (συνάξει) a holy people...."[46] Other references from the pseudepigrapha and rabbinic writings confirm this.[47] In the Synoptic Apocalypse the Son of Man will send out his angels, who on his behalf will gather

---

[42] Cf. LXX Zech 10:8, "I will redeem them."
[43] Sperber 3.491, Cathcart and Gordon 209.
[44] Cf. *Introduction* 388-389 on it.
[45] Albeck 239.
[46] *OTP* 2.667. On the dating, cf. R. Wright on pp. 640-641.
[47] Cf. the texts cited in Str-B 4.907-908.

(ἐπισυνάξουσιν) his elect from the whole world (Matt 24:31 par.).[48]

There thus may be a play on words in Matt 24:28 // Luke 13:37b. The Son of Man, who causes the elect to be "gathered" at the end of time, is the same as the vulture Messiah, who according to Judaic interpretation of Zech 10:8 will "gather" (the exiles from the diaspora). Of this vulture Messiah Matt 24:28 states in its original form: "Wherever the corpse is, there the vulture (*'ayiṭ*, the Messiah) will gather." The latter verb, συναχθήσεται in Greek, would be יִקָּבֵץ in Hebrew, or its Aramaic equivalent. After the vulture Messiah "gathers," he will cause his elect to be "gathered."

One reason I believe the vulture of Matt 24:28 was originally singular, suitable to the Messiah, is not only the singular "vulture" in Job 39:30, the biblical basis of the saying, and the Judaic tradition on the vulture Messiah cited in *b. Ḥull.* 63a above. Matt 24:28 also appears to have followed v 27 from the very beginning in Q: "For as the lightning comes from the east and flashes as far as the west, so will be the coming of the Son of Man." Here the Son of Man's "coming" would be the same as the vulture's (*'ayiṭ* – Messiah's) "gathering" in v 28, a fine parallelism. For theological reasons the Evangelist Luke separates the two sayings in 17:24 and 37b, unfortunately ruining their original parallelism.

IV. The Meaning of the Saying

The Q saying in Matt 24:28 and Luke 17:37b has been interpreted by scholars in a bewildering number of ways. At times one is tempted to agree with R. Bultmann that "it is impossible now to determine what was the original meaning...."[49] Several of the interpretations preferred are the following:

---

[48] Cf. also 13:41 for their negative counterparts.
[49] *The History of the Synoptic Tradition* (New York: Harper & Row, 1963) 169 in regard to Matt 24:28. Cf. also W. D. Davies and D. Allison, Jr., *The Gospel According to Saint Matthew* (Edinburgh: Clark, 1997) 3.355: "The meaning of this synthetic proverb is difficult." They list eight

1) J. Lightfoot believed that "Jerusalem, and that wicked nation which he [Jesus] described through the whole chapter, would be the carcase, to which the greedy and devouring eagles would fly to prey on it."⁵⁰ He interprets the eagles as the Roman soldiers with this bird on their standards.⁵¹
2) H. Meyer contended that the corpse / carcass are "the spiritually dead" who will incur the messianic punishment. The vultures are the angels the Messiah sends out.⁵²
3) W. F. Albright and C. S. Mann maintain that the Q saying appears to refer "either to the prostrate hopes of Judaism after A.D. 70, or to the apparent defeat of the Messiah in his death." They prefer the former.⁵³ To my knowledge no one else follows this interpretation.⁵⁴
4) W. Manson proposed that "Like vultures from carrion, judgment is inseparable from the body of sin and death."⁵⁵

---

possible interpretations. I. H. Marshall in *The Gospel of Luke* (Grand Rapids, Michigan: Eerdmans, 1978) 669 also relates several. H. Meyer in *Das Evangelium des Matthäus* (Meyers 1/1; Göttingen: Vandenhoeck & Ruprecht, 1844) 393 cites much earlier views.

⁵⁰ *A Commentary on the New Testament from the Talmud and Hebraica* (Peabody, MA: Hendrickson, 1989; original 1859) 2.319, referring to Matthew 24.

⁵¹ Cf. Josephus, *Bell.* 3.123 regarding Vespasian's army in Judea: "Next the ensigns surrounding the eagle, which in the Roman army precedes every legion, because it is the king and the bravest of all the birds: it is regarded by them as the symbol of empire, and, whoever may be their adversaries, an omen of victory." See also Pliny the Elder, *Natural History* X. 5, who assigns the eagle as the official badge of the legions to 104 BCE, although it also prevailed beforehand. Note also *b. Sanh.* 12a (Soncino 52, with n. 4).

⁵² *Das Evangelium des Matthäus* 392. Cf. L. Morris in *The Gospel according to Matthew* (Grand Rapids, Michigan: Eerdmans, 1992) 608: "The thought will be that the spiritually dead inevitably attract judgment."

⁵³ *Matthew* (AB 26; Garden City, New York: Doubleday, 1971) 296.

⁵⁴ Just as strange to me is L. T. Johnson's thought: "Vultures gather wherever there is carrion. The kingdom is wherever the people are gathered by God's word." Cf. his *The Gospel of Luke* (Sacra Pagina 3; Collegeville, Minnesota: The Liturgical Press, 1991) 267.

⁵⁵ *The Gospel of Luke* (Moffatts; London: Hodder and Stoughton, 1963) 200. Cf. also A. Schlatter, *Der Evangelist Matthäus* (Stuttgart: Calwer,

5) T. W. Manson noted the vulture's "almost incredible swiftness" and proposed that the Q saying draws attention to "the swiftness and suddenness of the coming of the day of the Son of Man."[56]
6) The Jewish scholar C. G. Montefiore maintained that "The Advent of the Messiah will be as little unnoticed by men as carcases are unnoticed by eagles."[57] J. Schniewind agreed, stating: "The Messiah will be apparent to all; just as certainly as carrion is espied by vultures, the Messiah will be seen by all."[58] J. Green similarly contends: "Just as the presence of carrion is indicated by circling vultures, so will his presence at the end be clearly evident."[59] D. Hagner notes that "as surely as you know that where you see vultures gathered there is a carcass, so you will not be able to miss the coming of the Son of Man."[60] Finally, A. Sand states that "the arrival

---

1929) 709: "Ist die Schuld reif und die Not so groß geworden, daß sie den Retter herbeiruft, dann wird er mit derselben unerwarteten aber völlig gewissen Sicherheit kommen, wie der Geier erscheint." W. Grundmann in his *Das Evangelium nach Matthäus* (THKNT 1; Berlin: Evangelische Verlagsanstalt, 1975[4]) 508 follows him at this point.

[56] *The Sayings of Jesus* (London: SCM Press, 1949) 147. In "The Gospel According to St. Luke" in *IB* (1952) 8.305, S. MacLean Gilmour notes that for Matthew the saying "seems to emphasize the suddenness with which the Son of man will appear." Cf. also F. Bovon, *Das Evangelium nach Lukas*, 3. Lk 15,1 – 19,27, p. 180: "Der Spruch unterstrich die Geschwindigkeit, mit der das Gericht Gottes kommen wird." Bovon maintains that in Q the saying must have had its place after the saying on lightning, so Matthew has the original order at this point.

[57] *The Synoptic Gospels* (New York: KTAV Publishing House, 1968) 2.313. He also calls attention to Job 39:30 here and offers two other possible interpretations.

[58] *Das Evangelium nach Matthäus* 244. Before this he compares the verse with the preceding one, saying that "the Son of man who comes from heaven appears like God himself, a judge whom no one can escape."

[59] *The Gospel of Luke* (NICNT 3; Grand Rapids, Michigan: Eerdmans, 1997) 636.

[60] *Matthew 14-28* (WBC 33B; Dallas, Texas: Word Books, 1995) 707, dealing with "the unmistakable character of the parousia."

of the Son of Man will be an event which cannot be missed."[61]

I have expanded on the sixth interpretation above because it agrees basically with my own view and seems to be gaining more and more adherents.[62] The Matthean connection with lightning appears to be the original sequence in the sayings source, Q. Both Matt 24:27 and 28 emphasize the clear nature of Jesus' future coming: it cannot be missed, just as one cannot miss something when lightning illuminates it at night, or when a very large vulture circles in the air over a particular site. Of course the Son of Man at his parousia will also later conduct judgment, yet the emphasis of the Matt 24:28 // Luke 13:37b saying on the Q level was on the clear character of Jesus' future coming: "You can't miss it!"

My own contribution to the above discussion lies on the originally Semitic level of Q,[63] which may have originated in a Jewish Christian community in Galilee near the Lake of Tiberias.[64] Hellenistic Jewish Christians later translated the *'ayiṭ* in the Semitic original into the plural, ἀετοί, vultures. There was precedent in the LXX for such a plural translation. Yet they did so because they were not cognizant of a Palestinian Jewish Semitic tradition which described the Messiah as a "vulture," *'ayiṭ*, singular. This is also the case for the vulture described in the Hebrew of Job 39:30, *nešer*, upon which the Q saying is primarily based, and for the vulture (*raḥam*) in Judaic tradition which by hissing announces the arrival of the Messiah, or

---

[61] *Das Evangelium nach Matthäus* (RNT; Regensburg: Pustet, 1965⁵) 488.
[62] Cf. it at the top of the list in W. D. Davies and D. Allison, Jr., *The Gospel According to Saint Matthew* 3.355-356, with n. 185.
[63] Against for example H. Guenther in "When 'Eagles' Draw Together" in *Forum* 5 (1989) 147, who speaks of the saying's LXX predecessors in Hab 1:8 and Job 39:27 and 30, and its inauthenticity. On the originally Aramaic background of traditions now found in Q, cf. now M. Casey, *An Aramaic Approach to Q. Sources for the Gospels of Matthew and Luke* (SNTSMS 122; Cambridge: Cambridge University Press, 2002).
[64] Cf. J. Reed, *Archaeology and the Galilean Jesus* (Harrisburg, Pennsylvania: Trinity Press International, 2000), chapter 6: "The Sayings Source Q in Galilee," pp. 170-196.

perhaps even its own arrival as the Messiah. The singular "vulture" in Matt 24:28 then correctly stands in parallelism to the Son of Man in v 27, with which it was originally connected in Q.

While no certainty can be attained in the matter, I see no compelling reason to deny the Q saying in Matt 24:28 // Luke 17:37b, as reconstructed above, to Jesus himself. Just as the *'ayiṭ* vulture tradition also lies behind John 8:56-58 (see the preceding chapter), and Jesus as a mother bird in Matt 23:37 // Luke 13:34 (see the next chapter), so here too the prophet from Nazareth employs imagery known to his fellow Palestinian Jews. They were both aware of, and appreciated, the Messiah described as a vulture. Unfortunately this knowledge was lost in the Greek-speaking Christian communities, already at the level of Greek Q. Finally, modern people of the Western world in general consider the vulture imagery of Matt 24:28 // Luke 17:37b to be grisly and gruesome, even "widerlich und abstoßend." If they become aware of its messianic significance, they will hopefully change their minds.

Chapter Seven

The Rejection of the Mother Bird Messiah in Luke 13:34b // Matt 23:37b

Introduction

In the Q passage Luke 13:34-35 // Matt 23:37-39[1] Jesus is represented as castigating Jerusalem[2] for killing the prophets and stoning those sent to it. Then he utters a sentence which became famous even before the advent of feministic theology: "How often have I desired to gather your (sing.) children together as a (mother) bird gathers her brood under (her) wings, but you (pl.) did not want it!" (Luke 13:34b // Matt 23:37b).

The latter statement has been described as "such words of poignant melancholy"[3] and "a most tender metaphor."[4]

---

[1] For relevant secondary literature, cf. U. Lutz, *Das Evangelium nach Matthäus (Mt 18-25)* (EKKNT 1/3; Zurich: Benziger; Neukirchen-Vluyn: Neukirchener, 1997) 376; W. D. Davies and D. Allison, Jr., *The Gospel According to Saint Matthew* (ICC; Edinburgh: Clark, 1997) 3.325; and F. Bovon, *Das Evangelium nach Lukas (Lk 9,51 - 14,35)* (EKKNT 3/2; Zurich: Benziger; Neukirchen-Vluyn: Neukirchener, 1996) 442-443.

[2] Cf. similar language in Luke 10:13-15 // Matt 11:21-24 employed of the towns Chorazin, Bethsaida and Capernaum in regard to the (day of) Judgment. Luke in 10:16 appends the motif of rejecting Jesus in this context.

[3] S. MacLean Gilmore, "The Gospel According to St. Luke" in *IB* (1952) 8.250.

[4] D. Hagner, *Matthew 14-28* (WBC 33B; Dallas, Texas: Word Books, 1995) 679. In contrast to him I see no "burst of warm sunshine" at this point in Matthew. See also T. Robinson, *The Gospel of Matthew* (Moffatt's; London: Hodder and Stoughton, 1928/1960) 193: the

M. Davies correctly notes that "This is the only metaphor in the Gospel which draws attention to a mother's rather than a father's care for children."[5] The following study presents the Palestinian Judaic background of the imagery present in this saying.

It has long been recognized that the pericope Luke 13:34-35 // Matt 23:37-39 is of Semitic origin.[6] Many commentators, like the NRSV, simply assume that a female chicken, a "hen," is meant by the Greek term ὄρνις here. In *Lev. Rab.* Kedoshim 25/5, commenting on Job 38:36, R. Levi, a third generation Palestinian Amora,[7] for example relates in Aramaic regarding a תַּרְנְגָלְתָּא [8] : "The hen, when its young are little, gathers them and puts them under its wings, warming them and picking before them."[9] This contains some of the imagery found in Luke 13:34b // Matt 23:37b.

Yet as others have pointed out, an ὄρνις is not necessarily a hen.[10] The primary meaning is "*bird*, including birds of prey and

---

pericope "is one of the most striking and impressive of the utterances of Jesus." U. Luz in *Das Evangelium nach Matthäus (Mt 18-25)* 378 notes the "Symmetrie dieses formvollendeten Unheilwortes...." T. Manson in *The Sayings of Jesus* (London: SCM Press, 1949) 126 speaks of it as "a passage of deep pathos."

[5] Cf. her *Matthew* (Sheffield: JSOT Press, 1993) 164.

[6] Cf. J. Wellhausen, *Das Evangelium Lucae* (Berlin: Reimer, 1904) 76; I. Marshall, *Commentary on Luke* (NIGTC; Grand Rapids, Michigan: Eerdmans, 1978/1992) 575; W. Grundmann, *Das Evangelium nach Lukas* (THKNT 3; Berlin: Evangelische Verlangsanstalt, 1984[10]) 289; J. Wellhausen, *Das Evangelium Matthei* (Berlin: Reimer, 1914) 115; A. Mc Neile, *The Gospel According to St Matthew* (New York: St Martin's Press, 1915/1965) 341-342; A. Sand, *Das Evangelium nach Matthäus* (RNT; Regensburg: Pustet, 1986) 475; and U. Luz, *Das Evangelium nach Matthäus (Mt 18-25)* 380, n. 30, who after noting specific features concludes: "The logion appears to be translated quite literally from the Semitic."

[7] Strack and Stemberger, *Introduction* 98.

[8] Jastrow 1700; תַּרְנְגוֹלֶת in Hebrew.

[9] Mirqin 8.65; cf. Soncino 4.317. P. Billerbeck had already called attention to this passage in Str-B 1.943.

[10] Cf. A. Mc Neile, *The Gospel According to St Matthew* 342; S. Johnson, "The Gospel According to St. Matthew" in *IB* (1951) 7.540; and R.

domestic fowls."[11] Only the context in the above Q saying shows that a "mother" bird is meant. The Semitic original could have been the Aramaic עוֹפָא, Hebrew עוֹף,[12] or possibly the Aramaic צִפּוֹרָא, Hebrew צִפּוֹר.[13] In the following, especially section III. on Deut 32:11, I propose that a specific bird of prey, the (mother) vulture, is meant in the Q saying. In section I., I briefly analyze Isa 31:5, in section II. Deut 22:6-7, and in section IV. I make suggestions as to the original meaning, setting and author of the unit Luke 13:34-35 // Matt 23:37-39.

I. Isa 31:5

One of the major passages in the Hebrew Bible dealing with the Lord's protecting Jerusalem is Isa 31:5.[14] Verse 4 first states that the Lord of hosts will come down to fight upon Mount Zion and upon its hill. The *Targum* renders this eschatologically by: "so shall the kingdom of the Lord of hosts be revealed to dwell upon Mount Zion, and upon the hill thereof."[15] Verse 5 then reads: "Like birds hovering, so the Lord of hosts will protect Jerusalem. He will protect and deliver, spare and rescue (it). "

The term "birds" here is the plural of צִפֹּר.[16] The *Targum* reduces this to the singular, עוֹפָא, "bird,"[17] adapting the image more closely to the singular "the Lord of hosts." It reads: "Like a bird which hovers, so shall the might (v. l. kingdom) of the Lord

---

Gundry, *Matthew*. A Commentary on His Handbook for a Mixed Church under Persecution (Grand Rapids, Michigan: Eerdmans, 1994²) 473: "ὄρνις may refer to any kind of mother bird."
[11] LSJ 1254. BAGD 582 do not mention the possibility of a bird of prey.
[12] Jastrow 1055. Cf. the עוֹפָא of *Targ*. Isa 31:5 cited in section I. below.
[13] Jastrow 1298 and 1295-1296.
[14] J. Jeremias in *The Parables of Jesus* (New York: Scribner's, 1962⁶) 167-168 even considers this the main biblical reference behind the Q saying Luke 13:34b // Matt 23:37b.
[15] Stenning 102-103.
[16] BDB 861-862. In *b. Ber.* 56b (Soncino 347-348) it is stated that if one dreams of a bird, this signifies peace, which is buttressed by Isa 31:5. The Lord's role as protector and deliverer is probably meant.
[17] Stenning 102-103.

of hosts be revealed over Jerusalem. He will protect and deliver, He will rescue and set (it) free."[18] Here too the eschatological period is meant.

The Hebrew participle "hovering" in v 5 is עָפוֹת , from עוּף, to fly. Here it means to "hover (protectingly)"[19] as in Deut 32:11, to be analyzed below in section III. The *Targum* renders it similarly.[20]

The Hebrew verb twice translated as "to protect" in Isa 31:5 is גָּנַן , which means to "cover, surround, defend."[21] The Lord's "covering" or protecting Jerusalem like a bird, together with His "hovering" over it, is one part of the background of Jesus' longing to gather Jerusalem's children, as a mother bird gathers her brood under her wings, in Luke 13:34b // Matt 23:37b.

II. Deut 22:6-7

Luke 13:34b speaks in regard to the mother bird of "her brood," τὴν ἑαυτῆς νοσσιάν , from νοσσιά .[22] The Matthean parallel in 23:37 reads τὰ νοσσία αὐτῆς, also "her brood," but from the plural of νοσσίον .[23] Both nouns are found only here in the NT.

The latter Greek noun, νοσσίον, is employed only once in the LXX, where, also in the plural, in Ps 83:3 (Heb 84:4) it translates the Hebrew אֶפְרֹחֶיהָ , "its [her] young ones, young,"[24] thus also

---

[18] *Ibid.*, slightly modified.
[19] BDB 733, 1. b.
[20] For this meaning of טוּס, cf. Jastrow 525 with an example of the soul "hovering" over the body. Against Stenning's "to fly swiftly," another possible meaning.
[21] BDB 170-171; Jastrow 260: to protect, surround. Cf. the saying of R. Ishmael (ben Elisha), a second generation Tanna (*Introduction* 79), in *Mek. R. Ish.* Pisḥa 7 on Exod 12:13 (Lauterbach 1.56) on the Lord's protecting in Isa 31:5. A parallel is found in Pisḥa 11 on Exod 12:23 (Lauterbach 1.87).
[22] Cf. BAGD 543 on νοσσιά, 2., as well as LSJ 1169 on νεοσσιά, νοσσιά, 2. "Nest" is not meant here.
[23] BAGD 543; LSJ 1169 on νεοσσίον , νοσσίον : nestling, chick.
[24] Cf. BDB 827 on אֶפְרֹחַ.

"brood." Jesus probably alludes to this psalm verse, "Even the sparrow finds a home, and the swallow a nest for herself, where she may lay 'her young'" (v 3, Eng.), in Luke 9:58 // Matt 8:20.

The very similar νεοσσός, "young bird, nestling, chick,"[25] is employed in the plural in LXX Job 39:30 of the vulture's "young ones," in Hebrew the sing. אֶפְרֹחָו, "its young ones" or "brood." Jesus alludes to the second part of this verse in Matt 24:28 // Luke 17:37b (see the preceding chapter).

The noun νεοσσός in the plural is found in LXX Deut 22:6 twice, where it also translates the Hebrew אֶפְרֹחִים . It thus seems very probable that the Lukan τῆς ἑαυτῆς νοσσιάν and the Matthean τὰ νοσσία αὐτῆς are translation variants of a Semitic original, either the Aramaic אֶפְרֹחַיָּה,[26] or the Hebrew אֶפְרֹחֶיהָ.[27]

When Semitic-speaking Palestinian Jewish Christians first heard the expression "its [her] brood" as found in the above Q saying, they would very probably have thought of Deut 22:6, together with Ps 84:4 and Job 39:30 one of only three occurrences of אֶפְרֹחַ, "brood," "young ones," "chicks" in the MT.

Deut 22:6-7 reads in the NRSV:

> 6) If you come on a bird's nest, in any tree or on the ground, with fledglings or eggs, with the mother sitting on the fledglings or the eggs, you shall not take the mother with the young.
> 7) Let the mother go, taking only the young for yourself, in order that it may go well with you and you may live long.

R. Simeon b. Yoḥai, a third generation Tanna,[28] taught that in comparison with honoring one's father and mother (Deut 5:16),

---

[25] LSJ 1169.
[26] Jastrow 108.
[27] Both the Hebrew New Testaments of Delitzsch (pp. 46 and 136) and the United Bible Societies (pp. 68 and 197) have this reading in the Matthean and Lukan verses. If the Semitic original was עוֹפָא or עוֹף, the suffix would of course also have been masculine. The context, however, showed that a mother bird was meant.
[28] Introduction 84.

the least onerous precept in the Torah is the above.²⁹ According to *m. Ḥull.* 12:1 it was binding in regard to non-captive birds "both in the Land [of Israel] and outside the Land, both during the time of the Temple and after the time of the Temple...."³⁰ *Deut. Rab.* Ki Teṣe 6/7 on Deut 22:6 states that "If you will fulfill this precept, you will hasten thereby the coming of the Messiah."³¹ The Deuteronomy passage is relevant to the Q saying in Luke 13:34b // Matt 23:37b in three respects.

1. Brood and Young Ones / Children

The term אֶפְרֹחִים in Deut 22:6 is translated "fledglings" in the NRSV. Above it was rendered "young ones," "brood," "nestlings" or "chicks." In verses 5 and 6 these are also labeled בָּנִים, literally "sons," also meant as "children" and the "young" of animals.³² It is the usual Hebrew background of τέκνα in the LXX.³³

The Q saying of Luke 13:34b // Matt 23:37b has Jesus address the city of Jerusalem with the words: "How often have I desired

---

²⁹ *Pesiq. R.* 23/24.2 (Friedmann 121b, Braude 495). Cf. also *Tanḥ.* B 'Eqeb 3 on Deut 3:12 (Buber 17, Bietenhard 2.462) and *Tanḥ.* 'Eqeb 2 (Eshkol 862), as well as *y. Pe'ah* 1:1, 3d (Neusner / Brooks 2.56) and *Deut. Rab.* Ki Teṣe 6/2 on Deut 22:6 (Mirqin 11.100, Soncino 7.122). For the small monetary value involved in keeping the precept, see *m. Ḥull.* 12:5 (Albeck 5.149, Danby 529).
³⁰ Albeck 5.148, Danby 528. The precept was known as שִׁלּוּחַ הַקֵּן, "Let [the mother bird] go from the nest."
³¹ Mirqin 11.102, Soncino 7.125. It is based on the term *shiluaḥ* in Isa 32:20, where the "donkey" is interpreted as that of the well-known messianic verse Zech 9:9. J. Rabbinowitz (7.125, n. 2) maintains that in his edition of *Tanḥuma* Vayyishlaḥ on Gen 32:6, the Messiah is referred to by Isa 32:20. The Eshkol edition (1.130) of *Tanḥ.* Vayyishlaḥ 1 on Gen 32:6 (Eng. 5) refers the "donkey" of the verse to the Messiah, the son of David, on the basis of Zech 9:9, as does *Tanḥ.* B Vayyishlaḥ 5 on the same verse (Buber 164, Bietenhard 2.183), with the King Messiah. Yet neither cites Isa 32:20. R. Huna, however, does associate Isa 32:20 with Deut 22:6-7 in *b. Ḥull.* 141b (Soncino 819-820).
³² BDB 121, 2. and 4.
³³ Cf. Hatch-Redpath 1340-1342. LXX Deut 22:6 has τῶν τέκτων, but in v 7 τὰ δὲ παιδία.

to gather 'your children' together as a mother bird gathers 'her brood' under her wings." As pointed out above, the Semitic original of her "brood" here was probably the Aramaic אֶפְרוֹחִין, or possibly the Hebrew אֶפְרֹחַ as a collective plural, or the pl. אֶפְרֹחִים. The Greek τὰ τέκνα σου, "your children," would have been the Aramaic בְּנַיְכִי or the Hebrew בָּנַיִךְ.[34]

Since Deut 22:6 has two of the only four occurrences of "brood" in the MT, it is probable that its parallelism there with "young ones / children" influenced the formulation of the Q saying in Luke 13:34b // Matt 23:37b, where the corresponding Greek terms are also parallel.

2. Often

The Tannaitic midrash *Sifre Ki Teṣe* § 228 on Deut 22:7 states that letting the mother bird go [while taking its brood / young ones from the nest] is a positive commandment. If one releases her and she returns (חזרה), [seeking to protect her young ones by brooding over them again], he must release her [a second time], and if she again returns (חזרה), he must release her [a third time]. Even if this happens "five times" (חמש פעמים), he is obligated to release her, as it is said: "You shall indeed release her."[35] In *m. Ḥull.* 12:3 on Deut 22:6-7, "even four or five times" (אפילו ארבעה וחמשה פעמים) is stated,[36] and *b. Meṣ.* 31a has "even a hundred times" (אפילו מאה פעמים).[37]

"Even if" (אֲפִילוּ)[38] five "times" (פְּעָמִים)[39] is the equivalent of "as often as five times." One could paraphrase the latter by "how often." 1 Kgs 22:16 (// 2 Chr 18:15) for example has "How

---

[34] Cf. the Hebrew New Testaments of Delitzsch and the United Bible Societies on these verses.
[35] This "indeed" is based on the doubling of the Hebrew verb: שלח תשלח.
[36] Albeck 5.149, Danby 529.
[37] Soncino 193.
[38] Jastrow 103.
[39] BDB 822, 3. a. on פַּעַם; Jastrow 1203.

many times...?" This is the Hebrew עַד־כַּמֶּה פְּעָמִים, which is translated in the LXX (3 Kgdms 22:16) as ποσάκις.[40]

I thus suggest that early Judaic tradition on the very well-known passage Deut 22:6-7, which later entered the Mishna at Ḥull. 12:3, provided the background for the expression ποσάκις in the Q saying of Luke 13:34b // Matt 23:37b. It reads: "'How often' have I desired to gather your children together as a mother bird gathers her brood under her wings." Here the term "how often" is associated with the "brood" and "children" of a mother bird, as is the similar expression "even ... times" with the other two terms in Judaic tradition on Deut 22:6-7.

3. Protective and Merciful Care

a) *Protective Care*

In *m. Ḥull.* 12:3, dealing with Deut 22:6-7, it is stated that the mother bird brooding on its nest must be let go "if the fledglings / young ones / brood 'need' their mother" (אַף הָאֶפְרוֹחִים צְרִיכִין לְאִמָּן). They are not yet able to fly (away in case of great danger).[41] B. *Ḥull.* 78b speaks of the parent "to whom the young clings" (בנו כרוך אחריו).[42] Such a fledgling only "hops away" as long as the nest is still in sight.[43] LXX Deut 22:6 notes that at this stage the mother bird still "warms" or "tends with fostering care" (θάλπω)[44] the fledglings. She protects them for

---

[40] Cf. the כַּמֶּה פְּעָמִים of Delitzsch in his Hebrew New Testament on Matt 23:37 (p. 46) and Luke 13:34 (p. 136), as well as the United Bible Societies' כַּמֶּה פְּעָמִים on the two verses (pp. 68 and 197).
[41] Albeck 5.149, Danby 529. T. *Ḥull.* 10:11 (Zuckermandel / Liebermann 512, Neusner 5.98) similarly speaks of "nestlings which have flown and do not require their dam." Here they are also called בנים. *Sifre Ki Teṣe* § 227 on Deut 22:6 (Finkelstein 259, Hammer 237) states that one may take the mother bird under the condition that "the young must be capable of survival."
[42] Soncino 438. Cf. Jastrow 668 on כָּרַךְ : cling to.
[43] Cf. *b. Beṣa* 11a (Soncino 51) with the verb דדי, דדה (Jastrow 280-281, with other references to young birds' "hopping" away from their nest).
[44] LSJ 783, heat, warm, keep warm; III. 2, tend with fostering care.

The Rejection of the Mother Bird Messiah

example from a cat,[45] a weasel,[46] a marten,[47] a hawk,[48] a falcon,[49] and of course humans (Deut 22:6–7). The above are all examples of a mother bird's tender, protective care of her fledglings / young ones / brood, especially when severe danger approaches.

b) Merciful Care

Lev 22:28 states that "you shall not slaughter, from the herd or the flock, an animal [a mother] with its young on the same day." Referring to this prohibition, *Deut. Rab.* Ki Teṣe 6/1 on Deut 21:10 and 22:6 notes: "in the same way that God 'had compassion' (רַחֲמִין ... נָתַן) upon the cattle, so too was God filled with 'mercy' (רַחֲמִים) for the birds," as in Deut 22:6.[50] That is, if one takes a nesting mother's fledglings, one is obligated to let her go free.

The Mishna at *Meg.* 4:9 refers to the above phenomenon. It states that if a man said [in his prayer]: "Even to a bird's nest do 'Your mercies' (רַחֲמֶיךָ) extend," he is to be put to silence.[51] The reasons are given in *b. Meg.* 25a[52] and *y. Meg.* 4:9, 75c.[53] Once a reader (in the synagogue) even prayed before Rabbah,

---

[45] Cf. *b. 'Erub.* 100b (Soncino 698); *B. Qam.* 15b (Soncino 67); *Ḥull.* 52b (Soncino 287-288); and *Cant. Rab.* 7:2 § 1 (Soncino 9.277).

[46] Cf. *b. Ber.* 60b (Soncino 380); *Pesaḥ.* 8b (Soncino 36); *Ḥull.* 53a (Soncino 288) and 56b (Soncino 310). A weasel's wounding a bird in the head is already found in *m. Ḥull.* 3:3 (5.124 in Albeck, 518 in Danby).

[47] Cf. *m. B. Bat.* 2:5 in regard to a dovecot (Albeck 4.121, Danby 367).

[48] Cf. *m. Ḥull.* 3:1 (Albeck 5.123, Danby 517). In *b. Ḥull.* 52b (Soncino 287) cat, hawk, marten and weasel are mentioned together. P. Bonnard in *L'Évangile selon Saint Matthieu* (CNT 1; Geneva: Labor et Fides, 1992³) 344 also notes a sparrow-hawk and a cat. T. Robinson in *The Gospel of Matthew* 194 had already called attention to a hawk in 1928.

[49] Cf. *m. Ḥull.* 3:1 (Albeck 5.123, Danby 517). The latter translates בַּז as vulture, but it is a falcon; see Jastrow 260, and 228 on בַּז.

[50] Mirqin 11.99, Soncino 7.121.

[51] Albeck 2.367-368, Danby 207.

[52] Soncino 149-150.

[53] Neusner 19.167. A parallel with "To [עַל, not עַד] a bird's nest..." is found in *m. Ber.* 5:3 (Albeck 1.22, Danby 6), *b. Ber.* 33b (Soncino 209), and *y. Ber.* 5:3, 9c (Neusner / Zahavy 1.211).

probably a third generation Babylonian Amora:[54] "You have shown 'kindness' (חֶסֶד) to the bird's nest, now show pity and 'mercy' (רַחֵם) to us."[55]

Early Judaic sources thus associate the precept of Deut 22:6-7 with God's "mercy" or compassion: רַחֲמִים.[56] Since the most common vulture found in Palestine was and is the רָחָם,[57] the statement found in *Pesiq. R.* 23/24.2 is understandable: "let the vulture (נֶשֶׁר), which is 'merciful' (רַחֲמָן),[58] come and eat" the eye of one who does not keep Deut 22:6-7.[59]

Another biblical passage which exemplifies the mother vulture's mercy in regard to its young is Deut 32:11, to which I now turn.

---

[54] *Introduction* 102.
[55] Cf. *b. Ber.* 33b (Soncino 209), with a parallel in *b. Meg.* 25a (Soncino 149-150).
[56] BDB 933, Jastrow 1468.
[57] See BDB 934, Jastrow 1467, and chapter six, section III. above.
[58] Jastrow 1468. Another example of the *neṣer's* merciful behavior is Tannaitic comment on Exod 19:4, "how I bore you on eagles' wings and brought you to Myself," in *Mek. R. Ish.* Baḥodesh 2 (Lauterbach 2.202-203). Other birds carry their young (בְּנֵיהֶם) between their feet since they fear the birds flying above them. Yet the *neṣer* only fears a human, who could shoot at him. It prefers that the arrow hit it rather than its young. As remarked above, *neṣer* can mean both eagle and vulture. People have observed an eagle's swooping down and catching its fledgling on its back when the latter falls out of the nest or is learning to fly. See V. Dröscher, ... *und der Wal schleuderte Jona an Land. Die Tierwunder der Bibel naturwissenschaftlich erklärt* (Goldmann; Hamburg: Rasch und Röhring Verlag, 1987) 80-83. He refers to Exod 19:4 on p. 80, and to Deut 32:11 (on a vulture) on p. 83.
[59] Friedmann 121b; I modify Braude 495, who translates "compassionate." G. R. Driver in "Birds in the Old Testament" in *PEQ* 87 (1955) 8 points out in regard to the *neṣer*: "griffon-vultures begin the consumption of their victims by attacking the eyes and other soft parts of the body before piercing the abdomen...."

III. Deut 32:11

In the "Song of Moses" (Deut 32:1-43), the Israelites are asked to "remember the days of old," to "consider the years long past" (v 7). To this period belongs the care God bestowed on His people after the exodus when they wandered in the wilderness for forty years,[60] vv 10-14.

In this wilderness waste the Lord "encompassed,"[61] "cared for"[62] and "guarded"[63] Israel as the apple of His eye (v 10). The Tannaitic commentary *Sifre Ha'azinu* 313 mentions at this point the well, manna, quails and the cloud of glory as examples of such divine care. Indeed, "everything was prepared and supplied to them."[64] *Num. Rab.* Bemidbar 2/6 on Num 2:2 asks in regard to the above verbs in Deut 32:10, "To what extent did He love them, to what extent did He guard them, to what extent did He preserve them [from dangers]? As it were, even as much 'as the apple of His eye.'"[65]

Deut 32:11 then makes a very positive comparison with the protective care a mother vulture renders to its fledglings / young:

> As a [mother] vulture stirs up its nest,
> hovering over its young,
> spreading out its wings,
> taking them and bearing them up upon its pinions.

---

[60] Cf. Exod 16:35.
[61] Cf. BDB 685-686 on סבב : surround, encompass, here with protection. See Ps 32:10 for its use with חֶסֶד, God's "lovingkindness" (339).
[62] Cf. BDB 107 on בִּין, po'el: "he attentively considereth him" (only here).
[63] Cf. BDB 665 on נצר, 2., guard from dangers, preserve.
[64] Finkelstein 355, Hammer 320. See also *Pesiq. Rav Kah.* 3 on Deut 25:17 (Mandelbaum 35, Braude and Kapstein 40), which mentions seven clouds of glory, manna, quail and "all they needed." On the latter, see the verb αὐταρκέω at LXX Deut 32:10 - to supply with necessities (LSJ 278).
[65] Mirqin 9.25, Soncino 5.27-28. Cf. similar traditions in *Tanḥ.* Bemidbar 13 on Num 2:2 (Eshkol 657) and *Tanḥ.* B 14 on the same verse (Buber 13, Bietenhard 2.206).

Verse 12a then concludes the above comparison: "[so] the Lord alone 'will guide him' [Israel]." Early Judaic tradition understood the latter verb (יַנְחֶ֑נּוּ),[66] in the imperfect, to refer to the future,[67] when the end[68] or the day of Judgment arrives,[69] when God will punish Esau (wicked Rome).[70] Since the verbs in v 11 are also in the imperfect, that verse also lent itself to being interpreted of the time to come, when judgment will take place. As in the NRSV, vv 11-12 belong together.

The נֶ֫שֶׁר of Deut 32:11 is not an eagle, as often assumed, but a vulture, more precisely the griffon vulture (*gyps fulvus*).[71] I suggest that this bird's protective care of its young provides a major part of the imagery behind the Q saying in Luke 13:34b // Matt 23:37b.

1. Desiring / Yearning / Longing

a) Luke 13:34b // Matt 23:37b has Jesus address Jerusalem with the words: "How often 'have I desired' (ἠθέλησα) to gather your children together as a mother bird gathers her brood under her wings, but[72] 'you were' not 'willing' (ἠθελήσατε)." The

---

[66] BDB 634 on נחה. This agrees with the imperfect form of the verbs in v 11.
[67] Cf. *Sifre* Ha'azinu 315 on this verse (Finkelstein 357, Hammer 321), *Pesiq. R.* 10/4 (Friedmann 36a, Braude 176), and *Tanḥ.* Terumah 9 (Eshkol 364).
[68] Cf. *Lev. Rab.* Aḥare Moth 23/5 on Lev 18:3 (Mirqin 8.46, Soncino 4.295).
[69] Cf. *Midr. Pss.* 2/14 (Buber 31-32, Braude 1.45-46).
[70] Cf. *Tanḥ.* B Tsav 4 on Lev 6:2 (Buber 15-16, Bietenhard 2.28). In *Tanḥ.* Shofeṭim 19 on Deut 20:10 (Eshkol 505), Deut 32:12 is associated with the messianic King and Isa 11:4.
[71] Cf. J. Feliks, art. "Vultures" in *EJ* (1971) 16.232-233. In regard to Deut 32:11 he states: "The fledgling develops slowly, and the parents tend it with devotion and train it to fly...." See also S. R. Driver, *Deuteronomy* (ICC 5; Edinburgh: Clark, 1960) 357: "Tristram's argument (see on 14, 12) that *nésher* is not the eagle, but the Griffon-vulture, seems irresistible...."
[72] The Semitic behind καί here was certainly *waw* (ו) meant as "but" (BDB 252, 1. e; Jastrow 371), not "and."

The Rejection of the Mother Bird Messiah

Greek θέλω means "wish (of desire)," "want" to do something.[73] Jesus frequently "wanted to / desired to" gather Jerusalem's children, but they did not "want / desire" this. The same term is thus employed here for the offer as for the rejection of the offer. The Semitic original was probably רצי , רצה ,[74] or possibly חפץ,[75] the same word in both cases.

Jesus' desiring / wanting here derives from Judaic tradition on Deut 32:11.

b) The Septuagint of Deuteronomy probably goes back to the third century BCE.[76] For the first half of 32:11 it reads: ὡς ἀετὸς σκεπάσαι νοσσιὰν αὐτοῦ καὶ ἐπὶ τοῖς νεοσσοῖς αὐτοῦ ἐπεπόθησεν... : "As a vulture 'wants to cover / protect' its brood and 'desires' its young...."

The first Greek verb is σκεπάσαι, the aorist optative of σκεπάζω, to cover / shelter / protect.[77] The optative expresses a wish.[78] Here it expresses the vulture's wish or desire to cover or protect its brood. The root of the second Greek verb is ἐπιποθέω, to desire or yearn for.[79] The vulture is represented as similarly "desiring," "yearning for" its young.

These two verbs are not found in the MT, which instead has the vulture "stir up" (עור)[80] its nest and "hover over" (רחף)[81] its young. That is, the (mother) vulture's wish to cover / shelter / protect her brood, her desiring or yearning for her young, is a very early Judaic interpretation of Deut 32:11.

---

[73] BAGD 354-355.
[74] Jastrow 1494 and 1493, 2).
[75] Jastrow 492. Cf. the Hebrew New Testament of Delitzsch, which employs both terms (46 and 136), as do the United Bible Societies (68 and 197).
[76] Cf. O. Eissfeldt, *The Old Testament. An Introduction* (Oxford: Blackwell, 1966) 605 and 702.
[77] Cf. LSJ 1606 on σκεπάζω. I thank Dr. U. Victor of Berlin for confirming my analysis of the verb here.
[78] Cf. BDF § 384 (p. 194).
[79] LSJ 652: desire besides or yearn after; feel the want of.
[80] BDB 734: rouse oneself, awake; hiphil *rouse, stir up* to activity.
[81] BDB 934: here the piel of a "vulture *hovering* over young."

I suggest that it (in Palestine) was the source of the very similar terminology of the Q saying described in a) above. A similar phenomenon occurred in regard to v 10, where the Hebrew "He *found* him in a desert land" was rendered by the LXX as αὐτάρκησεν, He "supplied with necessities" the Israelites in the wilderness. This term is reflected in *Sifre*'s comment on the verse described above: "everything was prepared and supplied to them."

2. Young

Deut 32:11 says the (mother) vulture hovers over "its young." This is the Hebrew גּוֹזָלָיו. The term גּוֹזָל, "young" of birds,[82] is only found here and in Gen 15:9 (see chapter five above on this verse). It is a synonym of אֶפְרֹחִים / אֶפְרֹחַ in *Targ*. Ps 84:4,[83] as well as in *Pal. Targ.*[84] and *Targ. Neofiti 1* [85] on Deut 22:6, analyzed above in section II. as part of the background of the Q saying in Luke 13:34b // Matt 23:37b. This aided the Palestinian Jewish Christian author of the latter saying in thinking of Judaic traditions on the two Deuteronomy passages, 22:6 and 33:11, in regard to a mother bird's protective care for her "young."

3. To Be Anxious About, Care For

Deut 32:11 states that the (mother) vulture "hovers" over its young. The Hebrew יְרַחֵף is the piel imperfect of רָחַף, to "hover."[86] While the text originally implied the mother bird's fluttering directly above its young[87] in order to encourage them to leave the nest and learn to fly, Palestinian Judaic tradition interpreted the verb differently.

---

[82] BDB 160, Jastrow 220.
[83] Merino 143, de Lagarde 50.
[84] Rieder 2.285.
[85] Díez Macho 5.185.
[86] BDB 934.
[87] Cf. *t. Hag.* 2:6 (Zuckermandel / Liebermann 234, Neusner 2.313), which has Ben Zoma, a second generation Tanna *(Introduction* 82), quote Deut 32:11-12 regarding the vulture's "fluttering above its nest, touching and not touching," as being similar to the extremely small distance between the upper and the lower waters.

The usually reticent *Targum Onqelos* here has מְתַחֲפֵף, from חפף.[88] The verb can mean to bend over, cover, but also "to be anxious, care."[89] The *Palestinian Targum* employs the same verb,[90] as does the *Fragment Targum*.[91] That is, when Palestinian Jews heard this rendering of a vulture's "hovering" over its young, they also thought simultaneously of the mother bird's concern, her "care" for the latter.

Here the mother vulture "hovers" over its young, it is anxious about / cares for them. The only other occurrence of the verb רחף in the MT occurs in Gen 1:2,[92] where the spirit of God "hovers" over the face of the waters at creation. This "spirit" (רוּחַ) of God was interpreted in Judaic sources of the Messiah.[93] The latter may have encouraged Palestinian Jewish Christians to have Jesus, their Messiah, speak in terms of Deut 32:11 in Luke 13:34b // Matt 23:37b. (For the messianic interpretation of Deut 32:11, see section 5. below.)

4. Wings as Protection

The Q saying of Luke 13:34b // Matt 23:37b has Jesus say: "How often have I desired to gather your children together as a mother bird gathers her brood under her 'wings.'" The latter is the plural of the Greek πτέρυξ, "wing."[94] With only one

---

[88] Drazin 275.
[89] Jastrow 492.
[90] Rieder 2.302. E. Clarke in *Targum Pseudo-Jonathan: Deuteronomy* reads: "and is anxious about its young."
[91] Klein 1.226 and 2.183 on MS "V." Cf. also the use of the verb חוּשׁ, to be anxious (Jastrow 441,3), for the vulture's being "anxious" about its nest in *Targum Onqelos* (Drazin 275) and the *Palestinian Targum* (Rieder 2.302).
[92] Cf. *t. Ḥag.* 2:6 in n. 87, where Ben Zoma cites both Gen 1:2 and Deut 32:11, with a parallel in *y. Ḥag.* 2:1, 77a-b (Neusner 20.44), as well as *Midr. Pss.* 93/5 on Ps 93:3 (Buber 414, Braude 2.126).
[93] Cf. the sources I cite in *"Caught in the Act," Walking on the Sea, and the Release of Barabbas Revisited* 110-115.
[94] BAGD 727.

exception this always translates the Hebrew כָּנָף in the LXX.⁹⁵ It is quite probable that the "wing" imagery above also derives from Deut 32:11. In *Mek. R. Šim. b. Yoḥ.* on Exod 19:4, for example, R. Eliezer b. R. Yose the Galilean, a third generation Tanna,⁹⁶ comments on Deut 32:11 by stating that "the way of the vulture is to be guardful of its young by using 'its wings' so that they should not be agitated."⁹⁷

In Deut 32:11 the mother vulture "spreads its wings": יִפְרֹשׂ כְּנָפָיו. The LXX also has πτέρυγας, "wings," at this point. The verb פָּרַשׂ means to spread out.⁹⁸ Here the mother bird spreads out her wings before teaching her young to leave the nest and fly. Elsewhere in the MT, wings express the Lord's protecting His people. Ps 91:4 states for example: "He will cover you with His pinions, and 'under His wings' you will find refuge." The same expression is found in Ruth 2:12. These two instances are similar to the phrase "under his wings" in the Q saying above.⁹⁹ In the First Temple in Jerusalem the cherubim "spread out their wings," signifying God's (protective) presence there.¹⁰⁰ When Jesus is represented as a mother bird gathering her brood under her wings, he at first sight appears to assume an attribute of God, who so protects His people.¹⁰¹

---

⁹⁵ Cf. Hatch-Redpath 1238. On the wing(s) of birds in the MT, see BDB 489, 1. a.
⁹⁶ *Introduction* 85.
⁹⁷ Epstein / Melamed 138. The verb form מסופף, "to be guardful," most probably derives from סַף (BDB 706), stand at or guard the threshold.
⁹⁸ BDB 831, with references to wings under 1.
⁹⁹ For other references to wings as expressing God's protecting His people, cf. BDB 489, 1. h. In Ps 36:8-9 (Eng. 7-8) "Your wings" is parallel to "Your house," the Jerusalem Temple. This is another reason for interpreting the "house" of Luke 13:35a // Matt 23:38 as the Temple.
¹⁰⁰ Cf. Exod 25:20; 37:9; 1 Kgs 6:27; and 8:7 (=2 Chr 5:8). On the cherubim, see the other references cited by T. H. Gaster, art. "Angels" in *IDB* 1.131.
¹⁰¹ In fact, he is represented as the Messiah, so described. Cf. the following section, 5. The imagery thus has nothing to do with the rabbinic expression "to bring someone under the wings of the Shekhinah" = to convert him. See for example *b. Sanh.* 99b (Soncino

5. The Messiah and Gathering

a) The Messiah

The Tannaitic midrash *Sifre* Ha'azinu 314 on Deut 32:11 comments on "As a (mother) vulture stirs up its nest": "this refers to the future, as it is said, 'The voice of my beloved! Look, he comes' (Cant 2:8). 'As it spreads its wings': as it is said, 'I will say to the north: Give them up, and to the south, Do not withhold' (Isa 43:6). 'Bears them aloft on its pinions': as it is said, 'And they shall bring your sons in their bosom' (Isa 49:22)."[102]

"The future" above is the Hebrew לעתיד לבוא, the time to come, or as P. Billerbeck correctly states, the days of the Messiah.[103] The latter is corroborated by other Judaic interpretation of the verse cited above, Cant 2:8.

Cant. Rab. 2:8 § 3 says that R. Yose the Galilean, a second generation Tanna,[104] and R. Eliezer b. Jacob, a third generation Tanna,[105] interpret "The voice of my beloved! Look, he comes" as the Messiah. He will say to Israel, "In this month [Nisan in Exod 12:2] you are to be redeemed."[106] It was standard Judaic

---

652). Against Str-B 1.943. For God as the vulture of Deut 32:11, see also *Pesiq. R.* 47/3 (Friedmann 190a, Braude 804) and *Eliyyahu Rabba* (22) 20 (Friedmann 119, Braude and Kapstein 298). *Cant. Zuṭa* 1/1 (Buber 6) says this is one of His seventy designations.

[102] Finkelstein 357; I modify Hammer at 321.
[103] Str-B 4.909. The same term is employed in regard to Deut 32:10 in *Sifre* 313 (Finkelstein 356, Hammer 320).
[104] *Introduction* 81.
[105] *Ibid.*, 85.
[106] Donsqi 66, Soncino 9.117. A dialogue ensues, ending with the quotation of Exod 12:2. The rabbis perceived the Song of Songs as a conversation between God and His people. Therefore "My beloved" is God's beloved. A parallel tradition is found in *Pesiq. Rav Kah.* 5/7 (Mandelbaum 89, Braude and Kapstein 101), dealing with Exod 12:2 and Cant 2:8. Commenting in 5/8 on Cant 2:9, R. Levi, a third generation Palestinian Amora (see n. 7), states that the first redeemer (Moses) is like the final redeemer (the Messiah) (Mandelbaum 92, Braude and Kapstein 104). On the latter, see also *Cant. Rab.* 2:9 § 3 (Donsqi 68, Soncino 9.120). Another parallel is found in *Pesiq. R.* 15/7 (Friedmann 71b, Braude 316-

belief that the Messiah was to appear on the fifteenth of Nisan, when the final redemption would occur.[107]

Cant. Zuṭa 2:8 interprets similarly: "these are the voices which in the time to come precede the Messiah."[108]

When *Sifre* interprets the (mother) vulture of Deut 32:11 in regard to the time to come, with Cant 2:8, the bird is thus thought to represent the Messiah. A similar interpretation is given of the bird of prey in Judaic tradition on Gen 15:11 (see chapter five above), and Job 39:30 is so interpreted in Jewish Christian tradition (see chapter six above).

b) *Gathering*

In *Sifre* Ha'azinu 314 on Deut 32:11, "As it spreads its wings" and "Bears them aloft on its pinions" are interpreted in terms of the mother bird's gathering of Israel's exiles in the future as exemplified by Isa 43:6 and 49:22. As indicated above, this bird is the Messiah, described in terms of a mother *nešer*, vulture.

In Isa 43:5-7 God promises to "gather" (קבץ, συνάγω LXX v 5) the exiles of Israel from all four directions. In Isa 49:22 God will cause the nations to do this when He raises His "signal" (נס) to them. This is a reiteration of the same motif already found in 11:10-12, where "on that day [in the eschatological future] the root of Jesse [David] shall stand as a 'signal' (נס) to the peoples" (v 10). At that time the Lord "will raise a 'signal' (נס, LXX σημεῖον) for the nations, and will assemble the outcasts of Israel, and 'gather' (קבץ, LXX συνάγω) the dispersed of Judah from the four corners of the earth" (v 12). Judaic tradition interprets the root of Jesse (David), the signal to

---

317). In *Tanḥ*. B Bemidbar 16 on Num 2:2 (Buber 14, with n. 138; Bietenhard 2.208), R. Levi employs Cant 2:8 of the world to come when "he comes who will redeem you." The Messiah is most probably meant.

[107] Cf. the sources cited above in chapter five, section IV. 2).
[108] Buber 23.

The Rejection of the Mother Bird Messiah

the peoples, to be the royal Messiah who "will come 'to assemble' (לכנס) the exiles of Israel...."[109]

The Messiah's assembling the exiles of Israel is found at the latest already in the first century BCE in Palestine, as exemplified in *Pss. Sol.* 17:26 with συνάγω. Other texts confirm this.[110]

For the above reasons I suggest that the mother vulture of Deut 32:11, described in the Tannaitic midrash *Sifre* as gathering Israel's exiles in the time to come, was considered to be the Messiah. This then was the source of a Palestinian Jewish Christian's imagery when he had Jesus say: "How often have I desired 'to gather' your children 'together' as a mother bird 'gathers' her brood under her wings..." (Luke 13:34b // Matt 23:37b). The present Greek of this Q saying has ἐπισυνάγω, a fuller form of the verb συνάγω noted above.[111] The Semitic behind this would be כנס / כנש in Aramaic,[112] or possibly קבץ in Hebrew.[113]

* * *

The above analysis of Palestinian Judaic traditions on Isa 31:5, Deut 22:6-7 and 32:11 shows that they provide the major background to the imagery found in the Q saying in Luke 13:34b // Matt 23:37b. The entire pericope Luke 13:34-35 // Matt 23:37-39 must now be examined in order to determine its original meaning.

---

[109] Cf. *Gen. Rab.* Vayechi 98/9 on Gen 49:11 (Theodor and Albeck 1260, Soncino 2.957), and 99/8 on the same verse (Theodor and Albeck 1280, Soncino 2.983).
[110] Cf. the references cited above in chapter six, section III. on gathering.
[111] Matthew has the verb twice, which is probably due to his own editing. He employs for example συνάγω twenty-four, Mark four, and Luke six times.
[112] Jastrow 649-650 and 651.
[113] Jastrow 1312. It is employed at this point in the Hebrew New Testaments of Delitzsch and the United Bible Societies.

IV. Protection from Judgment

Luke 13:34a // Matt 23:37a begins by having Jesus address the Judean capital: "Jerusalem, Jerusalem, she who kills the prophets and stones those who are sent to it!" The doubling of the city's name has nothing to do with the doubling of a person's name, as so often maintained.[114] Rather, it is modeled on Isa 29:1, where the prophet threatens the city of Jerusalem with destruction, saying: "Alas, Ariel, Ariel...."[115] The same kind of prophetic threat of destruction is found in Luke 13:35a, "See, your house is left to you." Matthew in 23:38 correctly adds the interpretation "desolate" (ἔρημος), probably based on Jer 22:5. The verb ἀφίεται in the present is meant as the prophetic future: "Your (Jerusalem's inhabitants') house will be left (desolate) to you." God will abandon the Temple (and the city) to judgment.[116] In this abandoned state its inhabitants will be easy prey to their enemies. They will lack the protective care of the Messiah, who like a mother bird would gladly have sheltered them from the coming severe danger.

The statement "And I tell you, you will not see me until the time comes when you say, 'Blessed is the one who comes in the name of the Lord'" (Luke 13:35, Matt 23:39 with only slight variants)[117] was also originally a veiled threat. The Jerusalemites

---

[114] Cf. "Abraham, Abraham" in Gen 22:11; "Jacob, Jacob" in 46:2; "Moses, Moses" in Exod 3:4; "Samuel, Samuel" in 1 Sam 3:10; "Lord, Lord" in Matt 7:21 // Luke 6:46; "Martha, Martha" in Luke 10:41; and "Simon, Simon" in 22:31.

[115] Cf. הוֹי in BDB 222 for "Alas," and אֲרִיאֵל in 72,1, as well as אֲרִאֵל as the altar hearth in the Temple (Ezek 43:15–16). See the analysis of this passage in chapter four, section VI., above.

[116] The verb (ἀφίημι in BAGD 126, 3.a.: leave, abandon) is in the divine passive. Cogent reasons for οἶκος as meaning "Temple" and not "city" are given by U. Luz, *Das Evangelium nach Matthäus (Mt 18–25)* 382. While it cannot be completely excluded, I doubt that Jerusalem stands here for all of Israel. The perspective is that of a Galilean Jewish Christian prophet addressing the inhabitants of his capital city (see below).

[117] On Lukan priority at this point, cf. the remarks of U. Luz, *Das Evangelium nach Matthäus (Mt 18–25)* 377, n. 4.

continue to "see" / encounter Jesus in the Gospel of Matthew after the unit 23:37-39, and they had already greeted him with these words from Ps 118:26 in 21:9. In Luke, Jesus speaks the unit 13:34-35 while he is still in Galilee, and the future occasion of reciting Ps 118:26 in v 35 is certainly not meant to be fulfilled in 19:38, just before Jesus weeps over Jerusalem (see chapter four above). Both Matthew and Luke borrowed the entire unit from Q and placed it where it seemed appropriate to them. Its original meaning thus should not be derived from the present contexts, although it now fits Matthew's better than Luke's.

U. Luz has convincingly shown that the thesis of divine wisdom's speaking the unit Luke 13:34-35 // Matt 23:37-39 should be "buried." There is no justification for continuing to maintain it.[118] Nor can Jesus himself have spoken these words. "How often have I desired to gather your children together" does not refer to frequent previous visits to Jerusalem, an additional Judean ministry not mentioned in the Synoptics.[119] Nor should it be softened down to mean Jesus' frequent "longing" or "yearning" while still in Galilee to go to Jerusalem and minister there.[120] Finally, as shown above, the Jerusalemites' greeting Jesus with the words of Ps 118:26 cannot refer to the "triumphal entry" into Jerusalem at the end of the Synoptic Gospels, but only to another, future occasion.

For the above reasons it is best to take the Q unit Luke 13:34-35 // Matt 23:37-39 as the words of a Palestinian Jewish Christian prophet spoken after Jesus' Resurrection.[121] He (and

---

[118] Ibid., 378-379. See also C. F. Evans, *Saint Luke* (Philadelphia: Trinity Press International; London: SCM Press, 1990) 564.

[119] John 2:13; 5:1; 7:10 and 10:23 should be treated with greater care in this respect.

[120] Against A. Mc Neile, *The Gospel According to St Matthew* 341-342. See also T. Manson, *The Sayings of Jesus* 127; D. Hagner, *Matthew 14–28*, 680-681; and J. Green, *The Gospel of Luke* (NICNT 3; Grand Rapids, Michigan: Eerdmans, 1997) 539.

[121] For early Christian prophets, cf. Acts 11:27 on those in Jerusalem, 13:1, 15:32, 21:10, 1 Cor 12:28 and chapter 14, as well as other references in G. Friedrich, art. προφήτης etc. in TDNT 6.828-861, and in D. Aune, *Prophecy in Early Christianity* (Grand Rapids, Michigan: Eerdmans, 1983). In "Der neutestamentliche Weheruf über Jerusalem

other followers of Jesus) had frequently ("how often") attempted to convince their fellow Jews in the capital city Jerusalem that Jesus was the long awaited Messiah, who had indeed already inaugurated the time of the final redemption. In spite of glowing reports in Acts (2:41; 5:14; 6:1, 7; 9:31; 21:20), there was only a relatively small congregation of Christians there. The great majority of Jerusalem's inhabitants (its "children") "did not want"[122] to be gathered together into the eschatological Christian community, which they did not consider to be part of the inbreaking of the kingdom of God. Their (primarily the religious leaders') vehement rejection of this invitation, including persecuting and even killing fellow Jews who had become Christians, led to a Jewish Christian prophet's formulating the sentence in the name of his risen and exalted Lord: "Jerusalem, Jerusalem, she that kills the prophets and stones those who are sent to it!" For him the first part referred primarily to prophets from the past like Isaiah and Zechariah the son of Jehoiada,[123] but the second part also in a more general sense to his Christian contemporaries.[124] For this reason he formulated his lament /

(Luk. 13,34–35 = Matt. 23,37–39)" in *TSK* 78 (1905) 455-460, M. Plath very improbably attributes the Q saying to a prophet of OT times, which somehow survived until being incorporated into this document. U. Luz in *Das Evangelium nach Matthäus (Mt 18–25)* 380 believes an itinerant prophet from Galilee's Q community speaks here in the name of the risen Lord. For this possibility, see earlier also E. Ellis, *The Gospel of Luke* (NCB 3; London: Oliphants, 1977) 191; D. Hill, *The Gospel of Matthew* (NCB 1; London: Oliphants, 1978) 315; and C. F. Evans, *Saint Luke* 565.

[122] This is well formulated by J. Ernst, *Das Evangelium nach Lukas* (RNT 3; Regensburg: Pustet, 1977⁴) 433: "Das Wort vom 'Nicht-Wollen' ist nicht nur Feststellung, sondern Anklage, die mit Bekehrung nicht mehr rechnet."

[123] Cf. the sources in Str-B 1.943, 940-942 and 3.747.

[124] Cf. the stoning of Stephen in Jerusalem in Acts 7:58-60; a severe persecution of the church there in 8:1, also by Saul (v 3; see 22:4; 1 Cor 15:9; Gal 1:13; and Phil 3:6); the killing of James the brother of John (Acts 12:2); and the stoning of Jesus' brother James and other Christians (Josephus, *Ant.* 20.200). The latter incident took place in 62 CE (Schürer, *The history* 1.468).

The Rejection of the Mother Bird Messiah

rebuke and threat of Jerusalem's later destruction in such a drastic way.

It is the Palestinian Jewish Christian prophet himself, rejected along with other Christian missionaries in Jerusalem, who threatens the city's inhabitants with words in Jesus' name: "And I tell you (pl.), you will not see me again[125] until the time comes when you say, 'Blessed is the one who comes in the name of the Lord.'" The time referred to will be that of the Judgment,[126] when Jesus at his parousia as the Son of Man will return and condemn all those who have done evil (such as those who kill the prophets and stone and persecute those sent to them), and will reward those who have done good. The Jerusalemites may then out of desperation greet Jesus with the words of Psalm 118:26, but it will be of no avail. They had the opportunity to accept Jesus and his message when he was once in their midst, and often later when Christian prophets and other missionaries were active among them. Now it is too late and they will be excluded from eternal life.[127]

---

[125] The (Galilean) prophet may have also meant himself here, believing that the Judgment would take place during his lifetime. It would begin in Jerusalem, and then they would encounter him there again.

[126] Cf. the Judaic interpretation of Deut 32:12a noted in section III., beginning; it was viewed as belonging together with the important verse 11.

[127] Cf. T. Manson in *The Sayings of Jesus* 128: "then it will be too late." See also Jesus' parable of the ten maidens, where "the door was shut" (Matt 25:10), and the early core of the parable of the judgment through the Son of Man in Matt 25:31-46, as well as 13:41-43; 16:27; 19:28; and Luke 21:36. See also the passages from Ethiopian Enoch cited by U. Luz, *Das Evangelium nach Matthäus* (Mt 18-25) 385. This sentiment obviously contrasts with statements such as Rom 11:26, "all Israel will be saved." However, just as Paul could also utter 1 Thess 2:15-16 because of severe persecution, so a Palestinian Jewish Christian prophet could formulate Luke 13:34a // Matt 23:37a because of severe persecution, and threaten the inhabitants of Jerusalem with complete exclusion from later participation in the kingdom of God. L. Sabourin, *L'Évangile de Luc* (Rome: Editrice Pontificia Università Gregoriana, 1985) 266 thinks the Q text may foresee a future conversion of the Jews. He even cites Rom 11:25. See also R. Gundry, *Matthew* 474, and W. D. Davies and D. Allison, Jr., *The Gospel According to Saint Matthew*

The words of Luke 13:34b // Matt 23:37b only receive their proper interpretation in light of the above future Judgment by the Son of Man.[128] Jesus is represented as a mother bird who frequently in a situation of extreme danger (a cat, a weasel, a marten, a hawk, falcon or other raptor, a human) is anxious about, cares for her young, yearning to gather and protect them when they have strayed from the nest and should dash back to the shelter of her wings in order not to be snatched, killed and devoured. Indeed, Judaic tradition on Deut 32:11 shows that the mother vulture there, well-known for the deep affection (mercy, compassion) it shows its young, was interpreted as the Messiah. It is thus not the LORD (God) who like a bird hovering over Jerusalem would like to protect and rescue the city (Isa 31:5 in section I. above), but Jesus the Messiah. Like a mother vulture, he yearns to preserve his "children," the inhabitants of the capital city, from the rapidly approaching Judgment, which he as the Son of Man will hold. Yet it is already too late for this, for they have refused to heed the mother bird's call, they have rejected him as the Messiah.

These "words of poignant melancholy" are not historical, as maintained by a number of commentators.[129] Rather, they were

---

3.323–324. H. van der Kwaak in "Die Klage über Jerusalem (Matt. xxiii 37-39)" in *NovT* 8 (1966) 156-170 interprets the ἕως ἄν of v 39 as conditional: "until" you say, i.e. the sentence is an invitation to conversion (p. 170).

[128] Numerous commentators in the past also thought here of the situation of judgment. Cf. W. Grundmann, *Das Evangelium nach Matthäus* (THKNT 1; Berlin: Evangelische Verlagsanstalt, 1975⁴) 496; R. Gundry, *Matthew* 473; A. Mc Neile, *The Gospel According to St Matthew* 341-342; and J. Jeremias, *The Parables of Jesus* 168. Jeremias includes this text in his section "4. The Imminence of Catastrophe." His next section, "5. It May Be Too Late," is closely related.

[129] Cf. T. Robinson, *The Gospel of Matthew* 193; R. Gundry, *Matthew* 473; L. Morris, *The Gospel According to Matthew* (Grand Rapids, Michigan: Eerdmans, 1992) 591; A. Mc Neile, *The Gospel According to St Matthew* 341-342; D. Harrington, *The Gospel of Matthew* (Sacra Pagina 1; Collegeville, Minnesota: The Liturgical Press, 1991) 330; J. Fitzmyer, *The Gospel According to Luke X–XXIV* (AB 28A; Garden City, New York: Doubleday, 1986) 1034-1035; and I. Marshall, *Commentary on Luke* 574.

originally spoken in a Semitic language by a Palestinian Jewish Christian prophet, probably from Galilee and perhaps even a member of the Christian community which produced "Q." This lament / rebuke and prophetic threat of destruction could have been uttered before the Temple ("your house") was razed by the Romans in 70 CE, yet after Jerusalem's inhabitants, especially the religious leadership, had not only frequently rejected the efforts of Christian missionaries, but also had persecuted and killed a number of them. Or, less probably, it could have been spoken shortly after the tragic events of the Jewish-Roman war, then very soon being incorporated into Q.

In spite of its original reference to the final Judgment by Jesus as the Son of Man, the pericope contains in Luke 13:34b // Matt 23:37b "a most tender metaphor" which conveys Jesus' longing to provide "maternal" protective care for his children. Indeed, he is the mother bird Messiah.

Sources and Reference Works

I. The Bible

Kittel, *Biblia Hebraica*, ed. R. Kittel et al. (Stuttgart: Privilegierte Württembergische Bibelanstalt, 1951⁷).
Rahlfs, *Septuaginta*, ed. A. Rahlfs (Stuttgart: Württembergische Bibelanstalt, 1962⁷).
Hatch-Redpath, *A Concordance to the Septuagint*, ed. E. Hatch and H. Redpath (Oxford: Clarendon, 1897; corrected reprint Grand Rapids, Michigan: Baker Book House, 1983), 2 volumes.
Nestle / Aland, *Novum Testamentum Graece*, ed. E. Nestle, K. Aland, et al. (Stuttgart: Deutsche Bibelgesellschaft, 1990²⁶).
The Greek New Testament, ed. K. Aland, M. Black, B. Metzger and A. Wikgren (London: United Bible Societies, 1966).
Hebrew New Testament, by F. Delitzsch (Berlin: Trowitzsch and Son, 1885).
Hebrew New Testament (Jerusalem: The United Bible Societies, 1979).

II. The Targums

Sperber, *The Bible in Aramaic*, ed. A. Sperber (Leiden: Brill, 1959), 4 volumes.
Aberbach and Grossfeld, *Targum Onkelos to Genesis*, trans. M. Aberbach and B. Grossfeld (Denver: Center for Judaic Studies, University of Denver; New York: Ktav, 1982).
McNamara, *Targum Neofiti 1: Genesis*, trans. M. McNamara (The Aramaic Bible, 1A; Edinburgh: Clark, 1992).
Maher, *Targum Pseudo-Jonathan: Genesis*, trans. M. Maher (The Aramaic Bible, 1B; Edinburgh: Clark, 1992). *Exodus*, 1994.

Drazin, *Targum Onkelos to Exodus*, ed. and trans. I. Drazin (New York: Ktav; Denver: Center for Judaic Studies, University of Denver, 1990).

Grossfeld, *The Targum Onqelos to Exodus*, trans. B. Grossfeld (The Aramaic Bible, 7; Edinburgh: Clark, 1988).

McNamara / Maher, *Targum Neofiti 1: Exodus, Targum Pseudo-Jonathan: Exodus*, trans. M. McNamara and M. Maher (The Aramaic Bible, 2; Edinburgh: Clark, 1994).

Díez Macho, *Neophyti 1*, ed. A. Díez Macho (Madrid: Consejo Superior de Investigaciones Científicas, 1968-1978), 5 volumes.

Drazin, *Targum Onkelos to Deuteronomy*, ed. and trans. I. Drazin (Hoboken, NJ: Ktav Publishing House, 1982).

Clarke, *Targum Pseudo-Jonathan: Deuteronomy*, ed. E. Clarke (The Aramaic Bible, 5 B; Edinburgh: Clark, 1998).

Rieder, *Targum Jonathan ben Uziel on the Pentateuch*, ed. with a Hebrew translation by D. Rieder (Jerusalem, 1984), 2 volumes.

Klein, *The Fragment-Targums of the Pentateuch*, ed. and trans. M. Klein (AnBib 76; Rome: Biblical Institute, 1980), 2 volumes.

Harrington and Saldarini, *Targum Jonathan of the Former Prophets*, trans. D. Harrington and A. Saldarini (The Aramaic Bible, 10; Edinburgh: Clark, 1987).

Stenning, *The Targum of Isaiah*, ed. and trans. J. Stenning (Oxford: Clarendon, 1949).

Chilton, *The Isaiah Targum*, trans. B. Chilton (The Aramaic Bible, 11; Edinburgh: Clark, 1987).

Hayward, *The Targum of Jeremiah*, trans. R. Hayward (The Aramaic Bible, 12; Edinburgh: Clark, 1987).

Cathcart and Gordon, *The Targum of the Minor Prophets*, trans. K. Cathcart and R. Gordon (The Aramaic Bible, 14; Edinburgh: Clark, 1989).

Merino, *Targum de Salmos*, ed. L. Merino (Madrid: Consejo Superior de Investigaciones Científicas, 1984).

Merino, *Targum de Job*, ed. L. Merino (Madrid: Consejo Superior de Investigaciones Científicas, 1984).

Mangan, *The Targum of Job*, trans. C. Mangan (The Aramaic Bible, 15; Collegeville, MN: The Liturgical Press, 1991).

Grossfeld, *The Targum Sheni to the Book of Esther*, ed. and trans. B. Grossfeld (New York: Sepher-Hermon, 1994).

Le Déaut and Robert, *Targum des Chroniques (Cod. Vat. Urb. Ebr. 1)*, ed. with a French translation by R. Le Déaut and J. Robert (AnBib 51; Rome: Biblical Institute, 1971).

McIvor, *The Targum of Chronicles*, trans. J. S. McIvor (The Aramaic Bible, 19; Edinburgh: Clark, 1994).

Lagarde, *Hagiographa Chaldaice*, ed. P. de Lagarde (Leipzig: Teubner, 1873; reprint Osnabrück: Zeller, 1967).

III. The Mishnah and Tosefta

Albeck, *Shisha Sidre Mishna*, ed. Ch. Albeck (Jerusalem and Tel Aviv: Bialik Institute and Dvir, 1975), 6 volumes.

Danby, *The Mishnah*, trans. H. Danby (London: Oxford University, 1933).

Neusner, *The Mishnah*, trans. J. Neusner (New Haven: Yale University, 1988).

Meinhold, *Die Mischna*, II.5. *Joma*, ed. with a German translation by J. Meinhold (Giessen: Töpelmann, 1913).

Zuckermandel, *Tosephta*, ed. M. Zuckermandel, with a supplement by S. Liebermann (Jerusalem: Wahrmann, 1970).

Lieberman, *The Tosefta*, ed. S. Lieberman (New York: The Jewish Theological Seminary of America, 1955-1992), 10 volumes.

Neusner, *The Tosefta*, trans. J. Neusner et al. (Hoboken, New Jersey: KTAV, 1977-1986), 6 volumes.

IV. The Talmuds

Soncino, *The Babylonian Talmud*, ed. I. Epstein, various translators (London: Soncino, 1952), 18 volumes and index.

Soncino, *The Minor Tractates of the Talmud*, ed. A. Cohen, various translators (London: Soncino, 1965), 2 volumes.

Higger, *Masseket Soferim*, ed. M. Higger (New York, 1937).

Goldschmidt, *Der Babylonische Talmud*, ed. with a German translation by L. Goldschmidt (Haag: Nijoff, 1933), 9 volumes.

Krotoshin, *Talmud Yerushalmi*, Krotoshin edition (Jerusalem: Shilah, 1969).

Neusner, *The Talmud of the Land of Israel*, trans. J. Neusner et al. (Chicago: University of Chicago, 1982-1995), 34 volumes.

V. Halakhic Midrashim

Lauterbach, *Mekilta de-Rabbi Ishmael*, ed. and trans. J. Lauterbach (Philadelphia: The Jewish Publication Society of America, 1976), 3 volumes.
Epstein and Melamed, *Mekhilta d'Rabbi Šim'on b. Jochai*, ed. J. Epstein and E. Melamed (Jerusalem: Hillel Press, 1955; reprint 1979).
Weiss, *Sifra*. Commentar zu Leviticus, ed. J. Weiss (Vienna: Jacob Schlossberg, 1862).
Winter, *Sifra*. Halachischer Midrasch zu Leviticus, trans. J. Winter (Breslau: Stefan Münz, 1938).
Neusner, *Sifra*. An Analytical Translation, trans. J. Neusner (BJS 138-140; Atlanta: Scholars Press, 1988), 3 volumes.
Horowitz, *Siphre ad Numeros adjecto Siphre zutta*, ed. H. Horowitz (Jerusalem: Wahrmann, 1976).
Neusner, *Sifre to Numbers*, trans. J. Neusner (BJS 118-119; Atlanta: Scholars Press, 1986), 2 volumes.
Kuhn, *Der tannaitische Midrasch Sifre zu Numeri*, German by K. Kuhn (Stuttgart: Kohlhammer, 1959).
Finkelstein, *Sifre on Deuteronomy*, ed. L. Finkelstein (New York: The Jewish Theological Seminary of America, 1969).
Hammer, *Sifre*. A Tannaitic Commentary on the Book of Deuteronomy, trans. R. Hammer (YJS 24; New Haven: Yale University, 1986).
Neusner, *Sifre to Deuteronomy*. An Analytical Translation, trans. J. Neusner (BJS 98 and 101; Atlanta: Scholars Press, 1987), 2 volumes.

VI. Haggadic Midrashim

Soncino, *Midrash Rabbah*, ed. H. Freedman and M. Simon (London: Soncino, 1939), 9 volumes and index.
Midrash Rabbah (Vilna: Romm, 1887).
Mirqin, *Midrash Rabbah*, Pentateuch. Ed. and vocalized by M. Mirqin (Tel Aviv: Yavneh, 1981), 11 volumes.

Sources and Reference Works

Theodor and Albeck, *Midrash Bereshit Rabba*, ed. J. Theodor and Ch. Albeck (Jerusalem: Wahrmann, 1965), 3 volumes.

Margulies, *Leviticus Rabbah*: Midrash Wayyikra Rabbah, ed. M. Margulies (Jerusalem: Ministry of Education and Culture of Israel, American Academy for Jewish Research, 1953–1960).

Donsqi, *Midrash Rabbah. Shir ha-Shirim*, ed. S. Donsqi (Jerusalem: Dvir, 1980).

Margulies, *Midrash Haggadol on the Pentateuch*, Genesis, ed. M. Margulies (Jerusalem: Mosad Harav Kook, 1975).

Buber, *Midrasch Tanḥuma*: Ein agadischer Commentar zum Pentateuch, ed. S. Buber (Vilna: Romm, 1885).

Bietenhard, *Midrasch Tanḥuma B*, German by H. Bietenhard (Judaica et Christiana 5–6; Bern: Peter Lang, 1980–1982), 2 volumes.

Midrash Tanḥuma, Eshkol edition (Jerusalem: Eshkol, no date).

Singermann, *Midrasch Tanchuma* (only Genesis), ed. with a German translation by F. Singermann (Berlin: Lamm, 1927).

Schechter, *Aboth de Rabbi Nathan* (A and B), ed. S. Schechter (Vienna, 1887; reprinted New York: Feldheim, 1945).

Goldin, *The Fathers According to Rabbi Nathan* (A), trans. J. Goldin (YJS 10; New Haven: Yale University, 1955).

Neusner, *The Fathers According to Rabbi Nathan. An Analytical Translation and Explanation*, trans. J. Neusner (BJS 114; Atlanta: Scholars Press, 1986).

Saldarini, *The Fathers According to Rabbi Nathan* (B), trans. A. Saldarini (SJLA 11; Leiden: Brill, 1975).

Mandelbaum, *Pesikta de Rav Kahana*, ed. B. Mandelbaum (New York: The Jewish Theological Seminary of America, 1962), 2 volumes.

Braude and Kapstein, *Pesikta de-Rab Kahana*, trans. W. Braude and I. Kapstein (Philadelphia: The Jewish Publication Society of America, 1975).

Neusner, *Pesiqta de Rab Kahana. An Analytical Translation*, trans. J. Neusner (BJS 122–123; Atlanta: Scholars Press, 1987).

Friedmann, *Pesikta Rabbati*, ed. M. Friedmann (Vienna, 1880; reprint Tel Aviv, 1962–1963).

Braude, *Pesikta Rabbati*, trans. W. Braude (YJS 18; New Haven: Yale University, 1968), 2 volumes.

Friedmann, *Seder Eliahu rabba und Seder Eliahu zuta*, ed. M. Friedmann (Vienna, 1902–1904; reprint Jerusalem, 1969).
Braude and Kapstein, *Tanna debe Eliyyahu*, trans. W. Braude and I. Kapstein (Philadelphia: The Jewish Publication Society of America, 1981).
Buber, *Midrasch Tehillim*, ed. S. Buber (Vilna: Romm, 1891).
Braude, *The Midrash on Psalms*, trans. W. Braude (YJS 13, 1–2; New Haven: Yale University, 1959), 2 volumes.
Buber, *Midrasch Mischle*, ed. S. Buber (Vilna, 1893; reprint Jerusalem, 1965).
Visotzky, *The Midrash on Proverbs*, trans. B. Visotzky (YJS 27; New Haven: Yale University, 1992).
Wünsche, "Der Midrasch Sprüche," German by A. Wünsche in *Bibliotheca Rabbinica* (Leipzig: Schulze, 1885) 4.1-77.
Eshkol, *Pirqe Rabbi Eliezer*, Eshkol edition (Jerusalem: Eshkol, 1973).
Higger, *Pirqe R. Eliezer*, ed. M. Higger in *Horeb* 8 (1944) 82–119; 9 (1946) 94–116; and 10 (1948) 185–294.
Friedlander, *Pirke de Rabbi Eliezer*, trans. G. Friedlander (New York: Hermon, 1970; original London, 1916).
Buber, *Midrasch Suta*, ed. S. Buber (Berlin: Mekize Nirdamim, 1894).
Albeck, *Midraš Berešit Rabbati*, ed. Ch. Albeck (Jerusalem: Mekize Nirdamim, 1940).
Buber, *Lekach tob* (Pesikta sutarta), ein agadischer Commentar zum ersten und zweiten Buche Mosis von R. Tobia ben Elieser, ed. S. Buber (Wilna, 1884).
Milikowsky, *Seder Olam. A Rabbinic Chronography*, ed. and trans. Ch. Milikowsky (1981 Yale University Ph.D. dissertation).
Jellinek, *Bet ha-Midrasch*, ed. A. Jellinek (Jerusalem: Wahrmann Books, 1967[3]), 6 volumes in 2.
Wünsche, *Aus Israels Lehrhallen*. German by A. Wünsche (Leipzig: Pfeiffer, 1907–1909; reprint Hildesheim: Olms, 1967), 5 volumes.
Yalquṭ Shim'oni, Genesis (Jerusalem: Kook, 1973), Leviticus (1984).

Kasher, *Encyclopedia of Biblical Interpretation*, vol. II, Genesis, ed. and trans. M. Kasher and H. Friedman (New York: American Biblical Encyclopedia Society, 1955).

* * *

Siegert, *Drei hellenistische Predigten*. Ps-Philon, "Über Simson," etc. German by F. Siegert (WUNT 20; Tübingen: Mohr / Siebeck, 1980).

VII. Apocrypha, Pseudepigrapha, Philo, Josephus and the Dead Sea Scrolls

Apocrypha: see Rahlfs, *Septuaginta*.

OTP. *The Old Testament Pseudepigrapha*, ed. J. Charlesworth (Garden City, New York: Doubleday, 1983-1985), 2 volumes.

APOT. *The Apocrypha and Pseudepigrapha of the Old Testament*, II. Pseudepigrapha, ed. R. Charles (Oxford: Clarendon, 1913).

Violet, B., *Die Esra-Apokalypse* (GSC 18; Leipzig: Hinrichs, 1910).

Harrington, *Les Antiquités Bibliques*, ed. D. Harrington, French by J. Cazeaux (SC 229–230; Paris: du Cerf, 1976), 2 volumes.

LCL, *Philo*, Greek and English translation by F. Colson, G. Whitaker, J. Earp and R. Marcus (Cambridge, MA: Harvard University, 1971), 10 volumes with 2 supplements.

LCL, *Josephus*, Greek and English translation by H. Thackeray, R. Marcus and A. Wikgren (Cambridge, MA: Harvard University, 1969), 9 volumes.

Martínez and Tigchelaar, *The Dead Sea Scrolls Study Edition*, ed. and trans. F. Martínez and E. Tigchelaar (Leiden: Brill, 2000), 2 volumes.

Martínez, *The Dead Sea Scrolls Translated*, trans. F. Martínez (Leiden: Brill, 1994).

Fitzmyer, J., *The Genesis Apocryphon of Qumran Cave 1: A Commentary* (Bib Or 18; Rome: Pontificial Biblical Institute Press, 1966).

Fitzmyer, J., *The Dead Sea Scrolls*. Major Publications and Tools for Study (SBLRBS 20; Atlanta: Scholars Press, 1990).

Charlesworth, *Graphic Concordance to the Dead Sea Scrolls*, ed. J. Charlesworth et al. (Tübingen: Mohr; Louisville: Westminster, John Knox, 1991).

VIII. The Early Church and Pagan Authors

Preuschen, *Origines Werke*, ed. E. Preuschen (Leipzig: Hinrichs, 1903), vol. IV.

Eusebius of Caesarea, *Das Onomastikon der biblischen Namen*, ed. E. Klostermann (Leipzig: Hinrichs, 1904; reprint Hildesheim: Olms, 1966).

Schwartz, *Kyrillos von Skythopolis*, ed. E. Schwartz (Texte und Untersuchungen zur Geschichte der altchristlichen Literatur 49.2; Leipzig: Hinrichs, 1939).

Price and Binns, *Cyril of Scythopolis: Lives of the Monks of Palestine*, ed. R. Price and J. Binns (Cistercian Studies series 114; Kalamazoo, MI: Cistercian Publications, 1991).

Aristotle, *History of Animals*, ed. and trans. D. Balme (LCL; Cambridge, MA: Harvard University Press, 1991), vol. III.

Pliny the Elder, *Natural History*, ed. and trans. H. Rackham (LCL; Cambridge, MA: Harvard University Press, 1940/1956), vol. III.

Marcus Terentius Varro, *Gespräche über die Landwirtschaft*, Buch 2, ed. D. Flach (Texte zur Forschung 66; Darmstadt: Wissenschaftliche Buchgesellschaft, 1997).

Varro, *The Farmer*. A selection from the Res Rusticae, trans. B. Tilly (London: University Tutorial Press, 1973).

IX. Dictionaries and Reference Works

BDB, *A Hebrew and English Lexicon of the Old Testament*, by F. Brown, S. Driver and C. Briggs (Oxford: Clarendon, 1962).

Jastrow, *A Dictionary of the Targumim, the Talmud Babli and Yerushalmi, and the Midrashic Literature*, by M. Jastrow (New York: Pardes, 1950), 2 volumes.

Levy, *Neuhebräisches und chaldäisches Wörterbuch über die Talmudim und Midraschim*, by J. Levy (Berlin and Vienna, 1924²), 4 volumes.

Krauss, *Griechische und Lateinische Lehnwörter in Talmud, Midrasch und Targum*, by S. Krauss (Berlin: Calvary, 1898–1899).

Hyman, *Torah Hakethubah Vehamessurah. A Reference Book of the Scriptural Passages Quoted in Talmudic, Midrashic and Early

Sources and Reference Works

Rabbinic Literature, by Aaron Hyman, second edition by Arthur Hyman (Tel Aviv: Dvir, 1979), 3 volumes.

Schürer, *The history of the Jewish people in the age of Jesus Christ (175 B.C. -A.D. 135)*, by E. Schürer, ed. G. Vermes, F. Millar and M. Black (Edinburgh: Clark, 1973-1986), 3 volumes.

Ginzberg, *The Legends of the Jews*, by L. Ginzberg (Philadelphia: The Jewish Publication Society of America, 1968), 6 volumes and index.

JE, The Jewish Encyclopedia (New York: Funk and Wagnalls, 1905), 12 volumes.

EncJud, Encyclopaedia Judaica (Jerusalem: Keter, 1971), 16 volumes.

Str-B, Kommentar zum Neuen Testament aus Talmud und Midrasch, by (H. Strack and) P. Billerbeck (Munich: Beck, 1924-1961), 6 volumes.

Strack and Stemberger, *Introduction to the Talmud and Midrash*, by H. Strack and G. Stemberger (Minneapolis: Fortress, 1992).

Nickelsburg, *Jewish Literature Between the Bible and the Mishnah*, by G. Nickelsburg (Philadelphia: Fortress, 1981).

LSJ, A Greek-English Lexicon, by H. Liddell, R. Scott and H. Jones (Oxford: Clarendon, 1966[9]).

BAGD, A Greek-English Lexicon of the New Testament and Other Early Christian Literature, by W. Bauer, W. Arndt, F. Gingrich and F. Danker (Chicago: University of Chicago, 1979[2]).

BDF, A Greek Grammar of the New Testament and Other Christian Literature, by F. Blass, A. Debrunner and R. Funk (Chicago: University of Chicago Press, 1962).

TDNT, Theological Dictionary of the New Testament, ed. G. Kittel and G. Friedrich (Grand Rapids, Michigan: Eerdmans, 1964-1976), 9 volumes and index.

PW, Realencyclopädie der classischen Altertumswissenschaft, ed. A. Pauly, G. Wissowa et al. (Stuttgart: Metzler, 1889-).

Chambers Murray, latin-english Dictionary, ed. W. Smith and J. Lockwood (Edinburgh: Chambers; London: Murray, 1986).

IDB, The Interpreter's Dictionary of the Bible, ed. G. Buttrick et al. (New York and Nashville: Abingdon Press, 1962), four volumes. Supplementary Volume, ed. K. Crim, 1976.

About the Author

Roger David Aus, b. 1940, studied English and German at St. Olaf College, and theology at Harvard Divinity School, Luther Theological Seminary, and Yale University, from which he received the Ph.D. degree in New Testament Studies in 1971. He is an ordained clergyman of the Evangelical Lutheran Church in America, currently serving the German-speaking Luthergemeinde in Berlin-Reinickendorf, Germany. The Protestant Church of Berlin-Brandenburg (Berlin West) kindly granted him a short study leave in Jerusalem, Israel, in 1981. His study of New Testament topics always reflects his great interest in, and deep appreciation of, the Jewish roots of the Christian faith.

Other volumes by Roger David Aus

The Stilling of the Storm. Studies in Early Palestinian Judaic Traditions (International Studies in Formative Christianity and Judaism; Binghamtom, NY: Global Publications, Binghamton University, 2000). Essays on Mark 4:35-41; 1:16-20; and Luke 24:13-35.

"Caught in the Act," Walking on the Sea, and the Release of Barabbas Revisited (South Florida Studies in the History of Judaism, 157; Atlanta: Scholars Press, 1998). Essays on John 7:53-8:11; Mark 6:45-52 par.; and 15:6-15 par.

The Wicked Tenants and Gethsemane (International Studies in Formative Christianity and Judaism, University of South Florida, 4; Atlanta: Scholars Press, 1996). Essays on Mark 12:1-9 par.; 14:32-42 par.; 2 Cor 12:1-10; and Judas' handing Jesus over to certain death through a kiss.

Samuel, Saul and Jesus. Three Early Palestinian Jewish Christian Gospel Haggadoth (South Florida Studies in the History of Judaism, 105; Atlanta: Scholars Press, 1994). Essays on Luke 2:41-51a; Mark 6:1-6a par.; and the prodigia at Jesus' crucifixion.

Barabbas and Esther and Other Studies in the Judaic Illumination of Earliest Christianity (South Florida Studies in the History of Judaism, 54; Atlanta: Scholars Press, 1992). Essays on Mark 15:6-15 par.; John 11:45-54; Luke 15:11-32; Matt 2:1-12; Gal 2:9; Isa 66:7, Revelation 12 and 2 Thessalonians 1; 2 Thess 2:6-7; Rom 11:25; and 2 Thess 1:3.

Weihnachtsgeschichte, Barmherziger Samariter, Verlorener Sohn. Studien zu ihrem jüdischen Hintergrund (ANTZ 2; Berlin: Institut Kirche und Judentum, 1988). Essays on Luke 2:1-20; 10:30-37; and 15:11-32.

Water into Wine and the Beheading of John the Baptist. Early Jewish-Christian Interpretation of Esther 1 in John 2:1-11 and Mark 6:17-29 (Brown Judaic Studies, 150; Atlanta: Scholars Press, 1988).

Index of Modern Authors

Adna, J. 71
Abel, F.-M. 72, 74, 77
Aḥituv, S. 114
Albeck, Ch. 115
Albright, W. F. 299
Allison, Jr., D. 298, 301,
.............................303, 325
Annen, F. 1, 91, 94, 99
Arav, R. 59
Aune, D. 323
Aus, R. 19, 57, 84, 90, 92,
...................105, 118, 130, 135,
...................137, 142, 147, 251,
.....................277-78, 282, 317
Avi Yonah, M. 72, 75, 81,
.............................136, 211
Baarda, T. 80, 254
Bacher, W. 26, 50
Barrois, G. 211
Bauernfeind, O. 84, 90, 99
Baumgarten, J. 114
Bayer, B. 19, 271
Beare, F. W. 291
Ben-Dor, I. 77
Ben-Yosef, Y. ....xiii, 72-74,
...............................81-82
Bernard, J. 254
Betz, O. 48, 69, 98
Bietenhard, H. 59
Billerbeck, P. 22, 26, 46,
....................134, 257, 278,
.............................304, 319

Black, M. 87-88
Blair, E. 155, 207
Bogaert, P.-M. 38
Boling, R. 22-23, 37, 193
Bonnard, P. 311
Bornhäuser, K. 124-125
Bovon, F. 101, 148, 150,
.............................289, 300, 303
Braslavi, J. 211
Braude, W. 181, 284
Brown, R. 164, 207, 277
Brun, L. 137
Buckwalter, D. 152
Büchler, A. 65, 119
Bultmann, R. 83-84, 89-90,
...............................244, 298
Burger, C. 156, 219
Burrelli, R. 6
Busse, U. 139, 143
Carrington, P. 98
Casey, M. ....xiii, 301
Cave, C. 21, 47, 60
Clark, K. 71
Cohen, A. 115
Craghan, J. 97
Crocket, L. 119
Dalman, G. 72, 76-77, 79,
........................134, 211, 215
Davies, G. 17
Davies, M. 304
Davies, W. D. 298, 301,
.............................303, 325

Deines, R. 118
Derrett, J. 10, 48, 67,
..............................91, 98, 207
Dibelius, M. 2, 83-84,
.................................89-90, 99
Dieckmann, B. 155
Dobsevage, I. 65
Dodd, C. H. 243
Donahue, J. ....…..........1
Dotan, A. ....…......195
Driver, G. R. 291-92,
.................................294, 312
Driver, S. R. 314
Dröscher, V. 312
Edersheim, A. 148
Eisenstein, J. 120
Eissfeldt, O. 255, 315
Elbogen, I. 10, 221, 286
Ellis, E. 141, 152, 239,
.................................244, 324
Enslin, M. S. 155
Ernst, J. 324
Evans, C. A. 219
Evans, C. F. 101, 132, 242,
..................….......244, 249, 323-24
Feliks, J. 290-92, 294,
................................296, 314
Fitzmyer, J. 105, 134, 141,
..............................148, 209, 239,
..........................241-42, 244, 246,
..........................261, 289, 326
Foerster, W. 6
Fohrer, G. 236, 277
Friedrich, G. 323
Fritz, V. 193
Fuller, R. 88
Gaechter, P. 291
Gärtner, B. 156, 187, 207
Gaster, T. 6, 318

Gaston, L. 231
Gealy, F. 16
Gilmour, S. M. 132, 227,
..............................300, 303
Ginzberg, L. ...19-21, 95, 156,
........................230, 256-57, 262
Glasson, T. 164
Glöckner, R. 6
Gnilka, J. 10, 34, 83-84,
..........................86, 89-90, 291
Gold, V. .....…..........31, 193
Goldin, J. ....…......117
Goldschmidt, H. ......….........155
Goodenough, E. …...........259
Gould, E. ....……........2
Grant, F. C. ....…......33, 90, 97
Gray, J. ....…........23, 75
Green, J. 141, 209, 252,
..............................300, 323
Greenberg, M. 120
Grundmann, W. 10, 48,
..........................97-98, 103, 125, 162,
..........................291, 300, 304, 326
Guelich, R. 2, 34, 84
Guenther, H. 301
Gundry, R. 21, 34, 71, 91,
..…...............94, 294, 305, 325-26
Guttmann, M. 156
Haenchen, E. 1, 83, 91, 170
Hagner, D. 300, 303
Harrington, D. 1, 19, 38,
..............................258, 326
Haugg, D. 207
Hedegärd, D. 120
Hengel, M. 118
Hengstenberg, E. 187
Henry, P. 260
Herr, M. 113, 119, 271
Hertzberg, H. ...184, 192, 216

Index of Modern Authors

Hill, D. 324
Hillers, D. 6
Hooker, M. 10, 90
Jacobs, J. 25, 65, 123
Jastrow, M. 182
Jeremias, J. 18, 124, 127,
....................143, 145, 246,
....................271, 305, 326
Johnson, Jr., E. 94
Johnson, L. 239, 299
Johnson, S. 304
Juel, D. 97, 162
Jung, L. 138
Kalmin, R. 156
Kapstein, I. 284
Kasher, M. 267
Kayserling, M. 182
Keel, O. 139
Klassen, W. 155, 194
Klauck, H.-J. 155, 194
Klausner, J. 193
Klijn, A. 264
Klostermann, E. 17, 33, 88
Kohler, K. 6, 8, 22, 156
Kollmann, B. 54
Kopp, C. 72, 133-34
Kremer, J. 209, 244
Küchler, M. 139
Lachs, S. 134
Lagrange, M.-J. 254
Landsberg, M. 221
Lane, W. 17, 91
Lapide, P. 66
Lauterbach, J. 19
Leaney, A. 102
Lieber, D. 120
Lightfoot, J. 17, 134, 299
Lohmeyer, E. 1, 17, 21,
....................86, 88

Lohse, E. 156, 219
Loisy, A. 210, 232, 250
Lona, H. 254, 257
Lüthi, K. 155
Luz, U. 71, 303-304,
....................322-25
Maloney, E. 87
Mangan, C. 265
Mann, C. S. 299
Mann, J. 65
Manson, T. 300, 304,
....................323, 325
Manson, W. 210, 243, 299
Marcus, R. 260
Markus, J. 2, 6, 48, 58,
....................84, 89, 91, 97-98
Marshall, I. 148, 244, 299,
....................304, 326
McCarter, Jr., P. 217
McNeile, A. 254, 304,
....................323, 326
Mendelsohn, I. 195
Metzger, B. 263
Meyer, H. 299
Milgrom, J. 114
Miller, M. 122
Montefiore, C. G. 300
Morris, L. 299, 326
Mowinckel, S. 247
Myers, J. 22
Neirynck, F. 101
Neusner, J. 265
Nolland, J. 101, 126-27,
....................209, 243, 246,
....................249-50, 289, 291
Nun, M. ....xiii, 52, 59,
....................70-73, 81-82
Oswald, N. ....xiii, 77
Paesler, K. 244

Page, C. 73
Perrot, C. 38, 65, 142
Pesch, R. 1, 83-84, 86,
....89, 98
Petzge, G. 244
Pixner, B. 72
Plath, M. 324
Plummer, A. 227, 232,
...............................244, 249-50
Pomykala, K. 219
Preisker, H. 16
Rabbinowitz, J. 121, 308
Rabinowitz, L. 6
Reed, J. ....…........80, 85, 301
Reeg, G. ......…..............72, 193
Rengstorf, K. ....…......134
Ridderbos, H. ....…254
Robinson, T. 303, 311, 326
Rothkoff, A. .....…...............19
Rothkopf, A. .....…..............120
Rousseau, J. ....…........59
Rubinkiewicz, R. 262
Rüger, H. 143
Sabourin, L. 249, 325
Safrai, S. ....…...120, 136
Safrai, Z. 16
Safren, J. 120
Sahlin, H. 97
Sand, A. 300, 304
Sanders, J. A. 122
Schlatter, A. 145, 242-43,
....299
Schmithals, W. 2, 33, 97,
....162
Schneider, G. 134, 244
Schniewind, J. 1, 97,
................................….291, 300
Schreck, C. 101

Schwarz, G. 54, 194,
....196, 207
Siff, M. 19
Sloan, Jr., R. 120
Sorensen, E. 89
Stein, E. 121
Stein, R. 243
Strobel, A. 120
Tate, M. 8
Taylor, V. 48, 84, 91
Tiede, D. 209, 242,
............................…......244-45, 249
Torrey, C. 187, 207
Trudinger, L. ....…......164
Twelftree, G. 89
Tzafaris, V. ....…............72-73
Urban, L. 260
Urman, D. 72
van der Kwaak, H. 326
van der Loos, H. 1
Victor, U. 315
Violet, B. 113, 124-25,
..................................144-45
Vogler, W. 155, 194
von der Osten-Sacken, P. .....
....xiii
Walker, W. 79
Weiser, A. 242, 247
Weiß, B. 97
Weiß, J. 2, 91
Wellhausen, J. 144-45,
..................................…250, 304
Wiefel, W. 148, 242, 245
Wintermute, O. 257
Wright, G. ......…..............193
Wright, R. 156, 297
Ydit, M. 22, 221, 286

STUDIES IN JUDAISM
TITLES IN THE SERIES

S. Daniel Breslauer
Creating a Judaism Without Religion. A Postmodern Jewish Possibility. Lanham, November 2001. University Press of America. Academic Studies in Ancient Judaism series.

Jacob Neusner
Dual Discourse, Single Judaism. Lanham, February 2001. University Press of America. Academic Studies in Ancient Judaism series.

The Emergence of Judaism. Jewish Religion in Response to the Critical Issues of the First Six Centuries. Lanham, April 2000. University Press of America. Academic Studies in Ancient Judaism series.

The Halakhah and the Aggadah. Lanham. February 2001. University Press of America. Academic Studies in Ancient Judaism series.

The Hermeneutics of Rabbinic Category Formations. Lanham, February 2001. University Press of America. Academic Studies in Ancient Judaism series.

Rivka Ulmer
Pesiqta Rabbati. A Synoptic Edition of Pesiqta Rabbati Based upon all Extant Manuscripts and the Editio Princeps, Lanham. January 2002. University Press of America. Academic Studies in Ancient Judaism series. Volume III

Edited by Jacob Neusner and James F. Strange
Religious Texts and Material Contexts. Lanham. August 2001. University Press of America. Academic Studies in Ancient Judaism series.

Leslie S. Wilson
The Serpent Symbol in the Ancient Near East. Nahash and Asherah: Death, Life, and Healing. Lanham. December 2001, University Press of America. Academic Studies in Ancient Judaism series.

Jacob Neusner
Talmud Torah. Ways to God's Presence through Learning: An Exercise in Practical Theology. Lanham, January 2002. University Press of America. Academic Studies in Ancient Judaism series.

Jacob Neusner

The Aggadic Role in Halakhic Discourses. Lanham. February 2001. University Press of America. Academic Studies in Ancient Judaism series. Volume I

The Aggadic Role in Halakhic Discourses. Lanham. February 2001. University Press of America. Academic Studies in Ancient Judaism series. Volume II

The Aggadic Role in Halakhic Discourses. Lanham. February 2001. University Press of America. Academic Studies in Ancient Judaism series. Volume III

A Theological Commentary to the Midrash. Lanham. April 2001. University Press of America. Academic Studies in Ancient Judaism series. Volume I. *Pesiqta deRab Kahana.*

A Theological Commentary to the Midrash. Lanham. March 2001. University Press of America. Academic Studies in Ancient Judaism series. - Volume II. *Genesis Raba.*

A Theological Commentary to the Midrash. Lanham. April 2001. University Press of America. Academic Studies in Ancient Judaism series. Volume III. *Song of Songs Rabbah*

A Theological Commentary to the Midrash. Lanham. April 2001. University Press of America. Academic Studies in Ancient Judaism series. Volume IV. *Leviticus Rabbah*

A Theological Commentary to the Midrash. Lanham. June 2001. University Press of America. Academic Studies in Ancient Judaism series. Volume V *Lamentations Rabbati*

A Theological Commentary to the Midrash. June 2001. University Press of America. Academic Studies in Ancient Judaism series.Volume VI. *Ruth Rabbah and Esther Rabbah I*

A Theological Commentary to the Midrash. June 2001. University Press of America. Academic Studies in Ancient Judaism series.Volume VII. *Sifra*

A Theological Commentary to the Midrash. July 2001. University Press of America. Academic Studies in Ancient Judaism series.Volume VIII. *Sifré to Numbers and Sifré to Deuteronomy*

A Theological Commentary to the Midrash. August 2001. University Press of America. Academic Studies in Ancient Judaism series. Volume IX. *Mekhilta Attributed to Rabbi Ishmael*

The Unity of Rabbinic Discourse. January 2001. University Press of America. Academic Studies in Ancient Judaism series. Volume I: *Aggadah in the Halakhah*

The Unity of Rabbinic Discourse. February 2001. University Press of America. Academic Studies in Ancient Judaism series. Volume II: *Halakhah in the Aggadah*

The Unity of Rabbinic Discourse. February 2001. University Press of America. Academic Studies in Ancient Judaism series. Volume III: *Halakhah and Aggadah in Concert*

Titles

Texts without Boundaries. Protocols of Non-Documentary Writing in the Rabbinic Canon, Lanham, 2002: University Press of America. Academic Studies in Ancient Judaism series. Volume Two. *Sifra*

Texts without Boundaries. Protocols of Non-Documentary Writing in the Rabbinic Canon, Lanham, 2003: University Press of America. Academic Studies in Ancient Judaism series. Volume Three. *Sifré to Numbers*.

Texts without Boundaries. Protocols of Non-Documentary Writing in the Rabbinic Canon, Lanham, 2003: University Press of America. Academic Studies in Ancient Judaism series. Volume Four. *Sifré to Deuteronomy*.

Texts without Boundaries. Protocols of Non-Documentary Writing in the Rabbinic Canon, Lanham, 2004: University Press of America. Academic Studies in Ancient Judaism series. Volume Five. *Genesis Rabbah*.

Texts without Boundaries. Protocols of Non-Documentary Writing in the Rabbinic Canon, Lanham, 2004: University Press of America. Academic Studies in Ancient Judaism series. Volume Six. *Leviticus Rabbah*.

Texts without Boundaries. Protocols of Non-Documentary Writing in the Rabbinic Canon, Lanham, 2004: University Press of America. Academic Studies in Ancient Judaism series. Volume Seven. *Pesiqta deRab Kahana*.

Texts without Boundaries. Protocols of Non-Documentary Writing in the Rabbinic Canon, Lanham, 2004: University Press of America. Academic Studies in Ancient Judaism series. Volume Eight. *Esther Rabbah and Ruth Rabbah*.

Texts without Boundaries. Protocols of Non-Documentary Writing in the Rabbinic Canon, Lanham, 2004: University Press of America. Academic Studies in Ancient Judaism series. Volume Nine. *Song of Songs Rabbah*.

Texts without Boundaries. Protocols of Non-Documentary Writing in the Rabbinic Canon, Lanham, 2004: University Press of America. Academic Studies in Ancient Judaism series. Volume Ten. *Lamentations Rabbah*.

Texts without Boundaries. Protocols of Non-Documentary Writing in the Rabbinic Canon, Lanham, 2004: University Press of America. Academic Studies in Ancient Judaism series. Volume Eleven. *Mekhilta Attributed to Rabbi Ishmael*.

Texts without Boundaries. Protocols of Non-Documentary Writing in the Rabbinic Canon, Lanham, 2004: University Press of America. Academic Studies in Ancient Judaism series. Volume Twelve. *Abot deRabbi Natan*.